CERTIFIED DREAMWEAVER DEVELOPER

Dreamweaver® MX
Developer Certification
Study Guide

CERTIFIED DREAMWEAVER DEVELOPER

Dreamweaver® MX Developer Certification Study Guide

Marc Campbell

McGraw-Hill Osborne

New York Chicago San Francisco Lisbon London Madrid
Mexico City Milan New Delhi San Juan Seoul Singapore Sydney Toronto

McGraw-Hill/Osborne
2600 Tenth Street
Berkeley, California 94710
U.S.A.

To arrange bulk purchase discounts for sales promotions, premiums, or fund-raisers, please contact **McGraw-Hill**/Osborne at the above address. For information on translations or book distributors outside the U.S.A., please see the International Contact Information page immediately following the index of this book.

Dreamweaver® MX Developer Certification Study Guide

1234567890 CUS CUS 01987654321

Book p/n 0-07-222371-5 and CD p/n 0-07-222372-3
parts of
ISBN 0-07-222370-7

Publisher Brandon A. Nordin	**Senior Project Editor** Betsy Manini	**Production** Apollo Publishing Services
Vice President & **Associate Publisher** Scott Rogers	**Acquisitions Coordinator** Jessica Wilson	**Illustrators** Michael Mueller, Lyssa Wald
Editorial Director Gareth Hancock	**Technical Editor** Jill Jodrey	**Series Design** Roberta Steele
Acquisitions Editor Timothy Green	**Copy Editor** Lisa Theobald	

This book was published with Corel VENTURA™ Publisher.

About the Author

Marc Campbell is a technology author, designer, and Macromedia Certified Dreamweaver Developer. He is best known for his work at DC Comics, where he designed and developed successful upgrades for the official DC Comics and MAD Magazine Web sites and launched *dckids.com*, a personal favorite. Marc went on to serve as Director of Creative Content for the National Information Consortium and Creative Director for SE Technologies before pursuing his passions for words, images, and the Web as a writer and instructor. You can find him in his adopted home of Philadelphia, where he lives with his wife, writing books like *The Complete Idiot's Guide to Web Animation* (Alpha Books, 2002), *The Complete Idiot's Guide to Computer Illustration* (Alpha Books, 2002), and *PageMaker 7.0 From A to Z* (Redmond Technology Press, 2001). If you drop him a line at *marc@taotezing.com*, he will reply.

About the Technical Editor

Jill Jodrey has been involved in the field of education for more than seven years. After graduating from Dalhousie University in Halifax, Nova Scotia, she taught in a private school in Nova Scotia and was fortunate to be able to design much of the curriculum for that program. Jill also taught overseas in language education and was a lead instructor for the Reading & Writing division where she designed and developed a program for new teachers.

Before joining the Learning and Instructional Development Center team at Simon Fraser University, she worked as a technical trainer in Denver, Colorado, and completed graduate studies specializing in adult and online education. Currently, she is Instructional Developer with Simon Fraser. Her work involves designing and facilitating virtual orientation workshops for the School of Business and designing and leading face-to-face workshops on e-moderation. As if this isn't enough, she develops and instructs Web and database design courses for Academic Computing Services. She also instructs graduate education courses online with Jones International University and is currently working on a PhD.

CONTENTS AT A GLANCE

Part IV
Appendixes

CONTENTS

Dreamweaver MX does it all. You want to build a Web site? Dreamweaver does that. You want to manage your site with speed and efficiency? Dreamweaver does that. You want to develop Web applications for dynamically driven content and integrate them into your site? Dreamweaver does that, too. This book helps you to learn how to use Dreamweaver MX, and it helps you to prepare for Macromedia's Certified Dreamweaver Developer exam. This exam tests your proficiency with Dreamweaver MX. It evaluates your conceptual understanding of the software as a whole as well as your practical knowledge about how best to use it. By reading this book, you come away with some of both.

Dreamweaver is easy to use. It's deceptively easy, if you think about it. You're not consciously aware of the sheer number of things that Dreamweaver can do until someone asks you exactly which command turns off an optional region in a template-based page or which buttons under the Forms tab of the Insert panel work only when you're in Code view.

Welcome to the Certified Dreamweaver Developer exam. If you're like me, when you first heard about the certification, you said something like, "How hard can it be?" I said this because I *knew* Dreamweaver. I'd used it nearly every day of my life since 1999. I felt very confident. I bragged to my editor that I could take the exam any time, any place. "Bring it on," I said, or something to that effect.

By the tenth question, I was regretting those words. The exam was trickier than I had expected. I realized just how much functionality I took for granted and how many mistakes the software had quietly tolerated nearly every day of my life since 1999. By the end of the test, I was seeing menus in my head, and I was ready for someone to reset *my* parameters.

As it turns out, I passed the exam, and I managed to log a respectable score, but it wasn't the 100% I had predicted. If only there had been a book like this to set me straight from the beginning!

Don't let my foolishness discourage you. The exam is challenging but not impossible. If you've never used Dreamweaver before, don't worry. This book will get you up to speed in time for the test—but if you, like me, have used Dreamweaver extensively on the job or at home, then this book is *especially* for you. This book will help you to channel your experience into the specific knowledge that Macromedia wants you to demonstrate. The size of this book attests to the fact that Dreamweaver isn't lightweight, and neither is the certification, but if you take the time to prepare for the exam carefully and thoroughly, I'm willing to bet money that you'll ace it.

Part of preparing for the exam is using Dreamweaver to build Web sites. Get a feel for the software. Figure out what it can do. Learn it well enough to predict what will happen when you click a certain button or execute a particular command. Going through the exercises in this book gives you a place to start. Even if you use Dreamweaver regularly, I recommend a back-to-basics approach to the software. A high number of Dreamweaver users are self-taught, and the demands of the marketplace often rule out such luxuries as sustained learning at your own pace. As a result, you might not realize the full scope of the software or the best ways to integrate it into your workflow. Part of the trick of the certification is figuring out exactly what Dreamweaver brings to the table in a professional Web development setting.

In This Book

I've taught Dreamweaver at least four different ways, and the structure and organization of the material in this book represents what has been the most successful method for my students. The early chapters focus on using Dreamweaver to set up a Web site and building the pages that go into the site. By the middle of the book, you're leveraging Dreamweaver's special features to streamline your workflow. The end of the book, you're ready to launch.

Along the way, in step-by-step exercises for each certification objective, you build a functioning site for a very important client, Mad Science LLC. The CD-ROM that comes with this book contains all the graphics for the site, but you develop the pages and make them work. Seeing a project through from start to finish gives you a sense of Dreamweaver's role in the production process that you might not get otherwise if you don't already work in the field.

At the end of each chapter are comprehensive reviews and practice questions much like the ones on the certification exam. There's also a lab question, in which you take the various threads of the chapter and pull them together to solve a typical on-the-job problem. A certified professional needs to be the guru in the workplace. When situations arise, you'll be the one who they pull into those frantic, closed-door meetings. The ability to apply your skills to save the day will increase your value to the team.

On the CD-ROM

This book includes a CD-ROM with assessment and training software, including online video training, two complete practice exams (one with free online registration) that simulate the actual Dreamweaver Developer exam, and an electronic copy of the book. The online training from LearnKey does not cover the Dreamweaver Developer exam, but we felt that offering additional instruction about how to integrate Dreamweaver, Fireworks, and Flash was a valuable addition to the book, meant to help you produce even more effective Web sites. For more information on the CD-ROM, please see Appendix B.

In Every Chapter

When you page through this book, here's what you find:

- **Certification Objectives** appear at the top of each chapter. These objectives provide a roadmap for the material that I cover, and they correspond to skill areas that the certification exam assesses.

- **Exam Watch** notes alert you to potential trouble spots or trick questions and offer ways to avoid falling into the trap.

- **Practice Exercises** come one per objective. Here's where you hone your hands-on skills. Nearly all the practice exercises relate to the task of building that Web site for your mad-scientist clients. I urge readers of all skill levels and experience to complete every exercise in order, step by step. Don't take your own personal shortcuts. Remember, Macromedia needs to assess your knowledge of the software, not your particular strategies for using it.

- **On the Job** notes put the material into the context of the workplace. Being a certified pro means applying your knowledge in creative ways to solve problems, not just memorizing commands and procedures.

- **From the Classroom** sidebars come from questions or issues that my students have raised. These sidebars often present the material of the chapter from competing perspectives, and I argue one side or the other. The goal of this is not to persuade you but to help you to make an informed decision.

- **Scenario and Solution** sections provide a quick reference for common problems and their solutions.

- The **Certification Summary** reiterates the main themes of the chapter and ties them together.

 ■ The **Two-Minute Drill** is a checklist of quick facts and exam topics. You can use these lists for last-minute review.

Q&A ■ The **Self Test** throws you 20 challenging certification-style questions per chapter and provides detailed explanations of the answers.

- The **Lab Question** asks you to apply what you learned to solve your daily nightmare scenario. I give my recommended results in the **Lab Answer** section.

Some Pointers

After you read this book and complete all the exercises, go back and review. The more time you spend in preparation for the exam, the better you'll perform. Here are some methods for reviewing the material:

1. Go over the Two-Minute Drills to reiterate the key points in each chapter.

2. Read the Exam Watch notes to prepare for trick questions.

3. Check the Scenario and Solution quick references for answers to common and hypothetical situations.

4. Redo the Self Tests in each chapter. Mark the questions that you answered incorrectly, and concentrate on these the next time, rereading the relevant sections of the chapter if the explanations in the Self Test Answers section don't make sense.

5. Do all the exercises in order, step by step.

6. Invent an imaginary client of your own, and prepare a Web site for this client using everything that you learned.

Marc Campbell

ACKNOWLEDGMENTS

This book comes with an extra feature that you won't find listed on the back cover. It comes with the talent, dedication, and hard work of professional people who made things happen.

Thanks to Neil Salkind, Jessica Richards, Stacey Barone, and everyone at Studio B. Thanks to Tim Green and Jessica Wilson for your guidance and support. Thanks to Jill Jodrey for keeping me on spec. Thanks especially to the production team at Osborne for the late nights and long hours of staring at these pages, making them work: Betsy Manini, Lisa Theobald, Michael Mueller, Jan Benes, Zora Dostalikova, Lindsay Mugglestone, and Alison de Grassi.

And thanks to Bobbi Jo for putting up with it all.

INTRODUCTION

This book helps you to prepare for Macromedia's Certified Dreamweaver Developer exam. To become a certified Dreamweaver developer, you must demonstrate your knowledge of Dreamweaver MX and your ability to use it to build professional Web sites. When combined with your patience, practice, and positive attitude, this book gives you everything you need to pass the exam, but this book doesn't become a doorjamb or paperweight after you attain certification. It contains tips, advice, and crib notes for any working Web professional. Keep this book on your shelf, and refer to it often. Its author wants you to succeed.

About the Certification Exam

The Certified Dreamweaver Developer exam consists of approximately 65 multiple-choice questions delivered under secure, proctored, timed conditions. To pass, you must answer at least 70 percent of these questions correctly. You can't bring any notes into the exam, you can't consult with your colleagues, and you aren't able to refer to the software. To succeed, you must be able to visualize Dreamweaver's interface and menus. You also need to know how to use Dreamweaver in a professional setting, and you should have a good working knowledge of Web production in general.

Macromedia recommends the following prerequisites:

- Two or more years' experience in Web development
- Job knowledge of HTML, JavaScript, and CSS syntax
- At least one year of experience using Dreamweaver version 3 or better
- Experience with hand coding
- Six months' experience with Web site management
- Six months' experience creating high-quality graphics for Web or print

Demonstrating Knowledge and Performance

There are two types of questions on the certification exam: knowledge-based questions and performance-based questions. The *knowledge-based questions* assess your familiarity with the commands, features, procedures, and controls of Dreamweaver MX. A typical knowledge-based question goes something like this:

In Dreamweaver, which panel shows the Library items for a particular site?

A.   The Site panel

B.   The Insert panel

C.   The Properties panel

D.   The Assets panel

The answer to this question is **D**, the Assets panel.

Notice that this kind of question doesn't ask you what a Library item is or how it can help you to speed up production. A knowledge-based question focuses solely on the software.

By contrast, a *performance-based question* requires that you put your knowledge of Dreamweaver into a practical context. These questions ask you to provide the reason for a particular strategy or the best method for achieving a certain result. Occasionally, you must choose the answer that makes the most sense from several reasonable and technically correct options. Here's an example:

When working with graphics on the Web, which file type is usually best for photographic images?

A.   BMP

B.   JPEG

C.   GIF

D.   PNG

The answer is **B**, because, in general, the JPEG format offers the best picture quality and the smallest file size for photographic images. You can save photographs in BMP format, but not all Web browsers support BMP images, and photos in GIF or PNG format often lose color information.

Notice how performance-based questions require you to draw from diverse but related knowledge areas. In this question, you needed to combine your knowledge of Web graphics with your knowledge of browsers and the file types that they support. Notice also that Dreamweaver didn't appear in this question at all. Expect a number of questions about the fundamentals of Web building.

Why You Are Doing This

The Web is a more complex place than it was five years ago. Back then, simple HTML pages were the rule, not the exception. If you were inclined, you could teach yourself HTML in a weekend, build a simple site as proof of concept, and compete with the pros for a Web building job. There was nothing to it.

Then public interest in the Web exploded, and millions upon millions of nontechnical people began hopping online. They liked what they found, but they demanded improvements. Better graphics. Easier navigation. More media. Interactivity. Web building became much more than a one-trick show. The learning curve of the coding became steeper. Professionals began to specialize. Some concentrated on the graphics, architecture, and user experience—the front end of the site. Others concentrated on the back end, learning JavaScript, CGI, ASP, Cold Fusion, CSS, DHTML, MySQL, ActionScript, Lingo, and a variety of other programming languages. Developing a site meant respecting the increasingly irreconcilable differences between Web browsers and understanding the strengths and weaknesses of client-side solutions.

Today, visitors expect to get as much functionality from a Web site as they find in a middleweight desktop application. For them, the Web is a software solution. They continue to be less and less technically savvy while increasing the tenor and frequency of their demands. They don't want to know why a feature won't work given the lack of state on the client side, so you had better come up with some server-side options.

The typical Web pro is no longer the person who takes a few hours from IT duties to post a few updates to the corporate site. Today's Web pro works on the site full time on a team of people with similar responsibilities. Web building has become an individual profession with new subspecialties emerging all the time. Not one Web pro can claim to do it all—not anymore. That employers would ask respective employees or service providers to demonstrate their particular set of skills was inevitable, especially given the excesses of the first big dot-com explosion and the very public drama of its subsequent implosion. The money people are far more cautious these days. If you want to be part of the Web's rebirth, you need to prove that you know what you're doing this time, from whence comes Dreamweaver developer certification.

You don't need certification to be a great Web pro. You'll build a career on the strength of your work, not the number of certifications that you cram into your resume. What certification provides is a context for your skills, a benchmark for your clients and employers. It won't substitute for shoddy work or bad references, but it gives them yet another reason to hire you if they like what they see in your portfolio.

Signing Up

VUE, or Virtual University Enterprise, administers the Certified Dreamweaver Developer exam on behalf of Macromedia. You must set up an appointment at an authorized VUE testing facility to take the exam. You probably won't have to travel far. VUE has more than 2500 authorized centers worldwide. I walked to mine in Center City, Philadelphia.

When you're ready to schedule your session, go to *http://www.vue.com/macromedia* or call 1-877-460-8679 in North America or 952-995-8833 outside North America. You choose the location, the day, and the time, and you pay $100 U.S. by credit card.

Taking the Test

If you prepare adequately, you have nothing to worry about. You'll pass the exam and earn your certification.

To beat the pretest jitters, you might try the following techniques:

- Choose a day and time for the exam when you don't have a hectic workload or other job-related distractions. Better yet, take the whole day off.

- Get a full eight hours of sleep the night before.

- Eat a modest, well-balanced meal before the test. Don't starve your brain!

- Spend some time calmly reviewing the material the day of the test, but leave your notes and this book at home. Don't cram! Do your studying beforehand.

- Plan to arrive to the testing center a half hour to 15 minutes early. You need to sign in and show some ID, but you also need a few minutes to relax, focus, and collect your thoughts.

■ During the exam, read each question and all the answers thoroughly before making your choice. Look carefully at the wording of the question, and eliminate obviously wrong answers. If you're stumped, move on, and come back to the question later.

■ If you have to guess at an answer, guess. You might get it right. Leaving a question blank is a guaranteed wrong answer.

■ You won't get extra points for completing the exam in 15 minutes, so pace yourself. You don't have to rush. Use every minute that they give you, too. If you finish early, go back and review the questions and your answers, but be careful about second-guessing yourself. Your first instinct was probably correct, so don't change your answer unless you're absolutely, undeniably certain that you made the wrong choice.

Remember also that the Certified Dreamweaver Developer exam isn't a life or death proposition. The absolute worst-case scenario is that you fail the test. Big deal—you can take it again, and you'll have the advantage this time, because you know what to expect.

The exam is challenging, but it's nothing that you can't handle. If you want to be certified and you're willing to work for it, you will be. I have every confidence. Good luck!

CERTIFIED DREAMWEAVER DEVELOPER

Part I

Design, Project Requirements, and Usability Techniques

1

Introducing Dreamweaver MX

CERTIFICATION OBJECTIVES

Dreamweaver MX allows you to build sophisticated Web sites quickly and reliably. For its power, it is remarkably easy to use. Getting productive with Dreamweaver doesn't require extensive knowledge of Web technologies or years of experience building sites by hand. In fact, people with no more Web production in their resumes than Expert Web Surfer find that they can put together Web pages with advanced features just by sitting down with the software for a few hours.

If you're already familiar with Dreamweaver MX and Web building in general, please feel free to skip ahead to Chapter 2. This chapter probably doesn't contain anything new for you. Be advised, though, that the certification exam asks general questions about Web building and the interface, so perhaps skimming through this chapter isn't a bad idea, even for crusty old pros.

Easy though it is, Dreamweaver isn't a toy; it's a tool. Like any tool, the more you know about it, the better it works when you want to use it. This chapter provides a quick tour of Dreamweaver's features and introduces you to the process of designing, developing, and deploying a Web site.

CERTIFICATION OBJECTIVE 1.01

What Dreamweaver MX Can Do

Macromedia Dreamweaver MX is a software application for designing and managing Web sites. You can use it to build a new site or maintain an existing one, and if you juggle several sites at once, Dreamweaver keeps track of them. In matters of Web production, Dreamweaver is indispensable. It helps you to organize your site and lay out the pages. At your command, it adds special effects like interactive images, dynamic text, and animation. It tests your site for technical problems and assists you in fixing them, and when you're ready to launch, it uploads your site to the Web.

At heart, Dreamweaver is an HTML editor. HTML, Hypertext Markup Language, is the code that a browser such as Internet Explorer or Netscape interprets and presents. The HTML contains the text of the page and the instructions for displaying the layout, but it doesn't include the actual images, sounds, or movies that the page might use. Instead, the HTML contains directions for finding the separate image, sound, and movie files, which you store elsewhere on your site. As the HTML loads, the browser collects these additional files, or *assets,* and puts them in the right place on the page. Incidentally, this is why certain Web pages appear with broken-image icons instead of graphics. The browser can't find the image files at the location in which the HTML tells it to look.

Given that a Web page is a collection of many different kinds of files, Dreamweaver's contribution is the source code. Dreamweaver lets you create the text and the layout of the page, and it allows you to position and manipulate such assets as images, sounds, and movies. However, to create most of the assets themselves, you need to use separate pieces of software. Dreamweaver integrates well with other Macromedia applications, such as Fireworks, Flash, and Director, all of which produce site assets. (Fireworks produces images, and Flash and Director produce movies.)

With Dreamweaver MX, you can also develop dynamic Web sites. For the purposes of this book, a *dynamic Web site* relies on server-side technology such as ColdFusion or ASP.NET to deliver personalized or customized information to the visitor while he or she browses the site—"on the fly," as we say in the business. Dreamweaver simplifies and speeds up the creation of *Web applications,* or *Web apps* for short, which are the pieces of code that manipulate the live data. This code is not HTML—what it is depends on the server-side technology you use. The Web application converts the live data into HTML, and this is what the visitor ends up seeing in the browser. Dreamweaver supports application development for five of the most popular software servers: ColdFusion, ASP.NET, ASP (Active Server Page), JSP (JavaServer Page), and PHP.

A quick reference for what Dreamweaver contributes is found in the next Scenario and Solution.

Each document that you create with Dreamweaver represents a single *Web page.* The page is what loads in your browser window when you follow a link or type a Uniform Resource Locator (URL) address. Constructing a Web page involves

SCENARIO & SOLUTION

What does Dreamweaver give you?	Source code (including Web apps), page layout, and text
What doesn't Dreamweaver give you?	Images, animation, movies, video, audio, and other media assets

designing the layout and adding the content, or the information that the page contains. Conscientious Web designers try to strike a balance between aesthetics and ease of use. A *Web site* is a collection of pages that share a similar design, theme, or purpose. Building a Web site has to do with arranging the HTML files and assets according to an architecture or structure and making sure that your visitors can navigate the pages effectively.

Dreamweaver allows you to work at both the page and the site levels. You create and edit individual Web pages with Dreamweaver's Web-building features, and you organize these pages into a site and upload them to the Web with Dreamweaver's site management features.

Exploring Dreamweaver's Web-Building Features

Dreamweaver gives you two ways to look at the Web page that you create: Design view and Code view. Design view shows you what your page will look like in a Web browser. Code view displays the underlying HTML. You can switch from one view to the other seamlessly, and you can work with both at the same time. Changes that you make in one view cause updates in the other. Graphics people usually find Design view more useful, while programmers tend toward Code view, but both views work equally well. Pick the one that makes the most sense for you, or mix and match as you prefer.

EXERCISE 1-1

Switching Between Views

I'm a firm believer in starting off with an easy exercise. Its confidence-building virtues are without compare. In the spirit of this, try switching from Design view to Code view and back again.

1. Launch Dreamweaver. Dreamweaver opens a new document window by default.

2. Open the View menu. If the Design option doesn't have a check mark next to it, click this option. The document window is now in Design view.

3. At the top of the interface, locate the button that looks like the one shown here. This is the Show Code View button. Click it. You are now in Code

view. The document window changes from an empty white screen to display a few lines of HTML code.

 4. Now click the button that looks like the one shown here. You're back in Design view. The HTML goes away, and the empty white screen reappears. Good job!

Working in Design View

Dreamweaver's Design view looks something like Figure 1-1. The large white area that takes up much of the screen is the *document window*. This is where you lay out your page and add its content. The collapsible *panels* and *panel groups* along the top and bottom and on the right give commands and options for building your page and organizing your site.

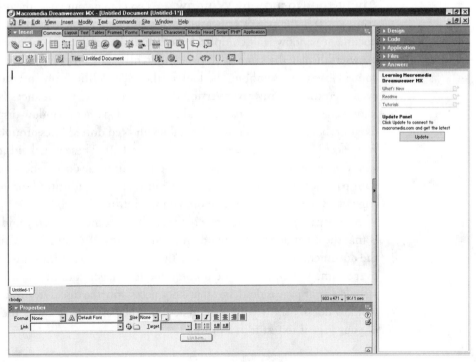

FIGURE 1-1

Dreamweaver's Design view lets you build a Web page more or less as it will appear in a browser window.

Go into the exam knowing the correct names for interface elements. You won't have the benefit of seeing the application on the screen while you take the exam, so you can't rely on your visual knowledge. Be able to call the parts of the interface by name.

Panels and panel groups are easy to use in that you can expand a panel group when you need it and collapse it when you don't. A panel group is collapsed when the arrow icon to the left of the name points to the right. To expand a panel group, click its arrow icon and click the tab of the panel that you want to see. To collapse the panel group, click the arrow icon again. You can expand a panel group and go directly to the panel of your choice by opening the Window menu and choosing the name of the panel that you want. Notice also that when a panel group is expanded, an options icon appears in the upper-right corner of the group. Click this icon for a context menu with commands for managing the panel group.

To enter Design view, choose View | Design or click the Show Design View button that you used in Exercise 1-1.

About the Document Window   As you build your page, the document window approximates the page's appearance in a browser. I say *approximates* because the document window isn't completely faithful in its rendering. For one thing, different browsers display the same Web page differently. Dreamweaver's document window comes closest to resembling the look of the page in Microsoft Internet Explorer, but even then the Dreamweaver version doesn't capture all the nuances (some would say idiosyncrasies) of the live page. In addition, the document window displays visual aids, like thin borders around borderless tables and red dotted lines around forms, to help you select the right page elements (see Figure 1-2). These visual aids don't appear in a browser at all. The bottom line is that you can trust the document window to present your page accurately most of the time, but there's no substitute for looking at your page in a variety of browsers before you send it to the Web.

Another important difference between the document window and a Web browser is that the document window doesn't behave like a Web browser. Clicking a link in the document window doesn't cause the target page to load, for instance, and rolling over an image with the mouse pointer doesn't trigger your interactive effect. It may seem like your page is dead, but that's not necessarily the case. Dreamweaver's document window doesn't show your page in action. The best way to check the functionality of your page is to test it in a browser.

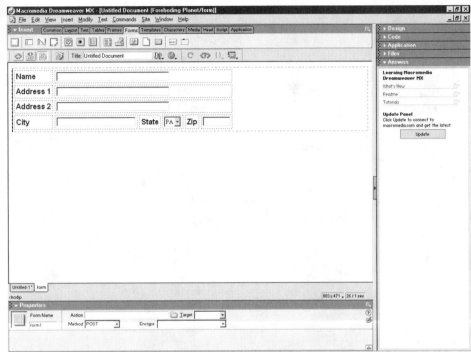

FIGURE 1-2

The visual aids around the form and table in Dreamweaver's document window disappear when you view the page in a browser.

To select a design element in the document window, simply click the element. The Properties panel at the bottom of the screen changes depending on the type of element you select (see Figure 1-3). Selecting an image, for instance, calls up the properties of the image in the panel. Modify the appearance or characteristics of the element by editing the values in the property fields. Make the Properties panel larger and smaller by clicking the arrow icon at the bottom right. The larger version of the panel shows more options.

About Live Data View Dreamweaver's Live Data view displays dynamic pages as they appear in their final form, after the Web application has converted all the live data to HTML. In regular Design view, Dreamweaver presents a dynamic page with placeholders that represent the content that the Web application will supply.

Turn on Live Data view by choosing View | Live Data or by clicking the button shown here. (You'll find this button on the screen to the right of the Show Design View button.) You can use Live Data view only if you're building a dynamic site. You can customize the options for Live Data view by choosing View | Live Data

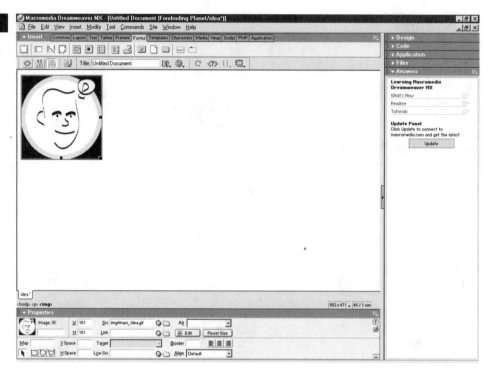

FIGURE 1-3

Use the
Properties panel
to modify the
appearance or
characteristics
of the selected
element.

Settings, but don't try to customize them now, as you'll need to define a dynamic site in Dreamweaver before this command will work. See Chapter 2 for details about how to define a site.

Using the Rulers   Choosing View | Rulers | Show causes horizontal and vertical rulers to appear in the document window, as shown in Figure 1-4. These rulers help you to space design elements precisely in the layout of the page. By default, the rulers measure in pixels, which is probably the most useful for HTML, but you can switch the units to inches or centimeters by choosing the corresponding option under View | Rulers.

Keeping Your Eye on the Code

When you work in Design view, it's often helpful to refer to the HTML code periodically. Certain elements of the page, such as the parts of a table, are difficult to select from the document window, but by selecting an element and then modifying

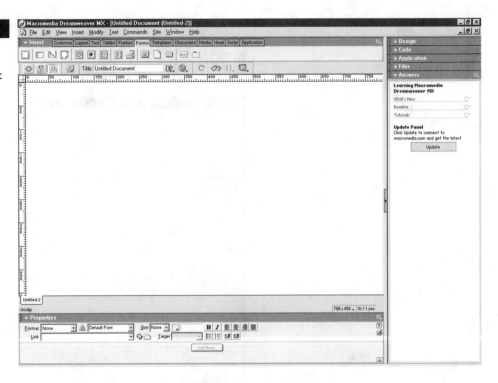

FIGURE 1-4

Use the rulers
in the document
window to
position design
elements
precisely.

the selection with one of Dreamweaver's code-watching tools, you can quickly draw
focus to a specific part of the page.

Using the Tag Inspector   Dreamweaver's Tag Inspector panel (Figure 1-5) shows
an outline of all the HTML *tags* in the page. An HTML tag marks a specific element
in the code. For instance, to display a paragraph, HTML precedes the text with the
paragraph tag, <p>. The closing tag, </p>, appears at the end of the text to signify
the end of the paragraph.

exam
ⓦatch

*The certification exam assumes passing knowledge of HTML. Brush up on your
tags before you take the test.*

Every tag corresponds to an element on the page. Some tags, like <body>, don't
appear in the Web browser as a discrete, identifiable design element like a table or a
paragraph of text. Nonetheless, these *invisible tags* are extremely important, since they
contain information about how the browser should display the page.

View the
structure of the
HTML code in
the Tag Inspector
panel.

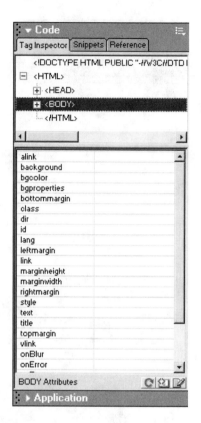

To open the Tag Inspector, expand the Code panel group and click the Tag Inspector tab or choose Window | Tag Inspector. When you select a tag in this panel, the *attributes* of that tag appear in list form. Attributes specify the particular properties of the tag, such as the background color of a table or the alternate text of an image, which is text that appears when a visitor hovers over the image with the mouse pointer. Set or modify the attributes of a tag by typing values into the attribute fields.

Using the Tag Selector   Another way to keep your eye on the code is to use the Tag Selector. The Tag Selector appears at the lower left of the document window (see Figure 1-6). When you select an item in the document window, the Tag Selector shows the HTML tags associated with that item. The tag in boldface represents the current selection.

By clicking a different tag in the Tag Selector, you move the selection to that specific tag. Use this feature to specify exactly which portion of the page Dreamweaver

FIGURE 1-6

The Tag Selector shows the HTML tags associated with the current selection.

should edit. For instance, if you click inside a table cell in the document window, the Tag Selector shows the all the HTML tags that create the table, and Dreamweaver highlights the table-cell tag, <td>, which corresponds to the cell that you clicked. Any changes you make apply only to that cell. If you want to make changes to the entire row instead, click the table-row tag, <tr>, in the Tag Selector.

Using the Quick Tag Editor   The Quick Tag Editor lets you make adjustments to a tag and its attributes much like the Tag Inspector, except the Quick Tag Editor gives you the tag and attributes as straight HTML, as you can see in in the following illustration.

```
Edit Tag: <table
          cellpadding="4"
          cellspacing="4">
```

To use the Quick Tag Editor, select a design element in the document window, and at the Tag Selector, choose the tag that you want to edit. Then go to the Properties panel and click the pencil-and-pad icon, or right-click the tag in the Tag Selector and choose Edit Tag from the context menu. Either way, a pop-up window appears containing the HTML code of the tag. Simply edit the code and close the pop-up window.

Using the Code Inspector Panel   The Code Inspector panel (Figure 1-7) is like a floating version of Code view with a few Site-panel buttons thrown in for good measure. If you work primarily in Design view, you might find it helpful to bring up the Code Inspector panel from time to time by choosing Window | Others | Code Inspector, or by pressing F10. Then again, you might find it equally convenient just to switch to Code view when you need to see the HTML. The Code Inspector panel doesn't give you any functionality that you can't find elsewhere in Dreamweaver.

FIGURE 1-7

The Code
Inspector panel
is like a floating
version of Code
view.

```
Code Inspector
1  <!DOCTYPE HTML PUBLIC "-//W3C//DTD HTML 4.01 Transitio
2  <html>
3  <head>
4  <title>Untitled Document</title>
5  <meta http-equiv="Content-Type" content="text/html; ch
6  </head>
7
8  <body bgcolor="#FFFFFF" text="#000000">
9  <form name="form1" method="post" action="">
10   <table cellpadding="4" cellspacing="4">
11     <tr>
12       <td><font face="Arial, Helvetica, sans-serif"><b
13       <td colspan="5"> <input name="textfield" type="t
```

Working in Code View

In Design view, the document window shows you what your Web page will look like
in a browser. In Code view, the page layout disappears and the document window
fills with the source code, as shown in Figure 1-8. To enter Code view, choose View
| Code, or click the Show Code View button that you used in Exercise 1-1.

*Be prepared to answer questions about multiple ways to perform the same
task. For instance, you can switch to Code view from Design view by clicking
the appropriate button on the interface or choosing View | Code.*

Comparing Types of Code   For most Web pages, much of the code in Code
view is HTML, but not all of it. Some of the code may be JavaScript, or some of
the code may be part of a Cascading Style Sheet (CSS). If you're building a dynamic
site, some of the code will be server specific. The type of code depends on the server
technology you use. If you're building a dynamic site for ColdFusion, for instance,
CFML is the server code.

In general, the HTML portion of the page contains the skeleton of the layout and
the guts of the content. JavaScript controls most of the interactivity on the page, from
swapping graphics to validating form data. JavaScript in Dreamweaver appears most
often near the top of the source-code listing. CSS code controls the look or style of the

FIGURE 1-8

Code view allows
you to edit the
source code
of a page.

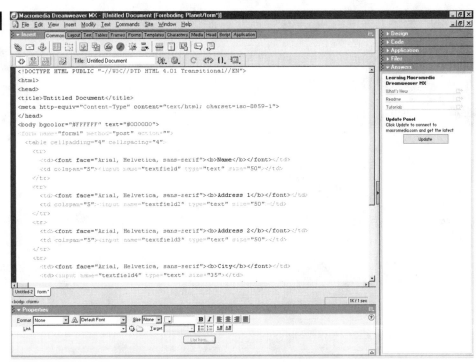

design elements in the page. Like JavaScript, it usually appears near the top of the source
(see Figure 1-9).

Server-specific code in a dynamic site is what drives the site's Web applications.
The Web server processes this code and outputs the results as HTML to the visitor's
Web browser. You can find the server code sprinkled throughout the HTML, usually
in small chunks.

Dreamweaver uses color to help you to distinguish the different kinds of code in
the page and to separate the code from text and other data. By default, text is black
in Code view and comments are generally gray. The code appears in a rainbow of colors.
By default, in an HTML document, the color for anchor tags is green, attribute values
and numbers are blue, form tags are orange, image tags and style tags are purple, table
tags are turquoise, comment tags are gray, object tags and script tags are brownish red,
and other tags are dark blue. You can change these color codes to suit your needs by
choosing Edit | Preferences. Choose the Code Coloring category.

Writing and Editing Code   Writing and editing code in Code view is much like
writing with a word processor or text editor. Position the cursor with the arrow keys
and start typing.

FIGURE 1-9

JavaScript and CSS code usually appear toward the top of the source listing, before the main chunk of HTML in the body of the page.

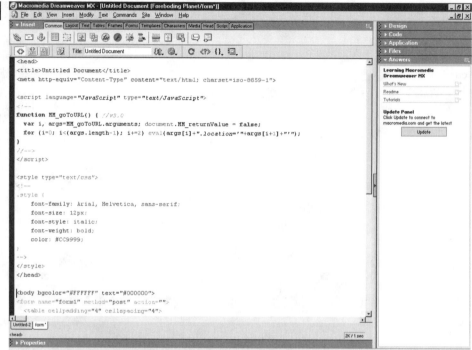

If you begin to type an HTML tag, Dreamweaver's Code Hints and Auto Tag Completion features kick in. Code Hints provides a drop-down list of common HTML tags and attributes from which you can choose, while Auto Tag Completion automatically supplies the matching closing tag to your opening one. You can disable or modify both features by choosing Edit | Preferences and clicking Code Hints from the Category list.

If you make a mistake in syntax, Dreamweaver doesn't flash an error message or a warning, so be careful. Use Code view's color conventions as a guide. If the code appears in black, Dreamweaver doesn't recognize it.

Another way to add tags to the source code is to use the Tag Chooser. The Tag Chooser dialog box (Figure 1-10) opens when you click the Tag Chooser button, which you can find under the Common tab of the Insert panel, shown here. Use the Tag Chooser to browse for and insert a specific tag.

The left pane of the Tag Chooser dialog box lists a hierarchy of categories of source-code tags. Find the specific tag you need by browsing the categories on the left and

FIGURE 1-10

Use the Tag
Chooser to
browse for and
insert a specific
HTML tag.

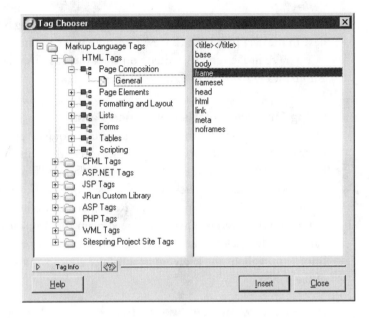

then double-clicking the tag in the pane on the right. If the tag you selected has no
attributes, the tag appears in the source code. If the tag you selected does have attributes,
the Tag Editor dialog box (Figure 1-11) appears, where you can fill in the most common
attributes of that tag. Click OK in the Tag Editor dialog box to insert the tag into the

FIGURE 1-11

Set the attributes
of the tag you
picked with the
Tag Chooser in
the Tag Editor
dialog box.

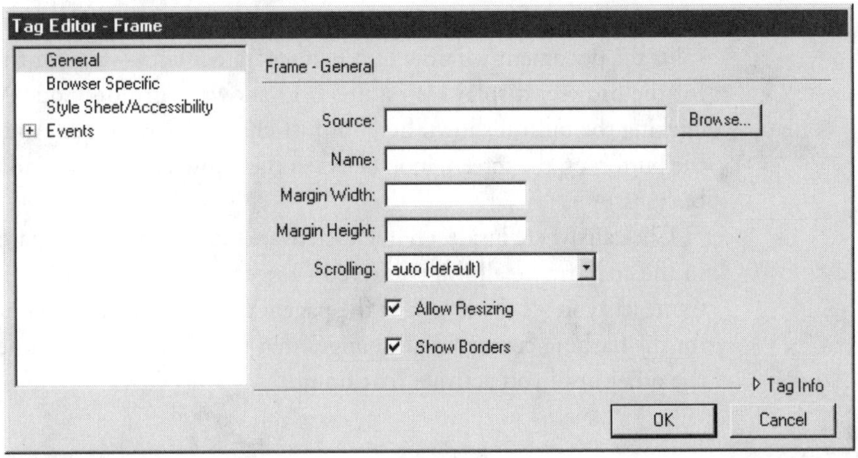

source code. In either the Tag Chooser or Tag Editor dialog box, click the triangle icon next to the Tag Info label to view Dreamweaver's online help for that particular tag.

If you're in Design view when you click the Tag Chooser button, Dreamweaver automatically switches to Code And Design view.

Using Dreamweaver's Reference Panel   To assist you in coding, Dreamweaver provides the equivalent of eight quick-reference books on HTML, JavaScript, CSS, and server languages. Access these in the Reference panel (see Figure 1-12). To open the Reference panel, choose Window | Reference, expand the Code panel group, and click the Reference tab; or click the Reference button in the bar just below the Insert panel. The Reference button looks like the one shown here.

Choose the reference book you need from the drop-down list at the top of the panel and then select a keyword and attribute or property from the lists below it. Information about the keyword or attribute appears in the window at the bottom of the panel.

on the **①ob**

Unfortunately, you can't use the Reference panel during the exam, but don't be a glutton for punishment on the job. Don't waste time tinkering with the code! If you have a question, look it up. I promise I won't think you're incompetent, and neither will anyone else.

Working in Code And Design View

Can't decide between Code and Design views? Do you prefer a little of both? Fortunately, you don't have to make a choice. Dreamweaver's Code And Design view splits the document window into two separate frames—one for the source and another for the browser display, as Figure 1-13 shows. Turn on Code And Design view by clicking the button shown here, or just choose View | Code And Design. (To find the button on the screen, look between the Show Code View and Show Design View buttons.)

Click anywhere inside a frame to activate the features of that particular view. Clicking in the code frame allows you to edit the code directly, while clicking in the design frame lets you see the layout of the page. (You can tell which frame is active by looking for the flashing cursor.) The changes that you make to one frame don't appear in the other until you activate that frame.

FIGURE 1-12

Use the Reference panel to help you figure out proper coding syntax.

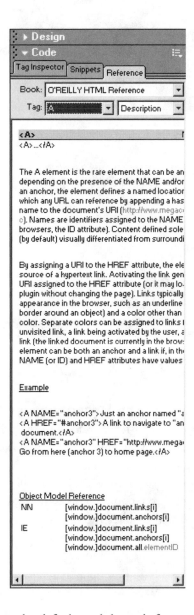

The design frame is larger by default, and the code frame appears at the top of the document window. If you need more room for code and less for design, drag the border between the frames. To switch the position of the frames, choose View | Design View On Top. This command appears in the View menu only when you're in Code And Design view.

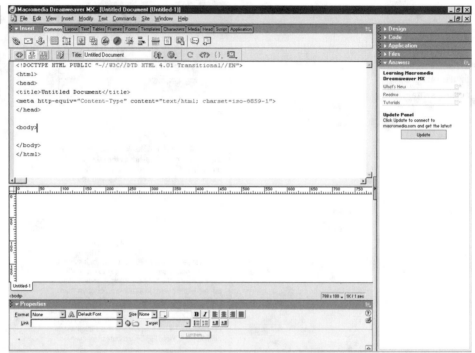

FIGURE 1-13

Dreamweaver's combined Code And Design view gives you the best of both worlds.

Switching to the Dreamweaver 4 Workspace

Dreamweaver MX for Windows sports a brand new interface design. If you're used to the traditional Dreamweaver look of floating panels everywhere, the new interface may take some getting used to.

Macromedia recommends that you use the new Dreamweaver MX workspace, but you can easily configure the software to resemble Dreamweaver 4. To do so, choose Edit | Preferences, click the General category, click the Change Workspace button, and set your workspace preference to Dreamweaver 4. The next time you start Dreamweaver, the floating panels return in all their glory, as Figure 1-14 shows. You can switch back to the MX workspace at any time.

Dreamweaver MX for Mac OS uses the Dreamweaver 4–style interface by default. In fact, Mac users don't have the option of the MX interface. It is available only in Windows.

FIGURE 1-14

If you feel disoriented or homesick, you can configure Dreamweaver MX for Windows to resemble Dreamweaver 4.

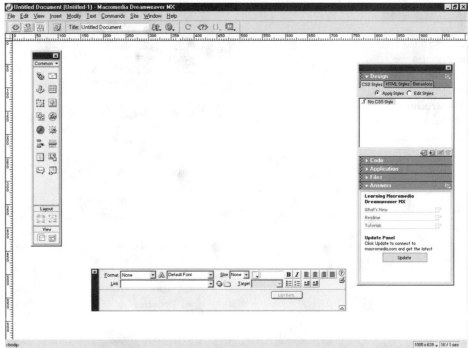

Exploring Dreamweaver's Site Management Features

Constructing individual Web pages is one side of the Dreamweaver equation. Organizing the pages into a site is the other. Dreamweaver MX integrates these two functions with intelligence. Most of the action happens on the Site panel, which you can open and view while you build pages. You can also manage a page directly from its document window.

About the Site Panel

For the best and most intuitive site management, look no further than the Site panel (see Figure 1-15) The Site panel appears when you choose Window | Site or expand the Files panel group and click the Site tab.

Unlike other panels, the Site panel has its own menu bar. Because of the huge number of commands and options you can use for managing a site, the specific menu bar is a convenient way to organize the panel—although having two different File, Edit, View,

FIGURE 1-15

Use the Site panel to organize the pages and assets of a Web site. The structure of your site is just a hierarchy of folders and files.

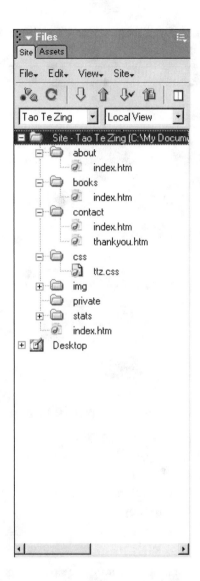

and Site menus on screen at the same time might cause confusion. As you might expect, the Site panel's menus provide commands and options to be used specifically for managing and maintaining your site. The commands and options in the main menus pertain mostly to individual Web pages, although they offer some site-management overlap. As a general rule of thumb, when managing your site, look in the Site panel's menus first.

By default, the Site panel shows the *local view* of the current Web site. The local view is the structure of the site as it resides on your hard drive or internal network. As Figure 1-15 shows, the structure of a site is nothing more than a hierarchy of folders and files. Contrast the local view with the *remote view,* which shows the structure of the live site on the Web.

The distinction between local and remote sites is crucial in Web building. The local site is the work version, accessible only by you and your colleagues, while the remote site is the live version that your visitors see when they point their browsers to your URL. When you update a page, you make the changes to the local version and then upload the modified page to the remote site. The next Scenario and Solution provides a quick reference for keeping these concepts straight.

To switch the Site panel to remote view, you must first connect to the Web server by clicking the button shown here. (It's the leftmost button in the Site panel.) Then look for the drop-down menus under the row of buttons, and choose Remote View from the drop-down menu on the right. The Site panel's main window reconfigures itself to shows the structure of the live site. If you're building a dynamic site, you can view the files on your application server from the Site panel by choosing the Application Server option from the same drop-down menu.

No matter the view, the basic functions of the Site panel are the same. Reorganize the structure of the site by dragging files from one folder to another, use the Site panel's File menu to create new folders and files or delete old ones, and exchange files between local and remote sites with the buttons under the Site panel's menu bar. You can also automatically *synchronize* your site from the Site panel or compare the local and remote sites and update the remote site with the most recent files. To edit a particular page in Dreamweaver, double-click its icon in the Site panel.

SCENARIO & SOLUTION

What is a local site?	The version of the site that you keep on your computer or your internal network. You make changes to the pages of the local site and then upload the modified pages to the remote site.
What is a remote site?	The live version of the site on the Web. You must upload new or updated pages from the local site to the remote site.

Expanding and Collapsing the Site Panel   The Site panel comes in two sizes: collapsed and expanded. The collapsed version appears in the Files panel group, and it shows only one view at a time. The expanded version takes up the entire Dreamweaver workspace, and it shows remote and local views simultaneously, as you can see in Figure 1-16. To expand the Site panel, click the button shown here. (Find it at the far right of the Site panel in the row of icons under the menu bar.) Collapse the Site panel by clicking the same button.

The expanded Site panel gives you a site map for checking and editing the navigation of your local site (see Figure 1-17). View the site map by clicking the button shown here. (Look for the third button from the left under the menu bar.) You can customize the appearance of the site map under View | Layout.

To go back to the files view, click the Expand/Collapse button shown here. (It's the first button on the left under the menu bar.)

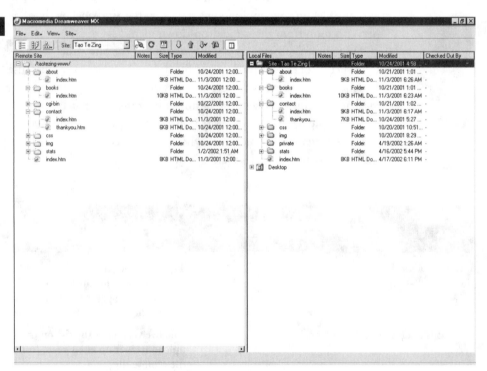

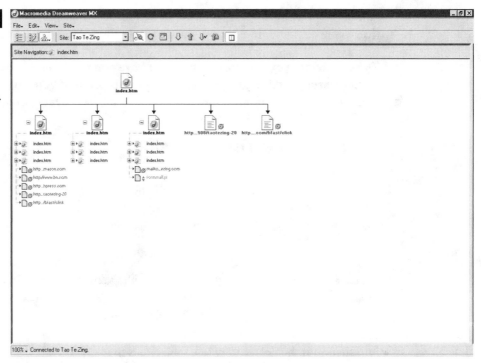

FIGURE 1-17

Check and edit the navigation of your local site with the site map.

About File Management in the Document Window

The Site panel is your best option for managing the files of your site, but you can also perform basic management functions on the current document window from Dreamweaver's main menu. Put the current page on the remote site by choosing Site | Put, or get the remote version of the page for your local site by choosing Site | Get. To find the page in the structure of the local site, choose Site | Locate In Site.

CERTIFICATION OBJECTIVE 1.02

What You Need to Know About Web Building

Dreamweaver is a tool for Web building, and it assumes that you have a certain amount of knowledge about the process of creating a site. If you have experience building Web sites in a professional environment, much of the material in this section should be familiar to you already. If not, think of this section as a crash course, but be aware that you're getting only a cursory introduction. Outside reading is recommended.

exam ⓦatch

The certification exam assumes that you have good working knowledge of Web-building practices and procedures. Don't be surprised if you get a few questions along these lines that don't have anything to do with Dreamweaver specifically.

Designing a Site with the Visitor in Mind

On the Web, the visitor is king. This means that the structure, navigation, design, and functionality of the site need to be usable above all else. No matter how cleverly you craft the graphics or how seamlessly you integrate the applications, the success of your site hinges on a single cardinal virtue: if your visitors can't use your site immediately and intuitively, they won't return.

Why? Because your site is a tool for accessing information. Your visitors want to access the information that your site provides. This is the most essential purpose of any site. Just as you wouldn't want to use a 300-pound hammer to drive a nail, you wouldn't want to use a Web site that makes accessing information confusing or bothersome. The degree to which your site facilitates its primary purpose of providing information is the degree to which your site is usable.

Usability begins with understanding your audience. By anticipating the expectations and technological tolerances of your visitors, your goals for the architectural and visual design of the site become clearer.

Perhaps the most essential ingredients to creating a usable site are as follows:

- Targeting an audience, including the technological preferences of this audience
- Building clear navigation
- Achieving design consistency
- Improving accessibility

Targeting an Audience

If Web building begins and ends with the visitor, the obvious first question becomes, "Who will be the visitors to this site?" The usual answer to this question is "Everybody on the Web." However, the Web is a worldwide medium, and Web surfers come to your site with a variety of languages, cultural biases, and personal tastes, not to mention browser and platform preferences and other technological tolerances. Some want animation, interactivity, and lots of graphics. Others want plain text and links. Some want to view your site on a desktop computer with a huge monitor. Others use laptops, handhelds, cell phones, and Web TV. How can you bring order to the chaos?

A good way to start is to target a specific audience for the site. No Web developer on the planet can create a single site to accommodate everybody. At the same time, no single person on the Web wants to visit every site. By figuring out which people are likely to visit your site, you get a better feel for the requirements, and you can design and develop the site accordingly.

Targeting an audience doesn't necessarily mean extensive market research. Much of it boils down to common sense. If you're building the site of an independent movie studio, for instance, you can make several safe assumptions about the visitors. For one, they aren't coming to the site for important information about their health or investments. They might want to learn more about their favorite movies, or they might be in the process of deciding whether to buy tickets for a new release. Whatever else you feature on the site, you should make it easy for your visitors to access movie information, reviews, clips, and perhaps even local show times.

Your visitors are coming to the site in their spare time, or maybe they're blowing off work, so they are bound to expect some entertainment value from their visit. If you have the resources, interactive games and polls might be fun. If the budget is tight, you might consider a few choice animations or even a clever navigation scheme. You could also think about giving your visitors a downloadable souvenir such as digital movie posters or sharable trailers.

Almost all your visitors enjoy movies. If they didn't, they wouldn't bother visiting your site. This means that they are likely to appreciate strong visuals, so a clear but decidedly graphical approach to the design makes sense. Not too many of your visitors will request a text-only version of your site—at least not all of it. Those local show times sound like they'd be a hit with the cell-phone-browsing set.

By targeting the audience in even the most general way, notice how your site begins to take shape. Your audience expects a strong visual component, so you know that you can design the site for standard monitor sizes and not worry so much about what the pages will look like on a handheld display. Your audience also expects some entertainment value, so you can assume that your visitors will already have a suite of media plug-ins for their browser of choice, which makes QuickTime clips and Flash and Shockwave movies fair game for your site. Since your site targets consumers of motion pictures, many of your visitors probably also enjoy television, in which case your potential Web TV client base may be higher than average. You can optimize the site for browser and monitor viewing, but you should also make sure that Web TV provides a passably satisfying user experience.

Working with Browsers A *user agent* is a tool for accessing a Web site. Browser programs, personal digital assistants (PDAs), cell phones, Web TV, and accessibility devices such as screen readers and Braille readers fall into this category, but the most common user agent by far is the browser.

There are all kinds of browsers on the Web, each with a unique personality—by which I mean that they all do things that they aren't supposed to, and none of them are idiosyncratic in quite the same way. Simply making your site compatible with the three major general-purpose browsers—Internet Explorer, Netscape, and Opera— can cause premature graying.

exam
Watch

You should be familiar with common incompatibility issues between Internet Explorer and Netscape to answer a few of the questions on the exam. I'll cover these situations as they come up throughout the book.

Just as you target an audience for your site, you should also optimize your site for one or two of the major browsers. At the same time, you should make sure that your site works passably well on the others. The best way to achieve this is to test your site extensively at every stage of production. Consider your site optimized when the user experience is flawless in the target browsers and adequate in the peripheral browsers. (An adequate user experience is one that works and supports the main purpose of your site.)

Choosing the best browsers for your site depends on which browsers your visitors use. If you expect a large percentage of your visitors to be casual computer users in North America, you can anticipate that Internet Explorer and Netscape will be the browsers of choice. Opera is popular in Europe, so optimize for this browser if you expect a sizable European audience.

As the builder of the site, you can suggest the best browser for your visitors to use, but you should avoid forcing your choice on them. Stay away from effects, features, and dialects of HTML that work only in a particular browser, even if that browser is your target. Remember, the goal is to make the user experience passable in other browsers, not exclusive to the target browser alone.

Working with Plug-ins A browser program displays HTML pages. Many browsers support images and client-side technology like JavaScript and CSS. The media goodies that you want to incorporate in your site—the Flash and Shockwave movies, the audio and video, the Adobe Acrobat files, and so on—don't work unless the visitor's browser has the right *plug-ins*. A plug-in is nothing more than a piece of software that enhances the functionality of some other piece of software. In the case of a Web browser, a plug-in enables the browser to display a media asset that it wouldn't ordinarily know what to do with.

Before you load down your site with special assets, make sure that your target audience is likely to have the necessary browser plug-ins. Macromedia's Flash plug-in is one of the safest bets, and many Web builders don't think twice about adding Flash content to their sites. QuickTime and Acrobat are also well supported. Still, whenever possible, your site should hold up for visitors who don't have the right plug-ins. Don't rely on media assets to drive the user experience of your site, in other words. Throw them in as nice extras, and add links to the plug-in manufacturer's Web site so that interested visitors can download the required software.

Building Clear Navigation

No matter the target audience, clear, intelligent, intuitive navigation is essential to any Web site. Remember the cardinal rule of usability: If a visitor can't use your site, the visitor won't use it.

The navigation scheme is the control panel of your Web site. Its purpose is to allow the visitor to find desired information quickly. You can't overestimate the importance of speed on the Web. Time works differently there for some reason. At the bank, a one-minute wait is nothing, but on the Web, if it takes one minute for a page in your site to load, your visitor has long since browsed away. Along the same lines, your visitor glances at the main navigation of your site for about a second. If the visitor doesn't know which option to choose, the visitor will probably leave.

To prevent this from happening, make the navigation obvious. The main navigation should occupy a place of privilege in the layout, usually across the top or down the left or right side of the page where the visitor is likely to see it. The navigation should also be visually distinct from the other elements on the page. Color and graphics are helpful but not necessary. Simply making textual navigation slightly larger or more prominent than the body text of the page can do the trick.

To facilitate browsing, organize the navigation into as few categories as possible on the home page, and draw the visitor toward more specific categories on interior pages. This helps first-time visitors to get a feel for the structure of your site, and it's the quickest way to lead them to the information they want. For click-conscious repeat customers, you should consider direct links to specific information, but don't include these choices in the main navigational scheme. Collect them elsewhere, such as in a *jump menu,* which is a drop-down list of frequently accessed pages. Think of these direct links as shortcuts for visitors who already understand the organization of your site.

A usable Web site should offer multiple schemes of navigation. Since different visitors have different reasons for their visit, give your visitors different ways to get around. Some visitors want to browse all the information on your site. Others want to go quickly to a specific area. To accommodate both types of visitors, most sites have at least three navigation schemes: the main navigation, which is usually hierarchical and built for browsing; a search function or jump menu for direct access to specific information; and text links at the bottom of the page that usually match the structure of the main navigation. Text links improve the accessibility of your site, but include them as a courtesy if for no other reason. They save your visitor the trouble of scrolling back to the main navigation at the top of the page.

If your site is large and complex, your visitors might also appreciate navigational tools such as *site maps* and *breadcrumb trails.* A site map is a special page with links to every other page in the site, usually organized by topic. A breadcrumb trail appears on every page and gives the visitor's current location in relation to the hierarchical structure of the site. For example, a visitor to the J.R.R. Tolkien page of a bookseller's Web site might see a breadcrumb trail like this: Home | Fiction | Fantasy | Tolkien, with links to the home page, the fiction page, and the fantasy page.

Achieving Design Consistency

A Web site should feel like a coherent whole. The pages should seem like they belong together. A consistent visual design satisfies this requirement nicely.

Design consistency is important from a stylistic standpoint but also from a navigational one. Most people find it extremely easy to get lost on Web sites. If the look of your site changes from page to page, your visitors have no clear way of figuring out where they are. But if you use a consistent design, your visitors know at least that they haven't left your site, which is a start. An intelligently consistent design goes further. If the main category pages of your site have a common design and the product information pages have a similar but distinct look, your visitors get an idea about where they are without reading any of the content on the page. The design itself suggests the location of the page in the site structure.

You can sum up design consistency with a single rule: *Use every visual element in the design the same way on every page of the site.* A visual element can be a color, a font, a text style like boldface, a link, the title of the page, the location of the main navigation, the copyright notice, and so on. Anything that the visitor sees on the page is a visual element.

Applying this rule is easy. If you decide that unvisited text links should be blue, make sure that all unvisited text links are blue throughout the site, and think twice before you make some other visual element the same shade of blue. Likewise, if you decide that the main navigation should appear at the upper left of every page, place the main navigation at the upper left of every page. Don't move it to the upper right on some pages. When a secondary page needs extra navigation, add these additional choices to the upper right if you like, but reserve the upper left for the main navigation.

You can improve the consistency of your design by using only the visual elements that you need. Less and fewer aren't nearly as fun, but they're usually for the best. For instance, in most cases, you need only a single background color for every page in your site, so choose one and stick with it. One or two font faces should suffice for most sites, so restrict your site to one or two fonts. If you select two, make sure you use them for different purposes, and respect their differences consistently. Avoid using different colors for normal text unless you can support it with a reason that reinforces your overall approach to the design. As long as you insist upon a method to your madness, the design of your site won't get out of hand.

Improving the Accessibility of Your Site

Usability also involves making your site accessible to people with disabilities. It's the polite thing to do, and, depending on where you live and the type of site you're building, it's required by law. All Web sites hosted by the United States government, for instance, must meet certain accessibility standards, so that visitors with disabilities receive equal access to the information on the site.

An accessible Web site offers a comparable user experience to all visitors. In terms of the process of Web building, this goal presents several interesting challenges, none of which is insurmountable. The key is providing a *comparable* user experience. To make an image accessible to visually impaired visitors, for instance, providing alternative descriptive text in the image's HTML tag is usually sufficient. Screen-reading software looks especially for this alternative text, so a visually impaired person gets the gist of the image. As an accessibility-conscious Web builder, you should strive to make the alternative text as descriptive and exact as possible so that the words and the image express the same idea or convey the same information. This is the concept of *text equivalence,* and it's the easiest and most graceful way to make buttons, icons, and other visual elements accessible. Text equivalence extends to such elements as charts and graphs as well, even if these images already contain text. If the captions are part of the image, screen readers can't access them, so make sure you summarize the

FROM THE CLASSROOM

Branding the Perfect Beast

One good way to achieve design consistency is to *brand* the site, by which you tie the visuals of the site to the general look and feel of the client's existing marketing materials. Not only do you help to ensure a coherent visual approach to the site, you also create the conditions for marketing synergy, and your client reaps the benefits of presenting a unified image. At the same time, nobody goes out of their way to see a commercial, unless it's during the Super Bowl. Some common questions arise: What is the best way to brand a site? And how much is too much?

The obvious place to start is with the client's logo. Put it on every page, but place it tastefully. Don't let it dominate the interior pages, where the content should be the focus of attention. You can get away with a large logo on the front page as a kind of identity-defining splash, but keep the logo smaller inside the site. Placing the logo somewhere in the neighborhood of the main navigation keeps it visible but out of the way. To justify its presence, make it clickable and link it to the home page.

An easy way to brand nonintrusively is to use the client's corporate colors in a significant way. If the client's marketing materials use a lot of red, for instance, make red the color of the navigation or the text links. Avoid using red for the background color of the pages, though. White is always best, whether or not it's a corporate color. If you need to get fancy, use a washed-out shade of a corporate color for the background. Make it as close to white as possible.

Utilize other branding elements creatively but subtly in the design. If the client has a recognizable symbol, like a pair of golden arches, perhaps, or a swoosh, appropriate it for small elements like the bullets in a bulleted list, or incorporate it into rollover effects for the navigation buttons. Again, keep the effect low key. Don't bludgeon the visitor with corporate iconography. The idea is to reinforce the content as part of the brand, not upstage it. The same holds true for catchphrases. Instead of emblazoning corporate slogans across the front page where they're completely out of context, try to weave them into the text of the page.

The bottom line is brand, but brand with taste and intelligence. Restraint makes the difference between a branded site and a crass commercialization.

information in text form, either as a caption to the graph or as part of the image's HTML tag. Providing redundant text links for graphical ones is also a good idea, especially if you use *image maps,* or images with separate clickable regions.

Labeling visual elements correctly is another method of improving accessibility. If a page in your site presents a table of data, for instance, make sure that you use the proper HTML markup. Label column heads with the table head tag, `<th>`, instead of the table data tag, `<td>`, and provide abbreviations for the table heads in the HTML. A table should have a summary, which you can also add to the HTML tag.

Accessibility becomes a stickier issue if you want to include media assets, such as Shockwave movies, in your site. Screen readers and other accessibility tools don't currently support text equivalence for most types of multimedia, so to be accessible, animations and video clips must provide separate audio tracks that narrate the visuals and describe the important information. Standards like this cause many accessibility-minded Web builders to shy away from multimedia altogether. Only the most recent version of Flash, Flash 6, supports basic test equivalence for its movies.

To aid you in addressing common accessibility issues, the next Scenario and Solution offers a quick reference.

The World Wide Web Consortium (W3C) provides a comprehensive list of accessibility guidelines and suggested methods for implementation at *http://www.w3.org/WAI/.*

SCENARIO & SOLUTION

What makes an image more accessible?	Providing text equivalence
What makes a graphical link more accessible?	Providing text equivalence and redundant text links
What makes an image map more accessible?	Providing text equivalence and redundant text links
What makes a chart or graph more accessible?	Providing a textual summary of the information
What makes a data table more accessible?	Observing the correct HTML markup, providing table-head abbreviations, and providing a textual summary
What makes multimedia more accessible?	Producing a narrative soundtrack or captions

Taking a Field Trip

Now that you're familiar with the essential philosophy of Web building, log on to the Web and explore two or three of your favorite sites with a critical eye. Evaluate the sites from a usability standpoint, and answer the following questions:

- What are the site's navigational strategies? How effectively does the navigation allow the visitor to access the information on the site? How would you improve the navigation?

- What visual elements does the design employ consistently across the site? Is the overall effect coherent or incoherent? Do you feel like you're in a well-tended garden or a carnival funhouse? How would you improve the consistency of the design?

- Visit the site in Internet Explorer and Netscape. How do the user experiences compare? Which browser seems to provide the better overall experience? Is this browser consistently better on this site, or on some pages is the other browser better?

- How and where does the site employ media assets like animation, audio, and video? Does the site use media effectively or ineffectively? Would any media be equally as effective as simple text or images?

Now, for one of the sites that you critiqued, write out a brief, one-page usability assessment. Start off with your positive findings, and gradually work in your negative findings. Offer possible solutions or suggestions to problem areas.

Find the e-mail link on the site you just critiqued, and send off your usability assessment to the Webmaster. Remember, when you're the visitor, you're the boss.

Understanding Web Production Workflow

Whether you're building a Web site for yourself, your employer, or your client, the process of producing the site follows more or less the same four steps:

1. Planning
2. Design and development

3. Testing and debugging

4. Going live

This procedure varies from builder to builder and project to project. Some builders prefer to combine design, development, testing, and debugging into a single, massive step, especially when working alone, and longer projects may call for a series of development, debugging, and launching phases, but the general rhythm remains essentially the same no matter where you go in the Web-building world.

Planning the Site

I can't stress enough the importance of good planning at the beginning of a Web project. The more fully you realize the idea of your site before you start building, the smoother the rest of production goes. Clients get itchy easily, and the natural tendency among time-constrained, deadline-conscious Web builders is to dive in headfirst and produce some results. Planning gets shortchanged and sometimes ignored altogether in this scheme, and the project almost always ends up running late and over budget. Make sure your boss or client realizes that while planning takes time up front, it allows you to draw up accurate schedules, make reliable estimates, anticipate problems, and turn in better results.

on the
Job

Expect a seemingly endless series of meetings in the early throes of the project while you hash out these details. It's better to have a few boring meetings now than to sweat out an extremely tense meeting later when you explain to the client why the site isn't up.

An important part of planning is determining what the site is going to be. Before anything else, define the purpose of the site. Draw up a list of strategic goals, and decide how the site will achieve them. Also determine the *functional requirements* of the site—the functions or procedures that the site needs to perform, such as keeping track of items in a shopping cart, logging a visitor in and out, or searching a database. Target an audience, and use the expectations of this audience to help you choose the best technology for implementing the functional requirements.

As the idea of the site takes shape, start drawing flowcharts. Organize the content of the site into categories and lay out the navigation. Make it easy for visitors to find the information that they want. Anticipate that first-time visitors will probably browse the site from the main navigation, and return visitors will appreciate shortcuts to specific information. If your site requires the visitor to sign in or check out, now is the time to determine exactly how these processes will work. Map them out from page to page. Always look for ways to reduce the number of steps.

Your site is planned when you have finalized its structure.

Designing and Developing the Site

With site structure in hand, production advances to the design and development stage. Designing the visual look of the site comes before developing the HTML, scripts, animations, and Web applications. If the same person does both, design and development often blend together. In a professional production environment, though, designers and developers usually work on different teams for different bosses. Cooperation between the two teams is essential. Production proper begins with the designers, so the designers should take great pains to hand off complete, clean, and usable work. The developers, in turn, should develop and not redesign. Adequate planning helps to ensure both. When design and development achieve harmonic convergence, it is truly a sight to behold.

Design begins with *page models,* or conceptual sketches of the layout. For the best design consistency, the structure of the site should inform the visuals, not the other way around. If the structure calls for three levels of pages, for instance, the design should incorporate three similar but distinct page models. The graphic design should also accommodate the functional requirements of the site. You achieve a more coherent design when you build the search field into the pages from the start instead of tacking it on as an afterthought.

Choose colors and styles for the visual elements, and describe these in a written style guide. Try to make the style guide as complete as possible. It should provide appearance guidelines for every visual element in the site. By collecting this information in a single document at the start of the project, you allow for quick and consistent design of any new or accidentally overlooked visual elements that crop up during production.

on the
(j)ob

Make sure everyone involved with the project gets a personal copy of the style guide: design, development, marketing, and don't just post it on the intranet. Print it out. Hard copy is easier to reference when the computer screen is full of Dreamweaver.

The design team hands over finished page models to the developers. In many cases, the designers also convert the models into skeleton HTML pages using software like Macromedia Fireworks, Adobe Photoshop, or Adobe ImageReady. Designers use a technique called *slicing,* which divides the page model into separate regions that fit together like the pieces of a puzzle. The software exports the slices as independent image files along with an HTML document that assembles the pieces correctly in a browser.

While the design team is busy building the page models, the development team usually gets a head start on writing the scripts and applications for the functional elements of the site. Development might also create CSSs from the style guide. Then, as the pages come in, development adds the content, programs the links, and integrates the functionality. Page by page, the first working version of the site appears on the *development server,* or the building and testing environment.

Dreamweaver's role in Web production is specifically the development portion of the design and development stage.

Testing and Debugging the Site

Developers do a fair amount of testing and debugging as they construct the pages. Checking a page for bugs in the target browser comes with the territory, and reviewing the page regularly in peripheral browsers is always a good idea.

When the first working version of the site is complete, the testing and debugging stage begins in earnest. Many times, the pages go from the development server to a *staging server,* or an environment that approximates the conditions of the live Web site.

The purpose of testing and debugging is to ensure that all the pages in the site work together as a functional whole. The entire production team assumes the role of the *malicious user* and tries to crash the site deliberately, which can be incredibly fun at the time, even if it causes programming headaches later. You also rate the performance of the site at this stage of production, and you optimize and finalize the coding.

Going Live

When the site on the staging server looks and behaves exactly as it should, the site moves at last to the *production server,* or the live Web environment, for the world to see.

Occasionally, sites go through a limited first launch for a final round of testing and debugging, much like a Broadway show opens in Boston first to work out the kinks. Visitors generally arrive to the limited release by invitation only, and they usually need a password to access the site.

The marketing team kicks into high gear during the launch. Many methods of promotion can be used, not the least of which is registering the site with popular search engines and directories. Adding the URL of the site to business cards, letterheads, and marketing material helps to generate traffic and word of mouth. Advertising is also an option, if an expensive one, and the returns are difficult to measure. It's more cost-effective to sponge off another department's advertising budget by getting your URL into their materials.

CERTIFICATION SUMMARY

This chapter introduced you to Dreamweaver and the general procedures for creating Web sites in a professional production environment.

You learned that Dreamweaver MX is a building and management tool for Web sites. Dreamweaver allows you to create Web sites from scratch or edit and manage existing sites. Dreamweaver contributes the source-code component of the site, including the HTML documents, the dynamic Web apps, the client-side scripting, and the CSSs. Dreamweaver can place and manipulate the assets, or external files that don't reside in the source code, but in all but a few cases, Dreamweaver can't generate these assets. You need different software to create site assets, such as Macromedia Fireworks MX or Adobe Photoshop for images and Macromedia Flash MX or Adobe LiveMotion for Flash movies.

Dreamweaver has two basic views: Design view and Code view. Design view approximates the appearance of a page in a live browser window. However, Design view isn't perfect in its rendering, and interactive elements such as links, rollovers, and forms don't work at all in this view. You should always review your work in a variety of actual browsers before uploading your site to the Web. Code view shows the source code of the page. Most static Web pages use HTML in the source, along with client-side scripting languages such as JavaScript and possibly also style definitions in CSS format. Dynamic Web pages combine HTML with server-specific languages such as CFML to achieve sophisticated functional effects.

You can switch between Design view and Code view with the click of a button. Changes that you make to one view appear in the other when you switch back. Dreamweaver also provides a hybrid Code And Design view, with one pane of the document window devoted to the source code and the other containing the visual layout of the page.

Dreamweaver provides a number of ways for you to keep your eye on the source code as you work in Design view, including the Quick Tag Editor, the Tag Selector, the Tag Inspector, and the Code Inspector panel.

The last part of this chapter focused on the essential characteristics of a well-designed site and the general production procedure in a professional Web-building environment.

You learned that your site is a tool for accessing information, which means that usability is the most important requirement of your site. If your site isn't usable, your visitors won't use it. Several techniques for improving the usability of your site were discussed, such as targeting an audience, maintaining design consistency, and using multiple navigation schemes.

You learned that Web production happens in a series of four steps: planning, design and development, testing and debugging, and going live. You should never underestimate the value of the planning stage. Going into design and development with a solid, well-constructed plan saves time for you and money for the client.

TWO-MINUTE DRILL

What Dreamweaver MX Can Do

❑ Dreamweaver MX is a software application for building and managing Web sites.

❑ Design view shows your Web page as it appears in a browser.

❑ Code view shows the source code of your Web page.

❑ Code-watching tools such as the Tag Inspector and the Tag Selector improve the accuracy of your selection when you work in Design view.

❑ Code view offers timesaving features like Code Hints and Auto Tag Completion.

❑ The Site panel allows you to organize individual Web pages and assets into a coherent Web site.

❑ The Site panel's local view shows the version of the site that you keep on your hard drive or development server.

❑ The Site panel's remote view shows the live version of the site on the production server.

What You Need to Know About Web Building

❑ Targeting an audience for your site helps you to determine the best strategies for design and development.

❑ Optimize your site for one or two common browsers, but make sure that your site offers an adequate user experience in other browsers.

❑ Don't rely on multimedia assets to drive the user experience of your site if these assets require special browser plug-ins.

❑ Provide multiple navigation schemes to appeal to visitors with different browsing preferences.

❑ Adhere to a consistent visual design to improve the coherency of your site.

❑ Provide text equivalents to visual information to improve the accessibility of your site.

❑ Web production typically happens in a four-step process: planning, design and development, testing and debugging, and going live.

SELF TEST

The following questions will help you measure your understanding of the material presented in this chapter. Read all the choices carefully because more than one answer may be correct. Choose all correct answers for each question.

What Dreamweaver MX Can Do

1. Which of the following features help you to improve the accuracy of your selections in Design view?

   A. Code Hints

   B. The Properties panel

   C. The Tag Inspector

   D. The Tag Selector

2. How do you make the Site panel appear?

   A. Choose Window | Site.

   B. Choose View | Site.

   C. Expand the Files panel group and click the Site tab.

   D. Expand the Panels window and click the Site tab.

3. Which of the following statements are true about the Properties panel?

   A. It allows you to modify the properties of an element on the page.

   B. It gives the property structure of the attributes.

   C. It shows the exact HTML tag of the selected element.

   D. It changes depending on what you select in the document window.

4. You want to switch from Design view to Code view. What do you do?

   A. Click the button that looks like this:

   B. Click the button that looks like this:

C. Click the button that looks like this:

D. Click the button that looks like this:

5. Which of the following could be site assets?

   A. Images

   B. Screen readers

   C. Accessibility

   D. Flash movies

6. Black text in Code view indicates what?

   A. A tag or keyword that Dreamweaver doesn't recognize

   B. A valid HTML tag

   C. Text to be displayed in the browser window

   D. JavaScript

7. You can use Dreamweaver to do what?

   A. Create Web sites

   B. Create images

   C. Create Web pages

   D. Create Cascading Style Sheets

8. You want to build a dynamic Web site using ColdFusion. You have Dreamweaver MX. What else do you need?

   A. The correct browser plug-ins

   B. The ColdFusion application server

   C. Any application server that supports ColdFusion

   D. You don't need anything else.

9. What does the local view in the Site panel show?

    A. The live version of your Web site

    B. The files on the production server

    C. The files on the application server

    D. The version of the site that you keep on your computer

10. What does it mean to synchronize your site?

    A. To test your site's download time over a variety of connections

    B. To check that all the hyperlinks work

    C. To coordinate the marketing push with the launch of the site

    D. To update the remote site with the latest versions of the local files

What You Need to Know About Web Building

11. You want to improve the accessibility of your site. What should you do?

    A. Use proper HTML markup.

    B. Add narrative audio soundtracks to Shockwave movies.

    C. Provide text equivalence for Shockwave movies.

    D. Provide text equivalence to images.

    E. Provide narrative audio soundtracks for table data.

12. Which of the following statements are true about usability?

    A. The only thing more important than usability is download time.

    B. To be usable, a site requires graphics.

    C. Consistent design improves usability.

    D. High-traffic sites are the most usable.

13. Which of the following is the best way to troubleshoot your site?

    A. Deliberately try to crash your site before it goes live.

    B. Launch the site and wait for user feedback to identify problem areas.

    C. Assume that you're a typical user, and go through your site carefully before you launch.

    D. Launch the site and then visit it using a variety of browsers.

14. You're building a Web site. Which of the following best describes the usual workflow?

    A. Production server, staging server, development server

    B. Development server, production server, staging server

    C. Staging server, development server, production server

    D. Development server, staging server, production server

    E. Staging server, development sever, staging server

15. What is the best text equivalent for the following image?

    A. A diagram

    B. A picture of a head

    C. Seven areas of the brain

    D. A diagram of a head with seven shaded regions showing different areas of the brain

16. When you're building a Web site for a client, which of the following happens first?

    A. You and the client develop the concept for the front page.

    B. You and the client establish the strategic goals of the site.

    C. You produce page models for the client's approval.

    D. You map out the navigation.

17. What is slicing?

    A. The process of creating separate clickable regions on an image map

    B. The appearance of the broken-image icon in the browser window

    C. The process of dividing a single graphic into two or more separate image files

    D. The process of cutting your site's advertising budget

18. On a large site, which of the following navigation strategies could provide shortcuts to specific information?

    A. Direct links

    B. Jump menus

    C. Search function

    D. Hierarchical content categories

19. What is the production server?

    A. The server that hosts the development files for the site

    B. The server that hosts the live site

    C. The server that hosts all the images and media assets for development purposes

    D. The server that hosts the production settings

20. Which of the following could be the functional requirements of a site?

    A. Round graphical buttons

    B. Dynamically driven content

    C. A shopping cart system

    D. Sign-in and sign-out procedures

LAB QUESTION

You're the sole member of the Web department where you work. You designed and developed your company's Web site, and you spend most of your time maintaining the site and making sure that your visitors have fresh and interesting new content to enjoy.

After reading in the newspaper about an unfavorable court decision involving a large and popular Web site and the inaccessibility of its information to people with disabilities, you decide that it's time for a usability upgrade. It's not that you're worried about being sued; the article simply helped to raise your awareness. You had never considered accessibility issues before.

You come from a graphic design background, and your site reflects your *visual bias*. (You learned that term from the newspaper article.) You notice that you often present concepts on the site with illustrations and icons instead of words. You also prefer to use graphics instead of text links—your site has none—and you prefer to show graphs and charts instead of dry tables of data. A few of the charts on your site are fairly complex.

Your site uses two Shockwave animations, which you also designed. The first is an animated logo, which appears on the front page. The second is a humorous tour of the office featuring a caricature of the owner. This movie appears on the About Us page. It's basically there for fun, but it does contain information about the history of the company that isn't available anywhere else on the site.

You present your idea, and the owner gives you the green light. You smell a bonus in your future. What do you do to make your site more accessible? Create a list of problem areas in the current site, and offer possible solutions. Check your list against mine in the Lab Answer section.

SELF TEST ANSWERS

What Dreamweaver MX Can Do

1. ☑ **C and D.** Both features provide quick access to the HTML, allowing you to fine-tune your selection from Design view.

☒ **A** is incorrect first because it applies to Code view and second because it doesn't improve the accuracy of your selection. **B** is incorrect because it shows the properties of the current selection. It doesn't help you to improve the selection's accuracy.

2. ☑ **A and C.** Use whichever method you prefer to open the Site panel. Both do the same thing.

☒ **B** is incorrect because the Site option is under the Window menu, not the View menu. **D** is incorrect because there is no feature called the Panels window in Dreamweaver.

3. ☑ **A and D.** The Properties panel allows you to modify the properties of the selected element, and the options on the panel change, depending on the type of element that you select.

☒ **B** is incorrect because it is full of empty jargon. It might sound good, but it specifies nothing. Watch out for choices like this on the exam! **C** is incorrect because the Properties panel doesn't show the exact HTML tag of the selection. You're thinking of the Quick Tag Editor.

4. ☑ **D.** The Show Code View button is the first button on the left at the top of the Dreamweaver interface.

☒ **A** is incorrect because it shows the button for expanding and collapsing the Site panel. **B** is incorrect because it shows the button for switching to Design view. **C** is incorrect because it shows the button for connecting to the remote site.

5. ☑ **A and D.** Both are excellent examples of site assets, or independent files that the HTML document places in the browser window.

☒ **B** is incorrect because a screen reader is a user agent, not an asset. **C** is incorrect because accessibility isn't an asset in the sense of being a separate file.

6. ☑ **A and C.** Code that Dreamweaver recognizes appears in a variety of colors.

☒ **B and D** are incorrect because valid tags and JavaScript appear in color.

7. ☑ **A, C, and D.** Dreamweaver is a good choice for creating all of these.

☒ **B** is incorrect because Dreamweaver doesn't create images from scratch, but it does allow you to place existing images in your page and manipulate some of their properties.

8. ☑ **B.** Without the ColdFusion application server, the CFML Web applications that you develop in Dreamweaver won't work.

☒ **A** is incorrect because ColdFusion is a server-side technology. The user's browser isn't involved in executing ColdFusion applications, so there is no special ColdFusion plug-in. **C** is incorrect because application servers are highly proprietary! The only app server that supports ColdFusion is the ColdFusion server. **D** is incorrect because the ColdFusion application server is required to execute ColdFusion Web apps. You can develop ColdFusion apps in Dreamweaver without the server, but the apps won't work.

9. ☑ **D.** The local view shows the development version of the site. You need to upload this version to the remote server in order to go live.
   ☒ **A, B,** and **C** are incorrect because these appear in the remote view, not the local view. Note that **A** and **B** signify the same thing.

10. ☑ **D.** Synchronizing the site means updating the remote files with the most recent local files. You can synchronize your site from the Site panel.
    ☒ **A, B,** and **C** are incorrect because these procedures don't describe synchronization.

What You Need to Know About Web Building

11. ☑ **A, B,** and **D.** These measures improve accessibility.
    ☒ **C** is incorrect because screen readers and other user agents don't currently support text equivalence for Shockwave movies. **E** is incorrect because audio soundtracks aren't required for table data. Using the proper HTML tags and providing a table summary is adequate.

12. ☑ **C.** Consistent design improves usability by decreasing the likelihood that your visitors will get lost or disoriented.
    ☒ **A** is incorrect because nothing is more important than usability, not even download time. **B** is incorrect because a perfectly usable site can have a purely textual interface. **D** is incorrect because simply having high traffic doesn't make your site usable. Usability can increase your site's traffic, though, and promote return visits.

13. ☑ **A.** Put on your malicious user hat and give your site the mother of all stress tests before you launch.
    ☒ **B** is incorrect because visitors who write in to complain won't be back any time soon. **C** is incorrect because the average user doesn't try to cause a crash. Treating your site nicely like this doesn't test its limits. Bang it around in the manner of a malicious user for a more reliable assessment of its robustness. **D** is incorrect because, while you should always view your site with a variety of browsers, you should do so on the development and staging servers before you go live.

14. ☑ **D.** Web production usually goes from development server to staging server to production server.

☒ **A** is incorrect because the production server hosts the live site, and you don't start with the live site. **B** is incorrect because the staging server comes before production server, not after it. Remember, the production server hosts the live site, so this server always comes in at the end. **C** is incorrect because the staging server comes after the development server, not before it. The development server is always first. **E** is incorrect because the development server comes first, not second, and the staging server should be the server in the middle.

15. ☑ **D.** Text equivalence means expressing the image with words as specifically and exactly as possible.

☒ **A, B,** and **C** are incorrect because they aren't specific enough.

16. ☑ **B.** If you don't start with a set of goals, you don't know what kind of site you're building or why.

☒ **A, C,** and **D** are incorrect because these steps, while important, should come after you establish the goals of the site.

17. ☑ **B.** Slicing divides a single graphic into separate image files.

☒ **A, C,** and **D** are incorrect because none of these describe slicing as it pertains to Web building.

18. ☑ **A, B,** and **C.** All of these are quicker alternatives to browsing the hierarchical structure of the site.

☒ **D** is incorrect because this method is slower and less direct. It isn't the best way to connect visitors to specific information that might be buried at the bottom of the hierarchical structure of the site.

19. ☑ **B.** The production server is the server that hosts the live site.

☒ **A** is incorrect because this describes the development server. **C** is incorrect because it describes one use of the development server. **D** is incorrect because it contains empty jargon and signifies nothing.

20. ☑ **B, C,** and **D.** All of these represent functions or procedures that the site needs to perform.

☒ **A** is incorrect because round graphical buttons in and of themselves aren't functions that the site needs to perform. They are interface elements that the designer creates.

LAB ANSWER

Making your site more accessible doesn't involve a drastic redesign. All it takes is better awareness about accessibility issues.

First, don't get rid of the images. Every last one of them can stay. To make them more accessible, provide text equivalence. For the illustrations and icons, provide alternative text that spells out what each image is and what is its significance. Include the text as captions under the images, or incorporate it into the HTML.

Second, provide text equivalence for the graphical links, and add redundant text links at the bottom of every page.

Third, provide text equivalence for the charts and graphs that summarizes their information. You should convert the more complex charts to HTML data tables, since summarizing them in prose form is probably too cumbersome. Be sure to use the correct HTML markup. Whether you replace the charts with the tables or present the tables in addition to the charts is up to you.

Fourth, don't worry about making the animated logo more accessible. A visitor who doesn't see it isn't missing anything important in terms of the information that your site contains. The office tour is another story. Even though it's mostly humorous, it does contain original and important information. You should add a narration soundtrack to the movie or at least make the same information available elsewhere on the site in a more accessible form.

Finally, go to the World Wide Web Consortium Web site at *http://www.w3.org* and read the documents about accessibility carefully. The W3C offers free tools for checking the accessibility of your site and gives practical suggestions for implementation.

2

Setting Up
a Web Site

As you know from Chapter 1, a *Web page* is a single HTML document that may or may not include external assets such as images and media, while a *Web site* is a collection of related pages that are organized in a hierarchy of folders and files. When you're working in Dreamweaver, which do you think you should tackle first: setting up the site or building the pages?

Common sense might suggest that you build the individual Web pages first and collect them into a Web site afterward, but the best approach is actually the other way around. Determining the characteristics and structure of the Web site at the beginning of the project, before you start building pages, makes it easier for you (and Dreamweaver) to keep track of the pages and assets. You can move files and modify the site structure at any time during production, and if you do, Dreamweaver automatically updates the links to keep the site functioning properly. This chapter takes you through the process of setting up a Web site in Dreamweaver.

CERTIFICATION OBJECTIVE 2.01

Defining a New Site

Setting up a Web site in Dreamweaver begins with the *site definition,* which is a collection of basic information about the site. You need to define the site only once, at the beginning of the project, before you do anything else. If you need to change the definition later, you can easily do so.

Because defining a site falls under site management, using Dreamweaver's Site panel is the most convenient way to get the job done. To begin, in the Site panel, choose Site | New Site, and the Site Definition dialog box appears, as you can see in Figure 2-1. Choosing Site | New Site from Dreamweaver's main menu opens the same dialog box.

Notice tabs for Basic and Advanced at the top of the dialog box. Under the Basic tab, a three-step wizard guides you through the process of defining the site. If you've never defined a site before, use this method. For Dreamweaver veterans, the Advanced method is better.

After you finish defining your site, click the OK button at the bottom of the Site Definition dialog box to save the definition or click Cancel to close the dialog box without saving.

FIGURE 2-1

Use the Site
Definition dialog
box to set up
your site.

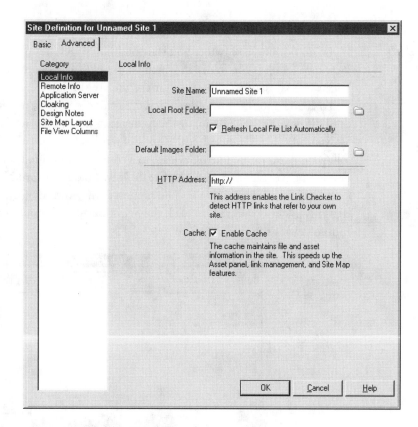

Setting Up Local Information

The first step in defining a site is providing the site's local information. This tells
Dreamweaver where and how to store your site on your hard drive or development
server.

To begin, provide a name for the site in the first field on the first screen (Basic)
or the first field in the Local Info category (Advanced). The name that you provide
here is the one that appears in the drop-down list of sites on the Site panel. You can
use any descriptive name that you want.

If you know the URL of the remote site, enter it in the HTTP Address field of the
Local Info category under the Advanced tab. If you don't know the URL, leave this
field blank for now; you can fill in this information later by editing the definition.

Dreamweaver keeps a *cache,* or a record of the files and assets of your site, which
helps to improve performance. Make sure that the cache is enabled for your site under
the Advanced tab.

Creating a Local Root Folder

If you do nothing else before you start building pages, define a *local root folder*. The local root folder is the folder in which all the HTML documents, Cascading Style Sheets (CSSs), scripts, and assets for the site are stored.

To create a local root folder, click the folder icon next to the second field in the Editing Files step (Basic) or the folder icon next to the Local Root Folder field (Advanced). The Choose Local Root Folder dialog box appears, as shown in the following illustration. Then, navigate to a convenient location on your hard drive or development server and click the Create New Folder button. Name the folder, and double-click its icon to open it. The caption at the bottom of the dialog box indicates that this folder is selected, so click the Select button to choose this folder as the local root folder for the site.

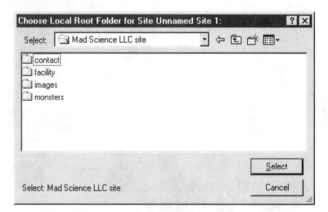

Creating the Default Images Folder

Now is an excellent time to create the default images folder for the site. I mentioned in Chapter 1 that image files are site *assets*—they're independent files that the HTML document positions on the page. It's universal practice for Web builders to store all the images for a site in a single folder called *images* or *img*. Keeping all the images in one folder makes the task of site maintenance much easier, at least when it comes to the graphics. If an image on your site is broken, for instance, you know exactly where to look for the file.

on the job

Feel free to store media assets such as Flash movies in the default images folder.

To create the default images folder, click the Advanced tab on the Site Definition dialog box, choose the Local Info category and click the folder icon next to the Default

Images Folder field. The Choose Local Images Folder dialog box appears. This dialog box works exactly like the one for choosing a local root folder.

Create the default images folder inside the local root folder. Navigate to the local root folder, double-click its icon to open it, and click the Create New Folder button. Name the new folder *images* or *img*. Don't use a different name! You won't crash the Web if you do, but it's best to adhere to standards in professional Web production as a courtesy to your colleagues, your client, and future developers.

After you create the folder, double-click its icon and click the Select button.

Connecting to the Application Server

If you're building a dynamic site, you need to provide connection information about the application server. Remember that in Dreamweaver a *dynamic* site is one that uses server-side technology such as ColdFusion for advanced interactive features. A site with client-side interactivity—JavaScript functions, CSSs—is a static site according to Dreamweaver, even though it may have a high level of interactivity. If your site is static according to Dreamweaver's definition, you shouldn't specify anything for the application server.

Define the connection to the application server in the Testing Files step of the Basic method or in the Testing Server category of the Advanced method. In the Basic method, make sure you answer Yes to the question about whether your site uses server-side technology. Answering No causes Dreamweaver to skip this step.

Choose your site's server technology from the drop-down list in the Testing Files step (Basic) or the Server Model drop-down list (Advanced). If you choose ColdFusion by way of the Advanced method, indicate in the second drop-down box whether the site contains Dreamweaver MX pages only, Dreamweaver UltraDev 4 pages only, or both types of pages. Making an accurate choice helps to improve Dreamweaver's performance.

After you select the appropriate technology, indicate the way that you connect to the application server from the Access drop-down menu and fill in the fields that appear. If you're following the Basic method, choosing the option to set up later essentially skips this step. After you complete the wizard, be sure to click the Advanced tab and look in the Testing Server category to configure the connection properly.

Setting Up Remote Information

The remote information of the site definition tells Dreamweaver how to connect to your production server or Web host. You need to supply this information if you want to use Dreamweaver to upload your site to the Web. Set up the remote information for your site in the Sharing Files step of the Basic method or under the Remote Info category of the Advanced method.

By the Basic method, indicate that, yes, you copy files to another machine, and then specify the way that you connect to it. Fill in the fields that appear. By the Advanced method, choose your connection type from the Access drop-down list and fill in the fields. Your network administrator or Internet service provider (ISP) can help you to configure the connection properly.

You can skip this step in the Basic method by choosing the option to set it up later. Until you define this connection, though, Dreamweaver can't upload your site. Click the Advanced tab after you complete the wizard and configure the connection.

Checking In and Out

Dreamweaver's Check In/Check Out feature helps you to maintain *version control*—that is, it allows only one developer at a time to work on a particular file. This way, you don't end up with multiple versions of the same Web page, each with a different set of improvements. When you work in a collaborative environment, always enable Check In/Check Out by answering Yes to the appropriate question in the wizard (Basic) or checking the check box for this option (Advanced).

Check In/Check Out works like a lending library. Checked-in files are the books on the shelves. They're available on a first-come, first-served basis. Checked-out files are the books in circulation. Someone has already signed them out. Try again later!

When you want to work on a file, check it out by clicking the Site panel button shown here. You can also choose the Check Out command from the Site panel's Site menu or the main Site menu. Once you check out a file, you take it off the shelves, so to speak, so make sure that no one on the team needs to work on it first.

After you finish, simply check in the file so that other developers can access it. To check in a file from the Site panel, click the button shown here, or choose the Check In command from either Site menu.

You can check in and out multiple files simultaneously by holding down CTRL (Windows) or COMMAND (Mac), selecting the files you want from the Site panel and clicking the Check In or Check Out button.

Cloaking Folders and File Types

Dreamweaver's cloaking feature effectively hides certain folders or file types in the local root folder from site-management operations. A cloaked folder isn't put on the production server, for instance, when you upload the site. By cloaking development files such as Fireworks PNGs or Flash FLAs, you can conveniently store these files in your site's local root folder without accidentally uploading them to the Web.

To illustrate the usefulness of cloaking, take the example of a Flash movie. When you create a Flash movie in Macromedia Flash MX, you end up with two files: an FLA version and an SWF version. The FLA version is unplayable; it's for editing purposes only. The SWF version is playable but not easily editable, and this is the version of your movie that belongs on the Web. The FLA version belongs offline. By cloaking FLA files in your site's definition, you can store an FLA alongside its SWF. This makes keeping track of your site's files easier while preventing the wrong version of the movie from going live.

Cloaking is automatically enabled when you define a site. Adjust the cloaking settings or turn off cloaking altogether by selecting the Cloaking category under the Advanced tab. You can also choose Site | Cloaking | Settings from the Site panel.

To cloak a folder, click it in the Site panel and choose Site | Cloaking | Cloak, or right-click the folder and choose Cloaking | Cloak from the context menu that appears. Dreamweaver "crosses out" the cloaked folder in the Site panel, as Figure 2-2 shows.

You can't cloak individual files, but you can cloak file types. To cloak a specific file type, open the cloaking settings for your site, select the Cloak Files Ending With check box, and enter the types of files that you want to cloak. Begin each file type with a period (.), and separate multiple file types with a space. Don't use commas or semicolons! With this is mind, to cloak PNG and FLA files, you would type **.png .fla** in the Cloak Files Ending With field.

exam
Ⓦatch

Go into the exam knowing familiar file-type extensions. The exam uses the abbreviations, not the spelled-out names, as a way to assess your knowledge of general Web-building practices.

The quick reference in the next Scenario and Solution box lists convenient and inconvenient file types to cloak.

SCENARIO & SOLUTION

What file types does it usually make sense to cloak?	Director development files (DIR), Fireworks development files (PNG), Flash development files (FLA), Photoshop files (PSD), and Word documents (DOC)
What file types does it usually not make sense to cloak?	Director movies (DCR), Web images (GIF, JPG), Flash movies (SWF), Web-page source code (HTML), Cascading Style Sheets (CSS), JavaScript source code (JS), and Adobe Acrobat documents (PDF)

FIGURE 2-2

When you cloak a folder, Dreamweaver crosses it out in the Site panel. Cloaked folders are invisible to site-management operations.

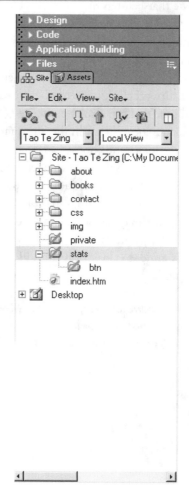

Dreamweaver's file-type cloaking is an all-or-nothing deal. You can't uncloak particular instances of certain file types. You can, however, divide development files into two separate folders. Put the files that you want to cloak in one folder—call it *Cloaked Work Files* or something like that—and put the files that you don't want to cloak in the other folder. Then, cloak the Cloaked Work Files folder. Everything inside becomes invisible to site management, saving you the hassle of bothering with cloaked file types and allowing you to upload certain development files to the Web server.

To uncloak an individual folder, click it in the Site panel and choose Site | Cloaking | Uncloak or right-click the folder and choose Cloaking | Uncloak from the context menu.

To uncloak a particular file type, open the cloaking settings of your site and remove the file type from the Cloak Files Ending With field. To uncloak all file types temporarily, deselect the Cloak Files Ending With check box. Checking the box restores the current list of cloaked file types.

To uncloak all the folders and file types in your site from the Site panel, choose Site | Cloaking | Uncloak All or right-click any folder or file and choose Cloaking | Uncloak All from the context menu.

You can cloak and uncloak multiple folders simultaneously by holding down CTRL (Windows) or COMMAND (Mac), selecting the folders, and choosing the Cloak or Uncloak command.

Using Design Notes

When you're working in a collaborative environment, it can be handy to attach messages to particular files. You may want to call attention to a bug in the functionality of the page or point out a visual element that doesn't match the style guide. You may want to leave a report of what you accomplished so that the next person can pick up where you left off. You may even want to congratulate your colleagues when they do an especially good job. Dreamweaver can keep track of these comments, or *Design Notes,* for you and the rest of the team. Even if you work alone, enabling Design Notes is a good idea because Dreamweaver uses this system internally for better integration with Fireworks and Flash.

on the
job

When you're working in a collaborative environment, enable both the Check In/Check Out and Design Notes features.

To enable Design Notes for your site, click the Advanced tab of the Site Definition dialog box, select the Design Notes category, and select the Maintain Design Notes check box. Select the second check box, Upload Design Notes For Sharing, if your team plans to use the system for passing information back and forth. With this option turned on, Dreamweaver automatically uploads a file's Design Notes whenever you put the file on the remote site.

To attach a Design Note to a folder or file, find and click the folder or file in the Site panel. Then choose File | Design Notes command from the Site panel's menu or the main menu. There's also a Design Notes command in the context menu that slides out when you right-click a folder or file in the Site panel.

No matter how you access the Design Notes command, the process for writing the message is the same. You invoke the command, and the Design Notes dialog box appears (see Figure 2-3). Choose the Basic Info tab. Set the status of the note, and click the calendar icon to insert the current date. Then type your notes. Select the check box under the Notes field if you want your Design Note to appear automatically when anyone opens the page. If you want to leave more detailed information, switch to the All Info tab and click the plus (+) button. Invent a category for the information, such as *sender,* and type this in the Name field. Then fill in the appropriate value, such as *Marc Campbell.* Now developers who switch to the All Info tab see immediately who left the message. When you're ready to submit the Design Note, click OK.

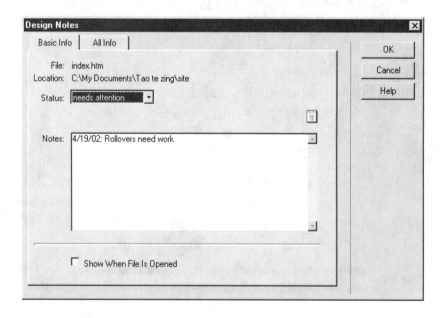

FIGURE 2-3

Use the Design Notes dialog box to leave messages to your colleagues about specific folders and files in the site.

To read a Design Note, expand the Site panel and look for the word-balloon icon in the Notes field, as shown in Figure 2-4. Double-click this icon to open the message, or choose File | Design Notes, or right-click the word-balloon icon and choose Design Notes from the context menu.

To edit a Design Note, double-click the word-balloon icon to open the message and click the All Info tab in the Design Notes dialog box. Select the information that you want to delete and click the minus (–) button. If you delete all the information from the message, the Design Note icon disappears from the Site panel.

FIGURE 2-4   Double-click the word-balloon icon in the expanded Site panel to open a Design Note.

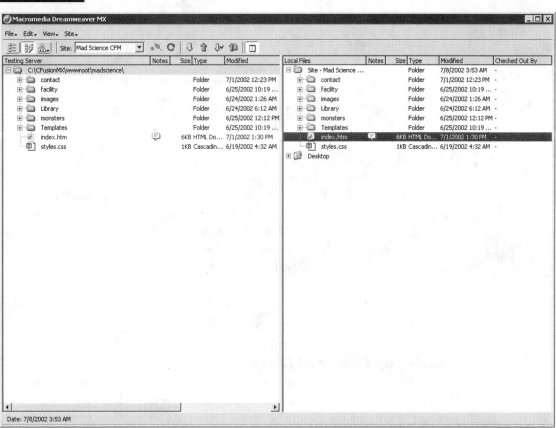

Editing the Site Definition

After you initially define your site, you can go back and make adjustments to the definition. To do so, choose Site | Edit Sites from the Site panel's menu, choose Site | Edit Sites from the main menu or choose Edit Sites from the drop-down list of sites on the Site panel. The Edit Sites dialog box appears, as shown here.

Pick a site from the list and click the Edit button to open the corresponding Site Definition dialog box. Make changes to the definition as necessary and click OK. Click Cancel to close the dialog box without saving the changes.

You can delete a site definition just as easily. Select the site from the Edit Sites dialog box and click the Remove button. Dreamweaver asks if you're sure that you want to remove the definition. This action isn't undoable, so think twice before you click Yes. Be aware also that removing the definition of a site does not delete the local root folder or any of the site files. The site itself remains safe and sound on your hard drive or development server.

When you're done editing sites, click the Done button at the bottom of the Edit Sites dialog box to close it.

Cleaning up Orphaned Design Notes

If, while building your site, you remove a folder or file that has a Design Note, Dreamweaver keeps the Design Note, just in case. You can delete these orphaned messages by clicking the Clean Up button under the Design Notes category of the Site Definition dialog box, as in Figure 2-5. Make sure you click the Advanced tab to see this category.

FIGURE 2-5

Click the Clean
Up button in the
Site Definition
dialog box to
delete orphaned
Design Notes.

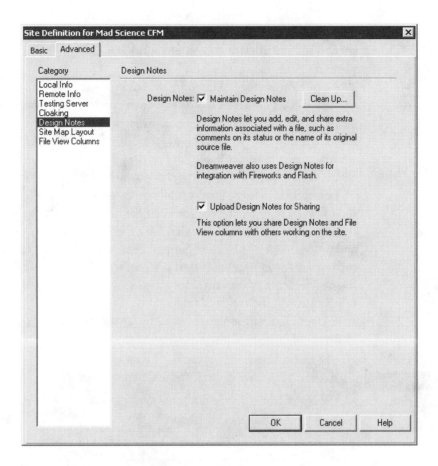

If you deselect the Maintain Design Notes check box before you click the Clean
Up button, Dreamweaver removes all Design Notes from the site.

Building the Site Structure

After you define your site in Dreamweaver, the next step is to build the site structure.
This is much easier than it sounds. As you know, the structure of a site is just a
hierarchy of folders and files. To build the structure, then, all you have to do is set
up this hierarchy.

Remember from Chapter 1 that Dreamweaver comes in at the design and
development stage of Web production. An important stage precedes design and
development: site planning. During planning, you outline the structure of the site

by organizing the content into categories and sketching out the navigation. Don't try to build the site structure in Dreamweaver until after you have completed the planning stage.

A common strategy to building the structure of a site is to create a folder for each of the top-level content categories, which correspond to the choices in your main navigation. Assume that your site has five major categories: Services, Clients, Portfolio, About Us, and Contact Us. The structure of your site calls for five folders—call them *services, clients, portfolio, about,* and *contact.* See how a little up-front planning makes all the difference in design and development?

To create the folders, go to the Site panel, select the local root folder, which is the top folder in the site, and choose File | New Folder. An unnamed folder appears in the site under the local root folder. Give the folder a name—*services,* for instance— and press ENTER or RETURN. Simply repeat this procedure four more times. Each time, don't forget to reselect the local root folder. If you don't, Dreamweaver adds the new folder to whatever folder is currently selected, which disrupts the structure of your site. All the top-level folders should be directly under the local root folder, as in Figure 2-6, not squirreled away inside some other folder. The default images folder should also be at the same level in the hierarchy.

FIGURE 2-6

A common way to structure your site is to create one folder for each choice in the main navigation. Put these folders directly under the local root folder of the site.

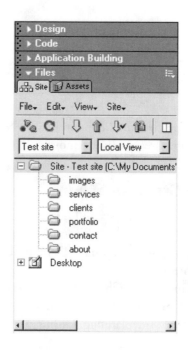

FROM THE CLASSROOM

Looking Beyond the Main Navigation

It's easy to visualize the main navigation of the site in terms of the site structure. If you have five main navigational choices, you create five folders. It takes about five seconds to do.

If your site has only five interior pages, your job is done. But many sites use the main navigation as a way to direct visitors toward more specific information. It's common for a main navigational choice—Books, for instance—to lead to a page with subnavigation, say to the Fiction and Nonfiction pages. Then the Fiction page might lead to further subpages: Mystery, Fantasy, Romance, Science Fiction, Horror, Classic Literature, Contemporary Literature, and so on. What's the best way to organize the structure of this kind of site beyond the first level of folders?

Different Web builders have different schemes. Some prefer flat site structures, where all the subpages appear inside the folder for the main navigational choice. In our example, the folder called *books* would contain files like fiction.htm, nonfic.htm, mystery.htm, romance.htm, scifi.htm, and so on, with no further structural organization, regardless of the navigational hierarchy. A site like this is fairly easy to maintain, since you don't have to put a great amount of thought into why you're doing what.

Other Web builders, including this one, believe that you'll never go wrong if you structure the site according to the navigational hierarchy. Therefore, the *books* folder would contain a folder called *fiction* and a folder called *nonfic,* and inside the fiction folder would be the files mystery.htm, romance.htm, scifi.htm, and the rest.

The great advantage to organizing a site like this is that the navigation becomes the outward expression of the underlying structure. As a result, these sites tend to solve their own organizational problems. You can see more easily which pages ought to link to which other pages, and you can figure out more quickly where best to add new pages. If you have too many steps in your navigation, you see it right away, because there are too many subfolders at a certain level of the site. Rearrange the structure of the site, and you know exactly how to rearrange the navigation.

The downside, of course, is that this structure requires more think-time up front, but a little think-time now can save you headaches later when you're trying to troubleshoot the navigation of your site. Looking at a folder of unstructured files six months later, you could easily forget what's supposed to link to what, much less figure out how to correct it, but if the structure and navigation are in synch, you can answer most of your questions simply by exploring the local root folder.

If you make a mistake, you can move a folder to a new location in the structure by dragging it with the mouse. You can also delete a folder by right-clicking it and choosing Delete from the context menu, or by left-clicking it and choosing File | Delete from the Site panel's menu.

EXERCISE 2-1

Defining the Mad Science LLC Site

In this book, you create a Web site for your client, Mad Science LLC, a full-service mutation, abomination, and aberration facility specializing in monsterification, machinification, creature development, and deployment. You know from your initial meetings with the client that the site has three choices in the main navigation: Our Facility, Monsters, and Contact Us. You choose Dreamweaver MX as your development tool.

In this exercise, you define the site.

1. Launch Dreamweaver.

2. Open the Site panel, and choose Site | New Site from the Site panel's menu. The Site Definition dialog box appears. Since this is your first Dreamweaver project, click the Basic tab to go through the wizard.

3. Type **Mad Science LLC** in the first field. This is the name of the project as it appears in the site list. Click the Next button.

4. Dreamweaver asks if you want to work with a server technology. Choose Yes and then choose PHP MySQL from the drop-down list. Click the Next button.

5. Dreamweaver asks how you want to work with your files during development. Choose the first option, the one for editing and testing locally.

6. Now, create a local root folder for the site. Click the folder icon to the right of the second field to open the Choose Local Root Folder dialog box, and navigate to a convenient location on your hard drive, such as My Documents on a Windows machine. Then, click the Create New Folder button, and provide a name for the folder, like *Mad Science LLC site*. Double-click the folder and click the Select button. The Choose Local Root Folder dialog box disappears.

7. Click the Next button at the bottom of the Site Definition dialog box.

8. Dreamweaver asks for the URL of the local root folder. Leave the default value in the field for now and click the Next button.

9. Dreamweaver asks if you copy your files to another machine when you're done editing them. Choose No and click the Next button.

10. Review the summary screen and click Done. Dreamweaver tells you that it's creating the initial cache for the site. Click OK.

11. The Site panel switches to the local root folder for Mad Science LLC. The local root folder should be highlighted in blue. If it isn't, click the folder's icon.

12. Now, create folders for the structure of the site. Remember that three categories are used in the main navigation: Our Facility, Monsters, and Contact Us. You need one folder for each of these categories in the site structure, plus a default images folder. Go to the Site panel's File menu and choose the New Folder command. Supply the name *facility* for the first folder and press ENTER or RETURN.

13. Repeat step 12 for the following folders: *monsters, contact,* and *images.* Don't forget to select the local root folder before you choose File | New Folder.

14. When you finish, check your Site panel against Figure 2-7. All four folders should be at the same level in the hierarchy, directly under the local root folder. If they aren't, just drag the interior folders to the local root folder—no harm, no foul.

15. Now, fine-tune the site definition. Choose Site | Edit Sites from the Site panel's menu and choose the Mad Science LLC site from the list. Click the Edit button, and the Site Definition dialog box reappears. Click the Advanced tab and select the Local Info category. Then click the folder icon next to the Default Images Folder field, navigate to the folder called *images* within the local root folder, double-click it, and click the Select button.

16. Click the Cloaking category. Enable cloaking and cloak Flash and Fireworks development files. Select the Cloak Files Ending With checkbox and type **.fla .png** in the field.

17. Click the Design Notes category. Make sure that both options are checked.

18. Click OK at the bottom of the Site Definition dialog box and click Done at the bottom of the Edit Sites dialog box. Well done!

FIGURE 2-7

When you finish,
your Site panel
should look
like this.

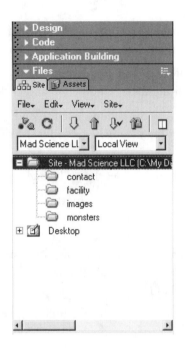

CERTIFICATION OBJECTIVE 2.02

Defining an Existing Site

The last objective assumed that you were building a Web site from scratch, but what if you've already developed a site? What if this site is already live on the Web? Are you seeking Dreamweaver certification in vain?

exam
Ⓦa t c h

You can define any site in Dreamweaver as long as the site has a local root folder, even if you built the site using a competing product.

Absolutely not! Dreamweaver doesn't care how you originated the project. It can manage any Web site. It doesn't matter whether you built the site by hand or created it with a different development tool, whether you just started the project or have long since completed it, or whether you have a local version on your hard drive or access only to the remote version. To manage the site in Dreamweaver, all you have to do is create a *definition.*

Creating the definition for an existing site is much like defining a new site. The same commands and procedures apply, with a few special considerations, which this objective covers. Keep in mind that whenever you define a site in Dreamweaver, the process hinges on the local root folder. If you don't have a local root folder for your existing site, you need to create one, as the next Scenario and Solution sums up.

Defining an Existing Local Site

You have an existing site on your hard drive or development server. How do you define this site in Dreamweaver?

Before you launch Dreamweaver, do a little housecleaning. Move all the folders and files for the site into a single folder and remove from this folder anything that doesn't belong to the site. This folder is going to be the local root folder in the site definition.

SCENARIO & SOLUTION	
How do you create a local root folder for a new site?	Open the Choose Local Root Folder dialog box from the Advanced tab of the Site Definition dialog box by selecting the Local Info category and clicking the folder icon next to the Local Root Folder field. Navigate to a convenient location and click the New Folder button.
How do you create a local root folder for an existing local site?	Move all the files and folders for the site into a single folder and remove everything from this folder that doesn't pertain to the site. Then, in Dreamweaver, open the Choose Local Root Folder dialog box from the Advanced tab of the Site Definition dialog box by selecting the Local Info category and clicking the folder icon next to the Local Root Folder field. Navigate to the folder that contains the site.
How do you create a local root folder for an existing remote site?	Proceed as if you were defining a new site.

Then, in Dreamweaver, open the Site Definition dialog box by choosing Site | New Site from the Site panel's menu or Site | New Site from the main menu. (Use the New Site command, even though the site already exists.) Click the folder icon next to the field for the local root folder and in the Choose Local Root Folder dialog box, navigate to the folder that contains the existing site. Double-click this folder's icon and click the Select button.

exam

ⓦatch

Remember that you use Site | New Site to open the Site Definition dialog box, even though you're defining an existing site. The exam may try to lure you with choices like Site | Define Existing or Site | Existing Site. Don't fall for these traps. Always use Site | New Site to define a site that's new to Dreamweaver, and use Site | Edit Sites to modify existing site definitions.

Now, fill in the rest of the definition fields. When you finish, click OK at the bottom of the Site Definition dialog box. Dreamweaver automatically analyzes the contents of the local root folder and displays the existing site structure in the Site panel. You may now manage the site, rearrange the structure, and edit its pages in Dreamweaver.

EXERCISE 2-2

Defining an Existing Local Site

In this exercise, you define an existing local site. To complete the exercise, you need to have an existing site somewhere on your local system. If you've built Web sites before, this shouldn't be a problem. If you've never built a Web site before, this still isn't a problem, because you have already begun the process in Exercise 2-1. Normally, you would never define an existing site that you already defined from scratch, but for the purposes of this exercise, the Mad Science LLC site works fine, even in its bare-bones state.

1. Before you launch Dreamweaver, prepare the local root folder for the site. Collect all the site files and folders into a single folder and remove anything that doesn't belong to the site. (If you're using the Mad Science LLC site, copy and paste the existing local root folder and give the copy a different name.)

2. Launch Dreamweaver.

3. Open the Site panel and choose Site | New Site from the Site panel's menu. Click the Advanced tab at the top of the Site Definition dialog box. Dreamweaver may give you a warning message that the local root folder is the same for a currently existing site. If this happens, just click OK. You'll choose the correct local root folder in step 4.

4. Click the Local Info category, and supply a name for the site. (If you're using the Mad Science LLC site, supply a different name than the one you used in Exercise 2-1.) Then click the folder icon next to the Local Root Folder field, and navigate to the folder you set up in step 1. Double-click this folder and click the Select button.

5. Click the folder icon next to the Default Images Folder field and navigate to the images folder within the local root folder. Double-click the images folder and click the Select button.

6. Leave the HTTP field blank, and make sure that you select the option to enable the cache.

7. Click the Remote Info category, choose the method that you use to connect to the remote server and fill in the rest of the fields. If you don't know the correct settings, choose None from the Access list.

8. If the existing local site is dynamic, click the Testing Server category and fill in the appropriate information. If the existing local site is static, skip this step. (If you're using the Mad Science LLC site, choose PHP MySQL from the Server Model list and choose None from the Access list.)

9. Set up cloaking and Design Notes as you require for the existing site.

10. Click OK at the bottom of the Site Definition dialog box. Dreamweaver tells you that it's about to create the initial cache. Click OK.

11. The Site panel switches to the existing local site. Mission accomplished. Congratulations!

Defining an Existing Remote Site

You have access to an existing site on the Web, but you don't have a local copy of the site. How do you define this site in Dreamweaver?

on the
job

Since Dreamweaver allows you to define existing remote sites, even if you don't have a local copy of the site, does this mean that you can define your competitor's site and use Dreamweaver to make unauthorized changes? Unfortunately, the answer is no, not unless you know how to configure the remote connection.

The process has two steps. The first step is to create a local root folder for the site and fill in the rest of the definition information. The second step is to connect to the remote site and copy the files to the local root folder. You can then manage the site locally and make updates to the remote site, just as you would for any other site.

Begin with the site definition. Pretend that you're defining a new site, so invoke the New Site command by your method of choice. Create a local root folder as you did before, and make sure that you correctly configure the remote connection. Pay particular attention to the Remote Info category under the Advanced tab. If you don't provide accurate information about the remote site, Dreamweaver won't be able to log on.

After you finish the definition, expand the Site panel so that you can see the remote and local views at the same time, and click the Connect button. Dreamweaver connects to the live site. Select the root folder in the remote view—this is the folder at the very top of the remote site's structure—and click the Get File(s) button, shown here. Dreamweaver asks whether you want to copy the entire site. Click Yes to proceed, and Dreamweaver downloads the entire site, structure and all, to the local root folder.

exam
Watch

Remember that getting is the same as downloading a file from a remote server, and putting is the same as uploading a file to a remote server.

Getting a Branch of the Site

If you don't want the entire site, you don't have to get it. You may copy only as much of the remote site as you want to manage in Dreamweaver.

Do this by holding down CTRL (Windows) or COMMAND (Mac) as you click to select folders and files from the remote view of the Site panel. If you want the entire contents of a folder, select the folder. If you want only specific files from the folder, select the files, but leave the folder unselected. Don't select the remote site's root folder, or you'll download the entire site. Deselect the root folder by clicking it.

When you click the Get File(s) button, Dreamweaver downloads the selected folders and files, building the structure of the local site to match that of the remote.

CERTIFICATION OBJECTIVE 2.03

Setting Up Preview Browsers

After you define your site in Dreamweaver, you're almost ready to start building pages. The last bit of preparation work is setting up the preview browsers.

You know from Chapter 1 that it's a good idea to test your site with a variety of user agents. Dreamweaver's Design view shows you reliably what the pages will look like in a browser, but Design view isn't perfect. It doesn't always give you a completely accurate representation of your page, and functional elements like links, forms, and rollovers don't work. As you build your Web site, preview the site often in a live browser window.

Dreamweaver allows you to choose preview browsers. While you build the pages of your site, you can launch a preview browser with the touch of a function key, and the live browser displays the current document window exactly as it appears on the Web. This section shows you how to set up preview browsers in Dreamweaver.

Choosing a Preview Browser

To define a preview browser, choose File | Preview In Browser | Edit Browser List from either the main menu or the Site panel's menu. You can also choose Edit | Preferences in the main menu and then choose the Preview In Browser category. The Preview In Browser screen of the Preferences dialog box appears, as shown in Figure 2-8.

Which browsers should you use to preview your site? Remember from Chapter 1 that when you target an audience, you also try to figure out which browsers your visitors are using and then you pick one or two of these browsers—the *target browsers*—and optimize the user experience of your site with these programs in mind. You also want to make sure that other browsers and user agents—the *peripheral browsers*—provide an adequate user experience. For the best results, set up all these browsers as preview browsers in Dreamweaver. At the least, set up the target browsers as preview browsers, but don't forget to look at your site in the peripheral browsers regularly outside Dreamweaver.

You can define as many as 20 preview browsers. To add one, click the plus (+) button next to Browsers in the Preferences dialog box. This calls up the Add Browser dialog box. Type the name of the browser in the Name field, as shown in the following

Set up preview
browsers in the
Preview In
Browser category
of the
Preferences
dialog box.

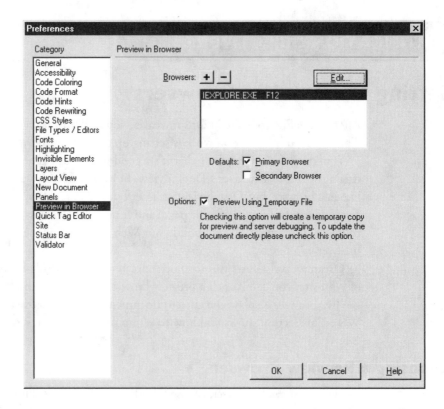

illustration. This is how the browser appears in the Preview In Browser menu, so
include the version number in the name, such as Netscape 6.2, to help you keep your
preview browsers straight. Then click the Browse button and navigate to your local
copy of the browser's EXE file.

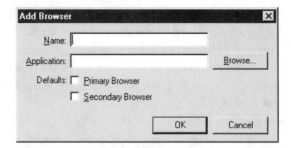

Dreamweaver lets you designate one preview browser as the primary browser and
another as the secondary browser. The advantage to defining primary and secondary

browsers is that these programs launch with a key sequence, saving you the trouble of opening the File menu. You press F12 to launch the primary browser and press CTRL-F12 (Windows) or COMMAND-F12 (Mac) to launch the secondary browser. If you want to designate a preview browser as primary or secondary, select the appropriate check box, but be careful, because if you have already designated a primary or secondary browser, Dreamweaver reassigns the browser without prompting you.

Click OK to set the preview browser. The Add Browser dialog box disappears, and the browser you specified appears in the list in the Preferences dialog box. To edit the definition of a preview browser, select the browser from the list and click the Edit button. To remove a browser entirely, select it and click the minus (–) button.

EXERCISE 2-3

Setting Up Primary and Secondary Browsers

In this exercise, you define two browsers, Microsoft Internet Explorer 6 and Netscape 6.2, as the primary and secondary preview browsers, respectively. You probably already have these applications. If you don't, you should download them from the Web. For Internet Explorer, check out *http://www.microsoft.com* and click the Downloads link. For Netscape, go to *http://www.netscape.com* and click the Download button.

1. Launch Dreamweaver.

2. Choose File | Preview In Browser | Edit Browser List from the main menu. The Preferences dialog box appears with the Preview In Browser category already selected.

3. One or both of the browsers may already appear in the list. For the purposes of this exercise, empty the browser list by selecting each browser and clicking the minus button. (Please note that you wouldn't ordinarily do this!)

4. The browser list should not contain Internet Explorer 6 or Netscape 6.2. Now click the plus button. The Add Browser dialog box appears.

5. Click the Browse button and navigate to the location of the browser's EXE file on your hard drive. Double-click this file.

6. Dreamweaver auto-fills the Name field with the name of the EXE file. Clear this out, and type the much more human-useful **Internet Explorer 6** in the field.

7. Designate this browser as the primary preview browser by selecting the Primary Browser check box.

8. Click OK. One down, one to go!

9. Click the plus button again, and this time navigate to the location of Netscape 6.2's EXE file. Double-click the file.

10. If Dreamweaver doesn't auto-fill a human-useful name, type **Netscape 6.2** in the Name field.

11. Check the Secondary Browser option and click OK. Your browser list should look like the following illustration. If it doesn't, select the browser that doesn't match up, click the Edit button, and change the Name field.

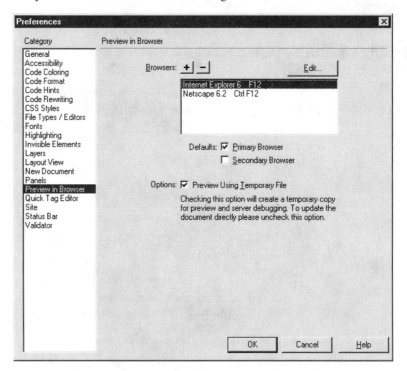

12. Click OK to close the Preferences dialog box. Good job!

Using Dreamweaver's Preview Feature

You can preview a page from Dreamweaver at any time during production.

To preview the current document window in the primary browser, click F12. To preview the current document window in the secondary browser, click CTRL-F12 (Windows) or COMMAND-F12 (Mac). If you want to use a different browser to preview the current document window, choose File | Preview In Browser from the main menu and select the browser from the submenu.

exam

ⓦatch

Remember that pressing F12 launches the primary preview browser. The exam may try to slip you up with alternative function-key references like F1 or F10. For your information, pressing F1 calls up Help, and F10 opens the Code Inspector panel.

To preview any page in the site, open the Site panel and select the page. Use F12 to launch the primary browser, use CTRL-F12 (Windows) or COMMAND-F12 (Mac) to launch the secondary browser, or choose File | Preview In Browser from the Site panel's menu and choose a browser from the submenu.

Notice the Preview Using Temporary File option in the Preferences dialog box. This is an important setting. When you check this option, Dreamweaver creates a temporary HTML file to present in the preview browser, which means that you don't have to save changes in Dreamweaver before you preview. However, the temporary file gives you a one-time-only view. If you make changes to the page and want to preview again, you can't just click the browser's Refresh button. Dreamweaver creates a new temporary file and opens a new instance of the preview browser. Unfortunately, you must close the old instances manually—and you should, because having too many browser windows open can provoke a crash if your system is low on resources.

Unchecking the Preview Using Temporary File option causes Dreamweaver to present the actual HTML document in a single instance of the preview browser, which eliminates the problem of having too many instances of the same browser running at the same time. However, unlike before, you must save the changes to the page before Dreamweaver gives you the preview. If you try to skip this step, Dreamweaver prompts you to save.

Should you check or uncheck the Preview Using Temporary File option? It depends on how you prefer to work. If you like the convenience of previewing a page before you commit the changes, check the option for temporary files. If you don't mind undoing unwanted changes in the interest of leaving the same browser window open,

SCENARIO & SOLUTION	
What are the pros of checking Preview Using Temporary File?	You don't have to save changes before previewing. It's the fastest way to get a preview of the page.
What are the cons of checking Preview Using Temporary File?	Dreamweaver opens a new browser window every time you preview. You have to close these windows manually.
What are the pros of unchecking Preview Using Temporary File?	Dreamweaver presents the previews in the same instance of the browser window. You don't have to keep closing browser windows.
What are the cons of unchecking Preview Using Temporary File?	You have to save changes before previewing. This can slow you down.

uncheck the option for temporary files. The Scenario and Solution above boils down the pros and cons of checking and unchecking the Preview Using Temporary File option.

CERTIFICATION SUMMARY

This chapter showed you how to prepare Dreamweaver for creating and editing your Web site. You learned that you should define your site before you start building pages. A site definition contains information about the structure and characteristics of your site. By defining your site from the get-go, you ensure that Dreamweaver's site-management features work at their peak capacity when you build the individual pages.

Essential to your site's definition is the local root folder, the folder on your system that contains all the folders and files of your site. You can use Dreamweaver's cloaking feature to exclude certain folders and file types in your local root folder from site-management operations. It's often convenient to cloak development file types such as Flash FLAs and Fireworks PNGs. Such file types belong in your local root folder for convenience's sake, but they don't belong on the live version of your site.

You can also define existing sites on your local system. Dreamweaver doesn't care whether you built the site in Adobe GoLive, Microsoft FrontPage, Macromedia HomeSite, or any other tool. As long as you store all the files and folders for your existing site in a single folder, you can assign this folder as the local root folder in Dreamweaver.

You can even define existing sites from a production server as long as you have access to this server. Create a local root folder for the site on your local system and then use Dreamweaver to download the entire remote site or just the folders and files that you need.

After you define a site, you should set up preview browsers in Dreamweaver. It's important to test your site often in live browser windows, since Dreamweaver's Design view isn't always 100 percent reliable in accurately representing your page. Moreover, interactive features such as links, rollovers, and forms don't work in Design view.

Choose preview browsers that your visitors are most likely to use. Choose one or two of the most common as the target browsers for your site, and optimize everything in your site for these browsers. These browsers should give your visitors the best possible user experience of your site. Don't forget about other browsers, though. Keep them on hand as peripheral browsers, and make sure that they provide an adequate user experience of your site.

TWO-MINUTE DRILL

Defining a New Site

❑ Define your site at the beginning of a Dreamweaver project.

❑ Use the New Site command to create the definition of your site.

❑ Store your site at the local root folder on your hard drive or development server.

❑ When you're working in a collaborative environment, enable Check In/Check Out and Design Notes.

❑ Use cloaking to hide folders and files in the local root folder from site-management operations.

❑ Use the Edit Sites command to edit and remove site definitions.

❑ Use the Site panel to build the structure of your site.

Defining an Existing Site

❑ Dreamweaver can manage any Web site as long as the site resides in a local root folder.

❑ Use the New Site command to open the Site Definition dialog box, even though the site already exists.

❑ To define an existing local site, navigate to the site's local root folder in the Choose Local Root Folder dialog box, and fill in the rest of the definition information.

❑ To define an existing remote site, create a local root folder, fill in the rest of the definition information, and then connect to the remote site and download it to the local root folder.

❑ If you want to define only certain branches of the remote site, you may choose the specific folders and files to download.

Setting Up Preview Browsers

❑ Use the Preview In Browser command to see your Dreamweaver page in a live browser window.

❑ Dreamweaver allows up to 20 preview browsers.

❑ The primary preview browser launches when you press F12.

❑ The secondary preview browser launches when you press CTRL-F12 (Windows) or COMMAND-F12 (Mac).

SELF TEST

The following questions will help you measure your understanding of the material presented in this chapter. Read all the choices carefully because there might be more than one correct answer. Choose all correct answers for each question.

Defining a New Site

1. When should you enable Design Notes for your Web site?

    A. You plan to integrate with Fireworks.

    B. You plan to integrate with Flash.

    C. You plan to build a dynamic site.

    D. You're working in a collaborative environment.

2. What is the local root folder?

    A. The folder at the top of your site structure in the Site panel

    B. The folder at the root, or bottom, of your site structure in the Site panel

    C. The folder where you store your site on the production server

    D. The folder where you store your site on the development server

3. What kinds of things can you cloak in Dreamweaver?

    A. Specific servers

    B. Specific folders

    C. Specific files

    D. Specific file types

4. Your Web site has five choices in the main navigation: Products, News, Partners, About Us, and Contact Us. Your site also contains graphics. Which of the following is the best structure for your site?

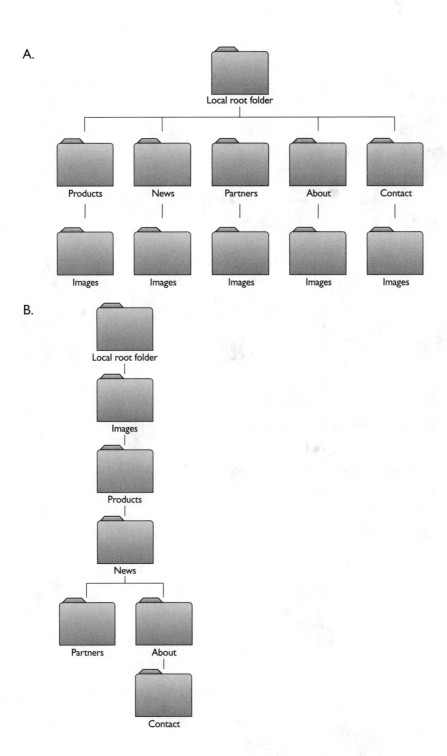

C.

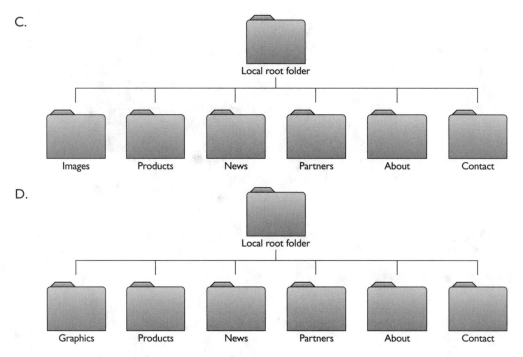

D.

5. You want to remove a folder from the structure of your Web site. How can you do this?

A. Open the Site panel, right-click the folder, and choose Delete from the context menu.

B. Open the Site panel and drag the folder to the bottom of the panel.

C. Open the Site panel, click the folder, and choose File | Delete from the Site panel's menu.

D. Open the Site panel, click the folder, and choose File | Delete from Dreamweaver's main menu.

6. Which of the following file types does it usually make sense to cloak?

A. CSS

B. HTML

C. FLA

D. PNG

7. You're managing a team of six developers building a Web site. Which Dreamweaver features should you enable when you define the site?

    A. Design Notes

    B. Check In/Check Out

    C. Roundtable Discussion Forum

    D. Progress Checker

8. Which of the following best describes *site definition* in Dreamweaver?

    A. A collection of information about the local site

    B. A collection of information about the Web project

    C. A hierarchy of folders and files

    D. An information resource on the World Wide Web

Defining an Existing Site

9. You want to define an existing site. What command do you use to open the Site Definition dialog box?

    A. Site | Existing Site

    B. Site | Import Site

    C. Site | New Site

    D. Site | Define Sites

10. What does it mean to get a file?

    A. To download the file

    B. To upload the file

    C. To select the file for downloading

    D. To select the file for uploading

11. You want to use Dreamweaver to manage a site. When do you have to create a local root folder?

    A. When an existing local site sits in a folder created by Microsoft FrontPage

    B. When you want to define an existing remote site and you don't have a local copy of the site

    C. When the folders and files of an existing local site are scattered throughout your hard drive

    D. When you want to build a site from scratch

12. Which of the following kinds of Web sites can Dreamweaver define?

    A. Sites created in Microsoft FrontPage

    B. Sites created by hand

    C. Sites created in Netscape Composer

13. You want to manage a remote site in Dreamweaver, but you want to store only a few branches of the site locally. After you connect to the remote site, what should you do?

    A. Select the root folder of the remote site.

    B. Select the root folder of the remote site, as well as the folders and files that you want to retrieve.

    C. Select only the folders and files that you want to retrieve.

    D. Nothing. You must retrieve the entire remote site.

14. Which of the following statements about root folders are true?

    A. The root folder of the remote site contains the entire remote site.

    B. The root folder of the remote site contains the entire local site.

    C. Dreamweaver doesn't usually show the remote root folder in the Site panel.

    D. Dreamweaver doesn't usually show the local root folder in the Site panel.

    E. The contents of the local root folder and the root folder on the remote site are often comparable, if not identical.

Setting Up Preview Browsers

15. What is the primary browser in Dreamweaver? Choose the best answer.

    A. Netscape 6.2

    B. The default preview browser

    C. The preview browser that launches when you press F12

    D. Microsoft Internet Explorer 6

16. While previewing a Web page using Dreamweaver's Preview In Browser feature, you notice a misspelling in the headline of the page. You correct the headline, save the page, go back to the browser window, and click the browser's Refresh button, but the browser window still shows the misspelled headline. What went wrong?

A. You didn't click the Refresh button twice.

B. The Preview Using Temporary File option is enabled.

C. Too many instances of the browser window are open.

D. You forgot to save the page.

17. How do you set up a preview browser in Dreamweaver?

A. Choose Edit | Preferences from the main menu and select the Preview In Browser category.

B. Choose Edit | Preferences from the Site panel's menu and select the Preview In Browser category.

C. Choose File | Preview In Browser | Edit Browser List from the main menu.

D. Choose File | Preview In Browser | Edit Browser List from the Site panel's menu.

18. Why should you preview your Web site in a browser?

A. Dreamweaver's Design view doesn't always display your page accurately.

B. Links, forms, and rollover effects don't function in Design view.

C. You have to use a browser to view the source code.

D. Dreamweaver doesn't display live data from Web apps.

19. You're setting up a preview browser in Dreamweaver, and you type **Internet Explorer 5.5** in the Name field of the Add Browser dialog box. Why did you do that?

A. Dreamweaver needs to know the version number of the browser.

B. You want to skip the step in which you navigate to the EXE file.

C. You are going to click the Browse button and navigate to the IE 5.5 EXE file.

D. It helps you to distinguish IE 5.5 from IE 6 in your preview browser list.

20. Which of the following are drawbacks to previewing pages using temporary files?

A. You don't see the most recent changes to the page until you click the Refresh button on the browser window.

B. Clicking the Refresh button on the browser window doesn't show you the most recent version of the page.

C. You have to save changes before previewing.

D. Every time you preview, you open a new instance of the browser window.

LAB QUESTION

You're a Web site builder by trade, and you decide after consulting your financial adviser that it's time to honor your New Year's resolution from three years ago and go into business for yourself.

Giving your two-week notice was the easy part. Now you have to think about attracting some clients. Building a Web site seems like the logical place to start. You want something sleek and cool, something that works as proof of concept for potential customers, so you know your site will include graphics, but you're also a conscientious Web builder, and you know that your site needs to be usable above all else. You need to figure out what's going to be on your site and how you're going to organize it before you start designing pages.

A dozen legal-sized scribble sheets later, you settle on the following categories for the main navigation: About the Studio, Portfolio, Resume, and Contact Me. In addition, you want to include subsections in the Portfolio category for your Web design work and print design work, figuring that you can crank out business cards and letterheads until the first big Web project comes through.

Assuming that you organize your site according to the recommendations in this chapter, what will the structure look like? And how will the structure change when you add a Clients category to the main navigation? Sketch the site structure in both cases.

SELF TEST ANSWERS

Defining a New Site

1. ☑ **A**, **B**, and **D**. Dreamweaver uses Design Notes to integrate better with Fireworks and Flash, and your development team uses Design Notes to exchange information about site files and folders.

   ☒ **C** is incorrect because you don't need to use Design Notes to build any kind of site, static or dynamic.

2. ☑ **A** and **D**. The local root folder is where you store your site on the development server (or your hard drive), and it's the top folder in the Site panel.

   ☒ **B** is incorrect because the bottom folder in the Site panel isn't called the root and also because the top folder in the Site panel is the local root folder. **C** is incorrect because the production server is live on the Web. It's a remote server. The local root folder must be local.

3. ☑ **B** and **D**. Dreamweaver's cloaking feature works on folders and file types.

   ☒ **A** is incorrect because cloaking applies to objects inside the local root folder. Servers aren't inside the local root folder. **C** is incorrect because you can't cloak individual files, but you can cloak all files of a given type.

4. ☑ **C**. This diagram represents the best choice because it has one folder for each of the main navigation items directly under the local root folder and a default images folder at the same level called *images*. You could also use a folder called *img* for the graphics.

   ☒ **A** is incorrect because the site should have only one default images folder. Create this folder at the same level as the five main folders. **B** is incorrect because all the main folders are inside the images folder, and some of the main folders appear inside other main folders. **D** is incorrect because, although the structure is sound, the default images folder is called *graphics*. Only use *images* or *img* as the name of this folder.

5. ☑ **A** and **C**. Use the Delete command in the context menu or the Site panel's File menu.

   ☒ **B** is incorrect because dragging the folder to the bottom of the Site panel simply repositions the folder in the site structure. **D** is incorrect because there is no Delete command in Dreamweaver's main File menu. Look in the Site panel's File menu for the Delete command, or right-click the folder and use the context menu.

6. ☑ C and D. Cloaking Flash (FLA) and Fireworks (PNG) development files in your local root folder is a convenient way to ensure that you don't accidentally upload them to the Web.
☒ A and B are incorrect because you almost always want to upload Cascading Style Sheets (CSSs) and Web-page source code (HTML) when you launch your site. Only cloak file types that you don't want to upload.

7. ☑ A and B. Enable Design Notes to share information about folders and files, and enable Check In/Check Out to maintain version control.
☒ C and D are incorrect because Dreamweaver doesn't have these features, although you could approximate them with Design Notes.

8. ☑ B. In Dreamweaver, the definition of a site is a collection of information about the project.
☒ A is incorrect because it's too specific. The site definition contains information about the local site, but it also contains information about the remote site, the application server, cloaking preferences, and so on. C is incorrect because it describes site structure, not site definition. D is incorrect because it's a quick definition of the term *Web site*. It doesn't describe the term *site definition*.

Defining an Existing Site

9. ☑ C. Find the New Site command in the Site panel's Site menu or the main Site menu.
☒ A, B, and D are incorrect because these aren't Dreamweaver commands. Use the New Site command to define an existing site.

10. ☑ A. To get a file means to download it.
☒ B is incorrect because uploading a file is putting it, not getting it. C and D are incorrect because selecting a file for upload or download is simply selecting it. You must actually download the file to get it.

11. ☑ B, C, and D. In essence, you need to create a local root folder when one doesn't already exist.
☒ A is incorrect because it doesn't matter to Dreamweaver who or what created the folder that contains the site. As long as such a folder exists, Dreamweaver can use it as the local root folder.

12. ☑ D. Dreamweaver can define any Web site as long as it resides in a local root folder.
☒ A, B, C, and E are incorrect because it doesn't matter to Dreamweaver where you originated the site. As long as it resides in a local root folder, Dreamweaver can define it.

13. ☑ **C.** Dreamweaver allows you to choose the folders and files to retrieve, but make sure that you deselect the remote site's root folder.

☒ **A** and **B** are incorrect because including the remote site's root folder causes you to download the entire remote site. **D** is incorrect because Dreamweaver allows you to retrieve specific folders and files from the remote site.

14. ☑ **A** and **E.** The root folder of the remote site contains the entire remote site, and the contents of this folder are similar if not identical to the contents of the local root folder.

☒ **B** is incorrect because the root folder of the remote site contains the remote site, not the local site. The local root folder contains the local site. **C** and **D** are incorrect because the Site panel always shows both the root folder of the remote site and the local root folder. These are the top items in the remote view and local view, respectively.

Setting Up Preview Browsers

15. ☑ **C.** The primary browser is the preview browser that launches when you press F12.

☒ **A** and **D** are incorrect because the primary browser doesn't have to be Netscape 6.2 or Microsoft Internet Explorer 6. You can designate any browser as the primary one. **B** is a reasonable answer, but **C** is more specific and therefore the best.

16. ☑ **B.** When you preview the page as a temporary file, you get a one-time-only view. Clicking the Refresh button doesn't update the view, even after you make and save changes to the original page. To correct this problem, open the Preview In Browser category in the Preferences dialog box and uncheck the Preview Using Temporary Files option.

☒ **A** is incorrect because you don't need to click the browser's Refresh button twice. Once is enough, but even if you click the button 100 times, it won't solve the current problem. **C** is incorrect because while too many browser instances can cause a crash, closing extraneous windows won't solve the current problem. **D** is incorrect because you did remember to save, as the question indicates.

17. ☑ **A, C,** and **D.** Call up the Preview In Browser category of the Preferences dialog box by choosing Edit | Preferences from the main menu or File | Preview In Browser | Edit Browser List from the main menu or the Site panel's menu.

☒ **B** is incorrect because there is no Preferences command in the Site panel's Edit menu. Use the main Edit menu instead.

18. ☑ **A and B.** Preview your site in Dreamweaver to double-check the layout and test functional elements such as links, forms, and rollover effects.

 ☒ **C** is incorrect, because, while you can view the page's source code in a browser, you can also view it in Dreamweaver by switching to Code view. **D** is incorrect because, if you're building a dynamic site, Dreamweaver's Live Data view supplies live data from a Web app.

19. ☑ **C and D.** You want to browse to the EXE file of Internet Explorer 5.5, and you want to distinguish this browser from Internet Explorer 6 in the Preview In Browser list.

 ☒ **A** is incorrect because Dreamweaver doesn't need to know the version of the browser. **B** is incorrect because what you type in the Name field doesn't determine the EXE file of the browser.

20. ☑ **B and D.** When you preview using temporary files, clicking the Refresh button on the browser doesn't update the page, and Dreamweaver opens a new instance of the browser every time you request a preview.

 ☒ **A and C** are incorrect because these are apply to previewing the actual file, not temporary files.

LAB ANSWER

Initially, the structure of your site looks like this:

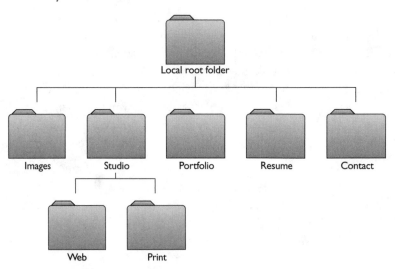

When you add a Clients category, the structure of your site looks like this:

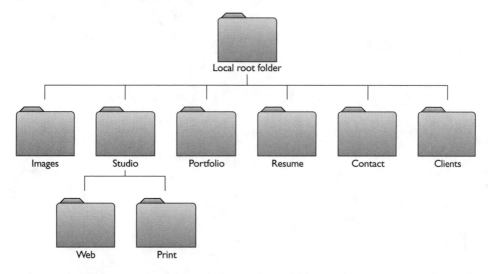

Notice that each of the main navigational choices has a folder in the structure, as do the Print and Web subcategories. Don't forget the default image folder.

Dreamweaver®

CERTIFIED DREAMWEAVER DEVELOPER

3

Opening a New Web Page

I n Chapter 2, you learned how to define a Web site in Dreamweaver. After you define the site, you can start building pages, and every page begins with a Dreamweaver document. This chapter shows you how to open a new document window.

Creating a Document

A Dreamweaver document contains the source code for a piece of your site. A document usually represents a single Web page, but you can create other kinds of documents, too, such as external Cascading Style Sheets and JavaScript listings.

You can create a new document window in Dreamweaver in two ways: The first way is to choose File | New from the main menu. This opens the New Document dialog box (see Figure 3-1), which allows you to specify exactly what kind of document you want to create. Pressing CTRL-N (Windows) or COMMAND-N (Mac) does the same thing.

FIGURE 3-1

The New Document dialog box gives you precise control of the type of document you create.

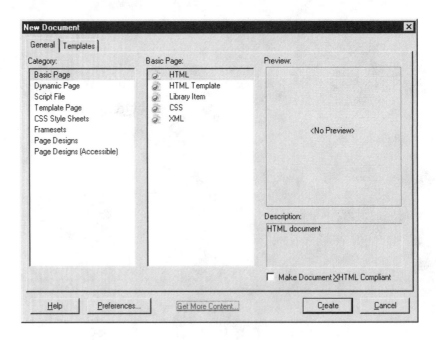

The second way is to open the Site panel, select the folder in which you want to create the document, and choose File | New File from the Site panel's menu. (You can also press CTRL-SHIFT-N in Windows or COMMAND-SHIFT-N in Mac, or you can right-click a folder and choose New File from the context menu.) A new file of the default type for your site appears in the highlighted folder. If you defined your site as static, the default type is an HTML file, in which case the New File command creates a new HTML file. If you defined your site as dynamic, the default type corresponds to the server-side technology you're using in your site. In a ColdFusion site, for instance, the New File command creates a new CFML file; in a PHP site, the same command creates a new PHP file.

Double-click the new file to open it in Dreamweaver. The file is completely blank—it contains no content and a minimal amount of coding, just enough to define it as a file of the default type.

There are advantages to using both methods. In the first method, the New command gives you precise control over the type of document that you create, but you have to deal with the dialog box before the new document appears. Also, the new document doesn't exist on your local site until you save your work. By comparison, the second method is faster. Invoke the New File command, and the default file type appears in the location that you specify—presaved, you might say. The new file exists on your local site from the start. At the same time, the second method creates only the default file type for your site. If you want to add a different kind of file, such as a static HTML file in a dynamic site or an external Cascading Style Sheet (CSS), the New File command can't help you.

When you want to create a new document, then, your first instinct should be to go for the New command, since this gives you the most options, but if you know that you want the new document to be of the default type for your site, go for the New File command. The next Scenario and Solution box spells it out.

SCENARIO & SOLUTION

When should you use the New command?	When you want to create any kind of Dreamweaver document
When should you use the New File command?	When you specifically want to create the default file type for your site

You can make the New command faster, at least when you use CTRL-N or COMMAND-N, by choosing Edit | Preferences, selecting the New Document category, specifying a default file type, and unchecking the option for showing the New Document dialog box. Now, when you use the control-key sequence, Dreamweaver skips the dialog box and automatically opens a document window with the default file type that you specified. This default type doesn't have anything to do with the New File command's default. If you change the New command's default type to CSS, for instance, invoking the New File command still creates an HTML file in a static site.

exam
ⓦatch

The New Document preference you specify under Edit | Preferences doesn't affect the type of file that the Site panel's New File command creates.

Choosing the Right Kind of Document

When you use the New command, the first pane of the New Document dialog box lists the eight categories of documents that you can create: Basic Page, Dynamic Page, Script File, Template Page, CSS Style Sheets, Framesets, Page Designs, and Page Designs (Accessible). Select a category by clicking it. Then choose a document type from the second pane and click the Create button, or simply double-click the document type. With either method, a new document window of the type you specified opens in Dreamweaver.

What type of document should you create? Several choices are available under each category. Using the New Document dialog box requires some brainpower. Fortunately, you have plenty to spare.

Creating a Blank Page

If you want to create a blank page like the kind that the New File command creates, select the Basic Page category for a static page or the Dynamic Page category for a dynamic page. If you select the Dynamic Page category, make sure you select the appropriate type of dynamic file for your site. Don't create a PHP document in a ColdFusion site and expect the PHP Web apps to work!

Creating a Cascading Style Sheet

A Cascading Style Sheet is a document that controls the appearance of textual elements and the layout of the page. You can set many of the same properties using HTML, but it's generally better to attach a style sheet. The World Wide Web Consortium (W3C) has pushed CSS hard for the last couple of years, and not without reason. CSS gives you more options and better control, and it makes site management easier, although browsers vary in their degrees of support. I'll talk more about CSS in Chapter 9.

CSS code can appear within the HTML document, or it can reside in a separate file. If you choose the separate-file strategy, you can create the file with the New command, which gives you two options: opening a blank CSS file under the Basic Page category or opening a predefined CSS file under the CSS Style Sheets category. As you might expect, a blank CSS file is *completely* blank. It has no preset style definitions of any kind. Create this type of style sheet when you want to build all the style definitions from scratch.

on the
ⓙob

Creating a separate CSS file means that all the pages in your site can reference its style definitions. If you build the CSS into the source code of a page instead, only that page can reference the styles.

A predefined CSS file saves you some work in that it provides style definitions for various page elements. Select the CSS Style Sheet category and choose the predefined style sheet of your choice. You are free to edit a predefined style sheet however you see fit. You may add style definitions, tweak existing ones, or remove styles entirely. These changes affect only the style sheet in your site. If you create a new, predefined style sheet based on the same model, Dreamweaver opens its default CSS file with the original definitions, not the customized version you created for your site.

It might seem odd that you should look under the Basic Page category instead of the CSS Style Sheets category when you want to create a blank CSS file. I won't argue with your logic. However, a good rule of thumb is that whenever you want a blank file, try the Basic Page and Dynamic Page categories first. If you don't find what you want, try a more specific category.

exam
ⓦatch

Remember that the CSS Style Sheets category of the New Document dialog box contains predefined Cascading Style Sheets only. If you want to open a blank CSS file, look under the Basic Page or Other categories.

Creating a Client-Side Script

Client-side scripts such as JavaScript and VBScript can infuse a degree of dynamism to an otherwise static site. Like CSS, scripts can appear within the HTML of a page or in separate files.

To create a blank client-side script file, select the Other category in the New Document dialog box. If you want a predefined client-side script, add a Dreamweaver behavior to an element of your page. I'll cover Dreamweaver behaviors in Chapter 8.

Creating a Template

A *page template* in Dreamweaver is a special kind of document that contains predefined content, such as the layout of a page or the main navigation. Using templates helps you to maintain design consistency throughout your site, but before you can use a template, you have to create one, build the predefined content into it, and save it as a template file. Afterward, you may use the template to create new pages for the site. When you do, the predefined areas of the page are locked—you can't edit them. This prevents you from making changes that would disrupt the consistency of the design.

The magic of templates happens when you update the template file itself. You can edit the locked regions, which represent the common elements on all the pages. Modify the template file, and all the pages that refer to it reflect your changes automatically! Now that's efficient Web building. The Template Page category gives you blank documents for creating templates for static and dynamic sites, not preexisting page designs. If you want preexisting page designs, try the Page Designs and Page Designs (Accessible) categories. Note also that you can create a static HTML template under the Basic Page category, as well as the Template Page category. You can create a blank template file from the Site panel. To do this, select an existing template file and invoke the New File command by your method of choice.

I'll discuss creating Dreamweaver templates in Chapter 10. Until then, just know what a template is and what procedures you can use to create one. Don't create a template just yet, or you may run into problems later on in this chapter.

Creating a Frameset

A *frameset* is a file that defines a system of HTML frames. Framing is a page-layout strategy that divides the browser window into separate areas. Each area, or frame, contains its own Web page. A list of navigational choices might appear in one frame, for instance, and the pages that correspond to these choices might appear in another frame.

Frames can be useful in certain circumstances, but they're often more trouble than they're worth, and in many cases they're an outright liability. I'll tell you all about it in Chapter 4. In the meantime, if you want to set up frames for your site, choose the

Framesets category and then choose from several common layouts. You can modify the frameset later to get the precise layout you need.

Creating a Predesigned Page

Dreamweaver provides two categories of predesigned pages: Page Designs and Page Designs (Accessible). Don't call the documents in these categories Dreamweaver templates, because they aren't. These documents simply have design elements built into them as a timesaving feature for you, much like the predefined Cascading Style Sheets in the CSS Style Sheets category. Unlike pages created from templates, you can freely edit the predefined design elements, and you should. You should edit them a lot, especially in a professional production environment. The page designs aren't bad, and they work well across different browsers, but they are pretty generic-looking; the last thing you want to do is give your client a generic-looking Web site. The Web is teeming with generic-looking pages. There's no better way to make your client's page blend into the background noise than to use one of these predefined designs as is. So use the predefined pages sparingly, when you need a quick guide or example. Don't build a Web site from these pages!

Having said that, glancing at the documents in the Page Designs (Accessible) category is a good way to learn practical techniques for improving the accessibility of your site.

EXERCISE 3-1

Beginning the Mad Science Home Page

In this exercise, you create the document that will serve as the home page for your client, Mad Science LLC.

1. Launch Dreamweaver, open the Site panel, and set the site to Mad Science LLC.

2. Even though you defined the Mad Science site as a dynamic one, you want the home page to be a static HTML page. (You're saving Web apps for the Monsters section of the site.) Go to the main menu and choose File | New. The New Document dialog box appears.

3. Select the Basic Page category, and double-click the choice for an HTML document. Dreamweaver opens a new document window.

4. Almost done! Now choose File | Save from the main menu. Since you haven't saved this file previously, the Save As dialog box appears, as shown here:

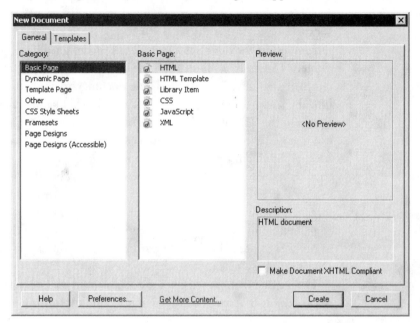

5. Make sure the Save In field shows the local root folder for the Mad Science site. Then type **index** in the File Name field. This is the usual file name for the home page of a site.

6. Click OK. Dreamweaver saves the file to the local root folder as *index.htm.*

7. To prove it, go back to the Site panel, and click the Refresh button, as shown here. The new file appears in the site list. Good job!

Creating a File from a Template

Once you build a page template, which you'll do in Chapter 10, you can use it as the basis for a new page in your site. Click the Templates tab, and the New Document dialog box becomes the New From Template dialog box, as shown in Figure 3-2.

The Templates For pane on the New From Template dialog box lists all the sites that you have defined in Dreamweaver. Select a site, and the templates that you created

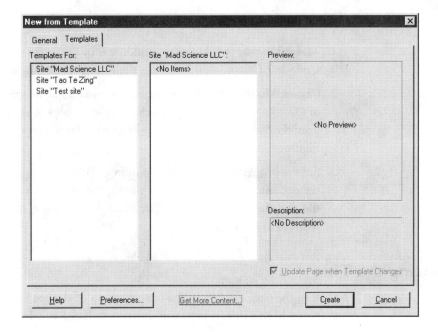

FIGURE 3-2

Create a new
page from an
existing template
with the New
From Template
dialog box.

for that site appear in the Site pane to the right. Choose the template that you want
to use and click the Create button, or double-click the template. A new document
window opens in Dreamweaver with the predefined template content in place.

If this sounds confusing, rest assured: You'll see these procedures in context in
Chapter 10.

CERTIFICATION OBJECTIVE 3.02

Setting Page Properties

You've opened a new Dreamweaver document. Now what?

If you're creating a Web page, now's the time to set the page properties. The *page
properties* in Dreamweaver are a collection of HTML tags and attributes that control
the overall appearance of the page. You find most of these tags and their attributes at
the top of an HTML document.

Here's how to set the page properties:

1. Make sure that the document window is in Design view. You can also use Code and Design view as long as the Design pane has the flashing cursor.

2. Choose Modify | Page Properties from the main menu, press CTRL-J (Windows) or COMMAND-J (Mac), or right-click in Design view and choose Page Properties from the context menu. The Page Properties dialog box appears, as shown in Figure 3-3.

3. Set the properties as your page requires. Click the Apply button to update the document window without closing the dialog box, or click OK to update the document and close the dialog box. Click Cancel to close the dialog box without making changes.

Setting the Title

The title of the page appears in the bar at the top of the browser window. All Web pages should have a title, even if you don't include the title in the design of the page. You don't have to use the file name of the HTML document as the title. In fact, the title can be anything you want, although you should try to make it meaningful to a human. For example, *About Us* is a better title than *about.htm*.

FIGURE 3-3

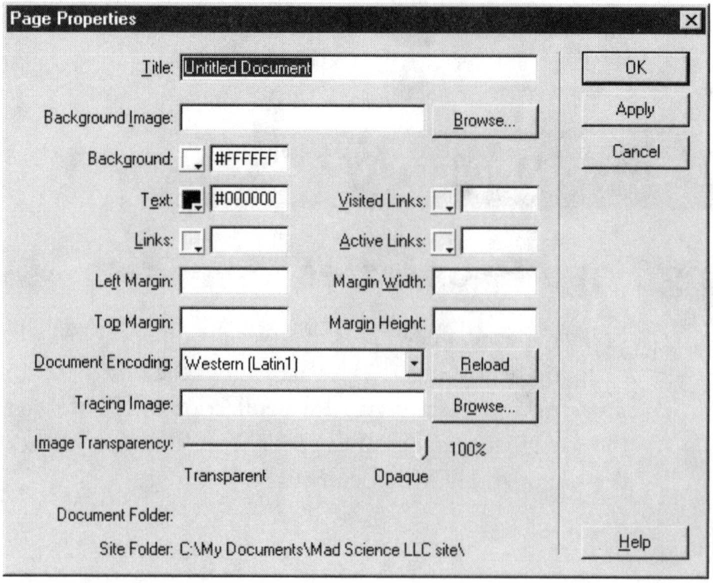

Set the general appearance of the page with the Page Properties dialog box.

Type the title of the page in the Title field of the Page Properties dialog box. You can also set the title in the Title field of the document window, as in the following illustration.

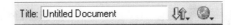

If you supply the title *About Us,* for instance, clicking Apply or OK prompts Dreamweaver to add the following HTML to your document:

```
<title>About Us</title>
```

exam
⚠atch   *The title tag has no attributes.*

Setting the Background Color

To set the background color of the page in the Page Properties dialog box, click the color square next to the Background field. Dreamweaver's Color Picker appears, as shown in Figure 3-4, and the mouse pointer becomes an eyedropper. Choose one of the color cubes in the Color Picker, or move the eyedropper into Dreamweaver and choose a color from the document window or even the software interface.

Notice that each color has a six-character code preceded by a number sign (#). This is the hexadecimal value of the color. If you know the hexadecimal value of the color that you want to use, you can type it directly into the field beside the color square.

Assuming that you choose a very pale blue (#CCFFFF) for the background color, clicking Apply or OK adds the following HTML:

```
<body bgcolor="#CCFFFF">
```

FIGURE 3-4

Choose colors
for visual
elements with
Dreamweaver's
Color Picker.

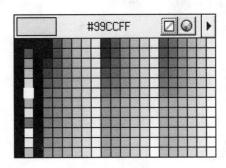

As you can see, the body tag's `bgcolor` attribute controls the background color. The closing body tag, `</body>`, appears at the bottom of the HTML listing.

FROM THE CLASSROOM

Safety First

The colors in the default view of the Color Picker are Web-safe. *Web-safe colors* are common colors that most Windows and Macintosh systems share. They're Web-safe in the sense that you can use them reliably—that is, they'll maintain the color when viewed in most Web browsers. Most of your visitors will have systems that can render these colors correctly.

The standard Web-safe palette comes from comparing Windows and Mac computers running in 256-color mode, of which there are 216 matches. That's a far cry from the 17 million colors that many computers can display, but 216 crayons still beats Crayola's best offering.

What happens if a visitor's system can't reproduce the colors of your page? The system does the best job it can, which usually results in an unappealing shade of brownish yellow. Using Web-safe colors reduces the risk of this happening.

Given that many people who visit your site have systems that are capable of displaying more than the usual Web-safe palette, restricting your color choices to the Web-safe 216 may be a needless limitation. Some Web builders ignore Web-safe colors altogether, pronouncing them a relic of a bygone age, when the typical surfer viewed the Web in 256 colors. There is some truth to this. I haven't run my computer in 256-color mode since 1995. Even so, plenty of clunkers are out there riding on the Information Superhighway. Not everyone buys a new computer every two years, and not everyone is savvy enough to go into the system settings and bump up the number of colors. Your Web site shouldn't discriminate against nonpower users. In fact, it should welcome them, since nonpower users already far outnumber those of us in the relative know.

Even with only 216 choices, the Web-safe palette is diverse enough to give you plenty of interesting combinations, so it's a good idea to use Web-safe colors whenever possible.

Setting the Text Color

The text color represents the default color for text on the page. In the Page Properties dialog box, click the Text field's color square to call up the Color Picker, or type the hexadecimal value for the color directly into the field.

The body tag's text attribute defines the text color in the HTML listing. So if you choose a darker blue (#000066) for the text, pressing Apply or OK tweaks the HTML as follows:

```
<body bgcolor="#CCFFFF" text="#000066">
```

Setting the Link Colors

The body tag has three more color attributes, and these correspond to the three states of links. The link attribute controls the color of unvisited links, which are links to pages that the visitor hasn't already seen. (The browser program keeps track of this information, not the Web server.) The vlink attribute controls the color of visited links, or links to pages that the visitor has already seen. The alink attribute controls the color of active links, or links that are in the process of being clicked. In most cases, the active-link color appears and disappears again quickly.

Set these colors by clicking the appropriate color square or typing the hexadecimal values in the fields. Making unvisited links blue (#0000FF), visited links purple (#660099), and active links red (#FF0000) inserts the following HTML when you click Apply or OK:

```
<body bgcolor="#CCFFFF" text="#000066" link="#0000FF" vlink="#660099" alink="#FF0000">
```

exam
ⓦatch

Look out for bogus tag attributes among the answer choices. There's no such attribute as ulink *for unvisited links, for instance.*

If you don't specify link colors in the body tag, the browser supplies default values. Unvisited links are generally blue, and visited links are purple or green. Active links are red in Netscape, but Internet Explorer and Opera don't display default colors for this state. These browsers draw a thin border around an active link unless you explicitly provide an active-link color in the body tag. It's wise not to stray too far from the

SCENARIO & SOLUTION	
What's the best color for unvisited links?	Blue
What's the best color for visited links?	Purple or green
What's the best color for active links?	Red or none

default link colors, since they have emerged as standards on the Web, and most Web surfers already understand what states these colors represent. If you opt for a different color scheme, make sure that your page looks passable with the browser-default colors anyway, since your visitors can override your color selections simply by setting their browser preferences.

The quick reference in the Scenario and Solution above provides recommended link colors based on browser standards.

If you define a color for the unvisited-link state, define a color for the visited-link state as well, and make it a different color.

Setting the Margins

The Page Properties dialog box allows you to set four body tag attributes that control the margins of the page: `leftmargin`, `topmargin`, `marginwidth`, and `marginheight`, as shown in the next Scenario and Solution.

Specify these values in the appropriate fields. For instance, to eliminate the margins of the browser window entirely in Internet Explorer, positioning the content of the page in the upper-left corner, supply **0** in the Left Margin field and **0** in the Top Margin field. Clicking Apply or OK emends the body tag as follows:

```
<body bgcolor="#CCFFFF" text="#000066" link="#0000FF" vlink="#660099" alink="#FF0000"
leftmargin="0" topmargin="0">
```

For best cross-browser compatibility, though, you would set values for all four attributes.

SCENARIO & SOLUTION

What does the `leftmargin` attribute do?	Sets the amount of space in pixels between the left edge of the browser window and the Web page (Internet Explorer)
What does the `topmargin` attribute do?	Sets the amount of space in pixels between the top edge of the browser window and the Web page (Internet Explorer)
What does the `marginheight` attribute do?	Sets the amount of space in pixels between the top and bottom edges of the browser window and the Web page (Netscape)
What does the `marginwidth` attribute do?	Sets the amount of space in pixels between the left and right edges of the browser window and the Web page (Netscape)

Setting a Background Image

Some pages use a repeating pattern as the background of the page in place of a solid color. This pattern is actually an image file called a *tile*. The browser repeats the image to fill the window.

on the job

Cascading Style Sheets allow you to control the position and repeat pattern of a background image.

If you want to use a background image, the first thing you should do is think twice. Background images are easy to misuse, often rendering the text on the page impossible to read. Make sure that the background image is faint and not distracting before you proceed.

To specify the background image, place the tile in your default images folder and then click the Browse button next to the Background Image field in the Page Properties dialog box. The Select Image Source dialog box appears. Navigate to the tile and either double-click it or click it and click the OK button. If you select a tile called *bgtile.gif*, for example, the body tag changes as follows:

```
<body bgcolor="#CCFFFF" background="images/bgtile.gif" text="#000066" link="#0000FF"
vlink="#660099" alink="#FF0000" leftmargin="0" topmargin="0">
```

The background image completely replaces the background color, unless you use a transparent GIF, in which case the background color shows through the transparent areas of the image.

Encoding the Document

The encoding information of the page indicates which character set the browser should use to display the text of the page. Character sets are divided by alphabet type: Western, Japanese, Cyrillic, and so on. Choose the best encoding for your page from the Document Encoding drop-down list. If you choose the Western (Latin1) encoding scheme, which works well with such languages as English, Spanish, French, and German, clicking Apply or OK adds the following HTML to your page:

```
<meta http-equiv="Content-Type" content="text/html; charset=iso-8859-1">
```

The content attribute of this meta tag gives the code for Western (Latin1).

exam
ⓦatch

Remember that document encoding doesn't provide the language of a Web page. It provides the character set (alphabet) that the language uses.

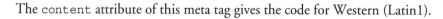

EXERCISE 3-2

Setting the Properties of the Mad Science Home Page

You created a blank HTML file for the Mad Science LLC home page in Exercise 3-1. In this exercise, you set the page properties of the document.

1. Launch Dreamweaver and open the Site panel.

2. Double-click the file *index.htm* to open the home page in Dreamweaver.

3. Choose Modify | Page Properties from the main menu. The Page Properties dialog box appears.

4. Type **Mad Science LLC: Home** in the Title field.

5. You don't want to use a background image, so leave the Background Image field blank.

6. The background color of the page is a slightly jaundiced mint green. It's washed-out enough to be unobtrusive. Type **#CCFFCC** in the Background field.

7. The default text color of the page is black. Type **#000000** in the Text field if this value isn't already there.

8. The unvisited-link color is an indigo blue. It's bright enough to stand out from the background. Type **#6600CC** in the Links field.

9. The visited-link color is a wine purple. Type **#990099** in the Visited Links field.

10. The active-link color is red with a touch of violet. Type **#CC0066** in the Active Links field.

11. Eliminate the margins of the page. Type **0** in the four margin fields.

12. Make sure to use Western (Latin1) for the document encoding.

13. Check your Page Properties dialog box against the one shown here. When yours matches, click the OK button.

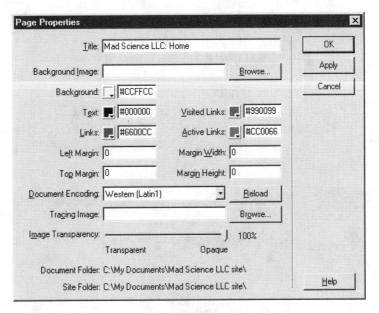

14. Choose File | Save from the main menu to commit the changes to the document in the local site, and you're done. Good going!

Using Preset Color Schemes

Dreamweaver provides several preset color schemes for the body tag attributes. If you want to use these instead of choosing your own colors, close the Page Properties dialog box and choose Commands | Set Color Scheme. This calls up the Set Color Scheme Command dialog box, as Figure 3-5 shows.

Choose a background color from the pane on the left and choose a scheme for text and link colors in the Text And Links pane.

Setting Page Properties in the Code

If you prefer to work in Code view, you don't have access to the Page Properties dialog box, but that doesn't mean you can't set page properties. For one, you can type them directly into the HTML listing of Code view. Experienced coders might prefer this to using the Properties dialog box.

Don't forget that Dreamweaver MX also provides the Tag Inspector in the Code panel group. Using the Tag Inspector is an excellent compromise between straight coding and opening the Page Properties dialog box. By selecting the body tag in the Tag Inspector, for instance, the various attributes appear, including `bgcolor`, `text`, `link`, `background`, `leftmargin`, and the rest, along with a few choices that don't appear in the Page Properties dialog box, like `bottommargin` and `rightmargin`. Simply tab through the attributes and supply their values.

FIGURE 3-5

Not feeling creative? Choose from several preset color schemes with the Set Color Scheme Command dialog box.

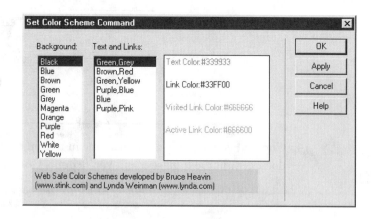

CERTIFICATION SUMMARY

In this chapter, you learned how to open a new document window in Dreamweaver. You learned about the two basic commands for creating new documents: New and New File. Use the New command when you want to create any kind of Dreamweaver document. The New command opens the New Document dialog box, from which you choose the category and type of document that you want to open. If you want to create the default file type for your site, you can skip the New Document dialog box and simply use the Site panel's New File command. This command is more direct but less versatile.

Among the choices in the New Document dialog box are several predesigned pages. While these pages can be useful for inspiration or as springboards for your own creations, you shouldn't rely on them for the finished look and feel of your site. These pages are generic by definition. You should strive to deliver something more unique and better suited to the particular goals for your site.

After you open the document window, you learned to set the properties of the page using Dreamweaver's Page Properties dialog box. Page Properties include the title of the page, the margin, the background color, the default text color, and the default link colors for all three link states: unvisited, visited, and active. Many of these properties appear as attributes of the opening body tag, `<body>`, in the source code. In addition, Dreamweaver provides several preset color schemes that automatically define many of the properties of the page.

TWO-MINUTE DRILL

Creating a Document

- ❏ The main menu's File | New command (CTRL-N or COMMAND-N) opens the New Document dialog box and allows you to create any kind of Dreamweaver document.

- ❏ The Site panel's File | New File command (CTRL-SHIFT-N or COMMAND-SHIFT-N) creates a new file of the default type under the selected folder.

- ❏ Edit the New Document category under Preferences to skip the New Document dialog box when you use the control-key sequence.

- ❏ Under the General tab of the New Document dialog box, choose a document category and then double-click the type of document that you want to create.

- ❏ Use the predesigned pages in the Page Designs and Page Designs (Accessible) categories as guides or examples.

- ❏ Create a new page template from the Basic Page or Template Page categories in the New Document dialog box or by highlighting an existing template in the Site panel and invoking the New File command.

- ❏ Look under the Templates tab to create a new document from the existing page templates for a particular site.

Setting Page Properties

- ❏ The page properties in Dreamweaver control the general appearance of the page.

- ❏ Use the Page Properties dialog box to set the properties of the page.

- ❏ The title tag `<title>` provides the title of the page as it appears in the title bar of the browser window.

- ❏ The body tag `<body>` contains attributes for controlling the text, link, and background colors, as well as the margins of the page.

- ❏ The body tag attributes `leftmargin` and `topmargin` apply to Internet Explorer, while `marginheight` and `marginwidth` apply to Netscape.

❑ The encoding information of a document tells the browser which character set to use in displaying the text.

❑ Dreamweaver provides a number of preset color schemes for background and link colors under Command | Set Color Scheme.

❑ If you know HTML, use the Tag Inspector to modify page properties quickly and accurately.

SELF TEST

The following questions will help you measure your understanding of the material presented in this chapter. Read all the choices carefully because more than one answer may be correct. Choose all correct answers for each question.

Creating a Document

1. What is a Dreamweaver template?

   A. A file from the Page Designs category of the New Document dialog box

   B. A file from the Basic Page category of the New Document dialog box

   C. A file from which you create new Dreamweaver pages

   D. A document that loads with editable predefined content

2. You want to create a blank Cascading Style Sheet in Dreamweaver. What should you do?

   A. Choose File | New from the main menu and look under the Basic Page category.

   B. Choose File | New from the Site panel's menu and look under the CSS Style Sheets category.

   C. Choose File | New from the main menu and look under the CSS Style Sheets category.

   D. Set the default file type to CSS under Edit | Preferences and choose File | New File from the Site panel's menu.

3. What kind of file does the Site panel's File | New File command create in a static site?

   A. CFML

   B. PHP

   C. A file of the type that you specify in the New Document category under Edit | Preferences

   D. HTML

4. Which of the following statements are true about documents with predefined content?

   A. These documents are Dreamweaver templates.

   B. You can edit the predefined content to suit your site.

   C. You can't edit the predefined content—what you get is what you get.

   D. Dreamweaver provides predefined page designs and predefined Cascading Style Sheets.

5. How do you create a blank HTML document for a static site in one step?

   A. Press CTRL-SHIFT-N (Windows) or COMMAND-SHIFT-N (Mac).

   B. Choose File | New File from the Site panel's menu.

   C. Choose File | New from the Site panel's menu.

   D. Press CTRL-N (Windows) or COMMAND-N (Mac).

   E. Right-click a folder and choose New File from the context menu.

6. The bean counters at your place of employment suggest that you save time and money by building a Web site for a paying client from Dreamweaver's predefined page designs. What's the fatal flaw of this plan?

   A. Dreamweaver's predefined page designs aren't compatible with different browsers.

   B. Dreamweaver's predefined page designs aren't accessible.

   C. Dreamweaver's predefined page designs are generic.

   D. Dreamweaver doesn't allow you to edit the layout of predefined page designs.

7. How do you create a new document from an existing template?

   A. Choose File | New from the main menu, click the General tab, and select the Template Page category.

   B. Open the Site panel, select the template file, and choose File | New File from the Site panel's menu.

   C. Choose File | New from the main menu, click the General tab, and select the Basic Page category.

   D. Choose File | New from the main menu, click the Templates tab, and select the site with the template that you want to use.

8. What is a frameset?

   A. The content of a frame on a Web page

   B. A file that defines a system of frames

   C. A file that contains the content of a frame

   D. The border around a system of frames

9. You want your static site to have more interactivity, so you decide to spruce it up with JavaScript. Where do you store the scripts?

   A. In a separate file

   B. In the source code of the page

   C. On the app server

   D. In a CSS file

10. Why is it a good idea to use Dreamweaver templates in your site?

    A. Templates provide instant, predesigned pages by top Macromedia designers.

    B. When you make changes to the template, the changes apply to all the pages that refer to it.

    C. Templates help you to maintain design consistency.

    D. Templates load faster.

Setting Page Properties

11. Which of the following statements are true about the `marginwidth` attribute?

    A. This attribute controls the left margin of the page.

    B. This attribute controls the right margin of the page.

    C. This attribute controls the top margin of the page.

    D. This attribute controls the bottom margin of the page.

    E. This attribute controls the margins of a page in Internet Explorer.

    F. This attribute controls the margins of a page in Netscape.

12. What information does the encoding of a Web page provide?

    A. The language of the page

    B. The character set that the browser should use to display the text

    C. The hexadecimal codes of the color scheme

    D. The security code key

13. You're building a Web page, and you decide that blue makes the most sense for the unvisited-link color. Why?

    A. The visitor's browser requires it.

    B. You also selected blue as the color for visited links.

   C. Blue has emerged as the standard color for unvisited links.

   D. Blue is also the background color of the page.

14. What is a Web-safe color?

   A. A color that displays properly in most browsers

   B. A color that displays properly on most computers

   C. A color that displays properly in most versions of Internet Explorer and Netscape

   D. A color that displays properly on most Windows and Macintosh computers

15. Which of the following are link-color attributes of the body tag?

   A. `alink`

   B. `vlink`

   C. `ulink`

   D. `link`

16. Which of the following lines of HTML gives the title of the file *contact.htm* as *Contact Us?* Choose the most correct answer.

   A. `<title name="Contact Us" file="contact.htm"></title>`

   B. `<title name="Contact Us">contact.htm</title>`

   C. `<title>Contact Us</title>`

   D. `<title file="contact.htm">Contact Us</title>`

17. When does it make sense to supply a background color, as well as a background image?

   A. When you specify values for the four margin attributes

   B. When the background image is a JPEG

   C. When the background image is a transparent GIF

   D. It never makes sense, because the background image tiles across the entire screen and completely covers the background color

18. How many colors are in the standard Web-safe palette?

   A. 215

   B. 216

   C. 217

   D. 218

19. Which of the following can appear in the body tag?

    A. Encoding information

    B. Default text color

    C. Background image

    D. Margin values

20. How do you choose a preset color scheme for background and link colors?

    A. Open the New Document dialog box and look under the Basic Page category.

    B. Open the New Document dialog box and look under the Color Schemes category.

    C. Choose Command | Set Color Scheme.

    D. Choose Edit | Color Scheme.

LAB QUESTION

You saw it coming. You knew from the initial meeting that the client's corporate colors were a big deal. The client made a point of mentioning it at least five times. "Talk about wrapping yourself in the company flag," you joked afterward. It was only a matter of time before the request came.

Sure enough, you see in an e-mail that the client wants you to use the corporate colors everywhere, not just in the graphical navigation of the site, as you had originally suggested. The client wants the background color, the text color, and the colors for all three link states to reflect the corporate palette, which is as follows: a vivid pink (#FF0066), a slate blue (#0066CC), a kind of indigo purple (#9900FF), a faint, washed-out blue (#99CCFF), and basic black (#000000).

As a conscientious Web builder, you want the client's site to be usable above all else. Your plan was to use standard link colors, since Web surfers already know what these colors represent. You wanted to make sure that the site had legible text and links, and you didn't want the background color to be too overpowering.

You're mulling over how to proceed when suddenly it hits you: There *is* a way to salvage your original plan and satisfy the client's color requirements at the same time. What brilliant scheme have you cooked up this time, and what does the body tag of the client's page look like as a result? Jot down the body tag, and check your result against mine in the Lab Answer section.

SELF TEST ANSWERS

Creating a Document

1. ☑ **B** and **C**. A Dreamweaver template is a file from which you build new Web pages. You can create a static HTML template under the Basic Page category, and you can create other kinds of templates, as well as an HTML template, under the Template Page category.

   ☒ **A** is incorrect because the documents under the Page Designs category aren't Dreamweaver templates, just sample page layouts. **D** is incorrect because it refers to a document from one of the Page Designs categories.

2. ☑ **A**. Choose File | New and double-click the CSS document under the Basic Page category.

   ☒ **B** is incorrect because there isn't a New command in the Site panel's menu, and even if there were, CSS Style Sheets is the wrong category for a blank CSS file. **C** is incorrect because you should look under the Basic Page category. The CSS Style Sheets category contains predefined CSS files, not blank ones. **D** is incorrect because the default file type that you set under Preferences has nothing to do with the default file type that the New File command uses.

3. ☑ **D**. The Site panel's New File command creates a file of the default type for your site. In the case of a static site, this is an HTML file.

   ☒ **A** and **B** are incorrect because they are dynamic file types. **C** is incorrect because the preference you express under the New Document category affects only the type of file that opens when you press CTRL-N (Windows) or COMMAND-N (Mac), not the default file type for your site.

4. ☑ **B** and **D**. Dreamweaver provides predefined page designs, as well as predefined CSS files, and these documents are completely editable.

   ☒ **A** is incorrect because these documents aren't Dreamweaver templates, even though they come with predefined content. These documents don't have the powerful site-management features of a template. **C** is incorrect because you can freely edit all the content that comes predefined in these documents.

5. ☑ **A**, **B**, and **E**. To create a blank HTML document for a static site, press CTRL-SHIFT-N (Windows) or COMMAND-SHIFT-N (Mac), choose File | New File from the Site panel's menu, or right-click a folder and choose New File from the context menu.

   ☒ **C** is incorrect because there isn't a New command in the Site panel's dialog box. The New command is under the main File menu. Also, this command opens the New Document dialog box, which requires more than one step to create a new document. **D** is incorrect because CTRL-N

(Windows) and COMMAND-N (Mac) open the New Document dialog box. You can create a blank HTML document this way, but it takes more than one step.

6. ☑ **C.** Dreamweaver's predefined page designs have a generic look about them. Don't rely on them to provide graphic-design services for your client.
   ☒ **A** is incorrect because the predefined pages work well across different browsers. **B** is incorrect because there is an entire category of accessible page designs. **D** is incorrect because you can freely edit the predefined content. You might be thinking of templates, which restrict editing.

7. ☑ **A and D.** Open a new document based on a template by invoking the New command and looking under the Templates tab of the New Document dialog box or by selecting an existing template file from the Site panel and invoking the New File command.
   ☒ **C and D** are incorrect because these procedures create new blank template files. They don't open a new document from an existing template.

8. ☑ **B.** A frameset is a file that defines a system of frames.
   ☒ **A** is incorrect because the content of a frame is a Web page, not a frameset. **C** is incorrect because the file that contains the content of a frame is a Web-page document such as an HTML file. **D** is incorrect because the border around a system of frames doesn't have a special name.

9. ☑ **A and B.** Store the scripts in a separate file or within the source code of the page.
   ☒ **C** is incorrect because there is no app server on a static site. **D** is incorrect because a CSS file contains a Cascading Style Sheet, not a client-side script like JavaScript.

10. ☑ **B and C.** Templates make short work of global changes, and they help you to maintain design consistency.
    ☒ **A** is incorrect because Macromedia doesn't design your templates—you do! You might be thinking of Dreamweaver's collection of predesigned pages. **D** is incorrect because a template loads no faster or slower than an ordinary Web page.

Setting Page Properties

11. ☑ **A, B,** and **F.** The `marginwidth` attribute controls the left and right margins in the Netscape browser.
    ☒ **C** is incorrect because it refers to the `topmargin` or `marginheight` attribute. **D** is incorrect because it refers to the `marginheight` attribute. **E** is incorrect because it refers to the `leftmargin` and `topmargin` attributes.

12. ☑ **B.** A document's encoding tells the browser which character set to use to display the text.
☒ **A** is incorrect because pages written in different languages can still use the same encoding. English and Spanish, for instance, both use Western (Latin1) encoding. **C** is incorrect because it refers to the body tag, not the encoding. **D** is incorrect because something called a "security code key," whatever that is, wouldn't be in the source code for anyone to see. That's not good security!

13. ☑ **C.** Blue has emerged as the standard color for unvisited links.
☒ **A** is incorrect because, while the visitor's browser can override your color choices, the browser doesn't require certain color choices. **B** is incorrect because visited links and unvisited links should appear in different colors. **D** is incorrect because if the unvisited-link color is the same as the background color, the visitor won't be able to read the links.

14. ☑ **D.** A Web-safe color is a color that displays properly on most Windows and Macintosh computers.
☒ **A** and **C** are incorrect because the visitor's browser has nothing to do with Web-safe colors. It depends on the computer hardware, not the software. **B** is incorrect because it's too broad. The Web-safe color palette comes from common Windows and Mac colors, not colors from other computer systems.

15. ☑ **A, B,** and **D.** The body tag has `link`, `vlink`, and `alink` link-color attributes.
☒ **C** is incorrect because there isn't an attribute called `ulink`. You may be thinking of the unvisited-link state, the attribute of which is `link`.

16. ☑ **C.** You're right in that the name of the file has nothing to do with the title of the page. **C** is the most correct choice.
☒ **A** and **B** are incorrect because they don't give the title as *Contact Us,* and also the HTML is terrible. Remember, the file name of the Contact Us page doesn't affect anything in the title tag. **D** is incorrect because, while it gives the title as *Contact Us,* it also adds the extraneous `file` attribute that the browser will ignore.

17. ☑ **C.** If you use a transparent GIF, the background color shows through the transparent areas in the image.
☒ **A** is incorrect because the margin values don't affect the background color or the background image. **B** is incorrect because a JPEG image doesn't support transparency. **D** is incorrect because, in the case of a transparent GIF, the background color shows through the transparent areas.

18. ☑ **B.** There are 216 colors in the standard Web-safe palette.
☒ **A, C,** and **D** are close but incorrect. The correct number is 216.

19. ☑ **B, C** and **D.** The default text color, the background image, and margin values can all appear in the body tag as attribute/value pairs.

 ☒ **A** is incorrect because the encoding information is part of a meta tag, not the body tag.

20. ☑ **C.** Choose Command | Set Color Scheme to pick from Dreamweaver's preset color schemes.

 ☒ **A** is incorrect because the Basic Page category doesn't offer preset color schemes. **B** is incorrect because there isn't a Color Schemes category in the New Document dialog box. **D** is incorrect because there isn't a Color Scheme command in the Edit menu.

LAB ANSWER

You realized that two of the colors in the client's corporate palette are similar to standard link colors. The rest was easy.

Remember that blue is the standard color for unvisited links, and purple and green are the standard colors for visited links. When you glance at the client's colors, you notice two shades of blue and one purple. Assuming that you make the visited-link color purple, which blue do you choose for unvisited links: the slate blue or the washed-out blue?

Looking at the other colors, it seems that the washed-out blue is the only real choice for a background. The darker and brighter colors would be too dark or too bright, but they all seem like they'd be legible enough in the foreground against a field of washed-out blue. This makes slate blue the link color.

Now for the text and the active-link state. You have two choices: bright pink text and black active links, or black text and bright pink active links. Bright pink seems like it would be hard on the eyes. It's best in small doses, like the split-second flash of an activated link. Besides, black makes better sense as the default text color.

Your job is done. The body tag looks like this:

```
<body bgcolor="#FFFFFF" text="#000000" link="#0066CC" vlink="#9900FF" alink="#FF0066">
```

The attributes may appear in any order.

CERTIFIED DREAMWEAVER DEVELOPER

Part II

Coding and Implementation

CHAPTERS

Dreamweaver®
CERTIFIED DREAMWEAVER DEVELOPER

4

Laying Out
the Page

A fter you open a document window, the next step is to build the *page layout*, which determines where different visual elements appear in the browser window. Page layout often begins with a rough thumbnail sketch on a piece of paper, perhaps also with sizes in pixels for the various sections, as shown in Figure 4-1.

When you're designing a layout, it's important to remember that the visitor might use a different screen width that yours. What looks like a nice fit on your screen could look spaced out and empty or, more likely, cramped and congested on the visitor's screen. The best way around this is to choose a target width for your design, either 800 or 640 pixels, since these are the most common screen settings. Not all your visitors have systems capable of displaying higher resolutions. You should also subtract 40 pixels from your target width to accommodate the browser window's interface and scrollbars. If your target width is 800, plan for a design width in the neighborhood of 760 pixels, similar to the one in the preceding illustration.

Your task is to copy the layout from your sketch into Dreamweaver using one of three techniques: tables, frames, or layers. This chapter shows you how to build layouts using all three.

CERTIFICATION OBJECTIVE 4.01

Achieving Page Layout with Tables

I don't know who first thought of presenting a Web page in an HTML table, but he or she was a genius. The table is the best, most consistent, and by far the most common method for achieving some semblance of graphic design in a browser window.

One gets the impression, though, that using tables for page layout irks standards committees like the World Wide Web Consortium (W3C). To be fair, nobody ever intended for the HTML table tags to be put to this kind of use. An HTML table is supposed to display rows and columns of data, as the name of the element suggests, so it only makes sense that a grassroots movement to expand the definition of what a table can and should be ends up ruffling some feathers. Then again, anyone who gets upset about using a tag in an unspecified way has never removed a screw with a hammer.

The W3C makes a better argument against *layout tables* (as they have come to be called, to distinguish them from the purely on-spec data tables) with regard to their

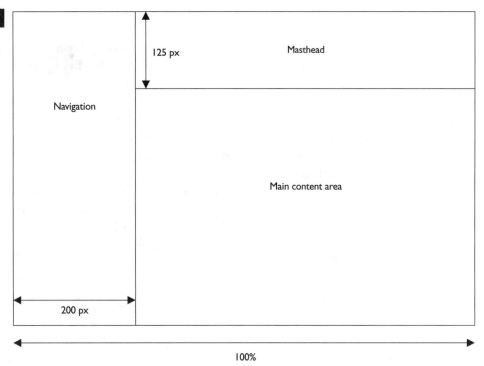

FIGURE 4-1

Page layout often begins with a rough thumbnail sketch like this.

accessibility. Screen readers and the like have a hard time figuring out which section of the page to read first, especially when layout tables are complex and highly designed. HTML table tags simply don't provide the right kinds of attributes for indicating this information, so the W3C and others point to Cascading Style Sheet (CSS)-powered layers as the better strategy for achieving graphic design on a Web page. As long as the layers appear in a linear, logical fashion in the source code, the layout is much more accessible, because screen readers convert text to speech from the top of the HTML document to the bottom. However, browsers vary in their degree and consistency of support for layers, and some browsers don't support layers at all, leaving Web builders with a serious dilemma. On the one hand, it's a virtue for your site to be cross-browser compatible. On the other, it's important to be aware of accessibility. Then again, even the W3C uses layout tables on its home page.

Who knows how this debate will eventually turn out? The fact remains that Web builders continue to create layout tables, and Dreamweaver gives you two ways of doing so: Layout view and Standard view.

Creating Tables in Layout View

Dreamweaver's Layout view allows you to draw tables and cells directly in the document window. Layout view is a mode of Design view. To enter Layout view, make sure that you're in Design view or Code and Design view first. (If you're in Design And Code view, make sure that you click in the Design partition, because you can't switch to Layout view from Code view.) Then, click the Layout tab in the Insert panel and press the Layout View button. You can also choose View | Table View | Layout View from Dreamweaver's main menu. A gray bar appears at the top of the document window to indicate that you're in Layout view.

To design a page in this view, you start by drawing a *layout table.* This represents the outer border of the design. Then you divide the layout table into regions by drawing *layout cells.* The layout cells become the containers, as it were, for the content of the page. Dreamweaver writes the HTML for you as you go.

Drawing Layout Tables

To draw a layout table, click the Draw Layout Table button, shown here. (This is the second button from the right under the Layout tab of the Insert panel.)

Then move the mouse pointer into the document window, hold down the mouse button, and drag the table. Release the mouse button to finish. The document window looks something like that shown in Figure 4-2. Dreamweaver marks the layout table with a green tab, which, of course, doesn't appear on the actual Web page.

Layout tables are easy to resize. First, select the layout table by clicking its green tab. You'll know the table is selected when a gray bar appears along the top of the table and square handles appear on its border. Then drag the handles. Another, more precise way, to resize the table is to select it and type new values in the Width and Height fields of the Properties panel.

Drawing Layout Cells

After you draw the table, you divide it into layout cells. As mentioned earlier, the layout cells hold the content of the page.

To draw a layout cell, click the Draw Layout Cell button, shown here. (This is the button to the right of the Draw Layout Table button.)

Move the mouse pointer into the layout table, hold down the mouse button, and drag the cell. When you release the mouse button, Dreamweaver adds your layout cell to the table and creates cells of its own to ensure the proper spacing, as shown

FIGURE 4-2

To design a page in Layout view, start by drawing a layout table.

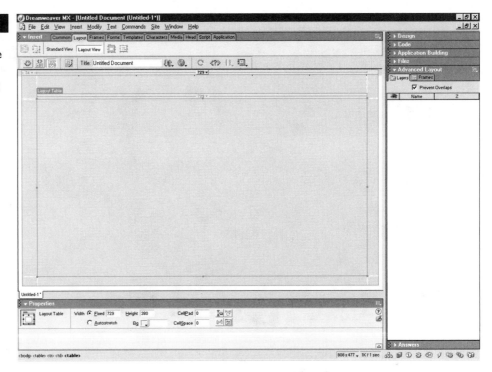

in Figure 4-3. In Layout view, you can add content only to the table cells that you specifically draw. By switching to Standard view, though, you can put content in any cell of the table.

To resize a layout cell, select it by clicking one of its borders. Square handles for you to drag appear around the cell. Notice that you can't drag the layout cell beyond the boundaries of the layout table Notice also that you can't drag a layout cell into the region of another layout cell. If you need more room for a cell, resize the table or adjacent layout cells first. You can also resize the cell mathematically by typing new values in the Width and Height fields in the Properties panel.

To move a layout cell, select it, and drag it by one of its sides. Don't drag it by a handle, or you'll resize the cell. Keep in mind that layout cells can't overlap. Dreamweaver won't let you drag a layout cell into another cell's screen space.

Using Autostretch

As you add layout cells, the gray bar at the top of the table divides into columns. The numbers in the columns show the column width in pixels. These widths are *fixed* in

Divide the table into content areas by drawing layout cells.

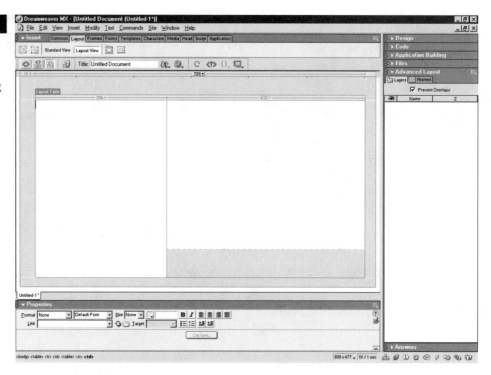

that they always display at this number of pixels, no matter the size of the visitor's browser window.

A common strategy in Web design is to make the main content area of the page *variable width,* so that this column of the table automatically stretches to fill the browser window, whatever its size. Using Dreamweaver's Autostretch feature, you can convert one column per layout from fixed width to variable width.

To do so, select the cell that you want to make variable width, go to the Properties panel, and click the Autostretch radio button. You can also click the width value of the appropriate column in the gray column bar and select Make Column Autostretch from the menu that drops down.

Before turning on Autostretch, Dreamweaver looks for a *spacer image* on your site; if it doesn't find one, it asks you to supply one by way of the Choose Spacer Image dialog box (shown in the following illustration). A *spacer image* is a small graphic file, usually a transparent GIF that's 1 pixel by 1 pixel in size. Dreamweaver uses this image to reinforce the structure of the layout table. Without the spacer image, complex layout tables or layout tables with a number of empty cells may seem to collapse when you test your page in a browser.

The Save Spacer Image File As dialog box gives you three options: Dreamweaver can create a spacer image for you, you can supply an existing spacer image, or you can opt not to use a spacer image at all. Unless you already have a 1 × 1 transparent GIF file in your site's default image folder, let Dreamweaver create the spacer for you. Don't even consider not using a spacer image unless all the layout cells already have content, especially image content—textual content in the fixed-width columns tends to get compressed when you switch to Autostretch. If you don't supply a spacer image, the layout can become distorted, which makes the table difficult to work with. In any case, adding the spacer is never a bad idea: it's small, so it downloads quickly; it won't overwrite any existing table-cell content; and it can improve the stability of the layout.

The W3C recommends that you supply descriptive alternative text for spacer images to improve the accessibility of your page. For a spacer, descriptive alternative text might read something like this: "Spacer image to pad out empty cells of layout table."

After you set a column for variable width, a wavy line replaces the width value in the column bar, and the Width field in the Properties panel grays out. Notice also that the width of the entire layout table becomes variable.

You can switch back to fixed width by selecting either the layout table or the autostretching layout cell and clicking the Fixed radio button. You can also click the wavy line in the column bar and choose Make Column Fixed Width from the drop-down menu.

If you want to use a different spacer image for your site or create a new spacer image, choose Edit | Preferences and choose one under the Layout View category.

Working with the Grid

Dreamweaver's grid is a matrix of horizontal and vertical lines that appears in the back of the document window, as Figure 4-4 shows. Call up the grid by choosing View |

FROM THE CLASSROOM

To Stretch or Not to Stretch?

Should the layout of your Web page use absolute or relative measurements? There are advantages to both.

If you use absolute measurements—that is, supplying pixel values for *width* and *height* attributes in a layout table—the design of your page doesn't break as easily. You can attempt more challenging layouts with less trial and error, and your page appears more consistently across browsers and platforms. That's the upside.

The downside is that, since you should design the layout for a screen width of 800 or 640 pixels, your Web page is constrained to this size. If a visitor with a 640-pixel width screen comes to your 800-pixel width site, the visitor sees an annoying horizontal scrollbar at the bottom of the browser window, which is a Web-design *faux pas* of the first order. On the other hand, if a visitor comes to your 640-pixel width site with a 1024-pixel width screen, which is a popular size for newer computers, the visitor sees large areas of empty space around your page.

You won't have these problems quite as often if you use relative measurements for the table and for at least some of its cells, supplying percentage values instead of pixels for *width* and *height* attributes. Set the table to display at 100 percent, and the table always fills the browser window—no matter what screen size your visitor uses.

You trade off a bit of intricacy of design with relative measurements. It's more difficult to get adventurous layouts to behave properly. However, this trade-off is well worth it. Your site looks more natural to the visitor when it fills the browser window. You reduce the likelihood of vertical scrollbars for visitors with the largest displays. Plus, as long as your site collapses gracefully to fit a 640-pixel width screen, you can consider the scrollbar problem solved for the majority of your visitors.

Remember that Web design is about usability. The usability of your site should drive every design choice, including that of layout. Setting absolute measurements for the layout table is like dictating to the visitor what screen size to use, which shouldn't be a requirement to browse the Web. Almost always, the more usable layout is the one that takes advantage of relative measurements.

Grid | Show Grid. The grid is a feature of the document window. You won't see the grid on the live version of your Web page.

Use the grid to help you create a table. By selecting View | Grid | Snap To Grid, layout tables and cells snap to the grid as you draw them or reposition them, ensuring a precise layout.

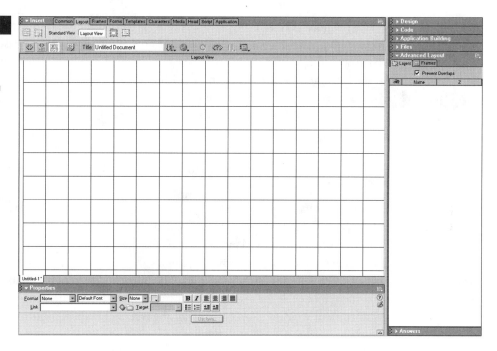

FIGURE 4-4

Use Dreamweaver's grid to help you draw a layout table.

If you want to change the color or spacing of the grid, choose View | Grid | Grid Settings. This opens the Grid Settings dialog box (shown next). Decreasing the value in the Spacing field makes the grid tighter. Increasing the value makes the grid looser. Notice also that you can choose between dotted lines and solid lines for the grid.

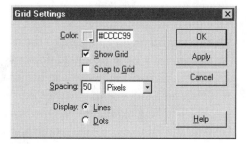

Using Tracing Images

A *tracing image* is a graphic that Dreamweaver places in the back of the document window—it's sort of like a background image, but not exactly. You can see the tracing image only when you work in Dreamweaver. It doesn't appear in a browser window on the finished page.

The purpose of the tracing image is to help you set up the layout of your page. Graphic designers who use Dreamweaver know all too well that it's easier to create a page layout in imaging software like Macromedia Fireworks, Adobe Photoshop, or Adobe Illustrator. The tools are more intuitive, and the software lets you experiment with the design more easily as you put it together.

With tracing images, Dreamweaver gives you the best of both worlds. You can lay out the page at full size in your favorite graphics application and save the image as a JPEG, GIF, or PNG file. Then bring the file into Dreamweaver as a tracing image. Build your layout table directly on top of the image to match your design.

Loading a Tracing Image   To place a tracing image in the document window, choose Modify | Page Properties to open the Page Properties dialog box. Click the Browse button next to the Tracing Image field, navigate to the tracing image from the Select Image Source dialog box, and click OK. Set the transparency of the tracing image by dragging the slider, and click OK in the Page Properties dialog box to save the settings and close the dialog. Dreamweaver adds the tracing image to the back of the document window. Remember that the tracing image appears in Dreamweaver only. It isn't part of the live Web page.

You can also choose View | Tracing Image | Load from Dreamweaver's main menu to call up the Select Image Source dialog box. When you select the tracing image and click OK, the Page Properties dialog box appears, allowing you to adjust the transparency of the image. Click OK to finish.

Dreamweaver references the tracing image in the HTML, even though the image doesn't show up in the actual page. When you set up a tracing image, Dreamweaver adds two custom attributes to the body tag, `tracingsrc` and `tracingopacity`. The `tracingsrc` attribute gives the path to the tracing image, while `tracingopacity` gives the transparency value from 0 (completely transparent) to 100 (completely opaque). Select the body tag in the Tag Inspector, and you can specify values for these attributes by hand. For that matter, you could switch to Code view and type them into the body tag manually. Web browsers don't recognize either attribute, so they skip over the values for `tracingsrc` and `tracingopacity` when displaying your page.

Modifying the Tracing Image   After you set the tracing image, you can tweak its transparency by choosing Modify | Page Properties again.

To move the tracing image around the page, choose View | Tracing Image | Adjust Position, and the Adjust Tracing Image Position dialog box appears. Type values into the X and Y fields of the dialog box, or hold down the arrow keys to move the image into place. (Custom body tag attributes `tracingx` and `tracingy` hold these values for those who prefer hand coding.)

To align the tracing image with your layout table, select the table and choose View | Tracing Image | Align To Selection.

To move the tracing image back to its default position in the upper-left corner of the document window, choose View | Tracing Image | Reset Position.

EXERCISE 4-1

Building the Layout for the Mad Science Home Page with a Table

In this exercise, you put together the layout of the home page for the Mad Science LLC Web site using a layout table. See Figure 4-5 for a sketch of the layout.

1. Launch Dreamweaver, open the Site panel, and set the site to Mad Science LLC.

FIGURE 4-5

Lay out the home page of the Mad Science LLC Web site like this.

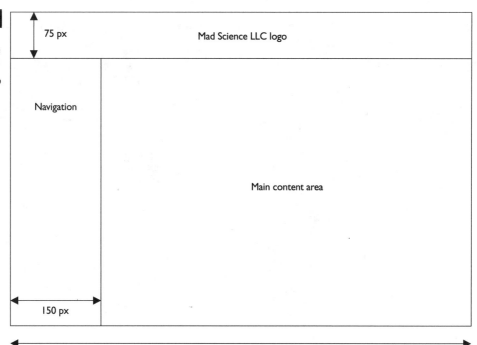

75 px — Mad Science LLC logo

Navigation

Main content area

150 px

100%

2. Double-click the file *index.htm*. This is the home page you created in Chapter 3. The home page opens in a document window.

3. Select the Layout tab in the Insert panel and click the Draw Layout Table button.

4. Draw a layout table in the document window to match the rough sketch in Figure 4-5. Don't worry about getting the size exactly right for now.

5. Now click the Draw Layout Cell button and draw layout cells to match the illustration. Again, don't worry about the sizes.

6. Select the layout cell on the bottom right, go to the Properties panel, and switch the width to Autostretch. A dialog box appears, in which Dreamweaver advises you to create a spacer image. Choose the first option on the dialog box, and click OK.

7. Double-click the images folder to save the spacer image there and click Save. Dreamweaver creates the spacer image in the default images folder, and your layout table expands to fill the entire document window.

8. Now select the cell on the bottom left, go to the Properties panel, and set the width to 150 pixels. Resize the cell on the right so that it sits snugly against the cell on the left.

9. Now select the cell along the top, and set the height to 75 pixels. You may have to make the bottom cells smaller at first. After you set the height, resize the bottom cells so that they sit against the top cell.

10. So much for the layout. Your design should look like the screen shown in Figure 4-6.

11. Choose File | Save to save the page as *index.htm*. Congratulations! You did it.

FIGURE 4-6

Here is the finished layout table for the Mad Science LLC site.

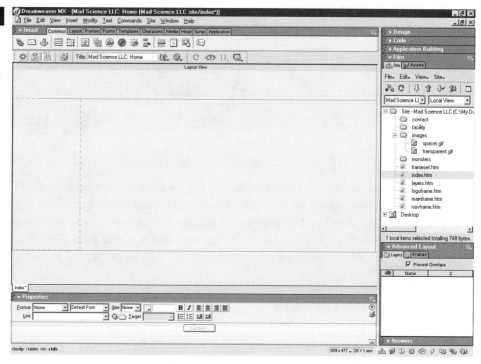

Creating Tables in Standard View

Layout view is fine for making quick tables, but if you want more precise control at the expense of some speed, Standard view is the view for you. To switch from Layout view to Standard view, click the Standard View button under the Layout tab of the Insert panel.

Inserting a Table

In Standard view, you don't draw a layout table; you insert it. You can find the Table button, shown here, under the Layout tab of the Insert panel as well as under the

Common tab. Click this button to insert a table, or choose Insert | Table. The Insert Table dialog box appears.

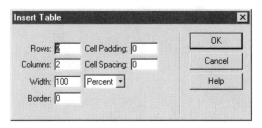

Normally, when you're in Layout view, you can't insert a table by clicking the Table button. In fact, if you look under the Layout tab of the Insert panel, you'll find that the Table button is disabled. However, if you look under the Common tab, the Table button isn't disabled, and it works fine. Click this button to insert a table instead of drawing one when you're in Layout view.

Specify the number of rows and columns for the table in the appropriate fields. A table must have at least one row and one column.

In the Width field, type the desired width of the table and choose the appropriate measurement from the drop-down list to the right. You have two options here: Percent, which creates a variable-width table, and Pixels, which creates a fixed-width table. If you don't supply a value for the width, Dreamweaver automatically creates a variable-width table, but the table appears compressed in the document window until you add content or specify a width.

In the Border field, type a value to represent the size of the table's border in pixels. You must specify at least a value of 1 to obtain a visible table border. To get rid of the border entirely, specify a value of 0. Leaving this field blank creates an invisible border around the table—the browser inserts a small bit of space around the table instead of a visible outline.

The Cell Padding field sets the amount of space in pixels from the interior of the cell to the cell's content. The higher the value, the more padded the cell appears. Browsers insert a small amount of padding by default, so set this value to 0 if you don't want any padding at all.

The Cell Spacing field sets the amount of space in pixels between table cells. Again, set this value to 0 if you don't want any space between cells. If you leave this field blank, the browser automatically inserts a small amount of space.

After you set up the table's attributes, click OK. Dreamweaver creates a table to your specifications in the document window. You can adjust the table's grid and attributes from the Properties panel. Select the table by clicking one of its outside borders. The Properties panel shows fields for the number of rows and columns, the table width, the table height, the border size, cell padding, cell spacing, and so on.

Even a small table requires a chunk of HTML code. A table tag, `<table>`, marks the beginning of the table. This tag contains the table's attributes, including `width`, `border`, `cellpadding`, and `cellspacing`. Each row of the table is marked with a table-row tag, `<tr>`, and the columns in that row are marked with table-data tags, `<td>`. For instance, if you create a table 600 pixels wide with no borders, no cell spacing, and no cell padding, which has two rows and three columns per row, the HTML in Code view looks something like this:

```
<table width="600" border="0" cellpadding="0" cellspacing="0">
   <tr>
      <td>Row 1 Col 1 goes here</td>
      <td>Row 1 Col 2 goes here</td>
      <td>Row 1 Col 3 goes here</td>
   </tr>
   <tr>
      <td>Row 2 Col 1 goes here</td>
      <td>Row 2 Col 2 goes here</td>
      <td>Row 2 Col 3 goes here</td>
   </tr>
</table>
```

The content for each cell of the table goes between the opening and closing table-data tags.

Merging and Splitting Cells

The table that you create from the Insert Table dialog box is great for organizing rows and columns of data. A layout table, however, almost never looks like a data table. A single row often stretches across several columns, or a single column straddles several rows. You can change the boring data-table structure into something more graphically interesting by merging and splitting cells.

To combine cells, you must first select them. Normally, you can select a cell by clicking inside it. However, since you need to choose multiple cells for merging, you hold down the CTRL key (Windows) or COMMAND key (Mac) while you click the cells. Then go to the Properties panel and find the Merge Selected Cells button, shown here. Click this button, and the cells fuse into one. You can also choose Modify | Table | Merge Cells to merge the cells, or you can right-click the selection and choose Table | Merge Cells from the context menu. Keep in mind that you can merge only contiguous cells—cells that touch each other in the table structure.

To split a single cell into several rows or columns, select the cell, go to the Properties panel and click the Split Cell button.

You can also choose Modify | Table | Split Cell or right-click for the context menu and choose Table | Split Cell. No matter how you get there, the Split Cell dialog box appears, as shown here. Indicate whether you want to split the cell into rows or columns, specify the number of rows or columns you want to create, and click OK.

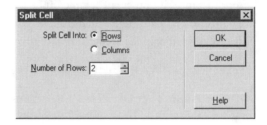

Dreamweaver achieves merging and splitting with the colspan and rowspan attributes of the table-data tag. The colspan attribute determines how many columns the current bit of table data should occupy. Similarly, the rowspan attribute determines the number of rows. A layout table with one large cell on the left for the navigation that straddles three content cells on the right has the following structure:

```
<table>
   <tr>
      <td rowspan="3">Navigation goes here</td>
      <td>First cell for content</td>
   </tr>
   <tr>
      <td>Second cell for content</td>
   </tr>
   <tr>
      <td>Third cell for content</td>
   </tr>
</table>
```

By comparison, a table with one large cell along the top for navigation that straddles two content cells beneath it looks something like this:

```
<table>
   <tr>
      <td colspan="2">Navigation goes here</td>
   </tr>
   <tr>
      <td>First cell for content</td>
```

```
      <td>Second cell for content</td>
   </tr>
</table>
```

Inserting and Deleting Rows and Columns

Three commands are used for inserting table rows and columns: Insert Row, Insert Column, and Insert Rows Or Columns. You can find these commands under Modify | Table in the main menu or in the context menu that appears when you right-click a table cell. To insert one row above the currently selected cell, choose Insert Row. To insert one column to the left of the currently selected cell, choose Insert Column. To insert a variable number of rows above or below the currently selected cell, or to insert a variable number of columns before or after, choose Insert Rows Or Columns. This command opens the Insert Rows Or Columns dialog box, shown next. Fill out the dialog and click OK.

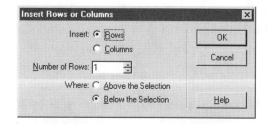

A quick reference to help you figure out which command to use for inserting rows and columns is found in the next Scenario and Solution.

Two commands are used for deleting table rows and columns—Delete Row and Delete Column, both of which appear in the same menus as the commands for inserting rows and columns. The Delete Row command deletes the row of the currently selected

SCENARIO & SOLUTION	
When should you use the Insert Row command?	When you want to insert one row above the currently selected cell
When should you use the Insert Column command?	When you want to insert one column to the left of the currently selected cell
When should you use the Insert Rows Or Columns command?	When you want to insert any number of columns or rows anywhere in relation to the currently selected cell

cell, while the Delete Column command deletes the column of the currently selected cell. Be careful! Deleting rows and columns also deletes any content contained therein.

Resizing the Table

When you select a table in Standard view, black handles appear along its outside border. Use these handles to drag the table to the size you need. Notice how the table cells change size as the table itself does.

You can set the size of an individual cell by selecting the cell, going to the Properties panel, and typing values in the W and H fields (W stands for width, and H stands for height). If you change the width of a cell, all the cells in the same column change to that width. Similarly, if you change the height, all the cells in the same row change to that height.

Dreamweaver sets the size of the table by specifying the width and height attributes of the table tag. The table-data tag also has width and height attributes, and this is how Dreamweaver sets the size of individual cells. For instance, a table 600 pixels wide and 400 pixels high has a table tag that looks like this:

```
<table width="600" height="400">
```

Meanwhile, a table cell 100 pixels wide by 300 pixels high looks like this:

```
<td width="100" height="300">
```

After you add content to the table, the width and height attributes might interfere with the way the browser displays the page. A quick way to eliminate all the W values from the table and its cells is to select the table, go to the Properties panel, and click the Clear Column Widths button, shown here.

Eliminate all the H values by selecting the table and clicking the Clear Row Heights button, shown here.

Alternatively, you can select the table and choose Modify | Table | Clear Cell Widths or Modify | Table | Clear Cell Heights. These commands aren't available in the context menu that opens when you right-click the table.

Converting the Width and Height Values   Dreamweaver lets you quickly convert all the width or height values in a table from pixels to percent and vice versa. To start, select the table and go to the Properties panel. Then, click the Convert Table Widths To Pixels button, shown here, to express all the W values in absolute pixel measurements:

Click the Convert Table Widths To Percent button to express all the W values as relative percentages:

Click the Convert Table Heights To Pixels button to express all the H values as pixels:

Click the Convert Table Heights To Percent button to express all the H values as percentages:

Look under Modify | Table in the main menu for similar commands.

Formatting Tables

In HTML, the table tags provide several attributes for changing the general appearance of a table. A few of them were mentioned already: `border`, `cellpadding`, and `cellspacing`. You can set these table attributes in Dreamweaver's Properties panel.

Working with Table Borders

To add a border to your layout table, select the table, go to the Properties panel, and type a value in the Border field. As you know, entering a value of 0 eliminates the border completely, while leaving the Border field blank causes the browser to display a small but invisible border.

The value you type in the Border field is the thickness of the border in pixels. For most purposes, you won't need a border thicker than 5 or 6 pixels, but you can supply any value you like. Keep in mind that the table border appears around the outside of the table and outlines every cell. It's an all-or-nothing deal.

A table with a 6-pixel border uses the following `border` attribute:

```
<table border="6">
```

Change the color of the border by clicking the color square next to the Brdr Color field on the Properties panel and choosing a color from the swatches. You can also type the hexadecimal color code of the desired border color directly into the Brdr Color field. A table with a 6-pixel blue border (#0000FF) looks something like this in HTML:

```
<table border="6" bordercolor="#0000FF">
```

Positioning the Table on the Page

By default, the browser displays a table flush left. You may want to position your layout table in the center of the browser window, or, less frequently, you might want to align it flush right.

To align the table, select it and choose a value from the Align drop-down list on the Properties panel. Notice that the drop-down list contains an option for Default as well as for Left. I can't think of a browser that doesn't default to the left automatically, but if you want to be absolutely sure that your layout table sits flush left, select the Left value.

The attribute at work here is the `align` attribute of the table tag. A table aligned to the center of the page looks like this in the HTML:

```
<table align="center">
```

If you choose Default from the drop-down list, the `align` attribute disappears entirely from the table tag.

Aligning Cell Content

You can also align the content of cells within the table. By default in most browsers, table cell content appears flush left horizontally and centered vertically. To align the contents of a table cell, select the cell, go to the Properties panel, and choose values from the Horz and Vert drop-down lists. The Horz list controls the horizontal alignment, obviously, and the Vert list controls the vertical alignment. You can also select a row of the table; setting the Horz and Vert values applies them to every cell in the row.

Horizontal alignment happens by way of the `align` attribute of the table-data or table-row tag, and vertical alignment happens by way of the `valign` attribute. Set the attributes of the table-data tag to align the content of a single cell, and set the attributes of the table-row tag to align the content of all the cells in the row.

Aligning table data horizontally in the center of a single cell, for example, requires the following HTML tag:

```
<td align="center">
```

Aligning table data vertically along the bottom of the cell for every cell in the row looks like this in the code:

```
<tr valign="bottom">
```

e x a m
🅦a t c h

Watch out, because there is no such thing as the `halign` *attribute. Use the* `align` *attribute for horizontal alignment in table cells.*

The alignment values in the Horz and Vert lists are self-explanatory, except perhaps for the Baseline option for vertical alignment. Baseline alignment works best when you apply it to the table-row tag. If you set up a row in your table this way, all the text in that row falls on a horizontal line, like on a sheet of notebook paper, only the line is invisible. This helps the table to look neater. Baseline alignment applies more to data tables than layout tables.

Coloring Cells, Rows, and Tables

You may recall that the `bgcolor` attribute of the body tag controls the background color of the page. The table tag, table-row tag, and table-data tag have `bgcolor` attributes also.

To set the background color of a table, row, or cell, select the desired element in the document window, go to the Properties panel, click the color square next to the Bg field, and choose a color from the swatches that appear. You can also type the hexadecimal code of the color directly into the Bg field.

CERTIFICATION OBJECTIVE 4.02

Achieving Page Layout with Frames

When you use frames, you divide the browser window into at least two separate rectangular regions, and each region contains its own Web page. A dead giveaway that frames have been used is a browser window has more than one set of scrollbars.

The main advantage to using frames is that the frameset, or the document that defines the separate regions of the browser window, controls the layout of the page. If you want to adjust the layout, all you have to do is change the values of the frameset. You don't have to touch the individual Web pages that appear inside the frames. Also, because the frameset controls the design, you don't have to bother with complex table layouts in the individual pages themselves.

Frames were popular in 1998. Web builders don't use them as often these days because of their limitations. For one, client-side interactivity like JavaScript doesn't always mix well with frames. You have to be exactly precise in the JavaScript code, even more so than usual, or the code doesn't work correctly. Search engines have problems indexing framed sites, too. The individual pages don't tell the search engine that they're part of a framed site, so the search engine links to the pages, not the frameset that controls the layout. If the navigation for your site appears in a different frame, you end up stranding your visitor on a page without links if your visitor arrives on your site by way of a search engine. What's more, frames aren't very accessible, and not all browsers can display them.

If you're trying to decide whether to use frames, ask yourself if you can achieve the same layout and functionality with tables or layers. If you can, don't use frames.

Creating a Frameset

A *frameset* is an HTML document that establishes the system of frames in the browser window. If you want to create frames in your site, you need a frameset.

Dreamweaver gives you several predefined framesets to use for common layouts. Use these, tweaking them as necessary, for faster development. You can also create your own customized frameset from the ground up.

Using Predefined Framesets

You may recall from Chapter 3 that Dreamweaver's predefined framesets appear in the Frameset category of the New Document dialog box. Open the New Document dialog box by choosing File | New from Dreamweaver's main menu and click the Frameset category to choose a layout.

The list of choices contains a bit of jargon. A *fixed frame* is a frame with an absolute width or height value in pixels. Fixed top and bottom frames have constant heights. Fixed left and right frames have constant widths. A fixed frame doesn't change size as the visitor minimizes or maximizes the browser window. For instance, if the main navigation for a page appears in the left region of the page, you could build a frameset with a fixed left frame. No matter what size browser window the visitor uses, the navigation always appears in a frame of the same width on the left side of the screen. Likewise, if your main navigation appears along the top of every page, you could build a frameset with a fixed top frame, a frame with a constant height value.

A *nested frame* further divides the browser window by placing a frameset inside one of the frames. The Fixed Bottom, Nested Right option in the New Document dialog box, for instance, creates a frameset with a fixed bottom frame. The top frame contains an additional frameset that divides this frame into left and right regions. The right nested frame in this scheme is fixed-width, and the left nested frame is variable-width (see Figure 4-7). By comparison, the Fixed Bottom, Nested Left option gives you a frameset with a fixed bottom frame, further dividing the top frame into a fixed-width left frame and a variable-width right frame, as shown in Figure 4-8.

Double-click the predefined frameset of your choice to create it in Dreamweaver. You can modify the size and attributes of the frames as you work.

The frameset tag, which sets up the frames, appears in its own HTML document. In skeleton form, a left frame with a fixed width of 80 pixels next to a variable-width right frame looks something like this:

```
<frameset cols="80,*">
    <frame src="left.htm">
    <frame src="right.htm">
</frameset>
```

on the
job

You can also supply relative percentage values instead of absolute pixel values for the columns and rows. This improves the page's chances of looking correct no matter what screen size your visitor uses.

FIGURE 4-7

The Fixed Bottom, Nested Right frameset gives you this layout.

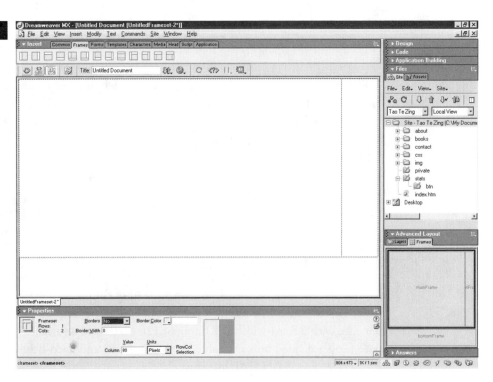

FIGURE 4-8

The Fixed
Bottom, Nested
Left frameset
gives you a
similar layout,
but notice that
Dreamweaver
has switched the
fixed and variable
regions of the
nested frame.

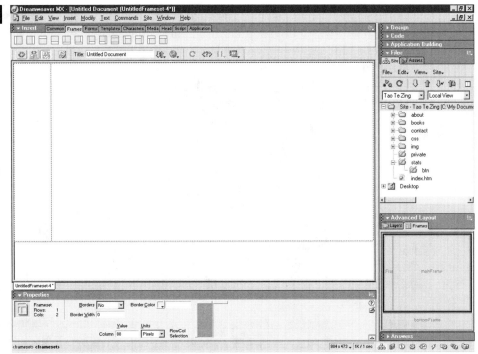

The cols attribute of the frameset tag creates left and right frames. The values of this attribute indicate that the frame on the left is 80 pixels wide, while the frame on the right is variable-width. The src attribute of the individual frame tags gives the Web page that loads inside each frame.

By comparison, a variable-width top frame and a fixed bottom frame 100 pixels high looks like this:

```
<frameset rows="*,100">
   <frame src="top.htm">
   <frame src="bottom.htm">
</frameset>
```

Notice that the rows attribute replaces the cols attribute in the frameset tag, dividing the browser window into rows instead of columns.

In a nested frameset, a frameset tag appears inside another frameset tag. Therefore, in a page with a fixed-width left frame of 120 pixels and a variable-width right frame that's further divided into a variable-height top frame and fixed-height bottom frame of 70 pixels, you get HTML like this:

```
<frameset cols="120,*">
   <frame src="left.htm"
   <frameset rows="*,70">
      <frame src="top.htm">
      <frame src="bottom.htm">
   </frameset>
</frameset>
```

Notice that the second frameset tag replaces the frame tag for the right frame.

Creating Your Own Frameset

To create your own frameset, start with a blank Web page, and click the Frames tab of the Insert panel. This panel shows icons for 13 different frame configurations to start you out. The blue areas in the icons represent variable-size regions, while the white areas represent fixed-size regions. Click the button to create the corresponding frameset.

Then, to add new or additional nesting frames to the layout, click inside a frame in the document window and choose another frame icon from the Insert panel. You can modify the width and height values and other properties afterward.

Choosing Modify | Frameset provides a submenu of frameset commands, including Split Frame Left, Split Frame Right, Split Frame Up, and Split Frame Down. Choosing Insert | Frames provides subcommands corresponding to the icons under the Frames tab of the Insert panel.

Adding Noframes Content

For browsers that can't display frames, it's a good idea to include noframes content. Browsers that can't display frames show the noframes content instead. Browsers that can display frames ignore the noframes content altogether.

To add noframes content, click any frame border, and switch to Code view. Look for the opening noframes tag, `<noframes>`, which falls immediately after the closing frameset tag, `</frameset>`. Dreamweaver adds the body tag, `<body>`, directly after the opening noframes tag, followed by an empty line; the closing body tag, `</body>`; and the closing noframes tag, `</noframes>`. Your noframes content goes between these body tags.

Click the empty line between the body tags and switch back to Design view. A gray bar at the top of the document window appears with the caption *NoFrames Content*. Create the content as if you were building a regular Web page. When you finish, switch to Code view again and click anywhere outside the noframes tags. When you go back to Design view, the noframes content disappears, and the system of frames reappears. As you might guess, Code And Design view works best when you're building noframes content. It allows you to switch between the views more easily.

Noframes content can be as simple as a line of text that says, "Your browser doesn't support frames. Upgrade to the latest version of Microsoft Internet Explorer or Netscape." This kind of noframes content is better than nothing. However, to make noframes content more useful, offer a link to your home page, and make sure that you build redundant links for the main navigation into the individual pages of the site. This way, visitors who prefer text-only browsers or older versions of Netscape or IE get a reasonable if not optimized user experience.

Managing Frames

Manage the layout of the frames in Design view. Dreamweaver lets you resize frames and alter frame properties easily. To resize a frame, drag its border in the document window. To delete a frame, drag its border outside the document window.

For more precise editing, or to modify the properties of the frameset, click the frame border and go to the Properties panel, which reconfigures itself with frameset options, shown in the next illustration. If you don't use nested frames, you can click anywhere on the frame border—the same properties appear in the Properties panel. If you use nested frames, though, make sure that you click the segment of the border that separates the frames you want to edit. Another way to select the frameset is to click the border in the thumbnail image on the Frames panel of the Advanced Layout panel group. This panel doesn't appear in Dreamweaver by default. You must choose Window | Others | Frames to open it.

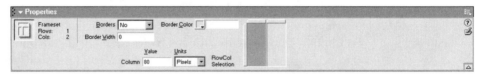

On the right side of the Properties panel, you find a rough thumbnail image of the frameset you're editing. This image is clickable. Click a frame in the thumbnail to see its width and height. If you want a relative-sized frame for the currently highlighted region in the thumbnail, type **1** or * in the Column or Row field and choose the Relative option from the Units drop-down list. If you want a fixed-width frame, type the value in pixels in the Column or Row field and choose the Pixels option from the Units drop-down list.

The frame borders in the document window don't necessarily appear on the live page in the browser window. To specify a visible border, select Yes from the Borders drop-down list. Select No to make the borders disappear in the live page, even though they still appear as visual aids in Dreamweaver. Select Default to allow the browser to use its default setting for frame borders, which is usually the equivalent of Yes.

The Border Width field gives the thickness of the border in pixels, and the Border Color field gives the color of the border. (Click the color square next to the Border Color field to choose a border color from a set of swatches or type the hexadecimal code of the color directly into the field.) If you leave these fields blank, the browser supplies default values. If you use nested frames, beware of frame borders in Design view! Dreamweaver doesn't always get border widths and border colors correct, especially when you use different widths and colors for different framesets. Always check the look of your frameset in a live browser. Don't trust Dreamweaver implicitly!

These border properties are attributes of the frameset tag. If you specify a border, Dreamweaver sets the `frameborder` attribute to `yes` in the code. If you specify that the frameset doesn't have a border, `frameborder` becomes `no`. The border-width value appears in the `border` and `framespacing` attributes, while the border color appears in `bordercolor`. Why two attributes for border width? The `framespacing` attribute is redundant. Internet Explorer prefers this attribute, although the more correct `border` has better cross-browser compatibility. It doesn't hurt to give both attributes, so that's what Dreamweaver does.

Here's an example of frameset attributes. The frameset for a fixed-width left frame of 200 pixels, a variable-width right frame, and a 12-pixel red (#FF0000) border looks like this in the code:

```
<frameset cols="200,*" frameborder="yes" border="12" framespacing="12" bordercolor="#FF0000">
```

Here's another example. This is the same frameset, only with no visible border:

```
<frameset cols="200,*" frameborder="no" border="0" framespacing="0">
```

Selecting and Editing Frames

So far, you've edited the properties of the frameset, but the individual frame tags inside the frameset also have attributes.

To edit them, you must first select the frame, not the frameset. Hold down the ALT button (Windows) or SHIFT-OPTION (Macintosh), and click inside the frame to select it. You can also click the corresponding frame in the thumbnail on the Frames panel. Select the frame, and the Properties panel changes accordingly. You may now edit the frame tag's attributes.

The Frame Name field provides the name of the frame, which links and client-side scripts reference. Always make sure you specify a name for each frame in the frameset.

If your frame is the main navigation for your site, for example, you might call it *navigation*, in which case your frame tag acquires the name attribute, like this:

```
<frame name="navigation">
```

The Src field gives the path and file name of the Web page that loads in the frame. Define a new source by clicking the folder icon next to this field and browsing for the Web-page file that you want. The path appears in the src attribute of the frame tag. If the source is a page called *nav.htm*, the HTML looks like this:

```
<frame name="navigation" src="nav.htm">
```

The Scroll field determines whether the frame gives the visitor scrollbars as needed to view all the content that the frame contains. Set this field to No if you never want the frame to provide scrollbars. Set this field to Yes if you always want the frame to provide scrollbars. Set this field to Auto or Default to give the visitor scrollbars as needed. The scrolling attribute of the frame tag controls this action, like this:

```
<frame name="navigation" src="nav.htm" scrolling="no">
```

By default, your visitor can resize a frame by dragging its border. Check the No Resize box to prevent the visitor from resizing the frame. Dreamweaver adds the valueless noresize attribute to the frame tag, as follows:

```
<frame name="navigation" src="nav.htm" scrolling="no" noresize>
```

If you don't check the No Resize box, Dreamweaver adds nothing to the frame tag.

exam
Watch

The noresize *attribute of the frame tag is valueless. Don't fall for a trick like* resize="yes" *or* resize="no" *on the exam. If you don't want the user to be able to resize the frame manually, give the* noresize *attribute with no value. Otherwise, do nothing to the tag.*

The Margin Width field indicates the amount of space in pixels between the left and right borders of the frame and the frame content. Likewise, the Margin Height field sets the amount of space between the top and bottom borders of the frame and the frame content. Set both values to 0 to remove frame margins entirely, and Dreamweaver adds the marginwidth and marginheight attributes as follows:

```
<frame name="navigation" src="nav.htm" scrolling="no" noresize marginwidth="0"
marginheight="0">
```

SCENARIO & SOLUTION

When should you select the frameset?	When you want to modify the size of the frames or the properties of the border
When should you select individual frames?	When you want to modify the frame's name, source, scrolling action, resizing action, or margins

Finally, notice that you can set `frameborder` and `bordercolor` attributes in the frame tag, just like you can in the frameset tag. Whatever values you supply for `frameborder` and `bordercolor` in the frame tag override the same attributes in the frameset tag, or at least they're supposed to. Many browsers offer spotty support of this, so set frame borders in the frameset tag, not the individual frame tags.

Now that you've seen the attributes of the frame tag in action, the quick reference in the Scenario and Solution above will help you decide whether to select the frameset or an individual frame when you want to modify the properties of the layout.

Saving Framesets and Frames

Since a framed site displays many pages at once, saving frames in Dreamweaver becomes trickier. You have to tell Dreamweaver exactly which page you want to save, which boils down to choosing the right command from the main File menu.

To save just a frame, click inside the frame and choose File | Save Frame, File | Save Frame As, or File | Save Frame As Template. Remember, the frame that you're saving is the one with the flashing cursor or the selected element.

To save just the frameset, select the frameset and choose File | Save Frameset or File | Save Frameset As.

To save everything—that is, the frameset and all the frames—choose File | Save All.

EXERCISE 4-2

Building the Layout for the Mad Science Home Page with Frames

In this exercise, you put together the layout of the home page for the Mad Science LLC Web site using frames. Refer back to the layout sketch in Exercise 4-1.

1. Launch Dreamweaver, open the Site panel, and set the site to Mad Science LLC.

2. Create a new document for the framed page, so that you don't overwrite your work on *index.htm* from Exercise 4-1. Choose File | New, select the Framesets category from the New Document dialog box, and double-click the Fixed Top, Nested Left document. This layout matches roughly the design in the layout sketch, as you see when the new document window opens.

3. Click the horizontal frame border that separates the top section of the page from the bottom. This selects the fixed-top frameset.

4. Go to the Properties panel, click the top frame in the thumbnail, and set the row height to 75 pixels.

5. Now click the vertical frame border that separates the left section of the page from the right. This selects the nested-left frameset.

6. Click the bottom frame in the thumbnail and make sure that the Units list shows the Relative option.

7. Go back to the Properties panel, click the left frame in the thumbnail and set the column width to 150 pixels.

8. Click the right frame in the thumbnail and make sure the Units list shows the Relative option. Your layout should look like Figure 4-9.

9. Choose Window | Others | Frames to open the Frames panel. Select the top frame by clicking the top frame of the thumbnail image in this panel.

10. Go to the Properties panel, type **logoFrame** in the Frame Name field (since this frame will contain the logo and masthead of the site) and press ENTER or RETURN. This replaces the more generic *topFrame* name that Dreamweaver supplied.

11. Go back to the Frames panel, and click the left frame. Type **navFrame** in the Frame Name field of the Properties panel and press ENTER or RETURN. This frame will contain the main navigation.

12. Click the right frame in the Frames panel. Glance at the Properties panel, and you'll see that Dreamweaver automatically supplied the name *mainFrame* for this frame. This name is descriptive enough for the main content area of the page, so leave it as is.

13. Now for the noframes content. Click anywhere along the frame border to select the frameset document, and switch to Code And Design view.

14. Look for the noframes tag in the code listing, followed by the body tag There should be a blank line between the opening and closing body tags. Click this

FIGURE 4-9

Here is the finished frame-based layout for the Mad Science LLC site.

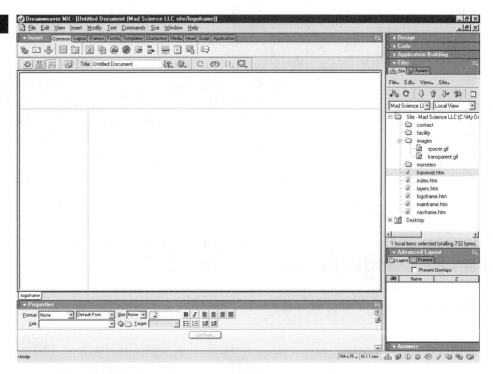

line. The Design portion of the document window should contain the caption *NoFrames Content.*

15. Double-click inside the Design portion of the document window. A flashing cursor appears. Type the following line: **Your browser doesn't support frames.** As you know, this isn't very helpful noframes content, but just go with it. If you were actually building a framed site, you would want to supply a link to the Web page in the appropriate frame. Click outside the body tag to see the frames again.

16. Now all you have to do is save the four documents: one Web page for each of the three frames and the frameset document. Save the top frame first. Click inside the top frame, and choose File | Save Frame. The Save As dialog box appears.

17. Type **logoframe.htm** in the File Name field and click Save.

18. Click inside the left frame and choose File | Save Frame again. Type **navframe.htm** in the File Name field and click Save.

19. Click inside the right frame, choose File | Save Frame and specify **mainframe.htm** as the file name. Click Save.

20. Now, save the frameset, and you're home free. Click anywhere on the frame border, and choose File | Save Frameset. The Save As dialog box appears, as before, and Dreamweaver prompts you for a file name. Normally, you would save this file as *index.htm,* but since you already have a home page and this framed layout was just for fun, type **frameset.htm** in the field and click Save. Excellent work! Another smashing success.

CERTIFICATION OBJECTIVE 4.03

Achieving Page Layout with Layers

The third strategy for designing page layouts is to use layers. A *layer* is a chunk of HTML code that contains the guts of a particular visual element on the page—a navigation bar, for instance, or the main content area. You assign a *style definition* to the layer, or a description of how and where this chunk of content should appear, and the browser takes care of the rest.

Once you define a visual element as a layer, editing becomes a breeze. If you want to move the element to a different position on the page, you simply modify its location coordinates. If you want to resize the layer, you simply change its width and height. The content of the layer automatically reflows.

You can achieve page layouts with layers that are impossible to create with tables or frames. For one thing, layers can overlap, like the windows of your operating system. For another, layers can be invisible. By adding behaviors to layers, as you will in Chapter 7, you can animate them, cause them to appear and disappear, or allow your audience to drag them across the browser window at will. Tables and frames don't come close to offering this kind of advanced interactivity.

Perhaps more important, pages with layers are often more accessible than pages with layout tables or frames. Since layers don't clog up the code with multiple tags and complex HTML constructions, screen readers and other accessibility tools have an easier time ignoring the purely visual layout information and concentrating on the guts of the page.

For all the reasons to use layers, there is one, extremely convincing reason not to use them: Not all browsers support them, and those that do offer inconsistent, contradictory, and generally unreliable support. If a browser doesn't support layers, your visitor still sees all the content of the page, but without any of the formatting, which can cause usability problems.

Should you use layers? Absolutely. Experiment with them whenever you get half a chance, but test them thoroughly in many different browsers before you deploy them.

Drawing Layers

Dreamweaver lets you draw layers in Standard view, similar to the way you draw layout tables and cells in Layout view. To draw a layer, go to the Insert panel and click the button, shown here, under the Common tab or Layout tab. |

exam

ⓦatch

When you're in Layout view, you can't draw layers. If you look under the Layout tab or the Common tab of the Insert panel, the Insert Layer button is disabled. If you want to draw layers, you need to switch to Standard view.

Then go to the document window, position the mouse pointer, hold down the mouse button, and drag the layer. Release the mouse button to finish. The thin border that appears around the layer (Figure 4-10) exists in Dreamweaver only as a visual aid. When you view your page in a live browser, no border appears. Dreamweaver also adds a gold icon to the top of the browser window. This represents the portion of code that controls the layer. Again, you don't see the gold icon in the live browser. (Incidentally, if you don't want Dreamweaver to display the gold icon, choose Edit | Properties and click the Invisible Elements category. Remove the check mark next to the Anchor Points For Layers option and click OK.)

To insert a generic, default-sized layer, choose Insert | Layer from the main menu. You can change the size and appearance of the layers that the Layer command creates by looking under the Layers category of the Preferences dialog box.

Superimposing Layers

One of the most interesting features of layers is that they can overlap. Therefore, you may draw a new layer on top of an existing one. If you don't want layers to overlap on your page, open the Layers panel by choosing Window | Others | Layers and check the box marked Prevent Overlaps or choose Modify | Arrange | Prevent Layer Overlaps. Use this feature if you plan to convert your layers to a table later on, since table cells can't overlap.

FIGURE 4-10

A layer appears like this in the document window. Notice the icon in the upper-right corner of the page, which represents the code that controls the layer.

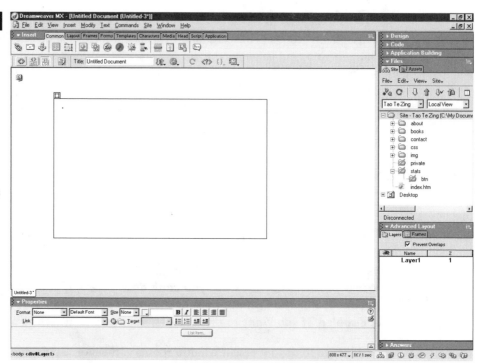

Be aware that the Prevent Overlaps feature works only when you draw layers manually. If you insert a layer with the Layer command, the new layer may overlap an existing one, and Dreamweaver doesn't stop it. Fix an overlapping layer by dragging it onto a blank area of the document window.

Nesting Layers

Remember that a layer is a container of HTML code, much like the cell of a table. A layer can contain anything: text, images, tables, and even other layers. A *nested layer* is a layer inside another layer. To nest a layer, hold down ALT (Windows) or SHIFT-OPTION (Mac) as you draw the new layer inside an existing layer. Dreamweaver puts the nested layer underneath its parent in the Layers panel and assigns the nested layer the same *z index,* or stacking position, as the parent.

Another way to create a nested layer is to drag the name of a layer in the Layers panel while holding down CTRL (Windows) or COMMAND (Mac). Drop the layer into another layer in the list.

To unnest a layer, drag it away from its parent in the Layers panel. You don't have to hold down any control keys. Just drag the layer away.

You can set up Dreamweaver to nest layers automatically when you draw them within existing layers. To do so, choose Edit | Preferences, click the Layers category, and check the option for Nest When Created Within A Layer.

Applying the Netscape Resize Fix

Version 4 of the Netscape Navigator browser loses the position of layers when the visitor resizes the browser window. Dreamweaver provides a JavaScript workaround that causes the browser to reload the page automatically after the user resizes the window, which repositions the layers where you want them. Unless you're designing for the most recent browsers only, be sure to include the Netscape Resize Fix on your page.

To add the resize fix manually, choose Commands | Add/Remove Netscape Resize Fix. Selecting this command again removes the resize fix from your page.

If you want Dreamweaver to add the resize fix automatically whenever you draw a layer, choose Edit | Preferences, select the Layers category, and check Add Netscape Resize Fix When Inserting Layer.

Modifying Layers

To modify a layer, you must first select it, and to select a layer, you can use several options: You can click the border of the layer. You can click the gold icon at the top of the browser window that corresponds to the layer. You can also click the name of the layer in the Layers panel.

A selected layer has a more prominent border with square handles and a tab along the top. To change the position of the layer, drag the tab. To resize the layer, drag the handles.

When you select a layer, the Properties panel gives you many options to tweak, as shown here:

The Layer ID field corresponds to the name of the layer. By default, Dreamweaver numbers the layers sequentially: Layer1, Layer2, Layer3, and so on. Give each layer a more useful name. If the layer contains the navigation, for instance, call the layer *Nav.* If the layer holds a form for sending e-mails, call the layer *emailForm* or something to that effect. Use a different name for every layer on the page.

Underneath the Layer ID field is the Tag drop-down list. This list indicates which HTML tag Dreamweaver uses to create the layer. You have four choices: div, span, layer, and ilayer. The layer and ilayer tags are Netscape-only tags that work in Netscape Navigator 4.0. Recent versions of the Netscape browser no longer support these tags, so stay away from them. The div tag is the best choice for creating layers, although the span tag is perhaps more forgiving in older browsers. Even still, if you're designing with layers, go with the div tag.

The quick reference in the next Scenario and Solution shows you which major browsers support which layer tags:

Assuming that you choose the div tag for your layer named Nav, Dreamweaver adds the following HTML to your page:

```
<div id="Nav"></div>
```

Notice that the name of the layer appears in the `id` attribute, not the `name` attribute that you find in many other HTML tags. The div tag has no `name` attribute.

The content for the layer appears between the opening and closing div tags. The rest of the layer's properties appear in the div tag's `style` attribute in the form of Cascading Style Sheet style definitions.

exam
Watch

CSS style definitions don't look exactly like HTML attribute/value pairs. A colon follows the attribute, not an equal sign; the value doesn't appear in quotes; and you always specify a unit of measurement. For instance, width:10px *and* width:50% *are correct in CSS—not* width="10" *or anything of the sort.*

SCENARIO & SOLUTION

Which major browsers support the div and span tags?	Microsoft Internet Explorer 4 and later, Netscape Navigator 4, Netscape 6, Opera 4 (shaky), Opera 5 (better)
Which major browsers support the layer and ilayer tags?	Netscape Navigator 4

Positioning the Layer

Dreamweaver uses *absolute* measurements to position the layer. It expresses these values as distances from the left side and the top of the page. These values appear in the L and T fields of the Properties panel. To change the distance of the layer from the left side of the page, type a new value in the L field. To change the distance of the layer from the top of the page, type a new value in the N field. Be sure to include the proper units abbreviation in the value, such as *px* for pixels, *in* for inches, and *cm* for centimeters.

If, for example, you specify the left and top distances as 10 pixels each, the div tag appears as follows:

```
<div id="Nav" style="position:absolute; left:10px; top:10px"></div>
```

Sizing the Layer

The W and H fields control the width and height of the layer, respectively. When you type values in these fields, make sure that you include the unit of measurement. Specifying a width of 2 inches and a height of 3 inches does the following to the div tag:

```
<div id="Nav" style="position:absolute; left:10px; top:10px; width:2in; height:3in"></div>
```

You can also create variable-width and variable-height layers by supplying a percentage value in the W and H fields instead of an absolute measurement such as pixels, inches, or millimeters. Make sure to type the percent sign (%) after the number.

Showing and Hiding the Layer

You can make layers visible or invisible, and client-side scripting can toggle this property, so that layers pop up from nowhere when the visitor mouses over a particular area of the page (more about this in Chapter 7). For now, declare the default state of the layer. If you want the layer to be invisible by default, set the Vis value to Hidden. Setting the Vis value to Inherit makes the layer acquire the visibility or invisibility of its *parent,* or the element that contains the layer. If you create a layer within another layer and set the visibility of the new layer to Inherit, its visibility depends on the visibility of the layer that contains it.

Assuming that you choose Visible as the default state of the layer, Dreamweaver adds a visibility definition to the `style` attribute as follows:

```
<div id="Nav" style="position:absolute; left:10px; top:10px; width:2in; height:3in;
visibility:visible"></div>
```

If you open the Layers panel, you should see an eye icon in the upper-left corner. This icon marks the visibility column. Click in this column to the left of a layer name to cycle through the default visibility options of that layer. An open eye generates `visibility:visible`. A closed eye generates `visibility:hidden`. No eye icon removes the visibility definition from the `style` attribute.

Clipping the Layer   When you clip a layer, you make a portion of it invisible. To do so, enter measurements in the L, T, R, and B fields of the Properties panel, which correspond to left, top, right, and bottom coordinates, respectively. These coordinates form a rectangle. Everything inside the rectangle is visible. Everything outside is clipped.

For example, assume that you have a layer 200 pixels square, and you want to hide all but a rectangular portion 50 pixels wide by 150 pixels high that starts 55 pixels from the left of the layer and 15 pixels from the top. You'd type **55px** in the L field to clip 55 pixels from the left side of the layer; type **15px** in the T field to clip 15 pixels from the top, type **105px** in the R field to extend the visible width by 50 pixels, and type **165px** in the B field to extend the visible height by 150 pixels.

Assuming that the position of this layer called `clippedLayer` is 400 pixels from the left side of the screen and 100 pixels from the top, the clipping values appear in the style definition as follows:

```
<div id="clippedLayer" style="position:absolute; left:400px; top:100px; width:200px;
height:200px; clip:rect(15px 105px 165px 55px);"></div>
```

The order of the values in the clip definition is top, right, bottom, and left.

Shuffling the Stacking Order

As you know, layers can overlap. The browser determines which layer overlaps which by way of the layer's z index. The layer with the lowest z-index value sits at the bottom of the stacking order. The layer with the highest z-index value sits on top. Set the z index for a layer in the Z-Index field of the Properties panel. If two layers with the same z-index value overlap, the layer that comes last in the HTML code sits on top.

You can also manage the z index by way of the Layers panel. The Layers panel lists all the layers on the page from the highest in the stacking order to the lowest. Drag a layer's name to a different position in the list to change the z-index value of this layer. Doing so also changes the z-index values of all the other layers on the page.

If you set 1 as the z index for the `Nav` layer, the code appears as follows:

```
<div id="Nav" style="position:absolute; left:10px; top:10px; width:2in; height:3in;
visibility:visible; z-index:1"></div>
```

Dreamweaver also provides two Arrange commands for resetting the stacking order. To send a layer to the bottom of the stacking order, giving it the lowest z index, choose Modify | Arrange | Send To Back. To send a layer to the top of the stacking order, giving it the highest z index, choose Modify | Arrange | Bring To Front.

Handling Content Overflow

If you put more content in a layer than the layer can accommodate, you create *overflow*. The Web browser can handle overflow in a variety of ways. Set your preference in the Overflow list on the Properties panel. Choosing the Visible option causes the layer to resize itself to display all the content. Choosing the Hidden option shows only as much content as the layer allows at its specified size. Choosing the Scroll option automatically places scrollbars inside the layer, even if the layer doesn't need them. Choosing the Auto option places scrollbars inside the layer as required.

If you choose Hidden from the Overflow list, for example, you add the following definition to the `style` attribute:

```
<div id="Nav" style="position:absolute; left:10px; top:10px; width:2in; height:3in;
visibility:visible; z-index:1; overflow:hidden"></div>
```

Setting the Background

From the Properties panel, you may specify a background color or background image for the currently selected layer.

To choose a background color, click the color square next to the Bg Color field and choose a color from the menu of swatches that pops up. You can also type the hexadecimal code of the color directly into the field.

To choose a background image, click the folder icon next to the Bg Image field. This opens the Select Image Source dialog box. Navigate to the image that you want to use, and double-click it. The background image tiles to fill the layer, just like the background image of the body tag.

In both cases, Dreamweaver adds three style definitions to the code for the best cross-browser compatibility. If you choose green (#00FF00) as the background color, for instance, the code appears as follows:

```
<div id="Nav" style="position:absolute; left:10px; top:10px; width:2in; height:3in;
visibility:visible; z-index:1; overflow:hidden; background-color:#00FF00;
layer-background-color:#00FF00; border:1px none #000000;"></div>
```

Notice definitions for `background-color`, `layer-background-color`, and `border`.

Similarly, if you specify the image *tile.gif* as the background image, the code appears as follows:

```
<div id="Nav" style="position:absolute; left:10px; top:10px; width:2in; height:3in;
visibility:visible; z-index:1; overflow:hidden; background-image:url(tile.gif);
layer-background-image:url(tile.gif); border:1px none #000000;"></div>
```

This time, the three style definitions are for `background-image`, `layer-background-image`, and `border`.

Aligning Layers

Many Web designers appreciate precision control over the layout of the page. Dreamweaver provides two quick ways to ensure that your layers sit exactly where you want them: the grid and the Align commands.

You explored the grid already when you created tables in Layout view. The grid works the same way for layers. Choose View | Grid | Show Grid to make the grid appear and select View | Grid | Snap To Grid to make layers snap to the grid as you draw them or reposition them.

You also get six Align commands in the Modify menu. To use them, hold down SHIFT and click the borders of the layers that you want to align. Then, choose Modify | Align | Left to line up the layers on their left borders. Choose Modify | Align | Right to line up the layers on their right borders. As you might expect, the Top and Bottom commands under Modify | Align line up the layers on their top and bottom borders, respectively.

Choosing Modify | Align | Make Same Width causes all the selected layers to snap to the width of the layer you selected last. Similarly, choosing Modify | Align | Make Same Height causes all the selected layers to snap to the height of the layer you selected last.

EXERCISE 4-3

Building the Layout for the Mad Science Home Page with Layers

In this exercise, you put together the layout of the home page for the Mad Science LLC Web site using layers. You'll use a different layout sketch this time. Note that the sketch shown in Figure 4-11 uses an absolute measurement instead of a percentage for the width of the layout:

1. Launch Dreamweaver, open the Site panel, and set the site to Mad Science LLC.

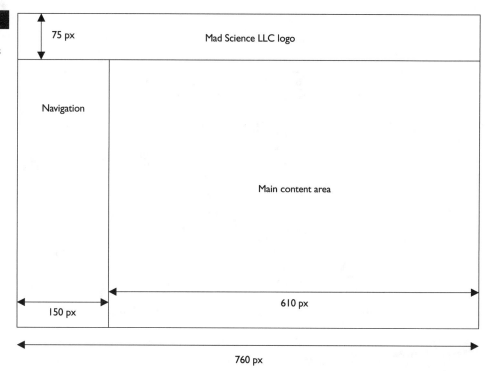

FIGURE 4-11

This sketch uses an absolute measurement instead of a percentage for the width of the layout.

2. Choose File | New, select the Basic Page category, and double-click the HTML document. A new document window opens.

3. Choose View | Grid | Show Grid and then View | Grid | Snap To Grid. This will help you to line up your layers. Also, choose Window | Others | Layers for the Layers panel and check the option for preventing overlap.

4. Select the Layout tab in the Insert panel and click the Standard View button.

5. Click the Draw Layer button under the Common tab of the Insert panel. Move the cursor into the document window and draw a layer for the top section of the design.

6. Click the Draw Layer button again and draw a layer for the bottom left section of the design.

7. Click the Draw Layer button yet again and draw a layer for the bottom right section of the design.

8. Now, click the top layer to select it. To position the layer, type **0px** in the L and T fields of the Properties panel. Type **760px** in the W field to optimize

the layer for an 800-pixel width screen, and type **75px** in the H field to set the height. This layer will contain the logo of the page, so type **Logo** in the Layer ID field.

9. Select the bottom-left layer and drag it so that it fits snugly against the top layer. Go to the Properties panel and make sure the L and T fields have the values *0px* and *75px,* respectively. Type **150px** in the W field and type **Nav** in the Layer ID field, since this layer will contain the main navigation.

10. Select the bottom-right layer and drag it so that it sits against the other two layers in the design. Go to the Properties panel. The L and T fields should have the values *150px* and *75px,* respectively. Type **610px** in the W field (that's 760 pixels for the screen size minus 150 pixels for the layer on the left), and type **Main** in the Layer ID field, since this layer is the main content area. Finally, set the Overflow list to Auto. This makes the browser provide scrollbars if you add more content than the layer can hold—a handy feature for the main content area of the page.

11. Your layout should look like Figure 4-12.

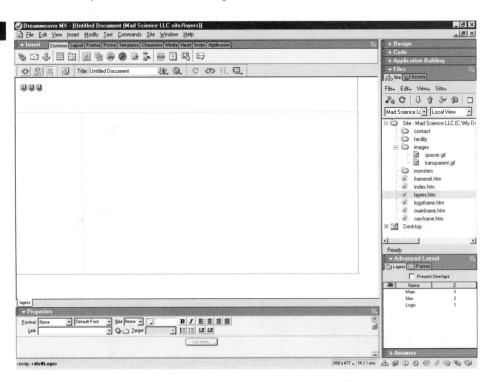

FIGURE 4-12

Here is the finished layer-based layout for the Mad Science LLC site.

12. Choose File | Save and supply the file name **layers.htm** in the Save As dialog box. Normally, you would save this file as *index.htm,* but since you already have a home page, go with the alternative file name. Click the Save button, and you're done. Nice job!

Converting Layers to a Table

Since browsers aren't consistent in their support of layers, you may find it easier to control the layout of your page with tables. What happens, though, if you already designed your page with layers? Do you have to start from scratch?

Not necessarily. Dreamweaver can convert layers to a table if the need arises. To do so, first save the current document under File | Save, or File | Save As. Then, hold down SHIFT and select all the layers that you want to convert. Finally, choose Modify | Convert | Layers To Table, and the Convert Layers To Table dialog box appears, as shown here.

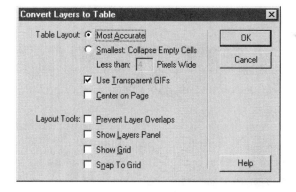

You should almost always choose the option Most Accurate. However, if your layout is complex or not precisely aligned, you might choose the option Smallest: Collapse Empty Cells to streamline the layout.

Check the option for using transparent GIFs as spacers. This prevents your table from collapsing if certain cells don't have any content.

Set the other options in the dialog as you prefer and click OK. Dreamweaver converts all the selected layers into a layout table. It also saves a file called *transparent.gif* in the same location as the current document. Open the Site panel and drag this image to the default images folder. (If you don't see it, click the Site panel's Refresh button.)

Dreamweaver automatically updates the code of the page so that your table continues to display correctly.

on the
Job

If your layout table is complex, Dreamweaver may have a hard time converting it to layers. Be prepared to make some manual adjustments and, as always, test the layout in a live browser.

You can also convert a layout table into layers by choosing Modify | Convert | Tables To Layers. The Convert Tables To Layers dialog box appears (shown in the following illustration). Set the options on the dialog box as you prefer and click OK. Dreamweaver converts the entire layout table into layers, preserving the content of the table cells. If a table cell in the layout doesn't have any content, Dreamweaver ignores it.

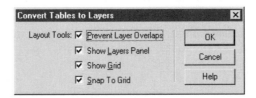

CERTIFICATION SUMMARY

This chapter presented three strategies for building the layout of a page: tables, frames, and layers. Of these three, tables are by far the most common and best supported feature. Frames give you the ability to adjust the layout quickly and easily, but they can cause problems with accessibility, search engines, and client-side scripting. Layers offer the most compelling layout possibilities, but browsers don't support them consistently and reliably.

You learned that Dreamweaver gives you two ways to create layout tables: Layout view and Standard view. In Layout view, you draw the table and its cells. This is the best way to create a layout quickly. In Standard view, you insert the table, and then you manipulate its structure by merging cells, dividing cells, adding rows and columns, and deleting rows and columns. Standard view offers more precise control of the table structure at the expense of speed, and its methods relate closely to the actual HTML that Dreamweaver generates.

With frames, you learned the difference between the frameset and the framed Web pages, and you saw how to add frames from the Insert panel. You also learned which to select—frameset or frame—when you want to modify a particular property of the layout and what commands to use to save different layout components.

You learned that layers use CSS style definitions to achieve a greater range of design possibilities than tables or frames provide. You saw that the Layers panel helps you to shuffle the stacking order of the layers on your page, make them visible or hidden, and nest them. I showed you various Dreamweaver commands for aligning and arranging layers, and you learned how to convert layers into a layout table and vice versa. While you should experiment with layers, you should also think of tables first when you consider the best layout strategy for your site.

TWO-MINUTE DRILL

Achieving Page Layout with Tables

❏ Tables offer the best cross-browser and cross-platform compatibility for page layouts, but they require off-spec markup practices and they can create accessibility issues.

❏ Layout view and Standard view are modes of Dreamweaver's Design view: Draw quick layout tables and layout cells in Layout view, and insert layout tables with greater precision in Standard view.

❏ The `colspan` and `rowspan` attributes of the table-data tag specify the number of columns and rows the cell straddles, respectively.

❏ The `cellpadding` attribute of the table tag controls the amount of space inside the cell between the cell border and the cell content, while the `cellspacing` attribute of the table tag controls the amount of space between cells.

❏ You can specify background colors for tables, table rows, and table cells.

Achieving Page Layout with Frames

❏ When you use frames, you divide the browser window into two or more regions, each with its own Web page.

❏ It's easy to update the layout of a page if you use frames, but frames can cause problems with accessibility, search engines, and client-side scripting.

❏ Set the properties of the frameset by clicking the border of the frame in the document window or the border of the frame in the thumbnail on the Frames panel.

❏ Set the properties of a frame by holding down ALT (Windows) or SHIFT-OPTION (Mac) and clicking inside the frame or by opening the Frames panel and clicking the corresponding frame in the thumbnail.

❏ Always specify noframes content in the frameset document so that visitors whose browsers don't support frames see something on your site.

Achieving Page Layout with Layers

❑ CSS-powered layers offer the most sophisticated page layout but are the least-reliable support across browsers.

❑ Draw layers in Design view's Standard view, not in Layout view.

❑ Use div or span tags to create layers, not Netscape Navigator 4's proprietary layer or ilayer tags.

❑ Select a layer by clicking its border in the document window by clicking the corresponding gold icon at the top of the document window or by clicking the name of the layer in the Layers panel.

❑ Apply the Netscape Resize Fix to your page if you expect that at least some of your visitors will use Netscape Navigator 4.

SELF TEST

The following questions will help you measure your understanding of the material presented in this chapter. Read all the choices carefully because there might be more than one correct answer. Choose all correct answers for each question.

Achieving Page Layout with Tables

1. You're designing a page for Microsoft Internet Explorer and Netscape, and you want to align the contents of a table cell to the left. What could the table-data tag look like?

   A. `<td>`

   B. `<td align="default">`

   C. `<td align="left">`

   D. `<td targetbrowser="MSIE, Netscape" align="left">`

2. In a table, what is cell padding?

   A. The amount of space between cells

   B. The amount of space inside a cell between the cell borders and cell content

   C. The amount of space between the border of the table and the table cells

   D. The amount of space between table rows

3. Which of the following statements are true about tracing images?

   A. Both a tracing image and a background image appear in the back of the document window.

   B. Both a tracing image and a background image appear in the back of the browser window.

   C. You can snap your layout cells to the lines of the tracing image under View | Tracing Image | Snap To Image.

   D. You can change the position of the tracing image under View | Tracing Image | Adjust Position.

   E. You can adjust the transparency of the tracing image from the Page Properties dialog box.

4. You're drawing a table in Layout view, and you decide to turn on Autostretch for the column that contains the main content of the page. A dialog box appears, asking if you want to add spacer images to your layout. Assuming that your layout table already has content in all its cells, should you add spacer images?

A. Definitely yes because the table will collapse if you don't.

B. Definitely no because the spacer images will delete the content of the cells.

C. Perhaps, leaning toward yes. Spacer images won't hurt, and they could improve the resiliency of your table.

D. Perhaps, leaning toward no. Spacer images take too long to download on slow modem connections.

5. Which button controls apply to creating and editing tables in Standard view?

A. The button that looks like this:

B. The button that looks like this:

C. The button that looks like this:

D. The button that looks like this:

E. The button that looks like this:

F. The button that looks like this:

6. You're in one of the endless meetings at the beginning of a Web project, where you try to decide how you're going to build the site. You're leaning toward using tables as the page-layout strategy, but a few of your colleagues from the development team keep raising objections whenever you try to get a word in edgewise. Which of their comments are valid?

A. Table tags aren't supposed to be used for page layout.

B. Layout tables look right only in Microsoft Internet Explorer.

C. Ever since layers came out, hardly anyone uses tables for design anymore.

D. Layout tables present accessibility problems.

7. Which HTML tag best represents the table cell on the left of this layout:

A. `<td colspan="2">`

B. `<td rowspan="2">`

C. `<td cols="1,2">`

D. `<td rows="*,2">`

Achieving Page Layout with Frames

8. You want to save the Web page in the top frame of the document window. What should you do? Choose the best answer.

A. Click the border of the frame and choose File I Save Frameset.

B. Click inside the top frame and choose File I Save Frameset.

C. Click the border of the frame and choose File I Save Frame.

D. Click inside the top frame and choose File I Save Frame.

E. Click the border of the frame and choose File I Save All.

F. Click inside the top frame and choose File I Save All.

9. You want to create a frameset with three columns: a fixed-width column 100 pixels wide, a variable-width column, and a fixed-width column 80 pixels wide. What is the corresponding HTML?

   A. `<frameset cols="100,80">`

   B. `<frameset cols="100px,80px">`

   C. `<frameset cols="100px,*,80px">`

   D. `<frameset cols="100,*,80">`

10. How do you prohibit the visitor from manually resizing a frame on your page?

    A. Add the `noresize` attribute to the frame tag.

    B. Set the `resize` attribute of the frame tag to the value *no*.

    C. Set the `resize` attribute of the frame tag to the value *0*.

    D. Set the `resize` attribute of the frameset tag to the value *no* or the value *0*.

    E. Add the `noresize` attribute to frameset tag.

11. What is noframes content?

    A. Content that appears in the `noframes` attribute of the frameset tag

    B. Content that appears in the `noframes` attribute of the frame tag

    C. Content that appears between noframes tags in the frameset document

    D. Content that appears between noframes tags in the framed Web page

12. How do you prevent a frame from displaying scrollbars?

    A. Hold down ALT (Windows) or SHIFT-OPTION (Mac), click inside the frame, and set the Scroll list in the Properties panel to No.

    B. Hold down ALT (Windows) or SHIFT-OPTION (Mac), click the frame border, and set the Scroll list in the Properties panel to No.

    C. Click the frame border and set the Scroll list in the Properties panel to No.

    D. Click inside the corresponding frame in the Frames panel and set the Scroll list in the Properties panel to No.

13. You begrudgingly accept that, in spite of serious problems, using frames for page layout has a few advantages. What are they?

    A. Frames are search-engine-friendly.

    B. To redesign the layout of the page, all you have to do is modify the frameset.

   C. Using frames often frees you from designing complex layout tables in the framed Web pages.

   D. You can usually implement client-side scripting with frames as easily as without.

Achieving Page Layout with Layers

14. Which of the following layer tags are compatible in both Internet Explorer 4 and Netscape Navigator 4?

   A. layer

   B. ilayer

   C. span

   D. div

15. In which Dreamweaver views can you draw layers?

   A. Code And Design view

   B. Code view

   C. Layout view

   D. Standard view

16. What code does Dreamweaver add to the `style` attribute of a layer tag to specify that the layer is invisible by default?

   A. `style="invisible"`

   B. `style="hidden"`

   C. `style:hidden`

   D. `style:invisible`

17. Why do layers give you more display options than HTML layout tables? Choose the best answer.

   A. Layers are inherently better than tables.

   B. Layers use Cascading Style Sheet style definitions.

   C. Layers are newer than layout tables.

   D. There are at least two cross-browser-compatible layer tags, while there is only one table tag.

18. Where should you store the transparent GIF that Dreamweaver creates when you convert layers to a table? Pick the best answer.

    A. Wherever Dreamweaver creates it

    B. In the default images folder

    C. In the spacers folder

    D. Anywhere, as long as you don't put it on the remote site

19. What is the Netscape Resize Fix?

    A. A JavaScript that prevents the visitor from resizing the browser window

    B. A JavaScript that displays nolayers content if the visitor attempts to resize the Netscape Navigator 4 browser window

    C. A JavaScript that reloads the page when the visitor resizes the browser window

    D. A JavaScript that prevents Netscape Navigator 4 from resizing the layers on a page

20. You want to bring the current layer to the top of the stacking order. How can you achieve this?

    A. Open the Layers panel and drag the name of the current layer to the top of the list.

    B. Open the Layers panel and drag the name of the current layer to the bottom of the list.

    C. Choose Modify | Align | Bring To Front.

    D. Choose Modify | Arrange | Bring To Front.

    E. Go to the Properties panel and adjust the z index.

    F. Switch to Code view and adjust the z index for the corresponding layer.

LAB QUESTION

You're the developer of a Web site. You and your partner, a graphic designer, decide on tables as the layout strategy after a long meeting on Friday afternoon.

The designer comes back Monday morning with a general design for the top-level pages (see Figure 4-13).

Your job is to convert this sketch into a layout table. Dreamweaver is your development tool, and you prefer to use Standard view for creating tables. What does the HTML for the table look like when you're finished? (Don't forget to clear the heights of the cells.)

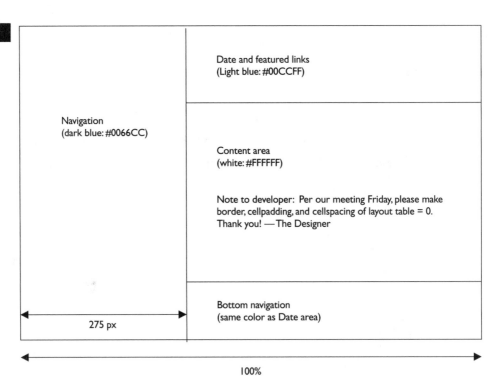

FIGURE 4-13

Your designer supplies this sketch of the layout.

SELF TEST ANSWERS

Achieving Page Layout with Tables

1. ☑ **A and C.** In Microsoft Internet Explorer and Netscape, table-cell content aligns to the left by default, so you can simply provide a table-data tag without attributes. To be absolutely clear, though, you can also use `<td align="left">` as the table-data tag.
   ☒ **B** is incorrect because `default` isn't a value that the browser recognizes for the `align` attribute. Use `<td align="left">` instead. **D** is incorrect because the `targetbrowsers` attribute doesn't exist.

2. ☑ **B.** Cell padding is the amount of space inside a cell between the cell borders and the cell content.
   ☒ **A** is incorrect because it describes cell spacing. **C** and **D** are incorrect because there aren't specific table-tag attributes for either of these, although they partly describe the `cellspacing` attribute.

3. ☑ **A, D,** and **E.** A tracing image appears in the back of the window, you can change its position, and you can adjust its transparency.
   ☒ **B** is incorrect because the tracing image doesn't appear in the background of a browser window. The tracing image is a visual aid that appears only in Dreamweaver. **C** is incorrect because there is no Snap To Image command. You're probably thinking of the Snap To Grid option.

4. ☑ **C.** Perhaps "leaning toward yes" is the best answer. Spacing images won't hurt, and they could help.
   ☒ **A** is incorrect because the table won't collapse completely if you already have content in all the cells. **B** is incorrect because the spacer images won't overwrite existing content. **D** is incorrect because the spacer image is a small, 1×1 GIF. It's minuscule by any definition. It downloads almost instantly, even over slow modem connections.

5. ☑ **D, E,** and **F.** These are the Table button, the Split Cell button, and the Convert Table Heights to Percent button, respectively. You can use them all in Standard view.
   ☒ **A** is incorrect because this is the Draw Layout Table button. It applies only to Layout view. **B** is incorrect because this is the Draw Layout Cell button. It applies only to Layout view. **C** is incorrect because this is the Draw Layer button. It applies to Standard view, but it creates a layer, not a table.

6. ☑ **A and D.** The main arguments against using tables for page layout is that this practice abuses table tags and poses problems with accessibility.

⊠   **B** is incorrect because tables offer the best cross-browser compatibility for page layout. **C** is incorrect because layers haven't made tables obsolete by any stretch of the imagination. The vast majority of sites still use tables for page layout.

7.   ☑   **B.** The `rowspan` attribute of the table-data tag causes the cell on the left to straddle the two cells on the right.
⊠   **A** is incorrect because the `colspan` attribute determines the number of columns that the cell straddles. In the diagram, the cell on the left straddles two rows, not two columns. **C** and **D** are incorrect because the `cols` and `rows` attributes apply to the frameset tag, not the table-data tag.

Achieving Page Layout with Frames

8.   ☑   **D.** Click inside the top frame and choose File | Save Frame.
⊠   **A** and **B** are incorrect because the Save Frameset command doesn't save any of the Web pages in the frames themselves. **C** is incorrect because you don't get the Save Frame command when you click the frame border. **E** and **F** are incorrect—or perhaps too correct—because they save the frameset and all the Web pages in the frames, not just the Web page in the top frame.

9.   ☑   **D.** Use the asterisk character to represent the variable-width column in the frameset.
⊠   **A** is incorrect because you forgot to specify the variable-width column in the middle. **B** and **C** are incorrect because you don't supply the units of measurement in the frameset tag. You're thinking of style definitions in a layer tag. Choice **C** is also incorrect because you forgot to specify the variable-width column.

10.   ☑   **A.** Add the `noresize` attribute to the frame tag.
⊠   **B, C,** and **D** are incorrect because there is no resize attribute of either the frame tag or the frameset tag. **E** is incorrect because you add the `noresize` attribute to the frame tag, not the frameset tag.

11.   ☑   **C.** Noframes content appears between noframes tags in the frameset document.
⊠   **A** and **B** are incorrect because there aren't `noframes` attributes of the frameset or frame tags. **D** is incorrect because the noframes tags appear in the frameset document, not the framed Web page.

12.   ☑   **A** and **D.** Hold down ALT (Windows) or SHIFT-OPTION (Mac) and click inside the frame, or click the corresponding frame in the Frames panel and set the Scroll list to No.
⊠   **B** and **C** are incorrect because clicking the frame border calls up the contents of the frameset tag. There isn't a Scroll list on the Properties panel in this case because there isn't a `scrolling` attribute in the frameset tag. Also, you don't need a key sequence to select the frameset, so choice **B** is doubly incorrect!

13. ☑ **B** and **C**. To modify the layout of the page, you can simply edit the frameset, and you probably won't need complex layout tables in the framed pages, since the frameset controls the main design of the page.
☒ **A** is incorrect because search engines have a hard time indexing framed sites correctly. **D** is incorrect because client-side scripting becomes more tedious and exacting when you work with frames.

Achieving Page Layout with Layers

14. ☑ **C** and **D**. The span and div tags apply to both browsers.
☒ **A** and **B** are incorrect the layer and ilayer tags apply to Netscape Navigator 4 only. Later versions of the Netscape browser don't support these tags.

15. ☑ **A** and **D**. You can draw layers in Code And Design view (in the Design partition, of course) and Standard view.
☒ **B** and **C** are incorrect because you can't draw layers in Code view or Design view.

16. ☑ **C**. This choice appears in CSS form, and the correct value is `hidden`.
☒ **A** and **B** are incorrect because they appear in standard HTML form. Style definitions should appear in CSS form. Also, choice **B** is incorrect because the value should be `hidden`, not `invisible`. **D** is incorrect because the value should be `hidden`, not `invisible`.

17. ☑ **B**. Layers give you more options because they use CSS style definitions.
☒ **A** is incorrect because, while layers offer many advantages, they aren't reliably compatible across browsers. The jury is still out as to whether layers are inherently better. **C** is incorrect because, while layers are more recent, it doesn't entirely explain why they have more display options. **D** is incorrect because the number of cross-browser-compatible layer tags has nothing to do with their display options.

18. ☑ **B**. Place the transparent GIF in the default images folder.
☒ **A** is incorrect because Dreamweaver creates the transparent GIF in the same location as the current document, which should never be the default images folder. **C** is incorrect because you don't need a separate spacers folder for transparent GIFs. Use the default images folder. **D** is incorrect because, if you don't upload the spacer image to the remote site, the visitor's browser can't use the spacer to pad out the layout.

19. ☑ **C**. The Netscape Resize Fix reloads the current page when the visitor resizes the browser window. This fix applies to Netscape Navigator 4.
☒ **A** is incorrect because the Netscape Resize Fix doesn't prevent the visitor from resizing the browser window, but it does cause the page to reload if the visitor uses Netscape Navigator 4.

B is incorrect because there is no such thing as nolayers content. **D** is incorrect because nothing prevents Netscape Navigator 4 from resizing the layers. This is a bug in the browser program. The Netscape Resize Fix offers a workaround, though.

20. ☑ **A, D, E,** and **F.** You can bring the current layer to the top of the stacking order by dragging the name of the layer to the top of the list in the Layers panel, by choosing Modify | Arrange | Bring To Front, by adjusting the z index on the Properties panel, or by adjusting the z index in Code view.

☒ **B** is incorrect because dragging the name of the current layer to the bottom of the list puts the layer at the bottom of the stacking order. **C** is incorrect because the Bring To Front command is under the Arrange submenu, not Align.

LAB ANSWER

From the look of things, you need a table with three rows and four cells, so that means three table-row tags and four table-data tags. The `border`, `cellspacing`, and `cellpadding` attributes go in the table tag, along with the width of 100%. This creates a table that shifts size to accommodate the browser window. Set the cell for the nav bar to 275, and make the background color `#0066CC`. Set the background color of the cells for the date and the bottom navigation to `#00CCFF`.

The only really tricky part is getting the rowspan right. Since the nav cell straddles three rows, add the `rowspan` attribute to this cell, and set the value to 3.

Here's the HTML, fresh from Code view:

```html
<table width="100%" border="0" cellspacing="0" cellpadding="0">
  <tr>
    <td width="275" rowspan="3" bgcolor="#0066CC">Navigation</td>
    <td bgcolor="#00CCFF">Date and featured links</td>
  </tr>
  <tr>
    <td bgcolor="#FFFFFF">Content area</td>
  </tr>
  <tr>
    <td bgcolor="#00CCFF">Bottom navigation</td>
  </tr>
</table>
```

The attributes of the tags can appear in any order.

5

Adding Content

C ontent is one of those words that people in the media game use all the time, and nearly everyone has a different definition for it. To some, content means the same as "anything, whatsoever," but this doesn't really help the present discussion. To others, content is what a Web site does, or it's the reason why someone visits a site; I think *functionality* and *strategic goals* are better terms for the concept of content. For the purposes of this book at least, content means specifically what appears in the guts of a Web page. If something identifiable sits on your page, even if it's broken and useless, then it's content. (And if it is broken and useless, it isn't very good content!)

Dreamweaver wouldn't be much of a development tool if it didn't let you add content to your page. In Design view, you simply click where you want to add content, and a flashing cursor appears. Then make sure that you choose an insertion point within the layout of the page: in a table cell, frame, or layer. If you click outside the structure of the layout, Dreamweaver puts the cursor at the nearest possible location, which is usually at the far left of the document window.

Unfortunately, because of the nature of HTML, Dreamweaver isn't a very good word processor or desktop publishing program. The software doesn't allow you to position content automatically in the middle of the page, for instance, unless of course you have a convenient table cell exactly where you want the content to be. In many cases, you can achieve basic formatting by inserting the content and then setting the alignment attribute of the corresponding HTML tag. Cascading Style Sheets give you more advanced formatting possibilities for *inline content,* as it's called, but you trade off reliable browser support in the process. For the best results, then, stick to the layout structure that you designed for the page. Don't put content outside the layout.

You'll recall from Chapter 1 that you can add two kinds of content to a page. The first kind, such as text and data tables, appears in the source code of the Web page itself. You don't need to store this kind of content in an external file because it already resides inside the HTML. The second kind of content, an *asset,* isn't part of the source code. An asset, such as an image or Flash movie, resides as an external file on your site. The source code tells the browser where to find this external file and where and how to display it on the page.

This chapter shows you how to add both kinds of content to your page and what happens in the source code when you do so.

Adding Content to the Source Code

Textual content of all kinds goes directly into the source code of your Web page. This content can be text that the visitor reads, scripts that the page runs to produce interactive effects, or descriptions that search engines use to index your page. In addition, you can use HTML markup to create visual elements such as lists, graphical rules, and floating frames.

Adding Text

To add text to your page, you simply choose an insertion point and type. To insert a special character such as the copyright symbol or the Euro currency mark, look under the Characters tab of the Insert panel. You can also choose Insert | Special Characters.

Select text for formatting by holding down the mouse button and dragging the mouse pointer. The Properties panel gives you several formatting and style choices, as the following illustration shows.

The Text menu, the Properties panel, and the right-click-activated context menu give you many of the same options, but also some different options. (See the next Scenario and Solution quick reference sidebar.)

When you're working in Code view, don't forget about the Text tab of the Insert panel (shown in the following illustration). It allows you to insert common HTML text tags. Click a button on the Insert panel to add the corresponding tag to your document's source code. You can also choose a tag from the Insert | Text Objects submenu.

SCENARIO & SOLUTION

What options for text editing can I access on the Properties panel?	Format, font face, font size, font color, bold and italic styles, alignment, indents, and outdents
What options for text editing can I access in the Text menu?	Format, font face, font size, font color, multiple styles, alignment, indents, and outdents
What options for text editing can I access in the context menu?	Format, font face, font size, multiple styles, alignment, and indents and outdents (in the List submenu)

Choosing a Format

HTML provides a few built-in text styles to use for paragraphs and headlines. The Properties panel's Format list allows you to specify one of these built-in styles for selected text. You can choose Text | Paragraph Format or right-click a text selection and choose Paragraph Format from the context menu to access styles.

To remove the formatting from a block of text, select the text and choose None from the Format list on the Properties panel.

About Headlines Six levels of headlines can be specified in HTML. They appear in the Format list as Heading 1 through Heading 6. Heading 1 is the largest and most prominent style. Heading 2 isn't quite as prominent as Heading 1, and Heading 3 isn't quite as prominent as Heading 2—you get the idea. Use headlines to give your visitors a sense of the structure of the page, just like this book uses different headline styles to reinforce the hierarchy of the information. Headings make it easier for users to tell at a glance what information goes with what section.

The six headlines correspond to the HTML tags <h1>, <h2>, <h3>, and so on. If you select a string of text and apply the Heading 1 format, for instance, Dreamweaver marks up the source code like this:

```
<h1>This is the text you selected for Heading 1.</h1>
```

About the Paragraph Format Choosing Paragraph from the Format list marks the selected text with paragraph tags, <p>:

```
<p>Here is a paragraph.</p>
```

A paragraph is just a regular block of text. When you mark a block of text as a paragraph, the browser usually inserts a carriage return between the paragraph and the item that follows it. The browser automatically inserts a carriage return between the paragraph and most other visual elements, as you can see in Figure 5-1. If you don't want a carriage return to follow a block of text, don't mark the block of text as a paragraph.

About Preformatted Text   Normally, the browser strips *whitespace,* or extra spaces and lines, from regular text, and it displays the text in a *proportional-pitch font,* which is a font whose characters have different amounts of space between them. In a proportional-pitch font, for example, the word *lit* takes up less space than the word *mow,* even though both words have three letters. That's because the lowercase letters *m, o,* and *w* are wider than *l, i,* and *t.*

By contrast, with *preformatted text,* the browser doesn't strip extra whitespace from the source code, and it usually displays this text in a *monospace* font, or a font whose characters take up the same amount of space, similar to the characters you type from

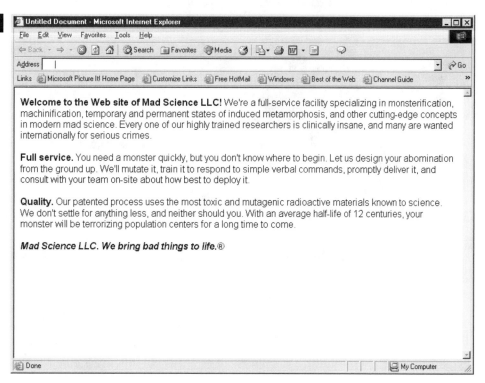

FIGURE 5-1

Carriage returns cause paragraphs to separate, like this.

a typewriter. In a monospace font, the words *lit* and *mow* take up exactly the same amount of space.

Use preformatted text when you want to preserve the internal formatting of a piece of text, such as for ASCII art (see the following illustration), where you represent pictures with keyboard characters and spaces, or in a data table whose columns are set up manually by spaces instead of with table tags. Preformatted text also works well when you want to display computer code, as we've done in this book.

 on the job

ASCII art isn't accessible on its own. In fact, it can easily confuse accessibility tools such as screen readers. If you use ASCII art on your page, be sure to include descriptive text as a caption, just as you would with a graphical image.

Choosing Preformatted from the Format list marks the selected text with preformatted-text tags, `<pre>`:

```
<pre>This is preformatted text.</pre>
```

Setting the Text Size

Change the size of selected text by pulling a value from the Size list. HTML provides two methods of sizing: absolute and relative. With absolute sizing, you specify exactly the size of the text that you want. With relative sizing, you express how much larger or smaller you want the text in relation to the current text size.

To return the text to normal size, select the text and choose None from the Size list.

About Absolute Sizing   Seven absolute sizes, ranging from 1 (the smallest) to 7 (the largest), are available. By default, unmarked text appears at size 3.

When you specify a size, Dreamweaver adds the font tag, `<font>`, to the source code. The `size` attribute of this tag determines the size of the text. Given a paragraph, if you set a particular word of the paragraph in size 5 text, the HTML looks like this:

```
<p>This paragraph has a word in <font size="5">larger</font> text.</p>
```

You can also set an absolute size by looking under Text | Size or by right-clicking the selection and choosing Size from the context menu.

About Relative Sizing   The relative options in the Size list are +1 through +7 and −1 through −7. These values determine how much the size of the marked-up text changes in relation to the regular size of the text.

For example, if the regular text is size 3, which it is by default, setting a selection to size +4 creates the effect of size 7, since 3 + 4 = 7. Similarly, if you have a block of text size 5 and set a selection within it to size −3, you get the effect of size 2, since 5 − 3 = 2.

Remember that only seven text sizes can be defined by HTML. If you start with a block of text size 6 and set a portion of it to size +7, you don't get size 13. You get size 7 instead, since size 7 is highest that HTML can handle.

Dreamweaver uses the `<font>` tag and its `size` attribute to denote relative sizing in the HTML, like this:

```
<p>This paragraph has a <font size="-1">smaller</font> word.</p>
```

You can also set relative sizing by looking under Text | Size Change or right-clicking the selection and choosing Size from the context menu.

exam
⚠ atch

The Text menu has two sizing submenus: Size for absolute values and Size Change for relative size values. However, the context menu has only one sizing submenu: Size, which contains both absolute and relative values.

Using Type Styles

HTML provides a number of style tags that you can use to modify the appearance of selected text. You can set the two most common, bold and italic, from the Properties panel. Find others under Text | Style.

Working with Bold and Italic   The B and I buttons on the Properties panel control boldface and italic type styles, which correspond to the HTML tags `<strong>` and `<em>`, respectively. (The `<em>` tag stands for *emphasis*.) A paragraph with one word in boldface and another in italic looks like this is the code:

```
<p>This paragraph has one word in <strong>bold</strong> and another in <em>italic</em>.</p>
```

In print publishing, it's usually the case that a punctuation mark like a period or comma appears in boldface or italic if the word that precedes it is in bold or italic. In Web publishing, it's usually just the opposite. Only the word appears in boldface or italic. The ending punctuation appears in normal style.

You can set multiple styles for the same text selection. A paragraph with a word that's both boldface and italic looks like this in the code:

```
<p>This paragraph has a <strong><em>word</em></strong> that's both bold and italic.</p>
```

Working with Other Type Styles   Choosing Text | Style or right-clicking a text selection and choosing Style from the context menu gives you several other style options, each corresponding to an HTML tag.

Web builders don't use these styles often, and browsers differ in their presentation of them. In general, though, you should use these special styles only for their intended purposes. If you have a citation in your text, for instance, feel free to use the Citation style. Don't use the Citation style for text that isn't a citation just because you like its formatting.

Under no circumstances should you ever use the Underline style! Underlining is a near-universal visual cue for a textual hyperlink. If you underline text that isn't a link, your visitors will try to click it. This leads to confusion and frustration when nothing happens.

Choosing Fonts

Dreamweaver uses the font tag, `<font>`, and its `face` attribute to mark selected text for a particular typeface.

In theory, you can specify any font you want in the `face` attribute, but in practice, you have to be extremely careful about it. The fonts that you might want to use on your page aren't necessarily the same fonts that your visitors have on their systems. If you specify an uncommon or unusual font like Space Toaster, for instance, only those who have Space Toaster will be able to see your page as you intended. If a visitor doesn't have Space Toaster, the browser automatically substitutes a more generic font of its choice, which can create formatting/readability headaches if the characters in the substitute font are smaller or larger than those in the font you specified.

You can use two strategies for avoiding these kinds of problems, and you should use them both. The first strategy is to provide a list of acceptable fonts instead of just a single typeface. As your Web page loads, the visitor's browser tries to use the first font in the list. If the visitor's system doesn't have it, the browser moves on to the next font in the list, and so on. The browser makes a substitution only if it exhausts all the fonts in the list, and you can even tell the browser exactly which kind of font to use as a substitute.

The second strategy is to restrict your font choices to the most common fonts—those that everyone on the Web is likely to have. If you use obvious typefaces, the chance of a visitor not seeing the page as you intend becomes small. Incidentally, this is why virtually all Web text is in Times New Roman, Arial, and Verdana. Guess which fonts are common to most Windows PCs? The next Scenario and Solution sidebar provides a quick reference of many of the most common fonts.

on the Job

A sans-serif *font, like the typeface you're reading right now, is a font whose characters don't have small typographic decorations, while a* serif *font, like most of the text in this book, uses these flourishes. Headlines look better in sans-serif fonts, but smaller text is easier to read when you set it in serifed font. The little feet on the characters help to guide the reader's eyes from one character to the next.*

Dreamweaver's default font lists implement both. The font list choices appear in the drop-down list to the right of the Format list and also under Text | Font and the Font submenu of the context menu. If you apply the first font list to a paragraph, for instance, the source code appears as follows:

```
<p><font face="Arial, Helvetica, sans-serif">This paragraph displays in Arial on most
Windows PCs.</font></p>
```

As you can see, the `face` attribute contains the list of desired fonts. Your first choice is Arial, which almost all Windows PCs have. Your second choice is Helvetica, a similar-looking Mac font. Your third choice is the generic font sans-serif, which doesn't apply to any one font in particular. The browser substitutes its default sans-serif font if neither Arial nor Helvetica is available.

SCENARIO & SOLUTION

Which serif fonts are the most common?	Times New Roman, Georgia (Windows), Times (Mac)
Which sans-serif fonts are the most common?	Arial, Verdana (Windows), Helvetica (Mac)
Which monospace fonts are the most common?	Courier New (Windows), Courier (Mac)

Creating Your Own Font Lists If you want to create a customized font list, choose the Edit Font List option, the last option in the drop-down list to the right of the Format list. The Edit Font List dialog box appears, as shown here.

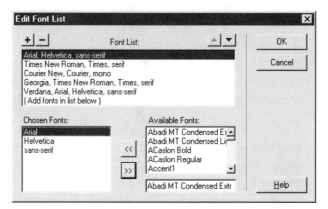

In the Font List area of the dialog box, select the font list that you want to edit. To delete an entire font list, select it and click the minus button. To change the position of a font list, select it and click the up-arrow and down-arrow buttons. To create a new font list, click the plus button.

To add a font to the list, choose a font from the Available Fonts pane and click the left-arrow button. At the bottom of the list of available fonts, you'll find generic fonts like sans-serif and monotype. The last choice of every font list should be one of these generic types. That way, if all else fails, the browser knows what type of font to substitute.

To remove a front from the Chosen Fonts list, select the font in the Chosen Fonts pane and click the right-arrow button.

To change the order of preference of a font in the font list, select the font in the Chosen Fonts pane and click the up-arrow and down-arrow buttons. The first font in the Chosen Fonts pane is your first choice. The second font is your second choice, and so on.

When you finish creating or editing the font list, click OK. Your font list appears in the Properties panel's drop-down list.

Choosing the Font Color

To set the text color of a selection, click the color square to the right of the Size list in the Properties panel and choose a color from the list of swatches that pops up, or choose Text | Color. You can also type the hexadecimal code of the color directly into the field to the right of the color square.

Dreamweaver creates the color with the font tag and its `color` attribute. If you set a word in a paragraph to display in red (#FF0000), Dreamweaver makes the following adjustments to the HTML:

```
<p>This paragraph has a <font color="#FF0000">red</font> word.</p>
```

You'll recall that the body tag has the `text` attribute, which defines the default text color of the page. The font color you specify in the font tag overrides the default text color. Set a font color for only a few words at most. If you want all the text to appear in a certain color, set the `text` attribute of the body tag instead.

Be extremely careful about using different colors for text on the same page! Your visitors can interpret colored text as links. In my creative-director days, I never let my designers get away with any additional text colors, not even for words like *Warning*. (I told them that color on a Web page is expensive, and I sent them phony bills for their overages.) Boldface and italic work much better anyway, and they're harder to misinterpret.

Setting Font Attributes in Code View

When you're in Code view, you have the option of using the Font Tag Editor shown in the following illustration to manage font tag attributes including `size`, `color`, and `face`. Launch the Font Tag Editor by looking under the Text tab of the Insert panel and clicking the first button on the left of your screen. (as shown here).

Aligning Text

You can align text horizontally by clicking one of the Properties panel's four alignment buttons, shown here. These are, from left to right, Align Left, Align Right, Align Center, and Justify.

Clicking one of these buttons defines the `align` attribute of the text's format tag, such as `<p>` or `<h3>`, like this:

```
<h1 align="center">This headline is centered.</h1>
```

If the selected text doesn't have a format tag, Dreamweaver places the text between `<div>` and `</div>` and sets the `align` attribute of the opening `<div>` tag, like this:

```
<div align="right">This unformatted text appears flush right.</div>
```

The default alignment for text depends on the browser, but all browsers to my knowledge use left alignment unless you specify otherwise.

Another way to set alignment for text is to choose Text | Align or right-click the text selection and choose Align from the context menu.

Using Outdents and Indents

The Text Outdent and Text Indent buttons, shown here, appear below the alignment buttons on the Properties panel.

To indent a selection, click the Text Indent button. Dreamweaver applies the blockquote tag, `<blockquote>`, to the HTML, like this:

```
<blockquote>
    <p>This paragraph is indented.</p>
</blockquote>
```

To increase the amount of indentation, click the Text Indent button more than once. This nests blockquote tags:

```
<blockquote>
    <blockquote>
        <blockquote>
            <p>The developer indented this paragraph three
times.</p>
```

```
        </blockquote>
      </blockquote>
</blockquote>
```

To remove levels of indentation (and thereby strip out blockquote tags), click the Text Outdent button.

You can also create indents and outdents by choosing Text | Indent or Text | Outdent or by right-clicking the text selection and choosing List | Indent or List | Outdent from the context menu.

Creating Lists

The Unordered List and Ordered List buttons, shown here, appear under the Bold and Italic buttons of the Properties panel.

Use these buttons to create bulleted (unordered) and numbered (ordered) lists. You can convert selected text to list format, or you can create the list as you go. Click the current list button again to switch back to normal text.

Dreamweaver marks up unordered and ordered lists with the `<ul>` and `<ol>` tags, respectively. It marks list items with `<li>`, like this:

```
<ul>
    <li>Bulleted item 1</li>
    <li>Bulleted item 2</li>
    <li>Bulleted item 3</li>
</ul>
```

exam

ⓦatch

Be wary of bogus tags like `<bl>` for bulleted lists and `<nl>` for numbered lists. The correct tags are `<ul>` for unordered lists (bulleted lists) and `<ol>` for ordered lists (numbered lists).

When you work in Code view and open the Text tab of the Insert panel, or choose Insert | Text Objects, you can insert the appropriate HTML tags for definition lists. *Definition lists* are list of terms and their descriptions, like those that appear in a glossary. Descriptions appear indented in most browsers.

Use the definition-term tag, `<dt>`, to indicate a term, and use the definition-description tag, `<dd>`, to indicate its meaning. Enclose the entire list in the definition-list tag, `<dl>`, like this:

```
<dl>
    <dt>Term 1</dt>
        <dd>Description of Term 1</dd>
    <dt>Term 2</dt>
```

```
    <dd>Description of Term 2</dd>
<dt>Term 3</dt>
    <dd>Description of Term 3</dd>
</dl>
```

To insert a definition list from Design view, choose Text | List | Definition List or right-click and choose List | Definition List from the context menu.

Nesting Lists

You can nest lists, or create lists within lists, by choosing an insertion point or selecting a block of text within a list and clicking the Text Indent button. This creates a nested list of the same type as the current list. Switch the type by clicking the opposite list button. To return to the main list from a nested list, click the Text Outdent button

In this example, the developer started with a bulleted list, created two bulleted items, clicked the Text Indent button to create a nested bulleted list, clicked the Ordered List button to change the nested bulleted list into a nested numbered list, added three numbered items, clicked the Text Outdent button to return to the unordered list, and finished with one more bulleted item:

```
<ul>
    <li>Bulleted item 1</li>
    <li>Bulleted item 2</li>
        <ol>
            <li>Nested numbered item 1</li>
            <li>Nested numbered item 2</li>
            <li>Nested numbered item 3</li>
        </ol>
    <li>Bulleted item 3</li>
</ul>
```

Inserting the Date

 Click the Date button, shown here, to add the current date to the document. Find this button under the Common tab of the Insert panel.

The Insert Date dialog box appears, shown in the following illustration. Choose the format for the date from the choices in the drop-down lists. If you want Dreamweaver to update the date automatically whenever you save the document, check this option and click OK. Having Dreamweaver automatically update the date completes sentences that read, "This page was last updated on . . . . "

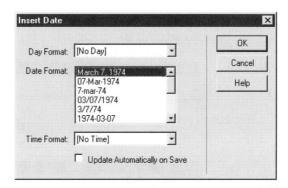

When you click the Date button, Dreamweaver inserts a static date on your page. That is, the date appears in plain text, as if you had typed it yourself. Your page doesn't keep track of the current date and time. If you added the date on May 3, for example, May 3 is what appears in the visitor's browser window, not whatever the current date happens to be. If you want a dynamic date, you need to add client-side scripting. Any JavaScript developer worth the asking price can write a function to retrieve the current date and display it on the page.

When you're working in Code view, you can insert the date by choosing Insert | Date.

Inserting Abbreviations and Acronyms

abbr. W3C

For abbreviations and acronyms, switch to Code view and look under the Text tab of the Insert panel. The last two buttons, shown here, correspond to the abbreviation tag <abbr> and the acronym tag <acronym>, respectively.

Use the abbreviation and acronym tags to improve the accessibility of your page. Screen readers and similar accessibility tools might not understand an abbreviation like *v.* for the word *very* or an acronym like W3C for *World Wide Web Consortium.* When you mark up abbreviations and acronyms with the appropriate tags, you embed the spelled-out text into the source code, allowing screen readers to skip the potentially confusing shortened form.

To insert abbreviation tags, highlight the abbreviation in the source code and click the Abbreviation button. The Abbreviation dialog box appears. Type the spelled-out form of the abbreviation in the Full Text field, and type the language of the spelled-out abbreviation, such as English, in the Language field. Click OK to insert the tag.

The Acronym dialog box works similarly, to make acronyms more accessible. These two dialog boxes are shown in the following illustrations.

In both cases, the spelled-out form appears in the `title` attribute, and the language appears in the `lang` attribute:

```
<p>I soon received an invitation to join the <abbr
title="Justice League of
    America" lang="English">JLA</abbr>.</p>
```

Remember that you have to switch to Code view to insert abbreviation and acronym tags this way, because the Text tab appears only in the Insert panel when you're working in Code view.

Another way to insert these tags from Code view is to select them from the submenu that appears when you choose Insert | Text Objects.

Inserting Horizontal Rules

 Click the Horizontal Rule button, shown here, on the Insert panel under the Common tab to insert a straight graphical line. Horizontal rules are helpful to use for separating different areas of the page.

When you select a horizontal rule, the Properties panel gives you a few options for modifying its appearance, as you can see in in the following illustration. Specify a width, expressed either in absolute pixels or relative percent measurements, in the W field. Specify a pixels-only height value in the H field.

Choose an alignment for the horizontal rule from the Align list. By default, browsers usually center horizontal rules.

If you don't want the rule to have shading, uncheck the Shading option. An unshaded horizontal rule looks less conspicuous than a shaded one, which makes it subtler and generally more aesthetically pleasing.

When you click the Horizontal Rule button, Dreamweaver adds the horizontal-rule tag, `<hr>`, to the source code. The W field of the Properties panel corresponds to the `width` attribute of this tag, while the H field corresponds to the `size` attribute—not `height`, as you might be tempted to believe. The Align list sets the `align` attribute. The valueless `noshade` attribute turns off shading. Therefore, a horizontal rule 33% wide and 6 pixels high aligned to the left without shading looks like this in the code:

```
<hr align="left" width="33%" size="6" noshade>
```

Notice that no closing horizontal-rule tag appears. This is one of the few HTML notations that doesn't require a closing tag.

exam 🐶 *atch*

Certification tests like to ask questions about horizontal rules, because the horizontal-rule tag throws several curve balls. First, the height of the rule is expressed by the `size` attribute, not the `height` attribute, and the size can't be a percentage. Second, the valueless `noshade` attribute turns off shading. There is no `shading="no"` or `shading="yes"` situation here. Third, no closing horizontal-rule tag is used. For your own good, get to know the HTML used for horizontal rules.

When you're working in Code view, you can insert a horizontal rule by choosing Insert | Horizontal Rule.

Adding Data Tables

You explored layout tables already in Chapter 4, and you may recall that standards bodies like the World Wide Web Consortium (W3C) get bent out of shape about tables because the W3C requires that table tags be used only for tabular data, not for other layout purposes. According to the W3C, the only completely acceptable use of table tags is to mark up *data tables,* or tables that present rows and columns of data.

You add a data table to your page exactly as you would a layout table, with the exception that you don't use Layout view. Stick with Standard view for layout tables, which means that you use the Table buttons under the Common and Layout tabs of the Insert panel or the Insert | Table command.

Where layout tables almost always set the `cellpadding`, `cellspacing`, and `border` attributes to 0, data tables almost always use a little of each. When in doubt, don't define any value for these attributes at all. Let the browser provide the default amounts of padding and spacing and an invisible border. If you find you need more, select the table and tweak the appropriate fields in the Properties panel.

Adding Headers and Captions

In addition to the usual table tags—`<table>`, `<tr>`, and `<td>`—data tables also use the table-header tag, `<th>`, and the table-caption tag, `<caption>`, to indicate different design elements of the table. A table header appears in place of a table-data tag, `<td>`, when the content of the cell represents a column head. You can include as many table-header tags in your table as you need, but typically you only use one per column or row. The table caption appears immediately after the opening table tag and gives a brief title or textual summary of the table's contents. For maximum accessibility, it's imperative that you provide table headers and a table caption for each data table in your site and that you do so with the appropriate tags.

To insert table-header and table-caption tags in Dreamweaver, you must first switch to Code view. You can't insert these tags in Design view. Position the cursor in the code and select the Tables tab of the Insert panel. Click the TH button to insert a table-header tag or click the CAP button to insert a table-caption tag. Alternatively, you can choose Insert | Table Objects | TH or Insert | Table Objects | Caption.

Here is a sample data table with the correct markup for the caption and table headers:

```
<table>
    <caption>Table 1: Results of y = x + 5</caption>
<tr>
    <th>x</th>
    <th>y</th>
</tr>
<tr>
    <td>0</td>
    <td>5</td>
```

```
    </tr>
    <tr>
       <td>1</td>
       <td>6</td>
    </tr>
    <tr>
       <td>2</td>
       <td>7</td>
    </tr>
    </table>
```

Formatting Data Tables

You can quickly add predesigned color and style schemes to a data table by selecting the table and choosing Commands | Format Table. (To select the table, click its outer border in Design view or click its table tag in the Tag Selector.) The Format Table dialog box appears, as shown in Figure 5-2.

Choose a style from the list in the upper-left corner of the dialog box. Customize the settings to your liking and click Apply to view the style without closing the dialog box—or click OK to set the style and close the dialog box.

FIGURE 5-2

Use the Format Table dialog box to add predesigned color and style schemes to a data table.

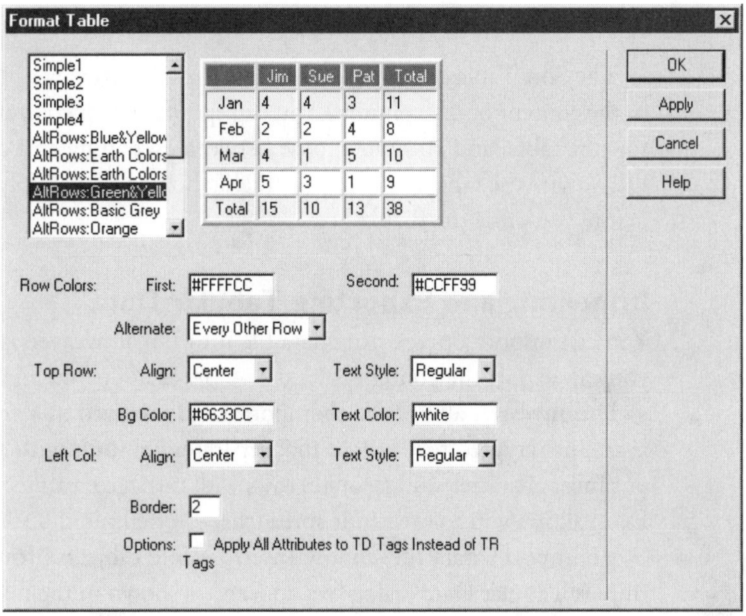

I'm not crazy about Dreamweaver's prepackaged formatting in any mode, so don't expect me to sing the joys of the Format Table dialog box here. If you're in a creative pinch, these styles can help you out, but the chance is next to zero that the colors and looks will match the ones you carefully chose and designed during the planning stage of your site.

Sorting Tabular Data

Use the Sort Table dialog box shown here, which opens when you select a table and choose Commands | Sort Table, to reorder the information in your data table.

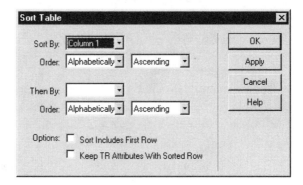

The Sort Table command rearranges the table-row tags in your data table according to the content of the columns. You can specify which columns Dreamweaver uses to sort the table, and you can choose between ascending and descending order. Click OK to sort the table and close the dialog box or click Apply to preview the changes before you close the dialog box.

Importing and Exporting Tabular Data

You can import a preexisting data file into Dreamweaver as a data table. Likewise, you can export the contents of a data table as a separate file.

Dreamweaver allows you to import data files saved in *delimited* text format, which is an unencrypted text format that separates columns with a tab, comma, semicolon, or similar character, and separates rows with carriage returns. Software such as Microsoft Excel allows you to save your spreadsheet in delimited text format.

To import a data file, choose Insert | Table Objects | Import Tabular Data. The Import Tabular Data dialog box appears, as shown in the following illustration. Click the Browse button to navigate to the data file on your system. Choose the file's delimiter character from the Delimiter drop-down list, specify the format of the data table in the remaining fields, and click OK. Dreamweaver reads the data file and creates a new data table from it. This operation doesn't delete or modify the existing file in any way. After Dreamweaver creates the table, you can change the values in the cells or edit the structure of the table exactly as you would if you had built the table by hand.

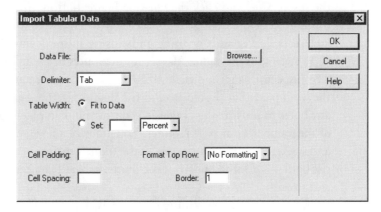

To export the contents of a data table in text-delimited format, select the table and choose File | Export | Table from Dreamweaver's main menu. The Export Table dialog box appears (see the following illustration). Choose the delimiter character that you prefer from the Delimiter list, and specify the style of line breaks. Go with the style that best matches the system with which you'll open the delimited text file. Click Export, and the Export Table As dialog box appears. Choose a convenient location for the file, supply a file name, and click Save.

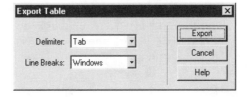

Adding Inline Frames

You remember frames from Chapter 4, where you used them to create page layouts. You can use another kind of frame as well: an *inline* or *floating* frame. This type of frame contains a separate Web page, just like the frames you constructed in Chapter 4. However, an inline frame doesn't come from a separate frameset file—you build it into the source code of the current page. What's more, the frame itself can appear anywhere on the page, and you can wrap content around it. In this regard, an inline frame behaves more like an image file.

To insert an inline frame, you must first switch to Code view. (You can't insert an inline frame from Design view.) Click an insertion point in the source code, and choose Insert | Frames | Floating Frame. You can also look under the Frames tab of the Insert panel and click the Floating Frame button, shown here. You didn't notice this button before because it appears only when you're working in Code view.

ifrm

Dreamweaver adds opening and closing inline-frame tags, <iframe> and </iframe>, to the source. To set the attributes of the inline-frame tag, open the Tag Inspector panel and click <IFRAME>. Set the src attribute to the location of the Web page that should load in the floating frame. Set the width and height attributes to provide the dimensions of the frame in pixels. Set the other attributes of the frame as your page requires. You'll notice a few familiar faces: marginwidth and marginheight for the size of the frame's margin, frameborder for the size of the border, id for the name of the frame, scrolling for how to handle scrollbars, and so on.

If, for example, you want to display a Web page called *ad.htm* in an inline frame called *floatingFrame* with a width of 300 pixels, a height of 150 pixels, and no scrolling, Dreamweaver adds the following HTML to your page:

```
<iframe id="floatingFrame" src="ad.htm" width="300" height="150"
    scrolling="no"></iframe>
```

Not all browsers support frames, much less floating frames. Type noframes content for the floating frame between the opening and closing tags, like this:

```
<iframe id="floatingFrame" src="ad.htm" width="300" height="150"
    scrolling="no">Your browser doesn't support inline frames.
    If it did, you'd see a very important message from our sponsor
    in this space.</iframe>
```

Adding Meta Tags

Meta tags contain descriptive information about the page or instructions for the HTTP header of the page. This information doesn't appear anywhere in the browser window. It's invisible by design. It shows up between the head tags, <head> and </head>. To make meta tags and other pieces of *head content* visible in the document window, choose View | Head Content from the main menu.

Use meta tags for a variety of purposes, including preparing your page for search engines, refreshing the page after a certain amount of time has passed, or redirecting the browser to a new URL. Find buttons for inserting meta tags under the Head tab of the Insert panel. If you're working in Code view, you can insert meta tags by choosing them from the submenu under Insert | Head Tags.

Adding a Keywords Element

A keywords element is a meta tag that contains indexing terms for the page. Some search engines use these meta tags to determine the relevance of your site against certain search phrases. For instance, if you set *balloons* and *ballooning* as keywords for your page, search engines may index your site so that it appears closer to the top of the list when someone searches for hot-air balloon rides.

To insert a keywords element, go under the Head tab of the Insert panel and click the Keywords button, shown here. In the Keywords dialog box (see the following illustration), type the indexing terms for the page, separating them with commas, and click OK.

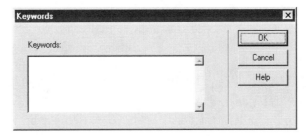

Assuming that you use *balloons* and *ballooning* as keywords, Dreamweaver adds the following HTML to your page:

```
<meta name="keywords" content="balloons,ballooning">
```

As you can see, the content attribute contains the list of keywords, while the name attribute specifies the kind of content that the meta tag provides.

Adding a Description Element

As the keywords element provides a list of indexing terms for the page, the description element provides a brief textual summary of the page and its content. Some search engines use this element to index your page as well. It often behooves you to keep the description short and sweet. Limit yourself to a sentence or two.

To insert a description element, click the Description button, shown here.

The Description dialog box appears, as shown in the following illustration. Type a brief description of your page in the window and click OK.

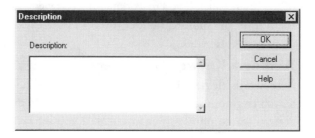

Dreamweaver adds something like this to your source code:

```
<meta name="description" content="Hot-air balloon rides. Low accident rating.">
```

Again, the name attribute determines what kind of content the meta tag provides.

Adding a Page-Refresh Element

Refreshing the page has nothing to do with search engine indexing or relevancy. Yet you can use a meta tag to achieve this effect. The page-refresh element reloads the current page or jumps to a new page after a specified amount of time elapses.

To insert a page-refresh element, click the Refresh button.

This opens the Refresh dialog box (see the following illustration). Type the delay in seconds in the Delay field. To redirect the browser to another page, choose the Go To URL action and specify the path to the page. To reload the current page, choose the Refresh This Document action. Click OK.

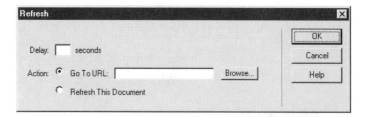

If, for example, you choose to redirect your visitor to a page called *index.htm* after 10 seconds have passed, Dreamweaver inserts the following meta tag:

```
<meta http-equiv="refresh" content="10;URL=index.htm">
```

If you choose to refresh the current page after the same amount of time instead, you get the following:

```
<meta http-equiv="refresh" content="10">
```

Notice this time that the `http-equiv` attribute determines the function of the meta tag instead of the `name` attribute of the keywords and description elements.

Defining Your Own Meta Tag

Since the attributes of the meta tag determine its purpose, you can create your own meta tags by supplying different values for the `name` or `http-equiv` and `content` attributes.

To create a meta tag, click the Meta button, shown here.

The Meta dialog box appears (see the following illustration). From the Attribute drop-down list, select the Name option to specify a `name` attribute, or select the HTTP-Equivalent option to specify an `http-equiv` attribute. The `name` attribute indicates that the content of the meta tag is some kind of textual description about the page. The `http-equiv` attribute indicates that the content of the meta tag is an instruction or a piece of information for the HTTP header. A meta tag can't have both `name` and `http-equiv` attributes.

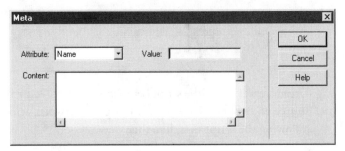

Give the value of the `name` or `http-equiv` attribute in the Value field, type the content of the meta tag in the Content field and click OK. For instance, if you create a meta tag that holds the name of the author of the Web page, your HTML looks something like this:

```
<meta name="author" content="JAK">
```

Inserting Client-Side Scripts

Use client-side scripts to enhance the functionality and interactivity of your page. Dreamweaver's behaviors give you a number of ready-made scripts for all kinds of functions. If you prefer to write your own scripts, though, choose Insert | Script Objects | Script or look under the Script tab of the Insert panel and click the Script button.

The Script dialog box will appear (see the following illustration). Choose the language of the script from the Language list and type the code of the script in the Content field. In the No Script field, specify *noscript content,* or content that appears in the event that your visitor's browser can't process scripts of the language you used. Click OK to insert the script.

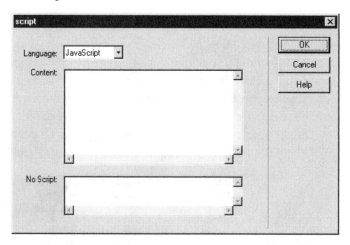

Dreamweaver places the script between script tags, `<script>` and `</script>`, in your source code. The noscript content goes between `<noscript>` tags immediately following the script tags, like this:

```
<script language="JavaScript" type="text/JavaScript">
   alert("This is a JavaScript.");
</script>
<noscript>There's a JavaScript on this page, but your browser can't
   process it. Either turn on JavaScript in your browser preferences or
   use a browser that supports JavaScript.</noscript>
```

The noscript content appears in the document window next to a golden shield icon that represents the script. Neither one appears in a live browser window, provided that the browser can process the script. To hide the noscript content in the document window, choose View | Noscript Content, which should have a check mark beside it. To hide the golden shield icon for the script, choose Edit | Preferences, select the Invisible Elements category, and remove the check mark next to Scripts.

exam
Watch

Only the current Web page can access a script built into the source code like this. If you want several pages to use the same script, save the script in a separate file and attach the script *to each page by defining the* src *attribute of the script tag.*

Adding Generic Noscript Content to the Page

If your page has several scripts, you may not want to supply noscript content for each of them. It probably makes more sense to add a single, generic noscript message in a prominent place.

To add generic noscript content, click an insertion point on the page. Then choose Insert | Script Objects | NoScript. Dreamweaver's Tag Editor appears. Type in the noscript content and click OK. In Code view, you can add noscript content after clicking the Noscript button under the Script tab of the Insert panel.

Adding Comments

Developers often comment their code with instructions or plain-text explanations about what the code does. In source code for a Web page, a developer might indicate different parts of the page with comments like *Content goes here* or *This is the main layout table.* Notes like these help to jog rusty memories when time has passed, and it allows others to make modifications faster and more accurately. Comments reside in the source code only; they don't appear in the browser window.

You can insert a comment in Design view or Code view. Choose an insertion point for the comment somewhere convenient on the page or in the HTML. Then look under the Common tab of the Insert panel and click the Comment button.

If you're working the Design view, the Comment dialog box appears. Type your comment in the field and click OK. Dreamweaver places a gold shield icon in the document window to mark the position of the comment. This icon is a visual aid— it doesn't appear in the browser window. You can ask Dreamweaver not to display comment icons in the document window from the Preferences dialog box, by choosing Edit | Preferences, choosing the Invisible Elements category, and unchecking the option for displaying comments. One advantage to keeping the comment icon, though, is that you can easily drag it to a new location on the page or click it to edit the comment's text in the Properties panel.

When you add a comment to your page, Dreamweaver inserts the proper HTML notation, such as the following:

```
<!--This is a comment-->
```

The comment appears grayed out and in italics when you look at it in Code view.

If you insert the comment in Code view instead of Design view, Dreamweaver adds the comment notation without any text inside. Simply type your comment between the comment marks. Code view also allows you to insert a comment by choosing Insert | Text Objects | Comment.

Commenting Out Code

Another indispensable use of commenting is to gray out troublesome blocks of HTML code without deleting them. This helps you to isolate problems faster. You can tell more easily which portions of the page are working and which portions need work.

To comment out a section of code, switch to Code view, select the code that you want to comment out, and click the Comment button. Dreamweaver inserts comment notation around the selection. This trick works only in Code view. If you try the same thing in Design view, the Comment dialog box opens instead.

EXERCISE 5-1

Adding Text to the Mad Science Home Page

In this exercise, you start adding content to the home page for Mad Science LLC.

1. Launch Dreamweaver, open the Site panel, and set the site to Mad Science LLC.

2. Double-click the file *index.htm*. This is the home page you created in Chapter 3. The home page opens in a document window.

3. Pop the CD-ROM from this book into your computer.

4. Choose File | Open from Dreamweaver's main menu. Navigate to the *examples/ch04* folder on the CD-ROM. Inside, you'll find a file called *text.txt*. Double-

click this file to open it in Dreamweaver. This is the text for the home page, supplied by your client.

5. Switch back to the document window for the home page. Click in the table cell on the bottom right, which is the main content area of the page. Look under the Common tab of the Insert panel and click the Horizontal Rule button to add a horizontal rule to the page. While the rule is selected, go to the Properties panel, type **1** in the H field, and remove the check mark next to the Shading option.

6. Now, click anywhere below the layout table and insert another horizontal rule to mark the bottom of the page. Go to the Properties panel, type **33** in the W field, change the units to Percent, type **1** in the H field, set the Align list to Left, and remove the shading.

7. Switch to the text document. Choose Edit | Select All and then choose Edit | Copy.

8. Switch back to the home page again. Select the horizontal rule in the table cell and press the down-arrow key. The flashing cursor appears to the far right of the rule. Choose Edit | Paste to fill the table cell with text.

9. Now to format the text. Click in each paragraph and notice that Dreamweaver assigned the Paragraph format to all but the first block of text. To change this, click anywhere in the first paragraph, go to the Properties panel and set the Format list to Paragraph.

10. Highlight all the text, go to the Properties panel and pull the first set of fonts from the font list. The text changes font.

11. Highlight the first sentence of the first paragraph and click the B button on the Properties panel. The sentence changes to boldface. Highlight the phrase *Full service* in the second paragraph, and make it boldface. Highlight the word *Quality* in the third paragraph and make it boldface. Highlight the entire fourth paragraph and make it boldface and italic.

12. Click to the right of the last period in the last paragraph and look under the Characters tab of the Insert panel. Click the button for Registered Trademark to insert this character next to the corporate slogan.

13. Highlight all the text again and click the Text Indent button on the Properties panel two times. This indents the text from the margins of the table cell.

14. Look under the Head tab of the Insert panel and add a keywords element to your page. Type the following the field: **monsters, mutation, mad science, creatures, fiends, abomination**s.

15. Now add a description element. Type the following in the field: **Corporate site for Mad Science LLC, a full-service monster design and development facility.**

16. Your finished page should look something like Figure 5-3.

17. Choose File | Save to save the page as *index.htm*. Well done! The client is pleased.

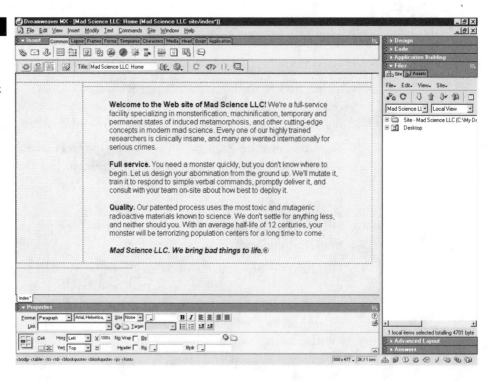

Adding Assets

Assets are pieces of content that come from external files. The source code of the Web page contains instructions for finding and displaying these external files. Dreamweaver allows you to place assets on your page, but, in all but a few cases, it doesn't allow you to create the external files themselves.

Adding Images

Most Web browsers can display images. GIF (Graphics Interchange Format) and JPEG (Joint Photographic Experts Group) images are the most common and best supported image formats for the Web, although some browsers display BMP (Windows bitmap) and PNG (Portable Network Graphics) images as well.

To add an image to your page, first make sure that the image file resides in your site's default images folder. Then choose an insertion point for the image in the document window, look under the Common tab of the Insert panel, and click the Image button.

This opens the Select Image Source dialog box. Navigate to the default images folder for your site and double-click the name of the image file that you want to insert. The Select Image Source dialog box closes, and Dreamweaver adds the image to your page.

To be more precise, Dreamweaver creates an HTML reference to the image file in the default images folder. The reference looks something like this:

```
<img src="images/picture.jpg">
```

The src attribute contains the path to the graphics file that you want to use. Notice that there's no closing image tag, a rarity in HTML.

Another way to insert an image is to choose Insert | Image or drag an image file from the Site panel into the document window.

If you want to change the source file of the image, click the folder icon next to the Src field on the Properties panel, navigate to the default images folder, and choose a new image file. You can also click the target icon to the left of the folder icon, hold

FROM THE CLASSROOM

Picture Perfect

Almost all Web graphics come in two varieties: GIFs and JPEGs. Both file formats are small and well optimized for the rigors of the Web. These formats are very different, though, and understanding their differences helps you to figure out which to use for a particular image on your site.

GIF is a proprietary image format owned by CompuServe, and it's been around longer than many Web builders. GIFs have built-in color palettes. Every pixel in the image uses one of the colors in the palette. The more colors you have, the more realistic the image looks, but the larger the file size becomes as a result. Even still, the maximum number of colors in the palette is 256. For this reason, the GIF format works best for images that have large areas of flat color, like most kinds of line art. If you can get away with 64 or even 128 colors in the palette, the image size drops and the graphic loads more quickly on your Web page.

GIFs aren't good for photographs. Photos contain a surprisingly large amount of color information. The range of lights and shades in even a high-contrast photo pushes well over the 256-color limit of the GIF. Enter the JPEG.

The JPEG image format doesn't have a built-in palette, which means that it doesn't have a limit to the amount of color information that it can contain. This makes it a better choice for photos or any kind of graphic with subtle degrees of color or shading. JPEGs keep the file size down by analyzing the source image and throwing out color information. In this sense, the JPEG is a *lossy* format. The amount of loss determines the size of the file. In a good JPEG, the loss is so subtle that the human eye can't easily detect it. In a poor JPEG, there's too much loss, and the image quality deteriorates noticeably.

JPEGs may be good for photos, but they don't do as well with large areas of flat color. There's less color information to begin with in these types of images, so there's less color information to throw out.

If you want to put a photo on your site, make it a JPEG. But if you want to put a typical diagram, logo, illustration, chart, or sketch on your page, GIF is usually the best way to go.

down the mouse button, and drag the pointer to the desired image file in the Site panel. Right-clicking the existing image and choosing Source File from the context menu calls up the Select Image Source dialog box, which gives you yet another way to change the image source.

Setting Image Properties

The image tag has many useful attributes. To set them, select the image. The Properties panel reconfigures itself for working with images, as the following illustration shows.

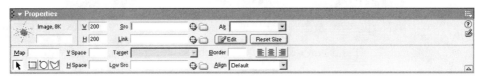

Setting the Dimensions of the Image

After you insert an image, you should first determine its width and height in pixels. Images with specified widths and heights load faster. If you don't see values in the W and H fields of the Properties panel, click the Reset Size button. Dreamweaver calculates the dimensions of the image and adds them to the image tag, like this:

```
<img src="images/picture.jpg" width="300" height="150">
```

The W and H fields of the Properties panel receive the appropriate width and height values. By changing these, you can stretch or compress the appearance of the image in the browser window. For example, specifying a height of 300 causes the image in the sample line of code above to stretch to twice its normal height while retaining its normal width. However, it's almost never a good idea to do this. Stretching a smaller graphic to make it larger decreases the image quality, and compressing a larger graphic to make it smaller wastes valuable downloading time—even though the image takes up less space on screen, the browser still has to download the full-sized version. The only time manual image sizing makes sense is when you want to increase the size of a spacer image. Since a spacer is usually just a 1×1 transparent GIF, you can stretch it to all manner of sizes without worrying about loss of image quality. There's no image quality to lose!

To resize an image visually instead of typing values into fields, select the image in the document window, and drag one of the image's handles. The handle along the bottom of the image resizes the height, and the handle on the right side resizes the width. The handle in the bottom right corner resizes the width and height proportionately.

After you resize the width and/or height of an image, the values in the W and/or H fields appear in boldface. Return the image to its original size by clicking the Reset Size button.

Setting Alternate Text

An image's alternate text (or *alt text*) displays while the image is loading or when the browser can't find the specified graphics file. Accessibility tools such as screen readers rely on the alternate text to provide accurate and succinct descriptions of the image's content.

Type alternate text for the image in the Alt field of the Properties panel. Dreamweaver adds the `alt` attribute to your image tag, like this:

```
<img src="images/picture.jpg" width="300" height="150" alt="A picture of a hot-air balloon.">
```

If you don't want to supply alternate text for an image, choose the Empty option from the Alt drop-down list. Dreamweaver adds `alt=""` to your image tag.

on the Job *Always provide alternate text for images! It improves the accessibility and usability of your page.*

Aligning the Image   You can align an image horizontally or vertically. To do so, select a value from the Align drop-down list in the Properties panel, or right-click the image and choose Align from the context menu. The `align` attribute of the image tag controls this action, so that if you align an image to the right, for example, you get:

```
<img src="images/picture.jpg" width="300" height="150"
    alt="A picture of a hot-air balloon." align="right">
```

When you align an *inline image,* or an image that appears inside a block of text, the surrounding text wraps around the image, as shown in Figure 5-4.

Another way to align an image horizontally is to place the image between `<div>` tags. This is the same technique that Dreamweaver uses to align blocks of text. If you want to center the image horizontally, use the `<div>` tag, because the Align list doesn't have a corresponding value.

exam Watch *Remember that the image tag's `align` attribute doesn't take the `center` value. Use `<div align="center">` to center an image.*

If you're aligning an inline image, the `<div>` tag affects the surrounding text as well as the image, which might not be the effect you want. On the other hand, if you want to align an inline image without forcing the surrounding block of text to wrap, the `<div>` tag provides an alternative.

To use `<div>` tags instead of the image tag's `align` attribute, click one of the alignment buttons to the right of the Border field on the Properties panel.

When you align
an inline image,
the surrounding
text wraps
around the image.

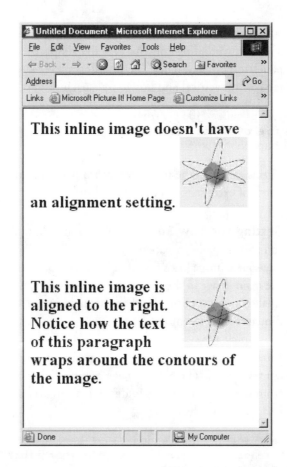

If you use layout tables, it's quicker and cleaner to align an image by setting the `align` *attribute of its layout cell. Don't fuss with adding* `<div>` *tags around the image.*

Adding a Border   If you want the browser to draw a solid border around the image, specify a value in the Border field of the Properties panel. This value represents the thickness of the border in pixels. In Microsoft Internet Explorer and Opera, this border is black. In Netscape 6.2, the border is the default text color.

Dreamweaver adds a `border` attribute to the image tag, like this:

```
<img src="images/picture.jpg" width="300" height="150"
   alt="A picture of a hot-air balloon." align="right" border="12">
```

Spacing the Image   You can add vertical and horizontal space between the image and its surrounding content. Use the V Space and H Space fields on the Properties panel, respectively. The corresponding `vspace` and `hspace` attributes of the image tag control vertical and horizontal spacing:

```
<img src="images/picture.jpg" width="300" height="150"
   alt="A picture of a hot-air balloon." align="right" border="12"
   vspace="8" hspace="4">
```

In this example, the image receives 8 pixels of extra space above and below it and 4 pixels of extra space to the left and right.

Setting the Low Source   If your graphics file is large in terms of file size, you can appease your impatient visitors by displaying a temporary *low-source image*. This low-source image loads first, and it remains on screen until the browser finishes loading the main image in the `src` attribute. Naturally, the low-source image should be much smaller in terms of file size than the main image, but it should have the same physical dimensions as the main image.

To pick a low-source image, click the folder icon next to the Low Src field in the Properties panel or right-click the existing image and choose Low Source from the context menu. The Select Image Source dialog box appears. Double-click an image from your default images folder. Dreamweaver adds the `lowsrc` attribute to your image tag, like this:

```
<img src="images/picture.jpg" width="300" height="150"
   alt="A picture of a hot-air balloon." align="right" border="12"
   vspace="8" hspace="4" lowsrc="images/lopic.jpg">
```

Another way to choose the low-source image is to click the target icon to the left of the folder icon, hold down the mouse button, and drag the pointer to the desired low-source image in the Site panel.

Adding an Image Placeholder

If you want to place an image on your Web page but don't have the actual image file yet, Dreamweaver can substitute an image placeholder for you until your designer delivers the goods. See Figure 5-5.

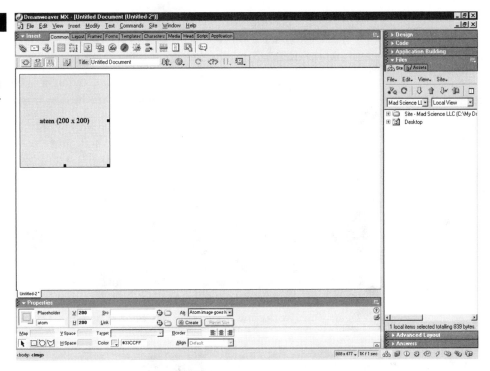

FIGURE 5-5

Use image placeholders to reserve space on your page for a forthcoming graphic.

 1. To insert an image placeholder, look under the Common tab of the Insert panel and click the Image Placeholder button, shown here. You can also choose Insert | Image Placeholder.

2. The Image Placeholder dialog box pops up, as in the following illustration. Type the name of the placeholder in the Name field. This is the text that appears inside the placeholder when you view the page in Design view.

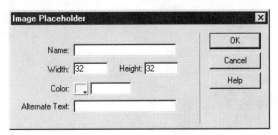

3. Type in the dimensions of the placeholder in the Width and Height fields. It behooves you to use values as close as possible to those of the final image.

4. Choose a color for the placeholder by clicking the color square and choosing a color from the set of swatches that pops up. You can also type the hexadecimal code of the desired color directly into the Color field.

5. Don't forget to supply alternate text for the placeholder. This is the text that appears in the browser window, along with the broken-image icon, when you view the page.

6. Click OK to create the placeholder. You can edit its properties just like an image by clicking it and going to the Properties panel.

An image placeholder in Dreamweaver is simply an image tag with no specified src attribute. It looks something like this in the code:

```
<img src="" width="300" height="150" alt="A picture of a hot-air balloon."
   style="background-color:#FF0000">
```

Notice the extremely interesting style attribute of the image tag. You've seen this attribute before—in Chapter 4, to be precise, when you explored layer tags. The style attribute works much the same way here. It defines a Cascading Style Sheet style for the placeholder's appearance. In this case, it sets red (#FF0000) as the background color.

To substitute an actual image for the placeholder, double-click the placeholder, or specify a value in its empty src attribute. Similarly, to change an existing image into a placeholder, select the image, remove its src attribute, and select a color for the placeholder from the Properties panel.

Adding Rollover Images

A *rollover image* is an image that appears to change when the visitor rolls over it with the mouse pointer. What actually happens is that the browser substitutes the default image of the page with a new one of the exact same dimensions. When the visitor moves the mouse pointer away, the browser shows the default image. A few short client-side scripts make it all happen.

Inserting a rollover image requires two graphics of the same width and height. Store both images in the default images folder. You might find it helpful to use the same file name for the replacement image, adding the suffix *_ro* just to keep things straight. For instance, if your default image is *balloon.jpg,* the rollover could be *balloon_ro.jpg.*

This way, there's no doubt as to which rollover goes with which default image. (When you have a folder full of graphics, you'll thank me for this advice.)

Here's how to insert a rollover image

1. Under the Common tab of the Insert panel, click the Rollover Image button, shown here. You can also choose Insert | Interactive Images | Rollover Image. Either method opens the Insert Rollover Image dialog box.

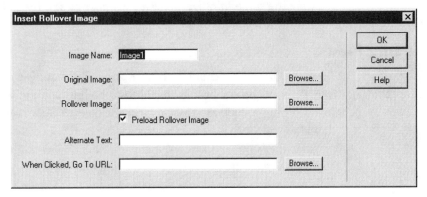

2. Your first and most important task is to provide a unique name for the rollover in the Name field. No two images on the same page should have the same name. The JavaScript that creates the rollover effect references the image by its name, so having two images with the same name can cause the rollover functions to behave strangely. Dreamweaver automatically provides a name for the rollover. It's generic, and it isn't useful for that reason, but it's also unique—so, when in doubt, go with Dreamweaver's suggested name.

3. Choose image sources for the original and rollover states by clicking the Browse buttons, navigating to the default images folder, and double-clicking the appropriate graphics files.

4. Check the option for preloading the rollover image to make the swapping effect happen faster at the expense of a little extra downloading time up front. If you don't check this option, the browser doesn't download the rollover right away. It waits until the visitor actually mouses over the original image. This causes a short but noticeable delay in the effect.

5. Supply alternate text for the rollover in the Alternate Text field, and if you wish, provide a hyperlink reference in the last field on the page. (I'll talk about linking and navigation in Chapter 6.)

6. Click OK to set up the rollover. Dreamweaver adds the necessary tags and JavaScripts to your page. The rollover functions appear between opening and closing script tags, `<script>` and `</script>`, at the top of the source code. There's also some JavaScript inside the anchor tag, `<a>`, which appears before the rollover's image tag in the body of the page.

The rollover doesn't appear to work if you test it in the document window. Preview the page in a live browser window to see the rollover in action.

Adding Media

Media in Dreamweaver are Web-page assets that require special browser plug-ins or, in the case of applets, Java-enabled browsers. If a visitor to your site doesn't have the required plug-in or Java capability, the media asset doesn't play. For this reason, you should use media sparingly on your Web site, and always include a link to the plug-in manufacturer's site so that interested parties can download the right playback software.

To make your life easier, store media files for your site in your default images folder. This way, you'll always know where to find them. The exception to this rule is the Java applet. Store applets in the same directory as the Web page that calls them.

Look under the Media tab of the Insert panel, and you'll see buttons for inserting various types of media.

Adding Flash Movies

Flash movies are short and often interactive animations in SWF (Shockwave Flash or Small Web File) format. To view Flash movies, your visitor needs the Flash Player plug-in from Macromedia. Macromedia estimates that nearly all the people on the Web today have at least some version of the Flash Player plug-in. If you want to use media on your site, Flash seems the safest and most reliable choice. Several applications create SWF files, including Macromedia Flash (the animation software, not the player plug-in), Adobe GoLive, Corel R.A.V.E., Macromedia Fireworks, and even Macromedia Dreamweaver.

To insert a Flash movie, choose Insert | Media | Flash or click the Flash button.

You can find this button under the Media tab of the Insert panel and under the Common tab as well. When you click the button, the Select File dialog box appears.

Navigate to your default images folder and double-click the SWF file you want to include. Dreamweaver puts a placeholder in the document window to represent the movie. To view the movie, select the placeholder and click the Play button on the Properties panel.

Dreamweaver uses the embed tag, <embed>, as well as the object tag, <object>, to reference the Flash movie in the source code. These tags are redundant. The embed tag is the older of the two. Netscape Navigator version 2 and Microsoft Internet Explorer version 3 adopted the embed tag, and newer browsers continue to support it. The object tag is the newer and more official construction for version 4 and later browsers. There's no harm in using both tags, so that's what Dreamweaver does.

The following example shows the code the Dreamweaver produces when you insert a Flash movie called *movie.swf* with a width of 300 pixels and a height of 400 pixels:

```
<object classid="clsid:D27CDB6E-AE6D-11cf-96B8-444553540000"
    codebase="http://download.macromedia.com/pub/shockwave/cabs/
    flash/swflash.cab#version=5,0,0,0" width="300" height="400">
        <param name="movie" value="images/movie.swf">
        <param name="quality" value="high">
        <embed src="images/movie.swf" quality="high"
            pluginspage="http://www.macromedia.com/shockwave/
            download/index.cgi?P1_Prod_Version=ShockwaveFlash"
            type="application/x-shockwave-flash" width="300"
            height="400">
        </embed>
</object>
```

Notice that the embed tag is nested between the object tags. The `classid` attribute of the object tag indicates what kind of media file you've inserted. There's no equivalent in the embed tag. The `codebase` attribute of the object tag and the `pluginpage` attribute of the embed tag give the URL of the Web page for downloading the Flash Player plug-in. The object tag also nests parameter tags, <param>, that give various properties of the movie. The embed tag defines the same properties in its own attributes. Edit the properties of the movie in the Properties panel.

Adding Flash Buttons

Flash buttons are SWF files that you use in place of regular graphical buttons. Because they're Flash movies, these buttons offer greater interactivity than you get with even JavaScript rollovers. However, because they're Flash movies, your visitors need the Flash Player plug-in to view them.

If you want to use Flash buttons, you don't need any additional software to install them. Dreamweaver creates the buttons for you and saves them as SWF files. This is one of the few cases in which Dreamweaver generates assets for your site.

Here's how to insert a Flash button:

1. Click the Flash Button icon under the Media tab. You can also choose Insert | Interactive Images | Flash Button.

2. The Insert Flash Button dialog box appears, as shown in Figure 5-6. Choose a style for the button's body from the Style list.

3. Type the text of the button's label in the Button Text field and set the font face and size. Since this text is part of the SWF file, you can present it using any font on your system. You don't have to limit yourself to the most common fonts as you do when you're inserting regular text on the page.

4. Set up the button's link in the appropriate fields and choose a background color for the button.

5. Finally, click the Browse button next to the Save As field to open the Select File dialog box. Navigate to your default images folder and specify a file name for the button, followed by the extension *.swf.*

6. Click the Save button on the Select File dialog box and click the OK button on the Insert Flash Button dialog box. Dreamweaver exports an SWF file for the button and inserts the object and embed tags in the source code.

To view the rollover effects of the button, preview your page in a live browser. To edit the button, select it in the document window, and click the Edit button on the Properties panel.

Adding Flash Text

Flash text is another Dreamweaver-generated asset for your site. It's an SWF file that contains a block of text. The advantage of using Flash text instead of regular HTML text is that the font you choose becomes part of the SWF file. Therefore, you can specify any font on your system; you don't have to limit yourself to the most common fonts. One disadvantage of using Flash text is that it loads more slowly than regular HTML text. Another is that it isn't as accessible. A third is that it requires the Flash Player plug-in. Exercise your own good judgment as to whether to use Flash text. If you do use it, use it sparingly, and don't rely on it to deliver all the text of your page.

FIGURE 5-6

Create animated buttons with the Insert Flash Button dialog box.

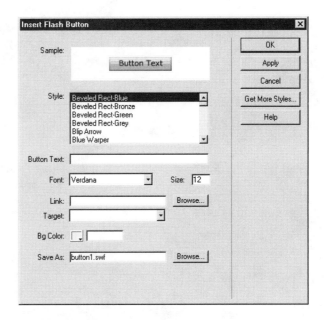

Here's how to insert Flash text:

1. Choose Insert | Interactive Images | Flash Text or click the Flash Text button.

2. The Insert Flash Text dialog box appears (see Figure 5-7). Specify the font face and size of the text and type the text in the Text field. Press ENTER or RETURN to insert a line break.

3. If you want the text to be interactive, supply a rollover color in the appropriate field. The text turns this color when the visitor mouses over it.

4. Set up the link for the text if you want it to be clickable and provide a background color in the Bg Color field.

5. Save the Flash text in your default images folder and give the file name the extension *.swf.* When you click OK, Dreamweaver creates a SWF file to your specifications and adds the object and embed tags to the source code of the page.

Preview the page in a live browser to test the rollover effects of the Flash text. Edit the Flash text by selecting it and clicking the Edit button in the Properties panel.

FIGURE 5-7

Create Flash text
with the Insert
Flash Text
dialog box.

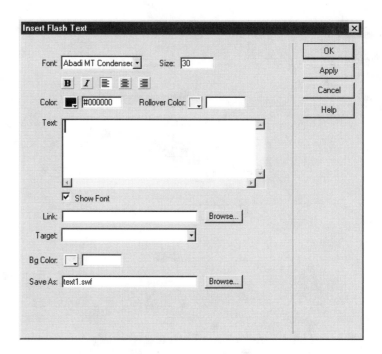

Adding Shockwave Movies

Shockwave movies are animations saved in DCR format. They are similar to Flash movies, although they're generally more robust in terms of interactivity. Your visitors need the Shockwave Player plug-in to view Shockwave movies. This plug-in isn't quite as ubiquitous as the Flash Player, but it's still common. To create Shockwave movies, you need Macromedia Director.

To insert a Shockwave movie, choose Insert | Media | Shockwave or click the Shockwave button.

The Select File dialog box appears. Navigate to your default images folder and double-click the desired DCR file. Dreamweaver adds the proper object and embed tags to your page and displays a placeholder image in the document window, just like with Flash. You can play the Shockwave movie and modify its properties from the Properties panel.

Adding Other Media Plug-In Assets

To add QuickTime video clips, RealAudio files, MP3s, and the like, choose Insert | Media | Plugin or click the Plugin button.

This calls up the Select File dialog box. Navigate to the source file and double-click it to add it to your page. Dreamweaver references the asset with the embed tag. Use the Properties panel to modify the embed tag's attributes.

Adding Java Applets

Applets are short applications written in Java. Your visitors need Java-enabled browsers to view applets. Netscape, Internet Explorer, and Opera are all Java-enabled, although the user can disable Java in the browser preferences.

To insert a Java applet, choose Insert | Media | Applet, or click the Applet button. The Select File dialog box appears. Navigate to the applet and double-click it. Dreamweaver uses the applet tag, `<applet>`, instead of embed or object tags, to refer to the applet in the source code, like this:

```
<applet code="appname.class" width="200" height="100"></applet>
```

A placeholder for the applet appears in the document window. To see the applet in action, preview the page in a live browser window.

Adding ActiveX Controls

An *ActiveX control* is a piece of code that, when used in a Web page, behaves like a Java applet or plug-in object. Your visitors need Microsoft Internet Explorer and the Windows operating system to view ActiveX controls on your page. If your visitors use Netscape, even if they run it on Windows, the ActiveX controls don't work.

To insert an ActiveX control, choose Insert | Media | ActiveX or click the ActiveX button.

Dreamweaver adds an object tag to your document's source code, like this:

```
<object width="32" height="32"></object>
```

As you can see, the object tag is completely "bald," except for width and height values. Set up the parameters and class ID for the ActiveX control by way of the Properties panel.

Inserting Parameter Tags

When you're working in Code view, a Parameter button appears under the Media tab of the Insert panel. Click this button to insert a parameter tag, `<param>`, into the source code. Dreamweaver's Tag Editor appears, allowing you to specify the name and value of the parameter tag.

Use the parameter tag to specify the properties of media files and Java applets that appear in the code as object or applet tags. The embed tag doesn't require parameter tags. You'll recall that media-file properties are expressed as attributes of the embed tag.

Make sure that your parameter tags fall between the opening and closing object or applet tags.

Attaching Scripts

By attaching script files to your Web page, your page can reference the scripts without them appearing the source code. This is the most efficient way to reuse frequently requested JavaScript functions and the like. Who wants to copy and paste the same functions into page after page?

To attach a script to your page, look under the Script tab of the Insert panel and click the Script button. You can also choose Insert | Script Objects | Script. Either way, the Script dialog box opens. Supply the language of the script, but don't type anything into the Content field; just click OK. Dreamweaver inserts a pair of script tags without content between them, like this:

```
<script language="VBScript" type="text/VBScript"></script>
```

Now open the Tag Inspector panel and select the opening script tag. Click in the `src` attribute and navigate to the script file in your site. Dreamweaver attaches a reference to the external script file in the source code as follows:

```
<script language="VBScript" src="script.vbs" type="text/VBScript"></script>
```

Adding Server-Side Includes

A *server-side include* is a snippet of source code saved in separate HTML file, usually with the extension *.shtm* or *.shtml*. The browser obtains this code from the Web server as the page loads, so that what you see in the window is a composite of the page's native source code and the code of the included file. You'll save yourself many headaches by storing the file to include at the same level as the main Web page or in a subfolder immediately below the main page. Don't store the file to include at a higher level. Many Web servers get unnecessarily cranky about this.

The included file has to reside on a Web server for server-side includes to work—in other words, you can't view server-side includes by previewing the page offline. You see the main content of the page but not the included file. However, Dreamweaver's Design view approximates what the composite page will look like, server-side includes and all.

To add a server-side include to your page, choose Insert | Script Objects | Server-Side Include or look under the Script tab of the Insert panel and click the Server-Side Include button.

The Select File dialog box appears. Navigate to the HTML code snippet that you want to include and double-click it. Dreamweaver displays the included code in the document window, as Figure 5-8 shows.

The instructions to the Web server appear in the source code between comment notations like this:

```
<!--#include virtual="inclfile.shtm" -->
```

When you click the included file in the document window, the Properties panel gives you a few options for modifying the server instructions, as shown in the following

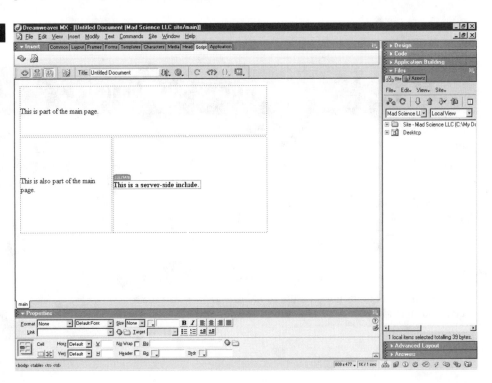

FIGURE 5-8

Dreamweaver's document window shows included files.

illustration. Change the source file to include by browsing for a new file. If your Web server is an Apache server, select the Virtual type on the Properties panel. If your Web server isn't Apache, chose Virtual, but test your page as soon as possible. If the include doesn't behave correctly (as it probably won't on a Microsoft IIS, or *Information Internet Server*), switch the type to File. If the include still doesn't behave correctly, contact your network administrator to troubleshoot the problem. It may be that the server needs some special configuration.

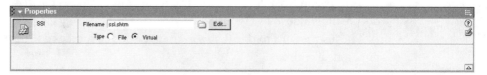

Now that you've explored several types of assets, the quick reference in the next Scenario and Solution will help you keep straight the various HTML tags and notations that Dreamweaver uses to reference the assets.

SCENARIO & SOLUTION

What tag does Dreamweaver use to reference images?	`<img>`
What tags does Dreamweaver use to reference media files?	`<object>` and `<embed>` for Flash and Shockwave movies; `<embed>` for other media plug-in files
What tag does Dreamweaver use to reference ActiveX controls?	`<object>`
What tag does Dreamweaver use to reference Java applets?	`<applet>`
What tag does Dreamweaver use to reference scripts?	`<script>`
What notation does Dreamweaver use to indicate a server-side include?	`#include`

EXERCISE 5-2

Adding Assets to the Mad Science Home Page

In this exercise, you continue adding content to the Mad Science LLC home page.

1. Before you launch Dreamweaver, insert the CD-ROM from this book into your computer, and navigate to the *examples/ch04* folder. Inside are several image files: *logo.gif, facility.gif, facility_ro.gif, monsters.gif, monsters_ro.gif, contact.gif, contact_ro.gif,* and *atom.jpg.* Copy these files and paste them in the default images folder of the Mad Science LLC site.

2. Now launch Dreamweaver, open the Site panel, and set the site to Mad Science LLC.

3. Double-click the file *index.htm* to open it.

4. Click inside the top cell in the layout table. Look under the Common tab of the Insert panel and click the Image button. The Select Image Source dialog box appears. Navigate to the default images folder and double-click the file *logo.gif.* Dreamweaver adds the logo to the top table cell.

5. While the image is selected, go to the Properties panel and type **Mad Science LLC logo** in the Alt field. Make sure also that values appear in the W and H fields. If no values appear in these fields, click the Reset Size button. The width should be 600, and the height should be 75.

6. Now click inside the bottom-left table cell, the one for the main navigation. Click the Rollover Image button in the Insert panel to open the Insert Rollover Image dialog box. Type **Facility** in the Name field. Choose *facility.gif* as the original image and *facility_ro.gif* as the rollover image by browsing to these files in the default images folder. (Be sure also to set the option for preloading rollover images.) Type **Our Facility button** as the alternate text and click OK. Dreamweaver adds the button to the navigation cell.

7. With the facility button highlighted, press the down-arrow key. Then, insert the next rollover button: *monsters.gif* and *monsters_ro.gif.* Type in the name **Monsters**, and make the alternate text **Monsters button**.

8. With the monsters button highlighted, press the down-arrow key. Insert the third rollover button: *contact.gif* and *contact_ro.gif.* The name should be **Contact**, and the alternate text should read **Contact Us button**.

9. Press F12 to preview the rollover effects in a browser window.

10. Now go back to Dreamweaver and click to the left of the first paragraph in the content area. Go to the Insert panel and click the Image button. Choose *atom.jpg* from the Select Image Source dialog box. Dreamweaver adds the image but pushes down the text, leaving some awkward blank space.

11. Select the image. Make sure that the W and H fields both show 200. If they don't, click the Reset Size button. Also, supply the alternate text **Picture of an atom**. To correct the layout problem, go to the Align list in the Properties panel. Choose Left from this list. The image stays on the left, and the text wraps around it.

12. Press F12 again to preview the finished page. It should look something like Figure 5-9 in Dreamweaver's document window.

13. Go back to Dreamweaver and choose File | Save. Well done!

FIGURE 5-9

In Dreamweaver's document window, you may preview your finished page.

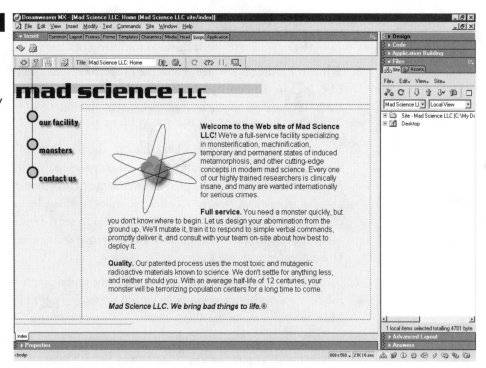

CERTIFICATION SUMMARY

This chapter showed you how to add many kinds of content to the layout of the page. You learned bout the two categories of content: content that resides in the source code of the page itself, and assets—content that resides in external files.

You learned to insert and format text, and you saw how Dreamweaver marks it up with HTML tags. I explained the importance of using at least one common font in your font list, since the browser uses the fonts on the visitor's system to render the page. I cautioned you against using multicolored text and the underline text style, since the visitor can easily confuse these for links.

You also saw how to add ordered, numbered, and definition lists in Design view and Code view. I showed you how to nest lists by using the Text Indent and Text Outdent buttons. I talked about the limitations of Dreamweaver's Date button and the subtleties of the horizontal-rule tag. You learned that you can add only certain elements like inline frames, table headers, and table captions when you're working in Code view.

You learned to insert assets like images and Flash movies by way of the Insert panel and modify their properties with the Properties panel. You worked with low-source images and image placeholders. I cautioned you against changing the dimensions of an image file, since it either degrades the quality of the image or creates needless extra download time. You saw that rollover images are really two separate graphics files that JavaScript functions swap. I showed you how to create assets like Flash text and Flash buttons with Dreamweaver, and I explained that these and other media assets require special browser plug-ins. If your visitors don't have the appropriate plug-ins, your media files don't play.

You saw that Dreamweaver uses different HTML tags to refer to different kinds of assets: `<img>` for images, `<object>` for media files and ActiveX controls, `<embed>` for media files, `<applet>` for Java applets, and `<script>` for scripts. You also saw that the object tag nests parameter tags, `<param>`, to describe the properties of an object, while the embed tag uses attributes for the same purpose.

Accessibility came up often. I explained that giving the full text for abbreviations and acronyms makes your text more accessible, and I recommended that you add table headers and table captions to data tables. I urged you to provide alternate text for all images in your page.

You explored two strategies for adding scripts to your page. The first strategy is to build the script into the source code, in which case only the current page can execute the script. The second strategy is to create a separate file for the script and then attach it to the page by way of the script tag's src attribute. This way, you can use the same script on more than one page.

Finally, you learned that server-side includes are snippet-files of HTML code that the Web server adds to an existing page. You can't view the results of a server-side include offline; however, you saw that Dreamweaver approximates what the combined page looks like.

TWO-MINUTE DRILL

Adding Content to the Source Code

❏ Source-code content appears within the Web document itself.

❏ Specify at least one common font for the text in your page to reduce the risk of a font substitution.

❏ Use horizontal rules to separate sections of the page.

❏ Use the Text Indent and Text Outdent buttons in conjunction with the Ordered List and Unordered List buttons to nest lists.

❏ Add table heads and table captions to data tables.

❏ Switch to Code view when you want to add table heads, table captions, and inline frames or comment out existing code.

❏ Dreamweaver's keywords element, description element, and page-refresh element use meta tags.

❏ When you build a client-side script into the source code of a page, only that page can reference the script.

Adding Assets

❏ Assets are pieces of content that exist as separate files.

❏ Always specify the width, height, and alternate text of images.

❏ Dreamweaver uses JavaScript to create rollover effects.

❏ Dreamweaver can generate Flash text and Flash button assets to your specifications.

❏ Dreamweaver uses redundant object and embed tags to refer to Flash and Shockwave movies, applet tags to refer to applets, object tags to refer to ActiveX controls, and embed tags to refer to media plug-in files.

❏ Attach scripts as separate files when you want to use the scripts on more than one page.

❏ Dreamweaver displays server-side includes in the document window, even though you don't see the included file when you preview the page offline.

SELF TEST

The following questions will help you measure your understanding of the material presented in this chapter. Read all the choices carefully because there might be more than one correct answer. Choose all correct answers for each question.

Adding Content to the Source Code

1. What kinds of lists can you create with buttons on the Properties panel in Dreamweaver's Design view?

   A. Definition lists

   B. Bulleted lists

   C. Numbered lists

   D. Outline lists

2. You have a script that you want to use on more than one page. What's the best solution?

   A. Click the Script button and type the script code in the dialog box that appears.

   B. Click the Script button, don't type the script code in the dialog box, and specify the `src` attribute of the script tag.

   C. Click the Script button, type the script code in the dialog box that appears, and specify the `src` attribute of the script tag.

3. Why is Arial a wise font choice for the text of your page? Pick the best answer.

   A. Arial is one of the most common Windows fonts.

   B. Arial is a sans-serif font.

   C. Arial is a serif font.

   D. Arial is available in boldface.

4. How can you change the size of a selected block of text?

   A. Choose a value from the Size list on the Properties panel.

   B. Choose Text | Size from the main menu.

   C. Choose Text | Size Change from the main menu.

   D. Right-click the selection and choose Size from the context menu.

   E. Right-click the selection and choose Size Change from the context menu.

   F. Drag the handles around the text object.

5. Which attribute controls the vertical size of the horizontal rule tag in HTML?

   A. `thickness`

   B. `size`

   C. `height`

   D. `vspace`

6. Which HTML tag appears at the start of a bulleted list?

   A. `<ul>`

   B. `<ol>`

   C. `<bl>`

   D. `<list type="bulleted">`

7. You want to present a block of text with its original whitespace. How should you mark it up in the code?

   A. Put it between `<p>` tags.

   B. Put it between `<ol>` tags.

   C. Put it between `<p spacing="orig">` tags.

   D. Put it between `<pre>` tags.

8. How do you add a table header to a data table in Dreamweaver?

   A. Right-click a table cell and choose Convert To Table Header.

   B. Switch to Code view and click the TH button under the Tables tab of the Insert panel.

   C. Switch to Design view and choose Insert | Table Objects | TH.

   D. Switch to Code view and choose Insert | Table Objects | TH.

   E. Switch to Layout view and draw a table header cell.

9. Which button do you click in the Insert panel to add a meta tag to your page?

   A. The button that looks like this:

   B. The button that looks like this:

C. The button that looks like this:

D. The button that looks like this:

10. What is an inline frame?

 A. A file that divides your page into a system of separate browser windows

 B. A frame created by `<div>` tags

 C. The opposite of a floating frame

 D. A frame that can appear anywhere on the page

Adding Assets

11. What types of assets can Dreamweaver produce?

 A. Scripts

 B. SWF files

 C. DCR files

 D. QuickTime video clips

 E. Spacer images

12. You place an image in a layout table. How can you align the image horizontally in the center of the cell?

 A. Select the image and choose Center from the Align list in the Properties panel.

 B. Select the image and choose Middle from the Align list in the Properties panel.

 C. Select the image and click the Align Center button on the Properties panel.

 D. Select the cell and choose Center from the Horz list in the Properties panel.

 E. Select the cell and choose Center from the Align list in the Properties panel.

13. What piece of software do your visitors need to have in order to open the DCR file on your site?

 A. Adobe Acrobat Reader

 B. Macromedia Flash Player

    C. Windows Media Player

    D. Macromedia Shockwave Player

14. Your all-text page is taking forever to load. What's the likely problem?

    A. You need at least one graphic on the page to make it load faster.

    B. You used way too much Flash text.

    C. You didn't specify `width` and `height` attributes for the text block.

    D. The browser doesn't recognize the language of the text.

15. When might you want to add an ActiveX control to your page?

    A. When you're building a site for an all-Netscape audience

    B. When you're building a site for an all-Internet Explorer audience

    C. When you're building a site for an all-Windows audience

    D. When you're building a site for an all-Macintosh audience

16. What makes Dreamweaver's rollover images work on a Web page? Choose the best answer.

    A. JavaScript functions

    B. Cascading Style Sheets

    C. HTML tags

    D. Server-side includes

17. What's a server-side include? Choose the best answer.

    A. An asset that sits on a Web server instead of a production server

    B. A snippet of HTML code saved as its own file

    C. Any file with the extension *.html*

    D. A client-side script

18. Which of the following can Dreamweaver display in the document window?

    A. Flash movies

    B. Shockwave movies

    C. Applets

    D. Server-side includes

    E. Images

    F. Rollover effects

19. How do you put a graphics file into an image placeholder in the document window?

   A. Specify the `lowsrc` attribute of the image tag.

   B. Double-click the placeholder.

   C. Remove the `src` attribute from the placeholder.

   D. Delete the placeholder and click the Image button in the Insert panel.

20. Which of the following statements are true about the object tag?

   A. Dreamweaver uses the object tag to insert Flash movies.

   B. Dreamweaver uses the object tag to insert ActiveX controls.

   C. Dreamweaver uses the object tag to insert rollovers.

   D. The object tag is older and better supported than the newer embed tag.

   E. The object tag uses many different attributes to express the properties of its object.

   F. The object tag nests `<param>` tags to express the properties of its object.

LAB QUESTION

You're a Web consultant and you arrive on site for a consultation. You put in a brief appearance with the brass (clueless), and then you head straight into the trenches. Your first stop: the poor sap who reads and answers the e-mail from site visitors. Your first question: "What do your visitors say about your site?"

"We get flamed all the time," comes the reply. "Every day I have to read at least 20 e-mails telling us to fix the links on this one page."

"Fix the links, and the problem's solved," you say.

"That's just it," says your client. "There aren't any links on that page! I checked it myself. There aren't any graphics, either. Just plain text."

Without looking at the page, you suggest two possible causes of the problem.

The Web page comes up, and your client gasps. "You're—you're right! How did you—?"

"All in a day's work," you say, and you bill the client for three hours instead of one for wasting your valuable time.

What were the two causes of the problem?

SELF TEST ANSWERS

Adding Content to the Source Code

1. ☑ **B and C.** You can create bulleted (unordered) and numbered (ordered) lists in Design view.
☒ **A** is incorrect because there is no Design List button on the Properties panel. **D** is incorrect because outline lists aren't specified in HTML.

2. ☑ **B.** Click the Script button to insert the script tag into the source code, but don't type the script in the dialog box that appears. Instead, specify the script tag's `src` attribute.
☒ **A** is incorrect because this procedure creates a script for the current page only. **C** is incorrect because you shouldn't retype the script in the dialog box.

3. ☑ **A.** Arial is one of the most common Windows fonts. Your visitors are likely to have this font on their systems, which means that their computers don't have to make font substitutions.
☒ **B** is incorrect because, while Arial is a sans-serif font, choice **A** is a better answer. **C** is incorrect because Arial is a sans-serif font. **D** is incorrect because, while Arial is available in boldface, choice **A** is a better answer.

4. ☑ **A, B, C, and D.** Use the Size list on the Properties panel, Text | Size, Text | Size Change, or Size from the context menu.
☒ **E** is incorrect because there is no Size Change item on the context menu. **F** is incorrect because text objects don't have size-change handles. You may be thinking of images.

5. ☑ **B.** The `size` attribute controls the height of the horizontal rule.
☒ **A** is incorrect because there isn't a `border` attribute in the horizontal-rule tag. **C** is incorrect because there isn't a `height` attribute in the horizontal-rule tag. **D** is incorrect because there isn't a `vspace` attribute in the horizontal rule tag.

6. ☑ **A.** The unordered-list tag, `<ul>`, appears at the top of a bulleted list in the source code.
☒ **B** is incorrect because `<ol>` is the ordered-list tag. **C** is incorrect because there is no `<bl>` tag in HTML. **D** is incorrect because there is no `<list>` tag in HTML.

7. ☑ **D.** To preserve the original spacing, put the text between preformatted-text tags, `<pre>` and `</pre>`.
☒ **A and B** are incorrect because these tags strip out extra whitespace. **C** is incorrect because there is no such `spacing` attribute in the paragraph tag.

8. ☑ **B** and **D**. Switch to Code view and either click the TH button on the Insert panel or choose Insert | Table Objects | TH.
   ☒ **A** is incorrect because no such choice exists on the context menu. **C** is incorrect because you have to be in Code view to insert a table header. **E** is incorrect because you can't draw a table header in Layout view. Table headers are for data tables anyway, not layout tables.

9. ☑ **A**. That's the Meta button.
   ☒ **B** is incorrect because it's the Server-Side Include button. **C** is incorrect because it's the Script button. **D** is incorrect because it's the Comment button.

10. ☑ **D**. An inline frame is a frame that can appear anywhere on the page.
    ☒ **A** is incorrect because this describes a frameset document, not an inline frame. **B** is incorrect because you use `<div>` tags to create layers, not inline frames. **C** is incorrect because a floating frame is an inline frame.

Adding Assets

11. ☑ **A**, **B**, and **E**. Dreamweaver can produce scripts, SWF files (in the form of Flash buttons and Flash text), and spacer images.
    ☒ **C** is incorrect because Dreamweaver can't produce DCR (Shockwave) files. **D** is incorrect because Dreamweaver can't produce QuickTime video clips.

12. ☑ **C** and **D**. You can center the image by selecting it and clicking the Align Center button or selecting the table cell and choosing Center from the Horz list.
    ☒ **A** is incorrect because there is no choice for horizontal centering in the Align list for images. **B** is incorrect because the Middle option is for vertical alignment. **E** is incorrect because there is no Align list for table cells in the Properties panel. There are separate lists for horizontal and vertical alignment.

13. ☑ **D**. To open DCR files, your visitors need the Shockwave Player plug-in.
    ☒ **A**, **B**, and **C** are incorrect because these pieces of software don't play back Shockwave movies.

14. ☑ **B**. Too much Flash text can cause a page to load slowly.
    ☒ **A** is incorrect because the more graphics you have, the longer it takes your page to load. **C** is incorrect because text doesn't have `width` and `height` attributes. **D** is incorrect because the language of the text by itself doesn't affect the download rate.

15. ☑ **C.** ActiveX controls work only in Internet Explorer on Windows systems.

    ☒ **A** is incorrect because the Netscape browser can't use ActiveX controls. **B** is incorrect because Internet Explorer on Macintosh can't use ActiveX controls. **D** is incorrect because Macintosh systems can't use ActiveX controls.

16. ☑ **A.** Dreamweaver uses JavaScript functions to create the rollover effect.

    ☒ **B** is an intelligent guess, but unfortunately it's incorrect because Dreamweaver relies on the more consistent support of JavaScript to create rollovers. **C** is incorrect because HTML tags don't perform the actual rollover effect. **D** is incorrect because server-side includes don't have anything necessarily to do with rollover images.

17. ☑ **B.** A server-side include is a snippet of HTML code stored as its own file (and then added to another Web page).

    ☒ **A** is incorrect because a production server is a type of Web server. **C** is incorrect because not all HTML files are server-side includes. Besides, server-side includes usually have the *.shtm* or *.shtml* extension. **D** is incorrect because the client, not the server, processes a client-side script.

18. ☑ **A, B, D** and **E.** Dreamweaver can display Flash movies, Shockwave movies, images, and server-side includes in the document window.

    ☒ **C** is incorrect because Dreamweaver doesn't display applets. You must preview your page in a browser to see the applet at work. **F** is incorrect because Dreamweaver doesn't display rollover effects. Preview your page in a browser to test the rollovers.

19. ☑ **B.** Double-click the placeholder to exchange it for an actual graphics file.

    ☒ **A** is incorrect because the `lowsrc` attribute of the image tag gives a temporary version of an image for the browser to load first. **C** is incorrect because the placeholder doesn't have a `src` attribute. In fact, that's what makes it a placeholder. **D** is incorrect because, while this procedure does get rid of the placeholder and add an image instead, it doesn't place an image in the existing placeholder.

20. ☑ **A, B,** and **F.** Dreamweaver uses the object tag to insert Flash movies and ActiveX controls, among other things. The object tag nests parameter tags, `<param>`, to describe the properties of its object.

    ☒ **C** is incorrect because Dreamweaver doesn't use object tags to insert rollovers. **D** is incorrect because the embed tag is older than the object tag. **E** is incorrect because the embed tag uses attributes to describe the properties of its object.

LAB ANSWER

You guessed that the client used multicolored text on the page. Visitors often assume that colored text is a link. When it isn't, they get frustrated and send nasty e-mails to the Webmaster.

You also guessed that the client used underlining on plain text. Underlining is a near-universal visual cue for a link. When visitors see underlining, they're liable to click, expecting a hotlink. When nothing happens, they get frustrated and send nasty e-mails.

Your client should refrain from using multiple colors for plain text and never, ever, underline anything unless it's a link. Suggest to your client that boldface and italic work better to call attention to certain phrases, and headline formats work better for dividing the page into logical sections.

Dreamweaver®

CERTIFIED DREAMWEAVER DEVELOPER

6

Linking and Navigation

T he Web is all about hyperlinks—the vehicle by which your visitors traverse your site. Chances are, links are also the way that visitors arrived on your site. As a Web builder, you can't pay too much attention to the links on your page.

Dreamweaver allows you to create links from text or images on your page. You can build links to URLs, links to named anchors, null links, and e-mail links with ease. The software also provides tools for adding different kinds of linking and navigational schemes, such as jump menus and image maps.

This chapter shows you how to define the various types of links in Dreamweaver.

CERTIFICATION OBJECTIVE 6.01

Adding Links

You add links in Dreamweaver by specifying the *path,* or instructions to the browser for loading the link, in the Link field on the Properties panel. You can use three kinds of paths: absolute paths, document-relative paths, and root-relative paths.

An *absolute path* is the full URL of the link's destination. For example, if you're linking to the Contact Us page of the Mad Science LLC site, the absolute path reads something like this:

```
http://www.madsciencellc.com/contact/index.htm
```

The absolute path is the same URL that you'd type in the address field of a live, connected browser window. This type of path is either correct or incorrect. It works (or doesn't work) no matter where you put it on your site. If the URL is correctly formatted and a page exists in the location specified, the link functions properly. If the URL is incorrectly formatted, or if a page doesn't exist in the location specified, the link doesn't work.

Web builders use absolute paths in *external links,* or links to pages outside the current site. In fact, for external links, absolute paths are a necessity, because you can't link to external resources by any other means. To test absolute paths, though, you have to be online, and the destination of the link needs to reside on a production server. These factors make absolute paths cumbersome for *internal links,* or links to pages within the current site, especially when you're in the process of building your site. The last thing you want to have to do when you're testing and troubleshooting is to upload your unfinished pages live to the Web.

A *document-relative path* contains a portion of the full URL expressed in relation to the visitor's current location in the site. If the visitor is currently sitting on the Mad Science home page, a link to the Contact Us page looks like this in document-relative format:

```
contact/index.htm
```

This path tells the browser that, from the current location, there's a subfolder called *contact,* and in this folder is a file called *index.htm.*

Unlike absolute paths, document-relative paths change depending on the page that contains the link. If there is no subfolder called *contact* from the visitor's current location—say, from the Our Facility page—the link doesn't work. With document-relative paths, you always have to explain to the browser exactly how to get to the destination page. Use the notation ../ to tell the browser to go one step up in the hierarchical structure of the site. Therefore, to link to the Contact Us page from the Our Facility page, a document-relative path looks like this:

```
../contact/index.htm
```

In plain English: "You're on the Our Facility page. Go up one level in the site structure, and you'll find a folder called *contact.* Inside this folder is a file called *index.htm.*"

Dreamweaver specifies document-relative paths by default. Most Web builders prefer using them, since they're simple and direct. More important, links with document-relative paths work perfectly well offline. Your pages don't have to reside on a Web server of any kind. You don't even need an Internet connection. This makes links with document-relative paths invaluable to the process of testing and troubleshooting your site. However, document-relative paths can be a pain to manage. If, for example, you change the position of a page in the structure of your site, all your document-relative links can break. Dreamweaver takes a bit of the sting out of the process by automatically updating document-relative links for you as long as you use the Site panel to rearrange the structure of your site.

Finally, a *root-relative path* contains a portion of the full URL expressed in relation to the root folder of the site. A root-relative path from the home page of Mad Science LLC to the Contact Us page looks like this:

```
/contact/index.htm
```

In plain English: "From the root folder of the site is a subfolder called *contact*. Inside this folder is a file called *index.htm*." Notice that the root-relative path begins with a forward slash (/). All root-relative paths begin this way.

Unlike document-relative paths, root-relative paths don't change if you move the page that contains the link. This makes root-relative paths especially useful if you maintain a large Web site containing pages that you often shuffle around. You don't have to worry about breaking the links on your pages.

The drawback to using root-relative paths is that you can't normally work with them offline, since the Web server, not the browser, keeps track of the site's root folder. For offline troubleshooting and testing, you need to have a personal Web server installed on your computer. Otherwise, you have to upload your pages to a staging server or the production server.

exam
ⓦatch

Be prepared to answer questions about the pros and cons of the three types of paths.

You can also invoke File | Preview In Browser from Dreamweaver's main menu. When you use this command, Dreamweaver temporarily converts any root-relative paths on the page to document-relative paths. This allows you to test the links on the page with more confidence.

See the following Scenario and Solution sidebar for a quick summary of the three types of paths and their pluses and minuses.

SCENARIO & SOLUTION

What are absolute paths?	Complete URLs. These paths don't change if you change the location of a page that uses them, but you have to be online to test them, and their destinations have to be live on the Web.
What are document-relative paths?	Paths expressed in relation to the visitor's current location on the site. You can test these paths offline, but they can easily break if you move a page that uses them.
What are root-relative paths?	Paths expressed in relation to the site's root folder. These paths don't break if you move a page that uses them. You can test these paths offline only if you have a personal Web server on your computer.

Linking to URLs

The most common link is one that goes to another URL. When the visitor clicks the *source* of the link, or the clickable element on the page, the browser follows the link's path and loads the page that it finds there.

You can specify two kinds of sources for the link: a text source or an image source.

Using a Text Source

A *text source* is a clickable piece of text that triggers a link. By default, the browser displays the text source with an underline and in a color corresponding to the state of the link: unvisited, visited, or active. You'll recall that you can define the default colors for all three link states by choosing Modify | Page Properties. You can also set the color for each link individually by selecting the link and choosing a font color from the Properties panel or choosing Text | Color.

To create a text source in Design view, highlight the text that you want to use as the link. Then go to the Properties panel. Type the path of the link directly into the Link field if you prefer. Follow this procedure if you haven't yet saved the current document.

If you have already saved the current document, Dreamweaver can figure out the correct document-relative path of the link for you. Use either the point-to-file icon or the folder icon.

To use the point-to-file icon, click it, and hold down the mouse button. Drag the icon to the Site panel, position the icon over the page to which you want to link, and release the mouse. Dreamweaver automatically computes the correct document-relative path and supplies it in the Link field.

To use the folder icon, click it, and the Select File dialog box appears (see Figure 6-1). Navigate to the page to which you want to link and double-click it. The Select File dialog box closes, and Dreamweaver fills in the correct document-relative path.

Notice the Relative To list in the Select File dialog box. When you use the folder icon to set the link, you can change the style of the path from document-relative to root-relative with this list.

If you use either the point-to-file icon or the folder icon and you haven't yet saved the current document, Dreamweaver creates a *file path,* a temporary path that begins with *file://.* A link with a file path functions correctly offline, but it does *not* work online, so don't upload your page if it has file paths. Once you save the current document, Dreamweaver permanently converts file paths to document-relative paths.

FIGURE 6-1

Use the Select
File dialog box
to navigate to
the page to which
you want to link.

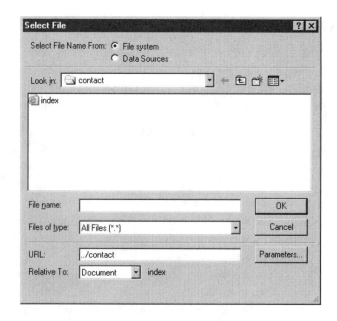

After you or Dreamweaver supplies a path in the Link field, the selected text source acquires the characteristics of a link. The text changes color and gets an underline. The text also becomes clickable, although you can't test this property in Dreamweaver's document window. Remember that the document window doesn't allow you to follow links. Preview the page in a browser, and you can click the text and make sure that the path leads to the correct destination.

In the HTML, Dreamweaver nests the text source inside anchor tags, <a> and </a>, and supplies the path of the link in the href attribute, like this:

```
This sentence contains a link to the <a href="../../about/index.htm">About Us</a> page.
```

In this example, the words *About Us* are clickable in the browser window. Clicking them directs the browser two levels up in the hierarchy of the site and into a folder called *about* for a file called *index.htm*.

Another way to set a text-source link is to highlight the text that you want to use and right-click the selection. Choose Make Link from the context menu. The Select File dialog box opens. Navigate to the destination page and double-click it.

FROM THE CLASSROOM

Click Here—or Not

It's difficult to imagine the Web without Click Here, that old standby of text-source links. *Click here* to go to the Products page. *Click here* for more information. *Click here* for your order summary. Click Here is everywhere, on personal home pages and high-profile Web sites. The phrasing seems straightforward and difficult to misinterpret. Or is it?

Usability experts tend to agree that Click Here is a terrible choice for the wording of a link. Why? Because, when taken out of context, Click Here loses its meaning.

Here's the theory. Web surfers dislike reading text on a Web page. Maybe it has to do with the inherent speed of the Web. Maybe the culprit is that strange time anomaly that I mentioned earlier, where 10 seconds on the Web seems like an eternity. Who knows? Usability studies show time and again that visitors skim online text instead of reading it.

Since your visitors are skimming, you had better make it easy for them to figure out what clicking a link is going to do. Your visitor's eyes are trained to look for visual cues, such as the color blue or an underline, to distinguish a link from the rest of the page. So while the rest of the page blurs into black, your visitor's eyes focus on the text of the link. If the link says "Products page," your visitor understands that clicking it causes the Products page to load. If the link says "Order summary," your visitor knows what to expect. But if the link says "Click here," the visitor has to slow down and reread the surrounding text more carefully to figure out what clicking here is supposed to do. There's nothing in the text of the link, in other words, that suggests the purpose of the link.

Furthermore, Click Here is redundant. The visitor knows already that the color and the underline are invitations to click. The words "Click here" aren't adding anything new. In fact, they're bogging down your speed-loving audience.

When crafting the phrasing for a link, you're better off sticking to one or two words that sum up what happens when the visitor clicks. This allows your visitors to skim unhindered, stopping to read carefully when they find what they need.

Using an Image Source

Like text, an image can act as the clickable element that triggers a link. Select the image in the document window, go to the Properties panel, and fill in the Link field, either manually or by using the point-to-file or folder icons. Dreamweaver nests the image tag, `<img>`, between anchor tags, as follows:

```
<a href="http://www.taotezing.com"><img src="images/button.gif" width="100"
    height="30" alt="A button that links to the Tao Te Zing Web site"
    border="0"></a>
```

The entire image becomes clickable when you specify it as the source of a link.

Notice the `border` attribute of the image tag. You used this attribute before to create a visible border around an image. When the image serves as the source of a link, this border appears in the color corresponding to the state of the link. For an image source that doesn't already have a specified border, Dreamweaver makes the border size 0 by default. If you want the image to have a border, which is helpful to the visitor if the image itself doesn't suggest that it is clickable, enter a value in the Border field on the Properties panel. If you already specified a border for the image, Dreamweaver leaves your value alone.

Give an image source a visible border if the image doesn't look clickable by itself. Buttons and the like don't need borders, because their appearance alone suggests "clickability" to the visitor, but photographs, charts, graphs, and other images that don't look clickable in and of themselves should get a visible border.

Inserting a Text-Source Link

To insert a text-source link without highlighting text in the document window, click to indicate an insertion point and choose Insert | Hyperlink or click the Hyperlink button under the Common tab of the Insert panel.

The Hyperlink dialog box appears, as shown in the following illustration. Type the text for the link in the Text field. Specify the path to the destination in the Link field or click the folder icon and navigate to the desired page. Choose the desired target value from the Target list (see "Linking to Frames," later in this chapter).

Hyperlink		✕
Text:		OK
Link:		Cancel
Target: Tab Index:		Help
Title:		
Access Key:		

This dialog box provides three fields for improving the accessibility of your link. Type a value in the Tab Index field to determine the order in which the browser highlights this link when the visitor presses the TAB key. Supply a title for the link in the Title field. The title appears when the visitor hovers over the link for a second or two. Use the title to provide alternate descriptive text for the link, such as "A link to the home page." Provide an access key in the Access Key field. An access key is a key that the visitor can press, usually in conjunction with ALT (Windows) or OPTION (Mac), to follow the link. If you supply values for these fields, Dreamweaver adds the `tabindex`, `title`, and `accesskey` attributes to the anchor tag accordingly:

```
This sentence contains a link to the <a href="../../index.htm"
    tabindex="1" title="A link to the home page. "
    accesskey="h">home page</a>.
```

In this example, the TAB key goes to this link first, since it has a tab index of 1, and pressing the H key on the keyboard causes the browser to follow the link.

exam

Watch

Remember that in the anchor tag, it's the `title` *attribute, not the* `alt` *attribute, that contains the descriptive text for the link. The* `alt` *attribute applies to images.*

author's

Note

Browsers and operating systems vary in their support of accessibility-enhancing features like tabindex, title, *and* accesskey *attributes. Don't be disappointed if they work poorly or not at all for the majority of your visitors. Before you add these attributes to every anchor tag on your page, test them out on one or two links.*

Removing a Link

To remove a link, click the source in the document window. Go to the Properties panel and clear the path in the Link field. You can also click the source and choose Modify | Remove Link or right-click the source and choose Remove Link from the context menu.

Picking a New Destination

To choose a new destination for a link, click the source in the document window and choose Modify | Change Link or right-click the source and choose Change Link from the context menu. This opens the Select File dialog box, where you can navigate to a new destination page.

You can also simply type a new URL into the Link field of the Properties panel or use the point-to-file or folder icons.

Opening the Destination in a New Window

If you want the browser to open the destination page of the link in a new browser window, choose the `_blank` option from the Target list on the Properties panel. Dreamweaver tweaks the anchor tag in the source code by adding the `target` attribute:

```
This sentence contains a link to an <a href="http://www.externalsite.com"
  target="_blank">external site</a> that opens in a new browser window.
```

You can also click the source of the link and choose Modify | Link Target | _blank, or right-click the source and choose Target Frame | _blank from the context menu.

exam
ⓦatch

If you prefer to work in Code view, don't forget to add the underscore character! The attribute/value pair `target="blank"` *means something different to the browser than the correct* `target="_blank"` *syntax. Briefly,* `target="blank"` *tells the browser to open the target page in a frame called* blank*. See the section called "Linking to Frames," later in the chapter, for more information.*

EXERCISE 6-1

Adding Links to the Mad Science Home Page

In this exercise, you add links to the home page of Mad Science LLC.

1. Launch Dreamweaver, open the Site panel and set the site to Mad Science LLC.

2. Double-click the file *index.htm*. This is the home page you created in Chapter 3. The home page opens in a document window.

3. Now for this exercise to work, you need to create some temporary files to represent the Our Facility, Monsters, and Contact Us pages. Go to the Site panel and select the folder called *contact*. Choose File | New File from the Site panel's menu. Dreamweaver adds a new file called *untitled.php*. Rename this file *index.htm*.

4. Repeat step 3 for the *facility* and *monsters* folders. Each time, rename the file *index.htm*.

5. Double-click the file in the *contact* folder. A new document window opens. Click an insertion point in the window and type **Contact Us page** or something to that effect. Choose File | Save and close the document window.

6. Repeat step 5 for the files in the *facility* and *monsters* folders, typing **Our Facility page** and **Monsters page** as appropriate. You'll eventually replace all three temporary pages with actual ones.

7. The document window for the home page should still be open. Select the Our Facility button. Go to the Properties panel and type **facility/index.htm** in the Link field. Typing the path by hand is one way to set the button's link.

8. Now select the Monsters button. Drag the point-to-file icon next to the Link field in the Properties panel to the *index.htm* file inside the *monsters* folder. Release the mouse button, and Dreamweaver supplies the path *monsters/ index.htm* in the Link field. This is another way to set a link in Dreamweaver.

9. Select the Contact Us button. Click the folder icon next to the Link field in the Properties panel. The Select File dialog box appears. Navigate to the *contact* folder and double-click the *index.htm* file inside it. The Select File dialog box closes, and Dreamweaver fills in the path *contact/index.htm* in the Link field. This a third way to set a link in Dreamweaver.

10. So much for the main navigation. It's always a good idea to have another navigation scheme, such as redundant text links at the bottom of the page matching the main navigation. Click to the right of the horizontal rule at the bottom of the document window. Press ENTER or RETURN and type the following: **HOME | OUR FACILITY | MONSTERS | CONTACT US**

11. Highlight the line of text you just typed, and set the font-face list to the first choice. This is the same set of fonts that you specified for the text in the main content area. Also set the Size list to −1.

12. Highlight the word *HOME* and type **index.htm** in the Link field of the Properties panel.

13. Highlight the words *OUR FACILITY* and type **facility/index.htm** in the Link field, or use the method that you prefer to set the link.

14. Highlight the word *MONSTERS* and type **monsters/index.htm** in the Link field, or use the method that you prefer.

15. Highlight the words *CONTACT US* and type **contact/index.htm** in the Link field, or use the method that you prefer. Your document window should look like Figure 6-2.

16. Choose File | Save.

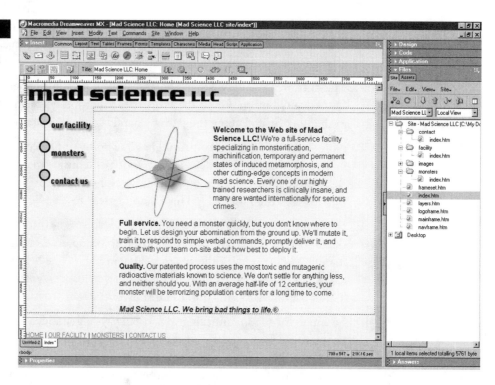

FIGURE 6-2

Your document window should look something like this.

17. Press F12 to preview the page in a browser window. When you hover over the links, the mouse pointer changes into a finger icon, signaling that you can click. Test every link on the page. Make sure they all link where they're supposed to link. Use your browser's Back button to return from your dead-end temporary pages.

18. Everything works? Close the browser window. You already saved the file, so you're done. Great job! Need to fix something? Make the necessary changes, and go back to step 16.

Using Named Anchors

A *named anchor* is an invisible element that marks off a section of a page. When you link to this named anchor, the browser jumps directly to that particular section. Web builders use named anchors to help visitors get around long pages of text.

Inserting a Named Anchor

 Before you can link to a named anchor, you have to insert one on the page. Choose an insertion point in the document window and look under the Common tab of the Insert panel for the Named Anchor button.

Click this button (or choose Insert | Named Anchor) for the Named Anchor dialog box (see the next illustration). Type the name of the anchor in the field and click OK. Dreamweaver places a golden anchor icon in the document window. This icon doesn't appear on the live page. If you don't want the icon to appear in the document window, choose Edit | Preferences, look under the Invisible Elements category and uncheck the option for named anchors.

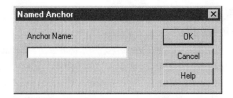

Assuming that you insert a named anchor called *details,* Dreamweaver adds the following source code to your page:

```
<a name="details"></a>
```

Notice that the closing anchor tag falls immediately after the opening tag. There's no text between the tags.

Linking to a Named Anchor

To link to the named anchor, select a source for the link and type a hash mark (#) followed by the name of the anchor in the Link field on the Properties panel. To link to the details anchor, type **#details** in the Link field. Alternatively, drag the point-to-file icon from the Properties panel to the golden anchor icon in the document window, and Dreamweaver fills in the correct path, hash mark and all.

The href attribute of a link to a named anchor looks like this in the code:

```
This sentence has a link to the <a href="#details">Details section</a>
    of the page.
```

If you guess that the anchor tag has two uses in HTML, you're absolutely correct. The first is to declare the destination of a link by way of the href attribute. The second is to serve as destination of a named-anchor link by way of the `name` attribute. The following example shows both uses of the anchor tag:

```
<!--Here, the anchor tag creates a named anchor.-->
<a name="details"></a>
<h2>The Details Section</h2>

<!--Here, the anchor tag directs a link to the named anchor declared above.-->
<p>This paragraph has a link to the <a href="#details">Details section</a>
   of the page.</p>
```

exam
Ⓦatch

Remember that the anchor tag has two functions: first, to supply the path for a link, and second, to supply the name of a named anchor. In the first sense, the anchor tag represents a link. In the second sense, the anchor tag represents the destination of a link.

See the next Scenario and Solution sidebar for a quick reference outlining the two functions of the anchor tag.

Using Named Anchors and URLs Together   You can link to a named anchor on another page by specifying the name of the anchor after the path to the page. For instance, to jump to the Disclaimer section of the About Us page, you would type something like **../about/index.htm#disclaimer** in the Link field of the Properties panel. This path tells the browser to go up one level in the site structure, look in the *about* folder, load the *index.htm* file, and then jump to a named anchor called *disclaimer*.

Jumping to the Top of the Page   To cause a link to jump to the top of the current page, specify a *null link,* which is nothing more than the hash character (#).

SCENARIO & SOLUTION

When is the anchor tag like a link?	When you specify a path in the `href` attribute
When is the anchor tag like the destination of a link?	When you specify the name of the anchor in the name attribute

Select a link source, and type # in the Link field of the Properties panel. The source code for such a link looks like this:

```
This sentence contains a link to the <a href="#">top of the page</a>.
```

Dreamweaver uses null links as triggers for JavaScript behaviors, as you'll see in Chapter 7.

Linking to Frames

When you use frames to build the layout of your page, you create what are, in essence, separate browser windows. Each frame contains its own Web page, and each Web page can have its own links.

By default, the destination of a link opens in the same frame as the page that contains the source of the link. This is fine if you have a link in the main content area of your page, but what about links in the navigation frame, for instance? By clicking a button in the navigation frame, the destination page loads by default into the very same frame, which causes the navigation buttons to disappear! Unless you're loony, this is not what you intend to do to the visitors of your site.

Fortunately, you can tell the link precisely which frame you want to use for the destination page by pulling a value from the Target list on the Properties panel. To do so, select the link source in the document window and choose the name of the destination frame from the Target list. (Dreamweaver automatically fills the list with the names of all the possible targets.) If a button in the navigation frame should load its target into the frame called Content, for instance, choose Content from the Target list. Dreamweaver adds the target attribute to the anchor tag in the source code, like this:

```
<a href="contact/index.htm" target="Content"><img src="images/contact.gif"
   width="50" height="50" alt="Contact Us button"></a>
```

HTML provides four standard target values that you can use in place of the actual name of the frame. These are _blank, _parent, _self, and _top. You've encountered the _blank target value already. This target causes the destination page to load in a new browser window. The _parent target causes the destination page to load in the parent frameset or the frameset in which the current frame is nested. Some of your frames may disappear if you use this option. The _self target causes the destination page to load in the current frame. This is the default setting. The _top target causes the destination page to replace the frameset in the current browser window. All the frames disappear on your page if you use this option.

When you link to an external site from your framed site, use the `_top` target for the link. This way, you don't wind up framing another site's content. Unscrupulous Web builders sometimes frame external content on purpose to make it seem like their sites are affiliated with the external site, but this practice is frowned upon in a professional environment. True partner sites are almost never framed.

To change the default target frame to something other than `_self`, insert a base element. See "Adding a Base Element," later in this chapter for more information.

You can also specify a target by selecting a link source and choosing Modify | Link Target from the main menu or by right-clicking the link source and choosing Target Frame from the context menu.

Beware! The `_top` target doesn't cause the browser to jump to the top of the page. For that, you need a null link: `<a href="#">`.

Adding E-Mail Links

The ever-popular e-mail link is a standby on most Web sites. When the visitor clicks an e-mail link, the visitor's default e-mail program opens a new message window.

To add an e-mail link to your page from a text source, choose an insertion point in the document window, look under the Common tab of the Insert panel, and click the E-mail Link button.

You can also choose Insert | Email Link. Either method opens the Email Link dialog box, shown in the following illustration. Type the text of the link in the Text field, and type the e-mail address of the recipient in the E-Mail field. This is the address that appears in the To field of the new mail window that opens. Click OK to set the link.

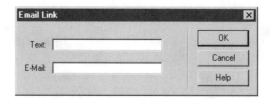

An e-mail link to the address marc@taotezing.com looks like this in the source code:

```
This sentence has an <a href="mailto:marc@taotezing.com">email link</a>.
```

As you can see, the `href` attribute of the anchor tag is at work here again, assisted by the `mailto:` notation. This notation signals the browser that what follows isn't a URL but an e-mail address.

A graphic can be the source of an e-mail link, too. Select the graphic, go to the Properties panel, and type **mailto:** plus the address of the recipient in the Link field.

Adding a Base Element

By default, document-relative paths tell the browser where to look to find the destination of a link in relation to the visitor's current location in the site. However, you can make document-relative paths relative to any location by inserting a base element.

Base elements have two functions. First, they specify the location to which all document-relative paths on the page refer. Second, they indicate the default target frame for links on the page.

To insert a base element, choose Insert | Head Tags | Base or look under the Head tab of the Insert panel and click the Base button.

The Base dialog box appears (see the following illustration). In the Href field, type the location to which all document-relative paths on the page should refer or click the Browse button and navigate to the desired location. For best results, give the location as an absolute path. If you use the Browse button, add the *http://www* portion of the full URL to the beginning of the path that Dreamweaver supplies. If you don't want to change the reference for document-relative paths, keep this field blank.

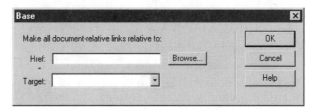

If you want to set a new default target frame, pick a value from the Target list. For example, if you choose the `_blank` option, all links on the page open in new browser windows by default. Leave this field blank if you want to use the browser's default, which is almost always `_self`.

Click OK to insert the base element. Dreamweaver adds the base tag, `<base>`, between the head tags of your source code, like this:

```
<base href="http://www.taotezing.com/img/" target="_blank">
```

This example bases all document-relative paths relative to the default images folder of the Tao Te Zing site. That is, the base element tells the browser where to start looking whenever it encounters a document-relative path. The path *../contact/index.htm* says to the browser, "Start in the default images folder. Go up one level in the site structure, look for a folder called *contact,* and load the *index.htm* file that's inside this folder." Without a base element, the browser would start at the visitor's current location in the site, not the default images folder.

Further, all link destinations open in a new browser window, since the base target is `_blank`.

on the
ʘob

The base element of a page affects document-relative paths only on that particular page. If another page of your site doesn't have a base element, the browser assumes the default scenario for that page, by which document-relative paths refer to the visitor's current location in the site.

CERTIFICATION OBJECTIVE 6.02

Creating Image Maps, Jump Menus, and Navigation Bars

Text-source and image-source links are the most common types of links, but they aren't the only types. Other image-source link types are image maps and jump menus. You can create both of these elements in Dreamweaver.

Dreamweaver also provides a Navigation Bar object. A *navigation bar* is a series of graphical buttons with links to the various pages of your site. Because they're graphical, nav bars work well as the site's main navigational scheme.

Creating Image Maps

An *image map* is a graphic with specific clickable regions or *hotspots*. Unlike a garden-variety image-source link, where the entire image is clickable, an image map might have only a single, small clickable region, in which case the rest of the image is inert. An image map can also have multiple clickable regions, so that clicking the image in different locations causes different pages to load.

Two kinds of image maps can be used: client-side and server-side. A *client-side image map* defines its hotspots, or clickable regions, in the source code of the Web page. Client software like a Web browser determines where on the image the visitor clicks. By comparison, a *server-side image map* relies on the Web server to process the visitor's image-map clicks. The source code doesn't contain information about the hotspots.

When you use Dreamweaver to create image maps, you create client-side image maps. Client-side image maps are faster than server-side maps, because the Web server doesn't have to get involved in figuring out where the visitor clicked. Client-side image maps are also easier to build, deploy, and maintain. However, the visitor's browser needs to understand the HTML markup that defines the hotspots. All the major graphical browsers have supported client-side image maps for a while now. Some extremely old browsers support only server-side image maps, so be aware that a small segment of your audience might not be able to use the client-side image maps on your site.

Brush up on the differences between client-side and server-side image maps. A client-side image map has HTML-defined hotspots. The client software figures out where the visitor clicked. In a server-side image map, the Web server intervenes to figure out where the visitor clicked. The HTML code doesn't contain information about the hotspots of a server-side image map.

To create an image map, insert the image that you want to use or choose an image that you already added to the page. Select this image and go to the Properties panel. At the bottom left, next to the label Map, you find a text field and four buttons, as shown here.

Type a name for the image map in the text field. If you don't supply a name, Dreamweaver assigns a generic one as soon as you start adding hotspots.

To add a hotspot to the image map, choose a hotspot tool: The Rectangular Hotspot tool lets you draw a rectangular hotspot on the image. The Oval Hotspot tool lets you draw a circular hotspot, and the Polygon Hotspot tool lets you draw a hotspot of practically any shape. Select the tool that you want by clicking the appropriate button. Move the mouse pointer onto the image you selected, and draw the hotspot. With the Rectangular or Oval Hotspot tool, hold down the mouse button and drag. (Hold down the SHIFT key with the Rectangular Hotspot tool to make the shape of the hotspot a perfect square.) With the Polygon Hotspot tool, click once and release to plot an anchor point for the shape. Move the mouse pointer to a new location and click again. Keep adding anchor points to define the shape.

The hotspot shows as a transparent field of blue on top of the image. This blue region appears only in Dreamweaver. When you view the page in a live browser, the hotspots are invisible.

After you draw a hotspot, the Properties panel reconfigures itself, as the next illustration shows. Type the path to the destination in the Link field or use the point-to-file or folder icons as before. If you want to target the destination, choose a value from the Target list drop-down menu. Be sure to specify alternate text for the clickable region in the Alt field. If you want to move the hotspot, click the Pointer tool from the Properties panel and drag the hotspot to a new location on the image. To change the size or shape of the hotspot, drag the square anchor points with the Pointer tool. To delete the hotspot entirely, select it and press the DELETE key or choose Edit | Clear.

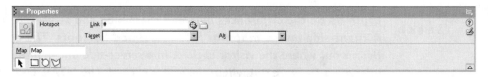

Continue adding hotspots to the image. You can include as many as you want. Be careful, though, that the hotspots don't overlap. Overlapping hotspots can confuse the browser, and the image map might not work the way you want. When you finish, preview the page in a live browser for testing and troubleshooting.

Here's how client-side image maps function in the source code. Dreamweaver adds the usemap attribute to the image tag, like this:

```
<img src="images/cake.gif" width="425" height="200" alt="A birthday cake
   with clickable candles" usemap="#candles">
```

The usemap attribute contains the name of the image map preceded by the hash character (#). In this example, the designer supplied the name *candles* in the Properties panel's Map field.

Dreamweaver also adds the map tags, <map> and </map>, to the bottom of the source code. Nested between these tags are area tags, <area>, one for each hotspot in the image map:

```
<map name="candles" id="candles">
   <area shape="rect" coords="150,170,200,220" href="presents.htm"
      target="_blank" alt="Link to the Presents page">
```

```
<area shape="circle" coords="50,50,25" href="party.htm" target="_blank"
    alt="Link to the Party page">
<area shape="poly" coords="12,15,14,18,13,7" href="wishes.htm"
    target="_blank" alt="Link to the Wishes page">
</map>
```

Notice that the name and id attributes of the map tag contain the same value, but these attributes have different purposes. The name attribute gives the name of the image map, which the usemap attribute of the image tag references. The id tag provides a unique identifier for the image map. Cascading Style Sheets and scripts can reference an image map by its id attribute but not by its name attribute, and elements with id attributes can be the destination of hyperlinks, just like named anchors. To link to an element with an id attribute, append the hash character (#) and the id value to the href attribute of the link:

```
<a href="birthday.htm#games">
```

Clicking this link would cause the browser to jump to this area of the birthday page, for example:

```
<img src="games.gif" id="games">
```

You can add the id attribute to most HTML tags, while the name attribute is more exclusive. In the case of image maps, Dreamweaver provides the same value for both as a convenience to you. There's no sense in having two different identifiers for the same element.

The shape attribute of the area tag determines the shape of the hotspot. The coords attribute defines the shape. In a rectangular hotspot, the coordinates represent the pixel positions of the left, top, right, and bottom anchor points. In a circular hotspot, the coordinates represent the horizontal position of the center point, the vertical position of the center point, and the radius. In a polygonal hotspot, each pair of coordinates represents the horizontal and vertical position of an anchor point. The href, target, and alt attributes work as they do in other HTML tags.

Inserting Jump Menus

A *jump menu* is a drop-down list of navigational choices. When the visitor selects an item from the jump menu, the destination page loads.

A jump menu is a combination of three elements: a form, a menu control, and a JavaScript. You need the form and the menu control to create the drop-down list that appears on the page. You need the JavaScript to process the linking action. When you insert a jump menu, Dreamweaver writes the JavaScript for you according to your specifications.

To insert a jump menu, choose an insertion point on the page, and then choose Insert | Form Objects | Jump Menu or click the Jump Menu button under the Forms tab of the Insert panel.

The Insert Jump Menu dialog box appears (see the following illustration). For every item that you want to add to the jump menu, click the plus button at the top of the dialog box. If you want to add five choices to the jump menu, for instance, click the plus button five times. Then select each unnamed item in turn. Supply the text of the choice in the Text field. The text is usually the name of the destination page, such as Contact Us or Products. Type the path to the destination page in the next field. You can also browse for the file, and Dreamweaver adds the correct document-relative path to the field.

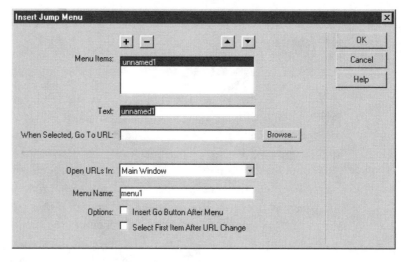

Jump menus are more useful when the first item in the list isn't a link but a prompt like "Pick a page..." or "Jump to...." If you decide to use a prompt for the first item in the list, don't supply a path for this item in the URL field. Keep the URL field blank.

You can rearrange the order of an item by selecting it and clicking the up and down buttons at the top of the dialog box. To delete an item, select it and click the minus button.

After you finish setting the text and paths of the choices, fill out the rest of the dialog box. The remaining choices apply to the entire jump menu, not individual menu items. Choose the target frame from the Open URLs In list. If your page doesn't use frames, you'll have only one choice in this list: the main browser window. Supply a name for the jump menu in the Menu Name field. This name must be unique in the sense that no other form objects on the page have it. Feel free to use the default name that Dreamweaver provides.

Finally, set the options for the jump menu. If you want to include a Go button next to the menu, check the option for this. Check the Select First Item After URL Change option if your site uses frames and you want the jump menu to reselect the first item in the list after a new page loads.

Click OK to create the jump menu. Dreamweaver adds HTML to the source code for the menu control and the Go button. The necessary JavaScript functions appear at the top of the code listing.

Notice that the jump menu sits inside a thin red dotted line in the document window. The dotted line indicates the presence of a form. This line doesn't show up on the live page.

Modifying a Jump Menu

To edit a jump menu after you insert it, select the menu control in the document window. Then, open the Design panel group and click the Behaviors tab for the Behaviors panel. You can also choose Window | Behaviors. Double-click the Jump Menu action in the behaviors list, and the Jump Menu dialog box appears, as shown next. Make changes to the menu settings and click OK.

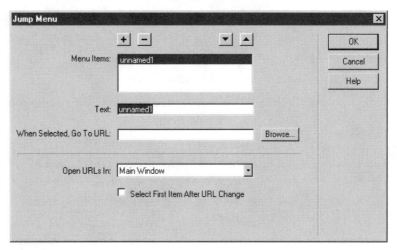

Unfortunately, you can't add or remove a Go button to the jump menu from the Jump Menu dialog box.

EXERCISE 6-2

Adding a Jump Menu to the Mad Science Home Page

In this exercise, you build a jump menu into the home page of Mad Science LLC.

1. Launch Dreamweaver, open the Site panel, and set the site to Mad Science LLC.

2. Double-click the file *index.htm*. The home page opens in a document window.

3. Select the horizontal rule at the top of the document window and press the right-arrow key. A flashing cursor appears at the far right of the rule.

4. You eventually want to align the jump menu to the right side of the screen. However, none of the objects that make up the jump menu have `align` attributes. To get around this problem, insert a nested layout table—that is, insert a table inside the existing table cell. You can put the jump menu inside the nested table's cell and then set the cell alignment. Select the Common tab of the Insert panel and click the Table button. In the Insert Table dialog box, specify a table 1 row by 1 column. Make the width 100% and set cell padding, cell spacing, and the border values to 0. Click OK to insert the table. Dreamweaver adds it directly below the horizontal rule.

5. Click inside the nested table's single cell. Set the Horz list on the Properties panel to Right. The flashing cursor jumps to the right side of the cell.

6. Now insert the jump menu. Switch to the Forms tab of the Insert panel and click the Jump Menu button. The Insert Jump Menu dialog box appears.

7. Click the plus button at the top of the menu four times. This creates a total of five unnamed items in the list.

8. Select the first item. In the Text field, type **Jump to...** as the linkless prompt. Leave the URL field blank.

9. Select the second item. Type **Our Facility** in the Text field. Click the Browse button next to the URL field and navigate to the *index.htm* file inside the *facility* folder. Double-click this file. Dreamweaver fills in the appropriate document-relative path in the URL field.

10. Select the third item. Type **Monsters** in the Text field. Browse to the *index.htm* file in the *monsters* folder or type **monsters/index.htm** in the URL field.

11. Select the fourth item. Type **Contact Us** in the Text field. Browse to the *index.htm* file in the *contact* folder or type **contact/index.htm** in the URL field.

12. Select the fifth item. Type **Home Page** in the Text field and type **index.htm** in the URL field.

13. Leave the other settings as they are by default. Click OK to create the jump menu. Your document window should look like Figure 6-3.

14. Choose File | Save.

15. Press F12 to test the jump menu in a live browser window. Make sure that all the items lead to the correct pages. Use your browser's Back button to return to the home page.

16. Close the browser window. If you need to make changes to the jump menu, select it, open the Behaviors panel, and double-click the Jump Menu behavior. If you don't need to make changes, consider your home page jump-menued. Bravo! You did it!

FIGURE 6-3

Your document window should look something like this.

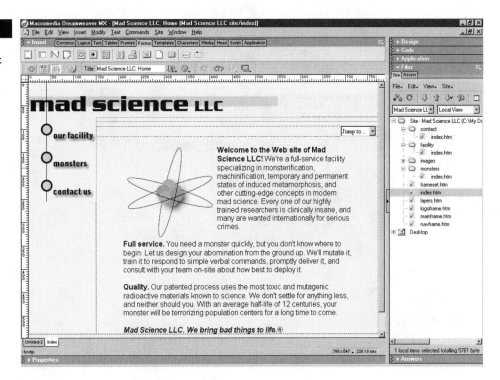

Building a Navigation Bar

Dreamweaver provides a command for adding a navigation bar to your page. However, you don't need this command to create a navigation bar. You proved that already in Exercise 5-2 when you added rollover images to the bottom left layout cell of the Mad Science LLC home page. Even still, the Navigation Bar command gives you a few extra options, and it may save you some time.

To invoke Dreamweaver's Navigation Bar command, select an insertion point, and choose Insert | Interactive Images | Navigation Bar or look under the Common tab of the Insert panel and click the Navigation Bar button.

This opens the Insert Navigation Bar dialog box, as shown in Figure 6-4. Type a name for the first navigational choice in the Element Name field. If the first button is the Our Facility button, for instance, type **facility** or something to that effect.

Then supply paths to the images that you want to use to represent the various button states. Click the Browse button next to the corresponding field, navigate to the default images folder of the site, and select the appropriate image file.

Supply alternate text for the button in the Alternate Text field. Type the path of the button's link in the URL field or click the Browse button and navigate to the

---

FIGURE 6-4

Use the Insert Navigation Bar dialog box to assemble a graphical navigation bar.

Insert Navigation Bar

Nav Bar Elements: unnamed1

Element Name: unnamed1

Up Image: Browse...

Over Image: Browse...

Down Image: Browse...

Over While Down Image: Browse...

Alternate Text:

When Clicked, Go To URL: Browse...   in   Main Window

Options: ☑ Preload Images
☐ Show "Down Image" Initially

Insert: Horizontally   ☑ Use Tables

OK   Cancel   Help

desired page. Dreamweaver fills in the correct document-relative path. If your site uses frames, choose a target frame for the drop-down list to the right of the URL field.

You can define as many as four different states for the nav bar buttons. The *up state* is the way the button looks normally. The *over state* is the way the button looks when the visitor rolls over the button with the mouse pointer. The *down state* is the way the button looks when the visitor clicks the button. The *over-while-down* state is the way the button looks when the visitor rolls over a down-state button. You must supply a graphic at least for the up state. The other three states are optional.

See the next Scenario and Solution sidebar for a quick reference to help you keep track of the four possible button states in a nav bar.

Button states are individual images. That is, you must create a separate graphics file for each state that you want to use. Store all these graphics in the default images folder. Unfortunately, Dreamweaver can't help you create the button images. However, Dreamweaver's counterpart, Fireworks MX, makes button creation a pleasure. Build the various button states in Fireworks, export the states as separate image files, and then select these image files from the Insert Navigation Bar dialog box.

Check the Preload Images option if you want the browser to download the button states initially. This improves the performance of the buttons at the expense of extra download time up front.

Your page presents the up state of the button by default. If you want your page to present the down state by default (because, for instance, the button represents the current page), check the option for this.

SCENARIO & SOLUTION

What is the up state?	An image that represents the button in its unpressed, unselected state. This is the default state for nav bar buttons.
What is the over state?	An image that represents the button when the visitor hovers over it with the mouse pointer. This is the same as the rollover state of a rollover image.
What is the down state?	An image that represents the button when the visitor clicks it. You can set this state as the default for any button in the nav bar.
What is the over-while-down state?	An image that represents the down-state button when the visitor hovers over it with the mouse pointer.

Go back to the top of the dialog box and click the plus button to add a new navigational choice. Fill in the middle portion of the dialog box as before. To rearrange the order of a nav choice, select it and click the up and down buttons. To remove a nav choice entirely, select it and click the minus button.

After you finish adding navigational choices, fill out the rest of the dialog box. To build the nav bar from left to right on your page, choose the Horizontally option from the Insert list. To build the nav bar from top to bottom, choose the Vertically option.

Finally, check the Use Tables option to create a layout table for the nav bar. Dreamweaver builds a table at the insertion point you chose and puts each button of the nav bar in a different layout cell. If you don't check this option, Dreamweaver inserts the nav bar directly into the page at the insertion point.

Click OK to build the nav bar. Dreamweaver generates a nice chunk of source code for you, including the layout table for the nav bar, the image tags for the buttons, and the JavaScript functions that control the button states.

To make changes to the navigation bar once you insert it, choose Modify | Navigation Bar to open the Modify Navigation Bar dialog box (Figure 6-5).

You can use Dreamweaver's Navigation Bar command only once per page. If you want to add a second navigation bar, you must build it by hand.

FIGURE 6-5

Make changes to your nav bar with the Modify Navigation Bar dialog box.

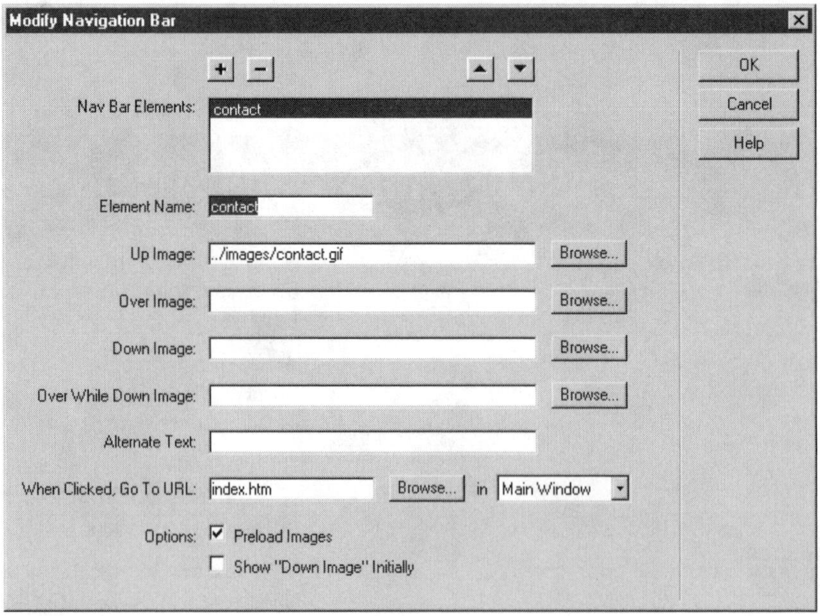

CERTIFICATION SUMMARY

You learned to create links and other kinds of navigation in this chapter. You saw that to change a string of text or an image into the source of a link, all you have to do is supply the path to the target page in the Link field of the dialog box. You learned the difference between absolute paths, document-relative paths, and root-relative paths, and I explained that when you use the point-to-file icon or the folder icon on the Properties panel, Dreamweaver automatically fills in the correct document-relative path.

You learned the two functions of the anchor tag in HTML: to give the destination for a link by way of the `href` attribute and to serve as a named anchor by way of the `name` attribute. I showed you how to insert and link to named anchors on your page.

I talked about the importance of specifying a target frame when you use frames for page layout. By default, the browser loads the destination page in the same frame as the link, which can cause problems if the visitor clicks a button in the navigation-bar frame, for instance. I went over the four standard targets that HTML provides: `_blank`, `_parent`, `_self`, and `_top`. You learned to set the default target frame and to change the location to which document-relative paths refer by inserting a base element on the page.

You created client-side image maps by drawing hotspots, or clickable regions, on images with the drawing tools on the Properties panel. I explained that you define the hotspots for client-side image maps in the source code of the page. This is what distinguishes client-side image maps from server-side image maps, where the Web server interprets the clicks on the image map.

You learned that a jump menu consists of three components: a form, a menu control, and a few JavaScript functions to make it work. You may also add a fourth component, a Go button, at your discretion.

You saw that Dreamweaver's Navigation Bar command gives you more graphical options than building the nav bar by hand with the Rollover Image command. However, Dreamweaver allows you to use the Navigation Bar command only once per page.

TWO-MINUTE DRILL

Adding Links

❏ To create a link from a text source, highlight the text and specify the path to the target page in the Link field of the Properties panel.

❏ To create a link from an image source, select the image and specify the path to the target page in the Link field of the Properties panel.

❏ When you use the Properties panel's point-to-file icon or the folder icon, Dreamweaver fills in the correct document-relative path.

❏ To insert a new text-source link, choose Insert | Hyperlink.

❏ Use named anchors to help your visitors navigate long pages.

❏ To insert a named anchor, click the Named Anchor button under the Common tab of the Insert panel or choose Insert | Named Anchor.

❏ When you use frames to create the layout of your page, specify a target frame if you don't want the destination page to load in the same frame as the link.

❏ To insert an e-mail link, click the E-mail Link button under the Common tab of the Properties panel or choose Insert | Email Link.

❏ A base element determines the location to which all document-relative paths refer and sets the default target frame.

Creating Image Maps, Jump Menus, and Navigation Bars

❏ Dreamweaver creates client-side image maps, or image maps defined by HTML tags in the source code of the page.

❏ Draw hotspots, or clickable areas, on a graphic with the drawing tools on the Properties panel.

❏ A jump menu consists of a form, a menu control, a few JavaScript functions, and sometimes a Go button.

❏ Edit an existing jump menu by selecting the jump menu, opening the Behaviors panel, and double-clicking the Jump Menu behavior.

❏ Dreamweaver's Navigation Bar command allows you to define up to four different button states: up, down, over, and over-while-down.

❏ You can insert only one navigation bar per page using the Navigation Bar command.

SELF TEST

The following questions will help you measure your understanding of the material presented in this chapter. Read all the choices carefully because there might be more than one correct answer. Choose all correct answers for each question.

Adding Links

I. How do you eliminate the visible border around a graphical link?

   A. Select the graphic and choose Modify | Remove Border from the main menu.

   B. Right-click the graphic and choose Remove Border from the context menu.

   C. Select the graphic and type **0** in the Border field on the Properties panel.

2. What does the base element do?

   A. It determines the destination for all links on the page.

   B. It sets the reference point for all document-relative paths on the page.

   C. It converts all document-relative paths to absolute paths.

   D. It determines the default frame for displaying destination pages.

   E. It treats document-relative paths as null links.

3. You want the destination page of a link to appear in a new browser window. What is the correct target value for this?

   A. `_new`

   B. `_top`

   C. `_open`

   D. `_blank`

   E. `_parent`

4. Your page has two frames: NavFrame, which holds the navigation bar, and ContentFrame, which is the main content area. What is the best HTML markup for a link in NavFrame?

   A. `<a href="partnerts.htm" target="ContentFrame">`

   B. `<a href="partners.htm" target="NavFrame">`

   C. `<a href="partners.htm" target="_ContentFrame">`

    D. `<a href="partners.htm" target="_NavFrame">`

    E. `<a href="partners.htm" target="#ContentFrame">`

    F. `<a href="partners.htm" target="#NavFrame" >`

5. You're building a Web site, or at least you're trying to. Your links don't work when you test the page offline. You're certain that the paths point to actual pages. What are the possible problems?

    A. The links use absolute paths.

    B. The links use document-relative paths.

    C. The links use root-relative paths.

    D. The links use file paths.

6. Which attribute of the anchor tag causes a short description of the link to appear in some browsers when the visitor hovers over the link with the mouse pointer?

    A. `alt`

    B. `title`

    C. `desc`

    D. `caption`

7. How do you insert a named anchor in your page?

    A. Right-click and choose Insert | Named Anchor from the context menu.

    B. Choose Insert | Named Anchor from the main menu.

    C. Click the Named Anchor button in the Insert panel.

    D. Drag the point-to-file icon into the document window.

8. How do you set the color of text links?

    A. Use the text-color square on the Properties panel.

    B. Use the link-color squares on the Page Properties dialog box.

    C. Choose Insert | Link Color.

    D. Choose Text | Color.

    E. Choose Color from the context menu.

9. What type of link causes the browser to jump to the top of the page?

   A. `<a href="top">`

   B. `<a href="_top">`

   C. A base element

   D. A null link

10. Which tab of the Insert panel has the E-mail Link button?

   A. Common

   B. Forms

   C. Media

   D. Script

Creating Image Maps, Jump Menus, and Navigation Bars

11. Which of the following shapes can you use to define hotspots on a client-side image map?

   A. Rectangle

   B. Circle

   C. Ellipse

   D. Polygon

12. What causes a Dreamweaver-created jump menu to jump?

   A. HTML

   B. CSS

   C. A Web app

   D. JavaScript functions

13. You want to assign an image map to a graphic called *image.gif*. Assuming that the map's name is *MyMap*, what is the correct HTML markup for the image tag?

   A. `<img map="MyMap">`

   B. `<img src="image.gif" map="MyMap">`

   C. `<img src="image.gif" map="#MyMap">`

   D. `<img src="image.gif" usemap="MyMap">`

   E. `<img src="image.gif" usemap="#MyMap">`

14. What is a hotspot? Choose the best answer.

   A. A button in a navigation bar

   B. A clickable region on an image map

   C. An HTML tag for creating image maps

   D. An item in a jump menu

15. When you insert a navigation bar with Dreamweaver's Navigation Bar command, which of the following states can you define for the buttons?

   A. Beside

   B. Up

   C. Next

   D. Down

   E. Over

   F. Over-while-out

   G. Down-while-up

   H. Over-while-down

16. Which of the following statements are true about Dreamweaver's Navigation Bar command?

   A. You can use this command to insert as many nav bars per page as you like.

   B. You can choose from more button states with this command that the Rollover Image command gives you.

   C. This command gives you seven different layout possibilities.

   D. This command can build a layout table for the nav bar.

17. What element of a jump menu does the Jump Menu dialog box prohibit you from adding or removing?

   A. Item names

   B. Item links

   C. Go button

   D. Target frame

18. You're drawing a rectangular hotspot on an image. What key do you hold down to make the rectangular hotspot perfectly square as you draw?

   A. SHIFT

   B. CTRL (Windows) or COMMAND (Mac)

   C. ALT (Windows) or OPTION (Mac)

   D. S

   E. ALT-S (Windows) or OPTION-S (Mac)

19. You want to edit a jump menu. What do you do?

   A. Select the jump menu, open the Behaviors panel, and double-click the Jump Menu behavior.

   B. Double-click the jump menu.

   C. Select the jump menu and choose Modify | Form Objects | Jump Menu.

   D. Select the jump menu and choose Insert | Form Objects | Jump Menu.

20. You want to edit a navigation bar. What do you do?

   A. Select the navigation bar, open the Behaviors panel and double-click the Nav Bar behavior.

   B. Choose Edit | Navigation Bar.

   C. Choose Modify | Navigation Bar.

   D. Right-click and choose Navigation Bar from the context menu.

LAB QUESTION

Around the office, they call you the Content Guru. You never asked for this title. You never even wanted it, but you're glad that your input seems to add some value.

You earned your moniker by taking ordinary content, no matter how dense, no matter how obtuse, and turning it into "Web magic," they say. You seem to have a knack for knowing how to make content work on the Web.

So when Ella, your colleague, intercepted some new text for one of the interior pages of your client's Web site, she forwarded it straight to you for advice. "Please see attached," her e-mail said. "We need to figure out where to put the links."

You know that Web magic is 90 percent common sense. You know that the site's visitors don't read, but skim. You know that their eyes skip over just about everything. You want the links to be efficient to make the page more usable.

The plan for the site calls for a general Services page, under which are subpages for Legal Services, Financial Services, and Personal Services. Underline the best phrasing for the links in the following paragraph, which appears on the home page of the site. Feel free to eliminate sentences that don't add anything to the text.

> The Sands Services Group wants nothing more than to serve you, our client. We have specialized in serving clients like you for the last 12 years. You'll find many helpful pages on this site explaining the many fine services we offer. Click here to visit the Services page. Our legal services include legal counseling, legal strategies, and legal planning. Click here to visit the Legal Services page. Among our financial services are fiscal responsibilities, fiscal management, financial management, and financial benefits. Click here to visit the Financial Services page. If you don't require legal or financial services at this time, perhaps we can interest you in our selection of personal services, including personal management, personal growth, life planning, and growth management. Click here to visit the Personal Services page. Trust the Sands Services Group, where our motto is "For a reasonable fee, anything is possible."

SELF TEST ANSWERS

Adding Links

1. ☑ C. Select the graphic and set its border value to 0.
☒ A, B, and D are incorrect because there isn't a Remove Border command in Dreamweaver.

2. ☑ B and D. The base element sets the reference point for all document-relative paths, and it determines the default frame.
☒ A is incorrect because if it were true, all links would point to the same destination, no matter what path you supply. C is incorrect because the base element doesn't convert document-relative paths to absolute paths. E is incorrect because if it were true, clicking any link on the page would force the browser to jump to the top of the page.

3. ☑ D. To cause the destination page to open in a new browser window, the correct target value is _blank.
☒ A and C are incorrect because HTML doesn't recognize these target values. B and E are incorrect because while both are acceptable target values, neither one causes the destination page to load in a new browser window.

4. ☑ A. The best HTML markup is the one that gives the target as ContentFrame without any extra characters.
☒ B, D, and F are incorrect because, if the target is NavFrame, the navigation buttons will disappear when the target page loads. Further, the underscore in D and the hash mark in F make these choices doubly incorrect. C is incorrect because of the underscore character. E is incorrect because of the hash mark.

5. ☑ A and C. Absolute and root-relative paths can cause problems with offline testing and troubleshooting.
☒ B is incorrect because correctly formed document-relative paths never cause problems offline. D is incorrect because file paths can cause problems online, not offline.

6. ☑ B. The title attribute unordered-list tag, `<ul>`, appears at the top of a bulleted list in the source code.
☒ A is incorrect, although it's an extremely good guess. The `alt` attribute holds the alternate text for images. C is incorrect because the `desc` attribute doesn't apply to the anchor tag. D is incorrect because the `caption` attribute applies to the table tag.

7. ☑ **B** and **C.** Either choose Insert | Named Anchor from the main menu or click the Named Anchor button in the Insert panel.

 ☒ **A** is incorrect because there is no Insert command in the context menu. **D** is incorrect because the point-to-file icon doesn't insert a named anchor. However, you can use this icon to generate the correct path to an existing anchor.

8. ☑ **A, B,** and **D.** Use the font-color square on the Properties panel, the link-color squares on the Page Properties dialog box, or choose Text | Color to set the color of the links.

 ☒ **C** is incorrect because there is no Insert | Link Color command. **E** is incorrect because the context menu doesn't have a Color command.

9. ☑ **D.** A null link (`<a href="#">`) causes the browser to jump to the top of the page.

 ☒ **A** and **B** are incorrect because the _top target value has to do with frames, not the top of the page. **A** is also incorrect because the target value should be in the `target` attribute, not the `href` attribute, and the target should have an underscore character in front. **B** is also incorrect because the target value should be in the `target` attribute, not the `href` attribute. **C** is incorrect because the base element isn't a kind of link. It's an element that determines how the browser should handle document-relative paths and default frames.

10. ☑ **A.** Find the E-mail Link button under the Common tab.

 ☒ **B, C,** and **D** are incorrect because the E-mail Link button appears only under the Common tab of the Insert panel.

Creating Image Maps, Jump Menus, and Navigation Bars

11. ☑ **A, B,** and **D.** Hotspots can be rectangular, circular, or polygonal.

 ☒ **C** is incorrect because HTML supports only circular hotspots, not elliptical ones.

12. ☑ **D.** JavaScript functions cause a jump menu to jump.

 ☒ **A** is incorrect because HTML doesn't provide the jumping behavior of a jump menu. HTML tags set up the form, the menu control, and the Go button, however. **B** is incorrect because CSS doesn't provide the jumping behavior of a jump menu, although you can use CSS to modify the visual properties of the jump menu. **C** is incorrect because jump menus in Dreamweaver are client-side functions, not server-side Web apps.

13. ☑ **E.** Use the `usemap` attribute and include a hash sign in front of the map name.
☒ **A, B,** and **C** are incorrect because there is no `map` attribute of the image tag. **D** is incorrect because the value of `usemap` doesn't begin with a hash character.

14. ☑ **B.** A hotspot is a clickable region on an image map.
☒ **A** and **D** are incorrect because these items aren't called hotspots. A hotspot is a clickable region on an image map. **C** is incorrect because the tags for defining image maps are `<map>` and `<area>`. There is no `<hotspot>` tag as such.

15. ☑ **B, D, E,** and **H.** The four nav bar button states are up, down, over, and over-while-down.
☒ **A, C, F,** and **G** are incorrect because there are no such states for nav bar buttons.

16. ☑ **B** and **D.** The Navigation Bar command gives you four button states, and Dreamweaver can build the nav bar in its own layout table.
☒ **A** is incorrect because you can only add one nav bar per page with the Navigation Bar command. **C** is incorrect because the Navigation Bar command gives you only two layout possibilities: horizontal and vertical.

17. ☑ **C.** You can't add or remove a Go button from the Jump Menu dialog box.
☒ **A, B,** and **D** are incorrect because you can add or remove any of these elements from the Jump Menu dialog box. The only element that you can't modify from this dialog is the Go button.

18. ☑ **A.** Hold down the SHIFT key to make the rectangular hotspot perfectly square as you draw.
☒ **B, C, D,** and **E** are incorrect because these keys and key sequences don't affect the hotspot at all while you're drawing.

19. ☑ **A.** To edit a jump menu, select it, open the Behaviors panel and double-click the Jump Menu behavior.
☒ **B** is incorrect because double-clicking the jump menu doesn't do anything. **C** is incorrect because there is no Form Objects submenu under the Edit menu. **D** is incorrect because, while there is a Form Objects submenu under the Insert menu, this command inserts a new jump menu. It doesn't allow you to edit an existing one.

20. ☑ **C.** Choose Modify | Navigation Bar. You don't have to select the navigation bar first, since you can only have one per page.
☒ **A** is incorrect because there is no Nav Bar behavior in Dreamweaver. **B** is incorrect because no Navigation Bar command appears under the Edit menu. **D** is incorrect because no Navigation Bar command appears in the context menu.

LAB ANSWER

The Sands Services Group needs a better copywriter, but there's no helping that now. The following paragraph is one possibility for the links, although the text still lags.

> The Sands Services Group wants nothing more than to serve you, our client. We have specialized in serving clients like you for the last 12 years. You'll find many helpful pages on this site explaining the many fine services we offer. Click here to visit the **Services** page. Our legal services include legal counseling, legal strategies, and legal planning. Click here to visit the **Legal Services** page. Among our financial services are fiscal responsibilities, fiscal management, financial management, and financial benefits. Click here to visit the **Financial Services** page. If you don't require legal or financial services at this time, perhaps we can interest you in our selection of personal services, including personal management, personal growth, life planning, and growth management. Click here to visit the **Personal Services** page. Trust the Sands Services Group, where our motto is, For a reasonable fee, anything is possible.

The following paragraph is better, because it trims some of the fat from the text. Notice that the links appear within the sentences of the paragraph, not separately in sentences of their own.

> The Sands Services Group wants nothing more than to serve you, our client. We have specialized in serving clients like you for the last 12 years. You'll find many helpful pages on this site explaining the many fine **services** we offer. Our **legal services** include legal counseling, legal strategies, and legal planning. Among our **financial services** are fiscal responsibilities, fiscal management, financial management, and financial benefits. If you don't require legal or financial services at this time, perhaps we can interest you in our selection of **personal services**, including personal management, personal growth, life planning, and growth management. Trust the Sands Services Group, where our motto is, For a reasonable fee, anything is possible.

Under no circumstances should you submit the text with all the Click Heres underlined. The visitor's roving eye sees nothing but Click Heres, all out of context, which does nothing to improve the usability of the links.

CERTIFIED DREAMWEAVER DEVELOPER

7

Creating Forms

A *form* is an element on a Web page that allows the visitor to submit information. Forms are used for many purposes on the Web, including logging in a visitor, asking for a search keyword, sending an e-mail, and taking an order. Some forms are simple, with just a few items to fill in or click. Some have multiple parts and occupy several pages of the site.

This chapter shows you how to add a form to your Web page with Dreamweaver.

CERTIFICATION OBJECTIVE 7.01

Building Forms

Building forms in Dreamweaver is easy. It's even easier when you understand how a form works, how Dreamweaver marks up the form using HTML tags, and how best to lay out the form on the page.

Understanding Form Components

Most forms have two components: a client-side component and a server-side component. The client-side component appears in the source code of the page. It contains the form's user interface, including the text fields, checkboxes, drop-down lists, buttons, and other visual elements. It usually also contains client-side scripts for processing and validating the information that your visitor submits. By contrast, the server-side component doesn't appear in the source code at all. It's a separate application like a common gateway interface (CGI) script that resides elsewhere on the Web server. The server-side component takes the information that the visitor submits and does something with it: sends it as an e-mail, stores it in a database, initiates an order, and so on.

Without a server-side component, you can't do much with the information that the visitor submits, but without a client-side component, there's no interface by which the visitor submits information. Both sides of this equation are equally important.

The commands and procedures that you'll see in this chapter deal with the client-side component of building a form. You'll learn how to create the visual interface that appears on a Web page. Keep in mind, though, that the interface is only half the story. Without a server-side component, precious little happens when the visitor clicks the Submit button.

Now, at the risk of contradicting myself, I should point out here that on occasion, certain forms don't need a server-side component. Think of the jump menu that you created in Chapter 6. The jump menu was a form, and the purely client-side JavaScript functions that Dreamweaver added to your Web page were sufficient to create the desired effect. You didn't need a CGI script or ColdFusion application to make the jump menu jump, in other words. If your form has a limited purpose, such as calling up a particular Web page or adding a series of numbers, client-side scripting often makes server-side scripting unnecessary, but if you want to retrieve the information that your visitor submits, client-side scripting can't help you.

Working with Form Tags

On the client side, in the source code, a form is a collection of HTML tags. Each interface element of the form—each text field, submit button, and the like—has a particular HTML tag that instructs the browser to display the corresponding control. These interface-element tags sit inside opening and closing form tags, `<form>` and `</form>`.

Whatever you do, don't attempt to build a form without first inserting these form tags on the page. Some browsers are exceedingly particular about form tags (imagine a cough here that sounds like "Netscape"). Such browsers won't display any of the interface elements in the form unless a pair of form tags surrounds them. During testing, if your form shows up in Internet Explorer but not Netscape, the most likely cause is that you forgot to place the opening and closing form tags around the set of interface elements.

Here's another important reason to include the form tags. The opening form tag tells the browser the location of the form's server-side script. Web builders who come from a development background don't often forget to include this piece of information. Web builders who come from a design background omit it all the time. Particularly if you're a designer, get into the habit of enclosing the interface elements in a pair of form tags.

Dreamweaver represents a pair of form tags as a red rectangle with dotted lines. All the interface elements of the form need to appear inside this red rectangle, as Figure 7-1 shows (in black-and-white). If they appear inside the rectangle, you know that the form has opening and closing form tags. If some of the interface elements sit inside the red rectangle and others sit outside, you need to move the outside elements inside, or these elements won't work properly. If you don't see a red rectangle in the document window at all, you need to add form tags.

FIGURE 7-1

The red rectangle represents opening and closing form tags.

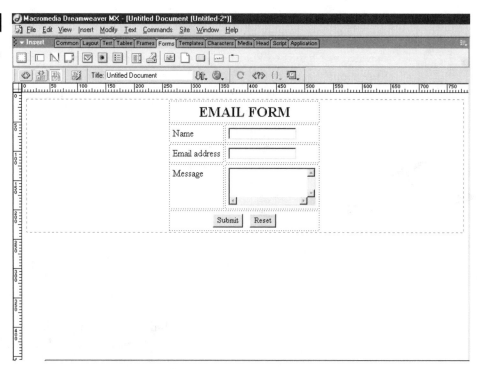

Inserting a Pair of Form Tags

To insert a pair of form tags, set the insertion point in the document window, switch to the Forms tab of the Insert panel, and click the Form button, shown here.

You can also choose Insert | Form. Dreamweaver adds the red rectangle to the document window and inserts form tags in the HTML. To set the attributes of the form tag, select the red rectangle, and go to the Properties panel, which gives you options for modifying the form tag's attributes and reconfigures itself to look like the following illustration.

Supply a name for the form in the Form Name field. Your page can have more than one form, but each one needs to have a different name. Replace the generic name that Dreamweaver provides with something more descriptive, like *Emailform* or *Orderform*. The value of the Form Name field goes in the name attribute of the form tag, like this:

```
<form name="Emailform">
```

The Action field gives the path to the form's server-side component. Type the path in this field, or click the folder icon to browse to the script or application that processes the form's results. The value of the Action field goes in the action attribute of the form tag:

```
<form name="Emailform"
action="http://www.taotezing.com/cgi-bin/email.cgi">
```

If your form doesn't have a server-side component, don't supply a value in this field, and Dreamweaver leaves the action attribute unspecified:

```
<form name="Emailform" action="">
```

If your site uses frames and your server-side script returns a Web page after processing your visitor's information, such as a Thank You page or an E-mail Sent page, you can indicate the target frame in which you want the return page to load by choosing a value from the Target list. Even if your site doesn't use frames, you can make the return page open in a new browser window by setting the Target list to _blank. The value of the Target list appears in the target attribute of the form tag:

```
<form name="Emailform"
action="http://www.taotezing.com/cgi-bin/email.cgi"
target="_blank">
```

The Method list determines how the browser submits the information to the Web server. Two choices are available: the get method and the post method. By the get method, the browser attaches the contents of the form to the URL. By the post method, the browser sends the contents of the form as a private message to the server. The get method is the default method for most browsers, but the post method is more secure, and you should use post whenever possible, especially when you pass confidential information like credit card numbers. Also, the get method limits you to a maximum of 8192 characters, so this method isn't a smart choice for submitting longer forms.

The value of the Method list goes in the method attribute of the form tag:

```
<form name="Emailform" action="http://www.taotezing.com/cgi-bin/
   email.cgi" target="_blank" method="post">
```

If your form doesn't have a server-side component, choose Default from the Method list, and Dreamweaver doesn't add a method attribute to the form tag. Keep in mind that if you choose Default from the Method list and you do have a server-side component, the browser usually assumes the get method. Check out the Scenario and Solution sidebar for a quick reference to help you differentiate between the two methods.

Finally, provide the MIME (Multipurpose Internet Mail Extensions) type of the form data in the Enctype field. You can type the value directly into the field, or you can choose a common value from the drop-down list. In general, you should use the *application/x-www-form-urlencoded* MIME type in conjunction with the post method, and you should use the *multipart/form-data* MIME type if your form includes a file field. The value of the Enctype field appears in the enctype attribute of the form tag:

```
<form name="Emailform" action="http://www.taotezing.com/cgi-bin/
   email.cgi" target="_blank" method="post" enctype="application/
   x-www-form-urlencoded">
```

All the interface elements of the form should appear between this pair of form tags. You need to include only one pair of tags per form.

Laying Out Forms

After you insert the form tags, create a layout table to arrange and align the interface elements of the form. Choose an insertion point inside the red rectangle. Then click the Table button under the Common tab of the Insert panel or choose Insert | Table.

A layout table helps to improve the appearance of the interface elements, which helps to improve the usability of the form. Notice the difference between the two forms in Figure 7-2. The top form doesn't use a layout table, and it shows. The text

SCENARIO & SOLUTION

What's the get method?	A method of form submission that adds the form information to a URL. This method is the default for most browsers, but it's less secure than the post method and truncates form data after 8192 characters.
What's the post method?	A method of form submission that sends the form information as a private message to the server. This method offers better security, and it works better with long forms.

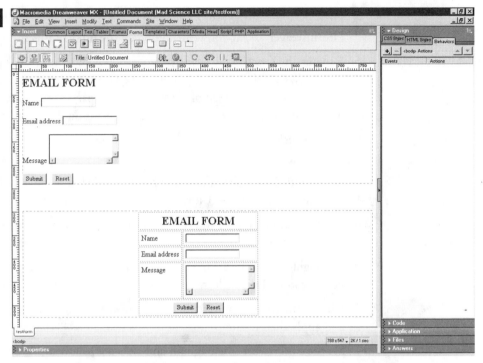

FIGURE 7-2

When you place a form's interface elements inside a layout table (bottom), the form tends to be easier on the eyes.

fields don't line up, which makes the form harder to follow, but the bottom form creates a nice left margin for the text fields, helping the visitor to fill out the form more quickly and with fewer questions. The bottom form also takes advantage of table-cell alignment to center the title and the Submit and Reset buttons.

EXERCISE 7-1

Starting a Form on the Mad Science LLC Contact Us Page

In this exercise, you begin building a form on the Contact Us page of the Mad Science LLC site.

1. Launch Dreamweaver, open the Site panel, and set the site to Mad Science LLC.

2. Click the file *index.htm*. In the Site panel, choose Edit | Copy. Then choose Edit | Paste to create a copy of *index.htm*.

3. Delete the placeholder *index.htm* file in the *contact* folder. You'll recall that this file is just a blank HTML page.

4. Drag the copy of the home page that you just made into the *contact* folder. Dreamweaver asks if you want to update the links in this file. Click Update.

5. Rename the copy of the home page *index.htm* by double-clicking the name of the file. Why did you create a copy of the home page and move it to the *contact* folder? It saved you a load of work. The home page has the layout table and the links. You don't have to reproduce these elements on the Contact Us page now.

6. Double-click the *index.htm* file in the contact folder. Dreamweaver opens a new document window.

7. In the Title field below the Insert panel, type **Mad Science LLC: Contact Us** and press ENTER or RETURN.

8. Select the atom graphic and then press the DELETE key or choose Edit | Clear from the main menu.

9. Highlight the text in the main content area of the page and press the DELETE key or choose Edit | Clear.

10. Choose the first set of fonts from Dreamweaver's font list, type **Contact Us** and apply the Heading 1 format to this text. Press ENTER or RETURN.

11. Set the Format list to Paragraph and type the following: **We look forward to hearing from you. Please fill out this form and click the Send Email button.** Press ENTER or RETURN.

12. Now look under the Forms tab of the Insert panel and click the Form button to insert a pair of form tags.

13. Go to the Properties panel and type **emailform** in the Form Name field.

14. Leave the Action field blank for the purposes of this exercise. Normally, you would type the path to the server-side script or Web app that processes the form.

15. Choose the post method from the Method list and choose the *application/x-www-form-urlencoded* MIME type from the Enctype list.

16. Switch to the Common tab of the Insert panel and click the Insert Table button. Type 7 in the Rows field and 2 in the Columns field of the Insert Table dialog box. Type **10** in the Cell Space field. Click OK to create the layout table for the form.

17. Your screen should look like Figure 7-3.

18. Choose File | Save. Good job!

FIGURE 7-3

Create a table for the interface elements of the form.

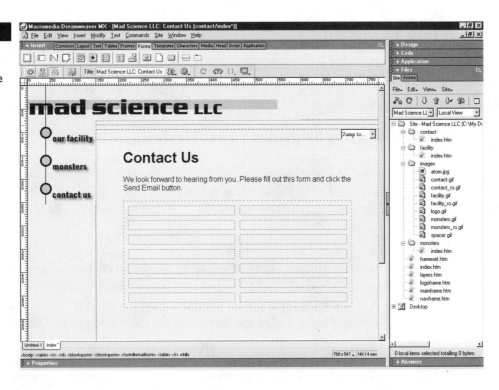

Inserting Form Objects

In Dreamweaver, *form objects* are the interface elements of the form. Place these form objects into cells of your layout table. The form objects that appear in Dreamweaver's document window are nonfunctioning placeholders. Clicking buttons that you insert, for example, doesn't cause anything to happen in Dreamweaver. Always test your form in a live browser window.

Another name for a form object is a widget.

Inserting Text Fields

Text fields are rectangular regions that allow the visitor to type in alphanumeric characters. You can use three kinds of text fields: single-line text fields, multiline text areas, and password fields.

Inserting Single-Line Text Fields

To insert a single-line text field, place an insertion point inside one of the cells in your layout table and choose Insert | Form Objects | Text Field or click the Text Field button under the Forms tab of the Insert panel.

Dreamweaver adds an input tag, `<input>`, to the source code of your page:

```
<input type="text">
```

The `type` attribute of the input tag defines the form object as a single-line text field by giving the value `"text"`.

Go to the Properties panel to set additional attributes for the text field (see the following illustration). Type a name for the form object in the TextField field. The name should be unique in the sense that no other form object in the form has it, and it should correspond to the name of the variable in the server-side script that references this particular bit of information. The name of the text field appears in the `name` attribute of the input tag:

```
<input type="text" name="yourname">
```

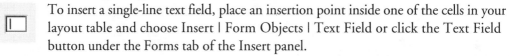

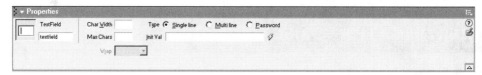

Coordinate with your application developer to make sure that you specify the correct names of form objects in the client-side code.

Type the width of the form object in the Char Width field. HTML measures the width of text fields in characters, not pixels, so if you want the text field to display roughly 30 characters at a time, type **30** in the Char Width field. However, since most browsers use a proportional-pitch font in single-line text fields, there's no telling exactly how many characters will actually appear in the object. Thirty lowercase *i* characters take up less space than 30 lowercase *m* characters, for instance. The value of the Char Width field appears in the `size` attribute of the input tag:

```
<input type="text" name="yourname" size="30">
```

Keep in mind that the size of the text field affects the appearance of the form object, not the amount of text it can hold. That is, a visitor can type more than 30 characters into a size=30 text field. If you want to limit the number of characters that the visitor can type, specify a value in the Max Chars field. To cut the visitor off after 60 characters, type **60** in the Max Chars field. In response, Dreamweaver adds the `maxlength` attribute to the input tag:

```
<input type="text" name="yourname" size="30" maxlength="60">
```

By default, the text field is blank when the page with the form loads. If you want the text field to display a piece of text instead, supply this text in the Init Val field. Dreamweaver adds your default text to the `value` attribute of the input tag:

```
<input type="text" name="yourname" size="30" maxlength="60"
    value="Please type your name here.">
```

Inserting Text Areas

A text area is a larger window that allows the visitor to enter multiple lines of text. To insert a text area, choose Insert | Form Objects | Textarea or click the Textarea button under the Forms tab of the Insert panel.

Alternatively, you can insert a single-line text field, go to the Properties panel, and switch the Type option to Multi Line.

A text area has a different HTML tag than the single-line text field. The text area tag, `<textarea>`, appears in the source code of your page:

```
<textarea></textarea>
```

Notice that there's a closing `</textarea>` tag, unlike the standalone input tag for single-line text objects.

Set the size of the text area in the Char Width field on the Properties panel. You can't specify the maximum number of characters for a text area, but you can determine the default number of rows of text that show on the screen at a time. Set this value in the Num Lines field, which corresponds to the `rows` attribute of the text area tag:

```
<textarea name="message" size="60" rows="5"></textarea>
```

You can supply default text for the text area in the Init Val field of the Properties panel. This text appears between the opening and closing text area tags, not in a `value` attribute:

```
<textarea name="message" size="60" rows="5">Type your message here.</textarea>
```

exam

Watch

The initial value for a text area doesn't appear in the value *attribute. Instead, it appears between the opening and closing text area tags.*

By default, the visitor needs to press ENTER or RETURN to move to the next line in the text area. Look under the Wrap list to choose a method of automatic word wrapping. With word wrapping enabled, the browser inserts a carriage return after the last complete word the visitor types past the right margin of the text area. Set wrapping to Virtual if you want the lines to end in carriage returns on screen only. Set wrapping to Physical if you want the lines to end in carriage returns on screen and in the submission to the Web server. The text area's `wrap` attribute contains the word-wrap setting:

```
<textarea name="message" size="60" rows="5" wrap="virtual">Type your message here.</textarea>
```

To change a text area into a single-line text field, choose the Single Line option from the Type area of the Properties panel.

Inserting Password Fields

A password field is a special kind of single-line text field that shows asterisk characters (*) or bullets no matter what the visitor actually types. (The type of character depends on the visitor's operating system.) Use this object to add a bit of visual security to your form.

To insert a password field, first insert a regular single-line text field and then select the Password option under Type on the Properties panel. A password field looks like this in the source code:

```
<input type="password">
```

As you can see, Dreamweaver uses the input tag again but sets the `type` attribute to `"password"` this time instead of `text`. A password field can have the same attributes as a regular text field, including `name`, `size`, `maxlength`, and `value`.

Inserting Checkboxes

A checkbox is a small, graphical square that the visitor can turn on and off with a click. When the checkbox is on, a check mark appears inside it. When the checkbox is off, the box is blank. Use checkboxes when you want the visitor to choose from a short list of options. Checkbox options aren't mutually exclusive. That is, the visitor can select as many or as few as he or she desires. If you want to require that the visitor choose one of several possibilities, only one of which can be true at a time, use radio buttons instead, as discussed in the next section.

To insert a checkbox, choose Insert | Form Objects | Check Box or click the Checkbox button under the Forms tab of the Insert panel.

Dreamweaver adds the input tag to your source code again, specifying the "checkbox" type in the `type` attribute:

```
<input type="checkbox">
```

The Properties panel gives you a few additional options for checkboxes, as the following illustration shows. Type the name of the checkbox in the CheckBox field.

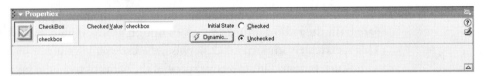

This value goes in the `name` attribute of the input tag:

```
<input type="checkbox" name="colorblack">
```

The Checked Value field contains the value that the form sends to the Web server if the visitor checked the box. The Checked Value field corresponds to the `value` attribute of the input tag:

```
<input type="checkbox" name="black" value="wantsBlack">
```

Under Initial State, determine whether the checkbox should be checked or unchecked when the page with the form loads. If you specify the Checked option, Dreamweaver adds the valueless `checked` attribute to the input tag, like this:

```
<input type="checkbox" name="black" value="wantsBlack" checked>
```

exam
Watch

The `checked` ***attribute of the input tag is valueless. Don't fall for choices like*** `checked="true"` ***or*** `checked="1"` ***on the exam.***

Inserting Radio Buttons

A radio button is a round form object that the visitor can turn on or off. When the radio button is filled, it's on. When the radio button isn't filled, it's off. Use radio buttons when the visitor has a short list of mutually exclusive choices. That is, only one of the choices can be true at the same time, such as shoe size 7, 8, or 9. Only one radio button in a given group can be turned on at a time. Selecting a new radio button automatically deselects the current radio button.

Dreamweaver allows you to insert radio buttons one at a time or in a group.

Inserting a Single Radio Button

To insert a single radio button, choose Insert | Form Objects | Radio Button or click the Radio Button button under the Forms tab of the Insert panel.
Dreamweaver adds the input tag to the HTML, this time with the `type` attribute equal to `"radio"`:

```
<input type="radio">
```

Specify the name of the radio button in the RadioButton field of the Properties panel. All the radio buttons in a given option group should have the same name. This is extremely important! Otherwise, the browser isn't sure which option belongs with which button. Dreamweaver specifies the name of the radio button in the `name` attribute of the input tag:

```
<input type="radio" name="shoesize">
```

In the Checked Value field, type the value that the browser returns to the Web server when the visitor selects the radio button. The Checked Value field corresponds to the `value` attribute of the input tag:

```
<input type="radio" name="shoesize" value="7">
```

One of the radio buttons in a group of options should always be preselected when the page with the form loads. To preselect a radio button, set the Initial State option on the Properties panel to Checked. Dreamweaver adds the valueless `checked` option to the input tag:

```
<input type="radio" name="shoesize" value="7" checked>
```

Inserting a Group of Radio Buttons

To insert a group of radio buttons at the same time, choose Insert | Form Objects | Radio Group or click the Radio Group button under the Forms tab of the Insert panel.

The Radio Group dialog box appears, as shown in the following illustration. Type the name of the option group in the Name field. This value goes into the name attributes of all the input tags. Type a label for each radio button under the Label list. The label appears in the HTML after the input tag; the label itself isn't an attribute of the input tag. Type a checked value for each radio button under the Value list. This is what appears in the value attribute of the input tag for that particular radio button.

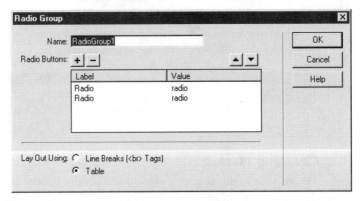

To add more radio buttons to the group, click the plus button. To remove a radio button, select it and click the minus button. Use the arrow buttons to change the order of the radio buttons in the group. Finally, determine how Dreamweaver should lay out the radio group. Select the Line Breaks option to format the radio group without a nested layout table. Select the Table option to use a nested layout table.

Click OK to create the group. Dreamweaver adds an input tag for every radio button in the group, nested between label tags, <label> and </label>, like this:

```
<label>
<input type="radio" name="shoesize" value="7">
Size 7</label>
```

Remember that a group of radio buttons doesn't allow multiple selections.

Inserting Lists and Menus

A list is a form element with multiple options showing simultaneously on the screen. The visitor may select one item or, at your discretion, any number of items in the list, as with checkboxes. A menu is a form element with a single option showing on the screen but with a list of other options in drop-down format. The visitor can choose only one menu item at a time, as with radio buttons. Use lists or menus instead of checkboxes or radio buttons when you have longer sets of options, since lists and menus are more economical in terms of screen real estate, especially in the case of menus.

 To insert a list or menu, choose Insert | Form Objects | List/Menu or click the List/Menu button under the Forms tab of the Insert panel.

When you select a list or menu object, the Properties panel gives you options for modifying the object's attributes, as shown next.

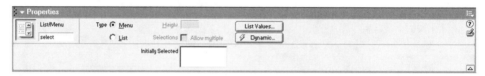

Creating Menus

To create a menu, set the Type option on the Properties panel to Menu. To fill in the options of the menu, click the List Values button, and the List Values dialog box pops up.

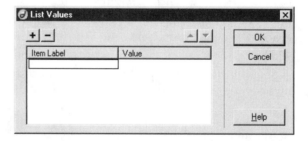

Insert a new menu item by clicking the plus button. Provide the text that appears in the menu under the Item Label column, and in the Value column, type the value that the form sends to the Web server if the visitor selects this item. To erase a menu item, select it and click the minus button. Reorder the menu items with the arrow buttons. Click OK when you finish setting the menu items. Then, in the Properties panel, look for the Initially Selected pane and click the menu item that should appear in the menu by default when the form loads. Provide a name for the menu in the List/Menu field.

Dreamweaver marks up the menu with the select tags. Each menu item appears between opening and closing option tags, like this:

```
<select name="shoesize">
   <option value="7" selected>Size 7</option>
   <option value="8">Size 8</option>
   <option value="9">Size 9</option>
</select>
```

The option tag uses the attribute selected *to indicate a preselected item, not the* checked *attribute of the input tag.*

As you can see, the name of the menu appears in the name attribute of the select tag. The value that goes to the Web server for each option appears in the value attribute of the option tag, and the valueless selected attribute appears in the default option. The text between the opening and closing option tags is the label of the menu item.

Creating Lists

If you want to create a list instead of a menu, set the Type option on the Properties panel to List. In the Height field, indicate the number of options that should appear on the screen simultaneously in the Height field. If your list has more items than the list object shows on screen, the list object automatically scrolls. To allow the visitor to select more than one list item, check the Allow Multiple option. Set the items of the list exactly as you would for a menu.

Dreamweaver uses the select tag to create the list object. The value in the Height field goes in the size attribute of the select tag. If you allow multiple selections, the valueless multiple attribute appears in the select tag, too, like this:

```
<select name="pizzaToppings" size="3" multiple>
   <option value="wantsMushrooms" selected>Mushrooms</option>
   <option value="wantsHotpeppers">Hot peppers</option>
   <option value="wantsXCheese">Extra cheese</option>
   <option value="wantsGreenpeppers">Green peppers</option>
   <option value="wantsOnions">Onions</option>
</select>
```

Remember that lists allow multiple selections and menus do not. Also, don't forget that the value of the Height field goes in the size *attribute of the select tag, not the* height *attribute. There is no* height *attribute in this tag.*

SCENARIO & SOLUTION

When should you use checkboxes?	When you have a short list of options that aren't mutually exclusive.
When should you use radio buttons?	When you have a short list of mutually exclusive options.
When should you use lists?	When you have a long list of options. Set the `multiple` attribute of the select tag when the choices aren't mutually exclusive.
When should you use menus?	When you have a long list of mutually exclusive options.

You've now seen four form objects for presenting options to the visitor: checkboxes, radio buttons, lists, and menus. See the Scenario and Solution sidebar above for a quick reference to help you figure out which form object to use.

Inserting File Fields

A file field is a combination text field and Browse button. This form object allows the visitor to attach and upload a computer file, such as an image or a resume, to the Web server.

To insert a file field, choose Insert | Form Objects | File Field or look under the Forms tab of the Insert panel and click the File Field button.

Dreamweaver uses the input tag once again, setting the `type` attribute to `"file"`:

```
<input type="file">
```

The visitor can type a path to the file for uploading or click the built-in Browse button and navigate to the file, in which case the Web browser automatically provides the correct path.

To set the properties of the file field, select it, and the Properties panel changes accordingly, as shown in the following illustration. Type the name of the object in the FileField Name field, which corresponds to the `name` attribute of the input tag. Specify the width of the text-field element inside this object in the Char Width field, which corresponds to the `size` attribute of the input tag. If you want to limit the number of characters that the visitor can supply, provide that number in the Max Chars field that corresponds to the `maxlength` attribute of the input tag, but be careful! There's no telling where the visitor has stored the file to upload, and the path to this file may be extremely long. You're better off not typing anything into the Max Chars field.

Here's a sample file field with a size of 40 characters but no maximum length:

```
<input type="file" name="uploadResume" size="40">
```

Inserting Hidden Fields

A hidden field is an invisible form object that contains information for the Web server's eyes only, so to speak, such as the forwarding address for e-mail submissions. Visitors don't see the value of the hidden field unless they view the source code of the page.

 To insert a hidden field, choose Insert | Form Objects | Hidden Field or click the Hidden Field button under the Forms tab of the Insert panel.

Supply the name and value of the hidden field by way of the Properties panel. Dreamweaver uses the input tag to create the hidden field. In this input tag, the `type` attribute has the value `"hidden"`. The `name` attribute holds the contents of the HiddenField field of the Properties panel, and the `value` attribute holds the contents of the Value field, like this:

```
<input type="hidden" name="sendTo" value="marc@taotezing.com">
```

Dreamweaver represents the hidden field in the document window with a golden shield icon. Click this icon to call up the properties of the hidden field. To hide the icon entirely in the document window, choose Edit | Preferences. Click the Invisible Elements category and uncheck the option for Hidden Form Fields.

Inserting Buttons

A button is a form object that the visitor clicks to execute a function. Three kinds of buttons are available in HTML: Submit buttons, Reset buttons, and scripting buttons.

FROM THE CLASSROOM

Keep It Simple, Sunshine

Typical form buttons come in two varieties: dull and boring. They're like Swedish furniture; they're supposed be functional, not stylish.

When you're designing a purely graphical button, such as a button for your navigation bar, you can make the button's shape and size help the visitor to figure out its purpose. Not so with form buttons. Since you don't have nearly as many design choices, you have to make absolutely certain that the button's label clearly indicates what happens when the visitor clicks it. The label is usually the only difference between a Submit button, a Reset button, and a scripting button.

It should come as no surprise after my attack on the Click Here's of the world that *Click This Button* is no respectable label. The button itself suggests that the visitor should click. Why restate the obvious?

It's far better if your button label just comes out and says what happens with a click. A simple *Submit* or *Reset* may suffice. However, these labels can be too vague, especially to people who don't surf the Web frequently. I've found that giving a little extra information without the computer jargon of submitting seems to play better. *Send E-mail* or *Place Order* are direct and to the point while conveying more about what the button does than a plain *Submit.*

Don't go much past three words for your label, though, if you can avoid it. Form buttons increase in size quickly, and screen real estate is always at a premium. Besides, a long, verbose Submit button next to a button that simply says *Reset* looks ridiculous.

Inserting a Submit Button

A Submit button sends the information in the form to the Web server. This button usually appears at the bottom of the form, but it doesn't have to. It can appear anywhere in the form.

To insert a Submit button, choose Insert | Form Objects | Button or look under the Forms tab of the Insert panel and click the Button button.

The Properties panel changes, as shown in the next illustration, allowing you to set the properties of the button. Type the name of the button in the Button Name field. Type the label, or the text that appears on the face of the button, in the Label field. Set the Action option to Submit Form.

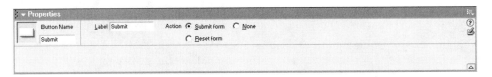

Dreamweaver inserts the input tag into the source code of your page, like this:

```
<input type="submit" name="sendButton" value="Send Your Email">
```

The `type` attribute set to `"submit"` is what makes the browser display a Submit button on the page. The `name` attribute controls the name of the button, and the label of the button appears in the `value` attribute.

There's no limit to the number of Submit buttons that you can place on a form, although you shouldn't need more than one.

Inserting an Image Field An image field is a special kind of Submit button, shown here, that uses your own graphic instead of the default button interface element. To insert an image field in place of a Submit button, choose Insert | Form Objects | Image Field, or click the Image Field button under the Forms tab of the Insert panel.

The Select Image Source dialog box appears. Navigate to your default images folder, and double-click the file of the image that you want to use. Dreamweaver inserts this image as an image field in your form, and the Properties panel changes, as shown here.

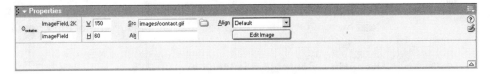

Dreamweaver fills in the width and height of the image in the W and H fields, respectively. You can change these values, but I don't recommend it. If you make the image larger than its original size, the image tends to look grainy or pixilated. If you make the image smaller than its original size, the visitor wastes time downloading the full-sized image.

The Src field contains the path to the image file. Click the folder icon to choose a different image as the image field. Don't forget to specify alternate text for the image in the Alt field.

You may choose an alignment option for the image field from the Align list, although if you inserted the image field into a layout-table cell, use the alignment options of the cell instead for better control.

Dreamweaver marks up the image field with the input tag, like this:

```
<input type="image" name="sendButton" src="images/send.gif" width="150"
   height="60" border="0" alt="The Send button for the e-mail form">
```

The type attribute's "image" value creates an image field, and the name attribute holds the value of the ImageField field on the Properties panel. The other attributes, like src, width, height, border, alt, and align (not shown above), are the same as the image tag's attributes.

on the job

You can use image fields to replace only Submit buttons. You can't use them in place of Reset buttons or scripting buttons.

Inserting a Reset Button

A Reset button erases the values of all the objects in the form and returns them to their default state. Like a Submit button, a Reset button can appear anywhere in the form. Not all forms have Reset buttons, mainly because this type of button isn't nearly as vital as the Submit variety. If your form is long, though, you should consider adding a Reset button to the form as a courtesy to your visitors.

You insert a Reset button in the same way that you insert a Submit button. Except, in the Properties panel, you set the Action option to Reset Form.

The type attribute of the input tag changes from submit to reset, but the other attributes—name and value—have the same functions. You can place as many Reset buttons on your form as you like, although you shouldn't need more than one.

Inserting Scripting Buttons

A scripting button is a button that launches a client-side script. You insert a scripting button in the same way that you insert a Submit button once again, except this time set the Action option in the Properties panel to None. The type attribute of the input tag becomes "button".

To specify the JavaScript that launches when the visitor clicks the button, open the Tag Inspector panel, and click the button in the document window. Go back to the Tag Inspector, find the onClick event, and type the name of the JavaScript function. Dreamweaver adjusts the input tag as follows:

```
<input type="button" name="spellCheckerButton" value="Launch Spell Check"
   onClick="spellCheck()">
```

You can add as many scripting buttons to your form as you need.

EXERCISE 7-2

Adding Form Objects to the Mad Science LLC Contact Us Page

In this exercise, you finish what you started in Exercise 7-1.

1. Launch Dreamweaver, open the Site panel, and set the site to Mad Science LLC.

2. Double-click the *index.htm* file in the *contact* folder. Dreamweaver opens the file in a document window.

3. Click inside the left table cell in the top row. Choose the first set of fonts from the font list on the Properties panel, turn on the boldface style, and type **Name** in the cell.

4. Click inside the table cell on the right in the same row. Switch to the Forms tab of the Insert panel and click the Text Field button. Dreamweaver adds a text field to the cell. In the TextField field of the Properties panel, type **name** as the name of the field.

5. Click inside the left table cell in the second row. Set the font and style as in step 3 and type **Email address** in the cell. Insert another text field in the adjacent table cell and type **email** in the TextField field of the Properties panel.

6. Click inside the left table cell in the third row. Set the font and style as you did in step 3 and type **Phone number** in the cell. Insert a third text field in the adjacent table cell, and type **phoneno** in the TextField field of the Properties panel. Type **14** in the Max Chars field. (Why 14? This allows for a 10-digit phone number plus parentheses for the area code, a space between the area code and phone number, and a dash.)

7. Click inside the left table cell in the fourth row. Set the font and style as in step 3 and type **Message** in the cell. Insert a text area in the adjacent cell with the Textarea button. Type **message** in the TextField field of the Properties panel. Type **40** in the Char Width field. Type **5** in the Num Lines field. Set the Wrap list to Virtual.

8. Click inside the left table cell in the fifth row. Set the font as in step 3, but don't apply boldface. Type **When is the best time to reach you?** In the adjacent table cell, click the Radio Group button on the Insert panel. Type **bestTime** in the Name field of the Radio Group dialog box. Add a third radio button to the group by clicking the plus button. Then, set the labels to Day, Evening, and Night and the values to isDay, isEvening, and isNight. Click the Table

option at the bottom of the dialog box to organize the radio group in a nested layout table. Click OK to insert the radio buttons. Select the Night radio button in the document window and set the Initial State option on the Properties panel to Checked.

9. Change the set of fonts for the radio-button labels to the first set in the font list.

10. Click inside the left table cell in the sixth row. Set the font as in step 8 and type **What types of monsters interest you?** Switch to the Common tab of the Insert panel. Click inside the adjacent table cell and add a new nested table with the Insert Table button. Type **2** in the Rows field and type **1** in the Columns field. Set the width to 100% and click OK.

11. Switch back to the Forms tab of the Insert panel. Click inside the top cell of the new nested layout table and insert a checkbox by clicking the Checkbox button on the Insert panel. Type **typeClassic** in the CheckBox field of the Properties panel. Type **likesClassic** in the Checked Value field. Then type **Classic** next to the checkbox in the cell. Set the font as you did in step 8.

12. Insert another checkbox in the bottom cell of the new layout table. Type **typeDesigner** in the CheckBox field. Type **likesDesigner** in the Checked Value field. Type **Designer** next to the checkbox in the cell and set the font as in step 8.

13. Hold down CTRL (Windows) or COMMAND (Mac) and select both cells in the bottom row of the form's main layout table. Click the Merge Cells button in the Properties panel.

14. Click the Button button in the Insert panel. Type **sendButton** in the Button Name field on the Properties panel. Type **Send Email** in the Label field and set the Action option to Submit Form.

15. Press the right-arrow key. The flashing cursor appears to the right of the Submit button. Choose Insert | Special Characters | Non-Breaking Space. Then click the Button button again in the Insert panel. Type **clearButton** in the Button Name field, type **Clear Form** in the Label field and set the Action option to Reset Form.

16. Press the right-arrow key. The flashing cursor appears to the right of Reset button. Go to the Properties panel and set the Horz list to Center. This centers the buttons in their cell.

17. Click the Send Email button and press the left-arrow key. The flashing cursor appears to the left of the Submit button. Press ENTER or RETURN to insert a carriage return. This separates the buttons from the rest of the form for purely aesthetic reasons.

18. Hold down CTRL (Windows) or COMMAND (Mac) and select the left table cells in the fourth, fifth, and sixth rows. Set the Vert list on the Properties panel to Top.

19. Hold down CTRL (Windows) or COMMAND (Mac) and select the left table cells in the first, second, and third rows in addition to the cells that you selected in step 18. Set the Horz list on the Properties panel to Right.

20. Your screen should look like Figure 7-4.

21. Choose File | Save.

22. Press F12 and test your form in a live browser window. Play with all the controls except the Submit button. (If you insist upon playing with the Submit button,

FIGURE 7-4

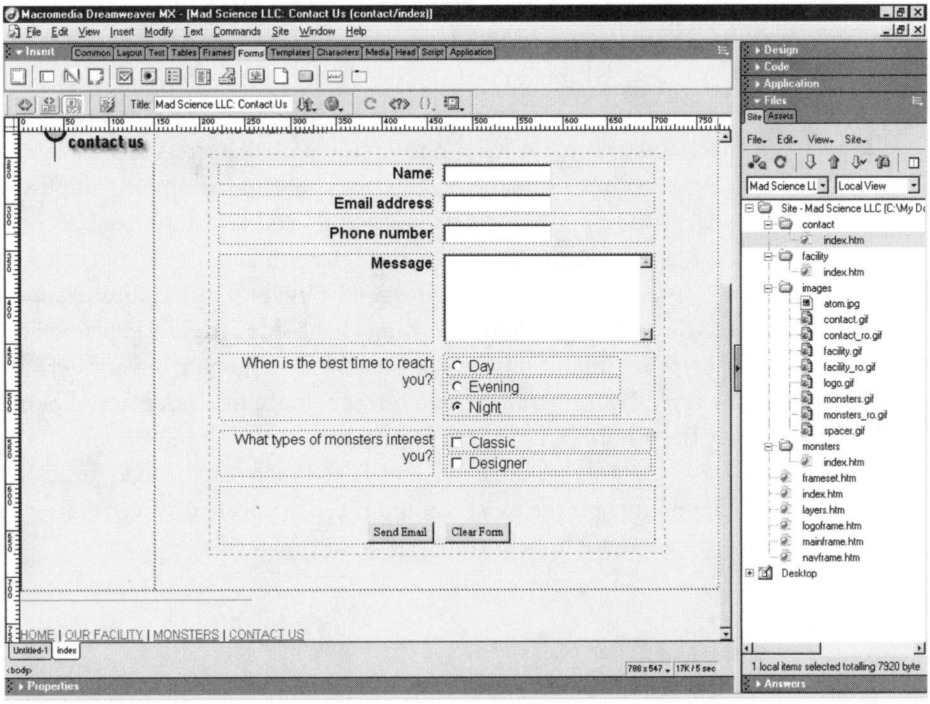

Add form objects and captions to the table cells.

like the technical editor of this book did, you won't do any damage, but you will find that the button doesn't work. Since your form tag doesn't have an `action` attribute, the browser doesn't know where to direct the form submission. Normally, you'd supply the path to the form's server-side component in the `action` attribute.)

23. Close the browser window. Well done!

CERTIFICATION SUMMARY

In this chapter, you learned how to create HTML forms. I explained that most forms have two components: a client-side component and a server-side component. The client-side component includes the visual interface elements of the form and client-side scripts for validating the form's data and performing simple tasks. The server-side component is the CGI script or Web app that retrieves the form data. I talked about the importance of adding form tags to your Dreamweaver document, and you saw the advantage to inserting form objects into cells of layout tables.

You learned about the various widgets or form objects available to you. I discussed the differences between single-line text fields and multiline text areas, and I told you that you can't set the maximum number of characters in a text area. You learned to use checkboxes and radio buttons for short lists of options and lists and menus for longer lists of options. Checkboxes and lists allow multiple selections, while radio buttons and menus allow only one selection at a time.

You learned that three actions can be used for form buttons: submitting form data, resetting form data, and launching client-side scripts. I explained that the image field is a type of Submit button that substitutes a graphic in your default images folder for the typical button design. You can use image fields in place of Submit buttons only, not Reset buttons or scripting buttons.

You learned that three different HTML tags can be used for inserting form objects. The input tag is the most common. See the Scenario and Solution sidebar for a quick reference to help you keep them straight.

SCENARIO & SOLUTION

Which form objects use the input tag, `<input>`?	Single-line text fields (`text`), password fields (`password`), checkboxes (`check`), radio buttons (`radio`), file fields (`file`), hidden fields (`hidden`), Submit buttons (`submit`), image fields (`image`), Reset buttons (`reset`), scripting buttons (`button`)
Which form object uses opening and closing text area tags, `<textarea>` and `</textarea>`?	Multiline text fields, also known as text areas
Which form objects use opening and closing select tags, `<select>` and `</select>`, with nested option tags, `<option>` and `</option>`?	Lists and menus

TWO-MINUTE DRILL

Building Forms

- ❑ Most forms contain a client-side component and a server-side component.
- ❑ The client-side component contains the interface elements of the form, as well as client-side scripts.
- ❑ The server-side component is the CGI script or Web app that retrieves and processes the form's information.
- ❑ All the interface elements of your form should appear between form tags.
- ❑ Dreamweaver's document window displays form tags as a red rectangle with dotted lines.
- ❑ The action attribute of the form tag contains the path to the server-side script or app.
- ❑ The method attribute of the form tag determines how the browser submits the form information to the server.
- ❑ Use the post method whenever possible to improve the security of the submission process.

Inserting Form Objects

- ❑ Use text fields, text areas, and password fields when you want the visitor to type information.
- ❑ Use checkboxes when you want the visitor to select multiple possibilities from a short list of options, and use radio buttons when you want to the visitor to select from a short list of mutually exclusive options.
- ❑ Use a list or menu object when you want the visitor to select from a longer list of options.
- ❑ A list object can take multiple choices simultaneously, while a menu object can take only a single choice.
- ❑ Use a file field when you want your visitors to upload files from their systems to the Web server.

❑ Use a Submit button to submit the information on the form and use a Reset button to return the form objects to their default settings.

❑ Replace standard Submit buttons with an image field.

❑ Use scripting buttons to launch a client-side JavaScript functions.

SELF TEST

The following questions will help you measure your understanding of the material presented in this chapter. Read all the choices carefully because there might be more than one correct answer. Choose all correct answers for each question.

Building Forms

1. You're clicking the Submit button on your form, but nothing happens. What's the likely cause of this problem?

    A. You didn't type anything in the Method field on the Properties panel.

    B. You didn't type anything in the Action field on the Properties panel.

    C. You didn't specify a target from the Target list.

    D. You didn't supply a name for the form.

2. Which form-submission method offers more secure transmission?

    A. get

    B. post

    C. The get and post methods both offer the same level of security.

3. Which form-submission method is better for long forms?

    A. get

    B. post

    C. The get and post methods are both fine for long forms.

4. What happens if you forget to place form objects inside a pair of form tags?

    A. You can crash the Web server.

    B. The form objects don't appear in some Web browsers.

    C. You can't submit the form.

    D. Your page doesn't display red dotted lines in a browser window.

5. Which of the following are possible server-side components of a form?

    A. CGI script

    B. ColdFusion app

    C. JavaScript function

    D. ASP.NET app

6. Which of these form functions can't you enable with client-side scripting?

   A. Checking that required fields are filled in

   B. Jumping to a new Web page

   C. Processing a password field

   D. Storing a credit card number in a database

7. How do you insert form tags in your page? Choose the best answer.

   A. Click this button:

   B. Click this button:

   C. Click this button:

   D. Click this button:

8. What's the usual MIME type for forms with a file field?

   A. *application/x-www-form-urlencoded*

   B. *multipart/form-dat*a

   C. *text/plain*

   D. None of the above

9. Why is it a good idea to build a form in a layout table?

   A. The form tends to look better.

   B. The form tends to be more usable.

   C. The Web server tends to have an easier time processing the form information.

   D. You can align form objects more easily.

10. How many pairs of form tags should a form have?

    A. One

    B. Two

    C. Three

    D. It depends on how many form objects you use.

Inserting Form Objects

11. Which attribute of the input tag controls the width of a text field?

    A. `length`

    B. `width`

    C. `size`

    D. `maxchar`

12. Which of the following properties doesn't Dreamweaver let you apply to a text area?

    A. Maximum number of characters

    B. Number of rows

    C. Character width

    D. Initial value

13. You want to define an image field for your form's Reset button. Why isn't Dreamweaver cooperating? Choose the best answer.

    A. You haven't selected the image field, so the Properties panel hasn't reconfigured itself for image-field options.

    B. You can't use an image field in place of a Reset button.

    C. You haven't added a Submit button yet.

    D. You already have a Reset button.

14. Which form objects use the select tag?

    A. Lists

    B. Menus

    C. Checkboxes

    D. Radio buttons

E. File fields

F. Radio groups

15. Your visitors purchase ice cream cones from your site. You offer small, medium, and large cones. When your visitor orders a single cone, which form object makes the most sense in determining the size? Choose the best answer.

A. Checkboxes

B. Text fields

C. Radio buttons

D. Image fields

16. Which property of a radio group must remain the same for all members of the group?

A. Name

B. Label

C. Value

D. Default checked state

17. Where does a menu item's label appear in the HTML?

A. In the `label` attribute of the select tag

B. Between label tags, `<label>` and `</label>`

C. Between option tags, `<option>` and `</option>`

D. In the `name` attribute of the option tag

18. Which of the following form objects allow the visitor to choose multiple options?

A. Checkboxes

B. Lists

C. Menus

D. Radio buttons

19. What does `wrap="virtual"` mean in the text area tag?

A. Word wrap is disabled.

B. Automatic carriage returns appear on screen only.

C. Automatic carriage returns appear in the server submission only.

D. Automatic carriage returns appear on screen and in the server submission.

20. What is a hidden field?

    A. A single-line text field where all the characters appear as asterisks

    B. A menu item that doesn't appear when the visitor opens the drop-down list

    C. A form object that appears only in the source code of the page

    D. A form object that doesn't appear in the browser window or the source code

LAB QUESTION

Your latest client, Pepe's Pizza, wants visitors to submit takeout orders via the Web. Pepe's offers pizza in three sizes: small, medium, and large. Toppings include mushrooms, green peppers, onions, extra cheese, hot peppers, pepperoni, black olives, and sausage. Soft drinks include cola, lemon-lime, orange, and root beer.

Build a form that asks for the customer's last name, ten-digit phone number, five-digit ZIP code, and order. Don't forget Submit and Reset buttons. Select size large and extra cheese initially, and allow the customer to choose multiple soft drinks.

SELF TEST ANSWERS

Building Forms

1. ☑ **B.** If you don't specify an action, the Submit button doesn't know where on the server to send the information.
☒ **A** is incorrect, because even if you don't specify a method, most browsers assume get. **C** and **D** are incorrect because not having these properties doesn't prevent the form from submitting its information.

2. ☑ **B.** The post method is more secure than the get method.
☒ **A** and **C** are incorrect because the get method appends form data to a URL.

3. ☑ **B.** The post method is better for long forms.
☒ **A** and **C** are incorrect because the get method truncates submission data after 8192 characters.

4. ☑ **B and C.** Some browsers don't display the form objects, and you can't submit the form.
☒ **A** is incorrect because the client, the Web browser, processes HTML code, not the Web server. **D** is incorrect because the red dotted lines appear only in Dreamweaver's document window, not the browser window.

5. ☑ **A, B, and D.** A CGI script, a ColdFusion app, and an ASP.NET app are all possible server-side components of a form.
☒ **C** is incorrect because JavaScript is a client-side scripting language.

6. ☑ **D.** Client-side scripting can't store a credit card number in a database.
☒ **A, B,** and **C** are incorrect because client-side scripting can handle all these tasks, none of which require the server to retrieve form data.

7. ☑ **A.** That's the Form button.
☒ **B** is incorrect because it's the Textarea button. **C** is incorrect because it's the Radio Group button. **D** is incorrect because it's the Hidden field button.

8. ☑ **B.** The MIME type *multipart/form-data* is the one for forms with a file field.
☒ **A, C,** and **D** are incorrect because the *multipart/form-data* MIME type is the usual MIME type for forms with a file field. Choice **A** is common to forms that use the post method, which could apply to forms with a file field. However, choice **B** is the better answer.

9. ☑ **A, B,** and **D.** A layout table improves the look, usability, and alignment options of the form.
☒ **C** is incorrect because the Web server doesn't care what the form looks like.

10. ☑ A. Each form needs only one pair of form tags.
    ☒ B, C, and D are incorrect because each form needs only one pair of form tags. Moreover, the number of form objects doesn't affect the number of form tags.

Inserting Form Objects

11. ☑ C. The size attribute controls the width of the text field.
    ☒ A and B are incorrect because a text field doesn't have a width or length attribute. D is incorrect because the maxlength attribute determines the maximum number of characters the visitor can type into the field.

12. ☑ A. Text areas don't have a property for controlling the maximum number of characters.
    ☒ B, C, and D are incorrect because text areas have these properties.

13. ☑ B. Image fields replace Submit buttons only, not Reset buttons.
    ☒ A is incorrect because the Properties panel for image fields doesn't give you an option for resetting the form. C is incorrect because you don't need a Submit button to insert an image field or a Reset button. D is incorrect because you can have more than one Reset button in your form.

14. ☑ A and B. Lists and menus use the select tag.
    ☒ C, D, E, and F are incorrect because these objects use the input tag.

15. ☑ C. Use radio buttons. A single cone can't simultaneously be small, medium, and large.
    ☒ A is incorrect because checkboxes allow the user to choose more than one size for the same cone. B is incorrect because text fields are too open-ended. Radio buttons are the better choice here. D is incorrect because an image field is like a Submit button.

16. ☑ A. The Name property must remain the same for all members of a radio group.
    ☒ B, C, and D are incorrect because each radio button in the group can have a different label and value, and only one radio button per group should be selected by default.

17. ☑ C. The label of a menu item appears between option tags.
    ☒ A is incorrect because the select tag doesn't have a label attribute. B is incorrect because the label tags don't apply to menus or lists. D is incorrect because the option tag doesn't have a name attribute.

18. ☑ A and B. Checkboxes and lists allow the visitor to select multiple options.
    ☒ C and D are incorrect because these objects allow the visitor to select only a single option..

19. ☑ **B.** With the `wrap` attribute set to `"virtual"` in the text area tag, automatic carriage returns appear on screen only.

☒ **A** is incorrect because `wrap="off"` turns off word wrap. **C** is incorrect because there isn't a `wrap` value that submits automatic carriage returns to the Web server only. **D** is incorrect because `wrap="physical"` causes automatic carriage returns on screen and in the server submission.

20. ☑ **C.** A hidden field appears only in the source code of the page.

☒ **A** is incorrect because this description applies to a password field. **B** is incorrect because all the options in a menu appear when the visitor opens the drop-down list. **D** is incorrect because the hidden field appears in the source code. A form object that doesn't appear in the browser window or the source code is not only hidden, it's nonexistent.

LAB ANSWER

See Figure 7-5 for my solution. Your form may look different, of course, but here are some guidelines for acceptability.

1. The text field for the phone number should have a maximum-character value of 10, and the text field for the ZIP code should have a maximum-character value of 5.

2. The Size field should either be a radio group or a menu, and Large should be preselected.

3. The Toppings field should either be a list or a series of checkboxes, and Extra Cheese should be preselected.

4. The Soft Drinks field should either be a list or a series of checkboxes. Nothing should be preselected.

5. You should include a Submit button and a Reset button.

   You can find the HTML code for my version of the form in the *examples/ch07* folder of the CD-ROM. Look for the file called *pepeform.htm*.

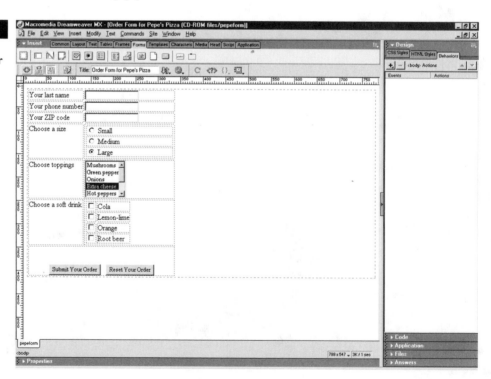

FIGURE 7-5

Here's the order form for Pepe's Pizza.

8

Using Behaviors

A *behavior* is a special interactive function that Dreamweaver achieves by way of client-side scripting. Even though adding behaviors to your site can significantly enhance your site's functionality, behaviors by themselves don't make a dynamic site, as Dreamweaver understands the term. Remember that a dynamic site is one that uses server-side scripting in addition to or in place of client-side scripting.

As you may recall from working with forms that you get a certain amount of mileage from client-side scripting alone. Some forms don't require a server-side component to function as you intend. Likewise, not all sites need to be dynamic. The arsenal of behaviors that Dreamweaver provides makes a compelling case for this point of view.

This chapter shows you how to enhance your site with client-side behaviors.

CERTIFICATION OBJECTIVE 8.01

Working with Triggers, Events, and Actions

Adding a behavior to your site involves choosing an element on one of the pages to serve as the trigger. This element can be a button, a hyperlink, a graphic, or even the body tag. You attach the desired behavior to this element so that when the element loads in the browser window, or when the visitor clicks the right button, image, or hyperlink, the behavior activates. It performs its function and returns its result.

Every behavior in Dreamweaver, then, has three components: the trigger, the event, and the action. The *trigger* is the element on the page to which you attach the behavior. The *event* is the thing that happens to the trigger to cause the behavior to activate, such as clicking the trigger, moving the mouse over the trigger, or simply loading the page that contains the trigger. Literally dozens of events are possible. The type and version of the visitor's browser determines which kinds of events can apply to the trigger that you select. In general, the more recent the browser, the greater the variety of events. Microsoft Internet Explorer 4.0, for instance, gives you six possible events for the Go To URL behavior. Internet Explorer 6.0 gives you 40 possible events for the same behavior.

Finally, the *action* is what happens when the event activates the trigger. These actions take the form of JavaScript functions, which work reliably in Internet

Explorer 4.0 and above, Netscape Navigator 4.0 and above, and most other JavaScript-enabled browsers.

exam
ⓦatch

Make sure you understand the purposes of the trigger, the event, and the action of a behavior.

Choosing a Trigger

To choose the trigger of a behavior in Design view, simply click the desired element. Use the Tag Selector at the bottom of the document window to fine-tune your selection. For instance, if you select a form object in the document window but you want to attach the behavior to the form itself, not the particular form object you selected, go to the Tag Selector and click the form tag.

To choose the trigger of the behavior in Code view, click the tag of the desired element in the HTML.

You can check to make sure you selected the correct trigger in the Behaviors panel. To open the Behaviors panel, choose Window | Behaviors or open the Design panel group and click the Behaviors tab. The trigger appears to the right of the minus button (see the following illustration). If you select a text field, for instance, the Behaviors panel says *<text> Actions*. If you use the Tag Selector to select the form tag instead, the Behaviors panel says *<form> Actions*.

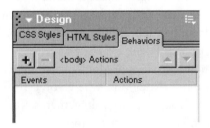

The trigger you choose determines the available events and actions. Not all triggers support the same behaviors. For instance, image and hyperlink triggers allow the Show Popup Menu behavior, while button triggers do not.

Using the Body Tag as a Trigger

Most triggers are easy to figure out. If you want to launch the Go To URL behavior when the visitor clicks a particular button, the button to click becomes the trigger.

If you want to open a pop-up window when the visitor hovers over a particular graphic with the mouse pointer, the graphic becomes the trigger.

However, you might want to attach a behavior to your page that doesn't seem to have a discernible trigger, such as a pop-up alert that appears whenever the page loads. The visitor doesn't click anything to activate this behavior. The behavior seems to activate itself.

In cases like these, attach the behavior to the body tag of the page. To select the body tag, go into Code view and click the opening body tag or click a blank area of the document window in Design view. Double-check that the Behaviors panel says *<body> Actions* before you attach the behavior. If not, select the body tag in the Tag Selector at the bottom of the document window.

Attaching an Action

After you select an element as the trigger, attach an action by clicking the plus button in the Behaviors panel. A menu drops down with the available actions, as shown in Figure 8-1. Grayed-out actions don't work with the particular element that you selected as the trigger.

Choose the action that you want to attach. A dialog box appears in which you can set the specifics of the behavior. Fill out the dialog box and click OK. The action appears in the Behaviors panel, to the right of the event that activates this action.

Dreamweaver adds the JavaScript functions that produce the action to the top of the document source. The functions appear between script tags, `<script>` and `</script>`, as Figure 8-2 shows.

To modify a behavior, double-click its action in the Behaviors panel. This copens the behavior's dialog box, where you can tweak the values you entered. To remove a behavior from your page altogether, select the behavior in the Behaviors panel and click the minus button at the top of the panel.

Changing the Event

Dreamweaver automatically assigns an event to the action that you attach. Perhaps the most common events are `onClick`, `onMouseOver`, `onMouseOut`, and `onLoad`. The `onClick` event signifies that the action launches when the visitor clicks the trigger element. The `onMouseOver` event signifies that the action launches when the visitor hovers over the trigger element with the mouse pointer. The `onMouseOut` event

FIGURE 8-1

Click the plus button on the Behaviors panel to attach a behavior to the selected element.

indicates that the action launches when the visitor moves the mouse pointer away from the trigger element after first hovering over it. The onLoad event means that the action launches when the trigger element loads in the browser window. The visitor doesn't have to do anything to launch the action, in other words. (See the Scenario and Solution sidebar for a quick reference listing several common events and their significance.)

FIGURE 8-2   Dreamweaver adds the JavaScript functions that produce the action to the top of the source code. Look between the script tags.

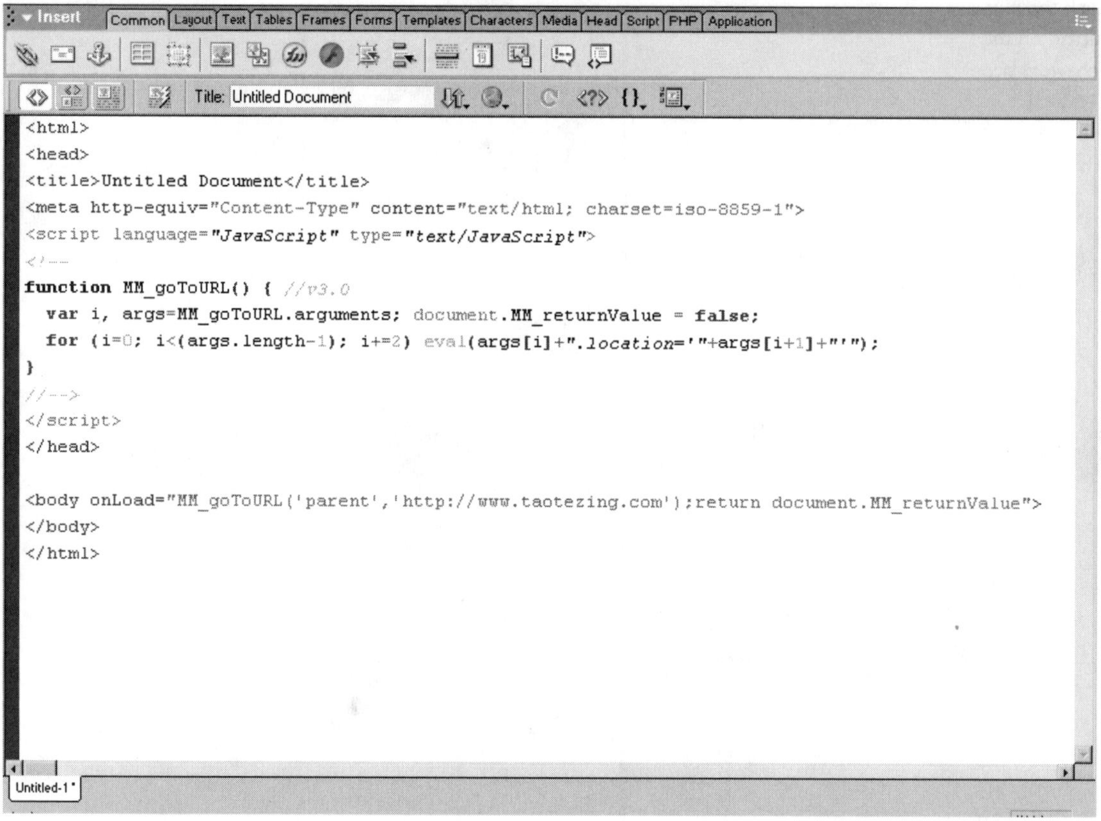

In most cases, you can change the event to suit your needs. To do so, click the corresponding behavior in the Behaviors panel. A gray button appears to the right of the event. Click this button to open a menu of events, as shown in Figure 8-3.

The event often appears inside the HTML tag of the trigger. For example, if you attach the Go To URL behavior to a button and specify the onClick event, the source code looks something like this:

```
<input name="Button" type="button" value="Go to Tao Te Zing"
    onClick="MM_goToURL('parent','http://www.taotezing.com');
    return document.MM_returnValue">
```

SCENARIO & SOLUTION

What causes the `onClick` event?	The visitor clicks the trigger.
What causes the `onMouseOver` event?	The visitor hovers over the trigger with the mouse pointer.
What causes the `onMouseOut` event?	The visitor moves the mouse pointer away from the trigger after hovering over it.
What causes the `onLoad` event?	The trigger loads in the browser window.
What causes the `onFocus` event?	The page gives control to the trigger element.
What causes the `onBlur` event?	The page's focus moves away from the trigger.
What causes the `onResize` event?	The visitor resizes the browser window.

FIGURE 8-3

Change the event
for a behavior by
clicking the
button to the
right of the event
in the Behaviors
panel.

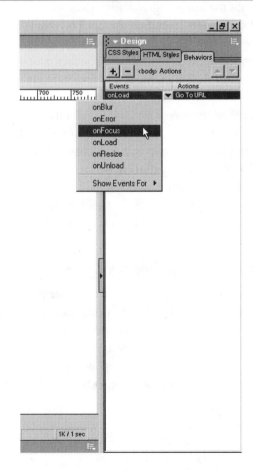

Here, a button with the label *Go to Tao Te Zing* launches the JavaScript function MM_goToURL when the visitor clicks. The items inside the parentheses are the values that the code passes to the function.

If the HTML tag of the trigger doesn't permit the JavaScript event you want, such as the onClick event for the image tag, <img>, in 4.0 browsers, Dreamweaver nests the trigger between a pair of anchor tags, <a> and </a>:

```
<a href="javascript:;" onClick="MM_goToURL('parent',
   'http://www.taotezing.com');return document.MM_returnValue">
<img src="img/zinglogo.jpg" width="150" height="50" border="0"
alt="Go to the Tao Te Zing site"></a>
```

I created this example by attaching the Go To URL behavior to an image and changing the event from onLoad to onClick. Dreamweaver added the anchor tags automatically. As you can see, the onClick event appears inside the opening anchor tag, not the image tag, although the end result is the same to the visitor. The visitor clicks the image to launch the Go To URL behavior.

Notice that the href attribute of the anchor tag gives the value "javascript:;" instead of a URL. This value is another type of *null link,* or a link without a URL definition. No URL loads when the visitor clicks a null link. You'll recall from Chapter 6 that the null link href="#" has the side effect of resetting the browser window to the top of the page. The null link href="javascript:;" has no such side effect. Earlier versions of Dreamweaver used the null link href="#" with behaviors. Dreamweaver MX uses href="javascript:;" instead.

When an event appears between parentheses in the menu that drops down when you click the button to the right of the event, that's your signal that the event applies to links only. Dreamweaver must nest the trigger element between anchor tags and apply the event to the anchor, not the trigger.

Targeting Browsers for Events

As I mentioned, the visitor's browser determines the kinds of events that you can reliably specify. Older browsers support just a handful of events. Newer browsers, particularly those from Microsoft, support a small army of them.

To choose from events for a particular browser, select a behavior from the Behaviors panel and click the down-arrow button to the right of the event. Then, select Show Events For and choose the target browser from the submenu that slides out.

Dreamweaver offers two generic choices in the menu: 3.0 And Later Browsers and 4.0 And Later Browsers. When you choose one of these targets, Dreamweaver limits your event choices to those that work in the 3.0 or 4.0 versions of Microsoft and Netscape browsers.

The newer the browser, the more events you get, and the most recent versions of Internet Explorer offer the most diverse set of events—far more than the competing versions of the Netscape browsers. Explorer-friendly events cause Web developers to drool, with options like onAfterPrint, which launches after the printer finishes a job, or onMouseWheel, which launches when the visitor uses the wheel control on newer Microsoft mouses. The interactive possibilities are extremely tempting. It's a good idea, though, not to get carried away with obscure, Microsoft-only events. You want to make your page compatible with as many user agents as possible, and Microsoft isn't the only browser maker in the world. Set Dreamweaver to display events for version 4.0 browsers and above. This way, you get the best possible assortment of events for the widest cross-section of the most popular browsers.

If you insist on trying the Microsoft-only events, make sure they control behaviors that aren't mission-critical to your site's success. A pop-up window that appears after the printer finishes a job might be a nice bonus for visitors who choose IE, and Netscape people won't necessarily know what they're missing. However, if the pop-up window contains vital information, like the address to which to mail the printout, you're better off finding a different event.

Along the same lines, don't choose the option for 3.0 And Later Browsers. Most of Dreamweaver's behaviors don't work in IE 3.0, and not all the behaviors work in Navigator 3.0. It's pointless to limit your events to 3.0 browsers if you want to appeal to users of Netscape, as well as IE. If a sizable contingent of your audience is still clunking around the Web in a 3.0 browser, my advice to you is not to use behaviors at all.

e x a m
ⓦ a t c h
Familiarize yourself with common events for 4.0 browsers, since version 4.0 is the usual baseline for working with behaviors in Dreamweaver. Commonly supported events for version-4.0 browsers include onClick, onMouseOver, onMouseOut, onLoad, onFocus, onBlur, *and* onResize.

Adding a Behavior to the Mad Science LLC Contact Us Page

In this exercise, you add the Validate Form behavior to the e-mail form on Mad Science LLC's Contact Us page.

1. Launch Dreamweaver, open the Site panel, and set the site to Mad Science LLC.

2. Open the folder *contact* and double-click the file *index.htm*. The Contact Us page opens in a document window.

3. Open the Behaviors panel. You can find this panel in the Design panel group or choose Window | Behaviors.

4. Select the Send E-mail button in the document window. The Behaviors panel says *<submit> Actions*, indicating that you've selected a Submit button as the trigger for the behavior.

5. Click the plus button of the Behaviors panel and choose Validate Form from the menu that drops down. This opens the Validate Form dialog box.

6. You'll set the options for this behavior in Exercise 8-2. For now, click the *Text "Name"* item in the Named Fields area of the dialog box and check the Required option to make the Name field a required field. Dreamweaver adds an *(R)* next to this item under Named Fields. Your Validate Form dialog box should look like this:

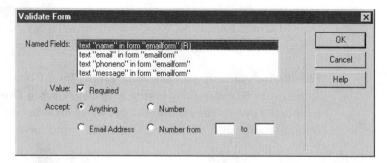

7. Click OK. Dreamweaver adds the behavior to the Behaviors panel.

8. Press F12 to test the page in a live browser. When you click the Submit button without typing anything into the Name field, the page alerts you that you need to fill in the name. Close the browser window.

9. Choose File | Save, and you're done. Good job!

Working with Multiple Behaviors

You can attach more than one behavior to the same trigger. Multiple behaviors on the same trigger can have the same event or different events. When they have the same event, like onClick, the behaviors launch in the order in which they appear in the Behaviors panel. The topmost behavior happens first. The bottommost behavior happens last. For instance, assume that you attach the Popup Message and Validate Form behaviors to a Submit button on your page, both of which specify the onClick event. If you attach the Popup Message behavior first and the Validate Form behavior second, the Popup Message behavior sits at the top of the Behaviors panel, which means that the pop-up message appears first, followed by the form validation, after the visitor clicks the Submit button. To change the order in which these behaviors occur, highlight a behavior and change its position using the arrow buttons on the Behaviors panel.

Watch out for multiple behaviors when you call new URLs or open new browser windows. Once the current page opens a new page, the old page passes control, or *focus,* to the new page, and the JavaScript on the old page stops working. As a result, pending behaviors on the old page don't launch. For this reason, if you attach multiple actions with the same event to the same trigger element, the Go To URL and Open Browser Window behaviors should always appear last in the Behaviors panel.

When multiple behaviors have different events, the behaviors don't launch in any specific order. Rather, the events determine which behavior activates. Therefore, the order in which the behaviors appear in the Behaviors panel isn't as important. For example, if a hyperlink has the Set Text behavior with the onMouseOver event and the PopUp Message behavior with the onClick event, the pop-up message appears when the visitor clicks the hyperlink, and the Set Text behavior happens when the visitor hovers over the link with the mouse pointer. No matter which behavior comes first in the Behaviors panel, your page functions exactly the same way.

Troubleshooting Behaviors

All Dreamweaver behaviors work because of JavaScript, which is processed by the visitor's browser, not the Web server. Behaviors reduce the amount of strain on your overtaxed Web server by delegating some of the processing duties.

Because behaviors are JavaScript-driven, behaviors work only in JavaScript-enabled browsers. All the most popular browsers like Netscape, IE, and Opera have been JavaScript-enabled for many years now. The user, however, can easily turn off JavaScript processing in the browser preferences, which renders your behaviors useless. Your behaviors disappear without warning in this case, unless you specify noscript content. See Chapter 5 for a refresher course in adding noscript content to your page.

on the **J**ob

Remember that your visitor can disable all the behaviors on your page simply by turning off JavaScript in the browser preferences.

CERTIFICATION OBJECTIVE 8.02

Exploring Behaviors

Now that you know what behaviors are and how they work, you can explore the array of behaviors that come with Dreamweaver MX. This section organizes Dreamweaver behaviors according to function, which is often but not always the name of the action in the Behaviors panel. The functions are as follows:

- Opening new browser windows
- Creating pop-up messages
- Calling URLs
- Controlling images
- Playing sounds
- Controlling movies
- Checking for specific browsers and plug-ins

- Changing the status bar
- Calling JavaScripts
- Controlling layers
- Changing frame content
- Controlling forms
- Creating pop-up menus

As you experiment, keep in mind that Dreamweaver's document window doesn't show behaviors in action. You must preview your page in a live browser window to test your behaviors.

Opening New Browser Windows

The Open Browser Window behavior opens a new browser window and loads up a specified Web page. You can control the appearance and attributes of the new browser window, shown next. By leaving all the attributes in the Open Browser Window dialog box unchecked and specifying relatively small width and height values, you create what is essentially a pop-up window.

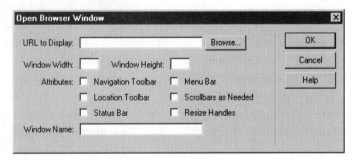

Creating Pop-Up Messages

A pop-up message differs from a new browser window in that the message appears in a system dialog box. This message contains text only—you can't add images, links, or other design elements. Pop-up messages work well for quick FYIs or alerts to the visitor.

FROM THE CLASSROOM

The Other Shoe Dropping

There's no doubt about it. Dreamweaver behaviors are cool. The ability to add quick, cross-browser–compatible, client-side scripts is one of the reasons I switched from hand coding to Dreamweaver in the first place. And these behaviors have strong magic. They do many, many things. Once you start adding them, it's hard to stop.

In spite of their inherent coolness, though, behaviors aren't always the perfect solution to your client-side-scripting needs. Here's why.

First, behaviors produce generally cumbersome code. Their JavaScript isn't as concise as it could be, since it has to take in account features and customization options that you might not even use in your deployment of the behavior. While these functions generally work as advertised, you can often improve immensely on their size and complexity by writing JavaScript functions of your own, tailor-made to the specific needs of your site.

Second, behaviors always add their code to the source of the page. If several pages on your site use the same behavior, like a Swap Image behavior in a nav bar, the same function appears on every page of the site. The visitor, in turn, downloads the same functions again and again. As you know, it's more efficient to add repeated functions to a separate script file and then link the script file to each page.

Third, behaviors are relatively generic. They give you some options but not all the options you might need for professional results. The Validate Form behavior, for instance, is better than nothing, but you can create more precise validation tests for your particular form by writing your own JavaScript functions.

In the end, Dreamweaver behaviors are prepackaged content. They're great quickie solutions, and they're undeniably cool. However, just like you shouldn't use Dreamweaver's built-in Web designs to deploy the look and feel of your client's site, you should also write your own JavaScript functions from scratch.

To create a pop-up message, apply the PopUp Message behavior. The PopUp Message dialog box appears. Type the text to display in the Text field and click OK.

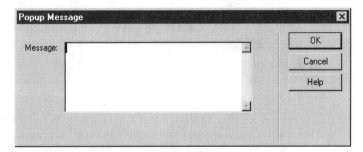

Calling URLs

The Go To URL behavior loads a specified Web page in the current browser window. Type the address of the Web page in the URL field of the Go To URL dialog box (see the following illustration). If you site uses frames, go to the Open In area and select the frame in which you want the URL to load.

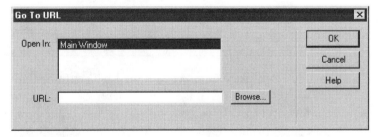

It's not necessary to attach this behavior to a trigger element like a hyperlink, since the `href` attribute of the anchor tag, `<a>`, already gives you this ability with much less bravado. Use the Go To URL behavior for triggers that don't have the `href` attribute built in, such as scripting buttons.

Controlling Images

A number of Dreamweaver behaviors give you additional control over the images on your page. Among these behaviors are Preload Images, Swap Image, Swap Image Restore, and Change Property.

Preloading Images

The Preload Images behavior causes the browser to cache specified image files from your site. By preloading images, rollovers and animation effects appear smoother, since the browser doesn't have to pause to download the necessary image files while the effects are happening.

When you apply the Preload Images behavior, the Preload Images dialog box appears. Type the path to the image file in the Image Source File field, or click the Browse button, navigate to your default images folder, and select the image that you want to preload. To preload another image, click the plus button at the top of the dialog box and type the path or browse to the image file. To remove an image, highlight it in the top half of the dialog box and click the minus button.

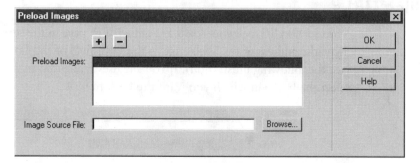

When you create rollovers with the Rollover Image button under the Common tab of the Insert panel or by accessing it after choosing Insert | Interactive Images | Rollover Image, the Insert Rollover Image dialog box gives you an option for preloading the images. Checking this option is the equivalent of adding the Preload Images behavior to the body tag of the page. If you already checked this option, you don't need to attach the Preload Images behavior for that particular rollover. However, if you want to preload a different image for another purpose, you should either choose a different trigger element and attach the Preload Images behavior to it or modify the body tag's existing Preload Images behavior.

Remember that the Preload Images behavior by itself doesn't create rollover effects. However, you can use this behavior in conjunction with behaviors like Swap Image to improve the performance of rollover effects.

Swapping Images

The Swap Image behavior switches one image file on the page for another. If you preload the image that you swap in, the effect is almost instantaneous for most visitors. If you don't preload the image, the browser pauses to load it the first time the behavior launches. The Swap Image Restore behavior switches the swapped-in image back to its original image. You can attach Swap Image Restore only to triggers that already have the Swap Image behavior. You can't apply Swap Image Restore by itself.

When you choose the Swap Image behavior, you open the Swap Image dialog box (see the following illustration). The top half of the dialog box lists all the images on the current page. The highlighted image is the one that the behavior will swap. In the Set Source To field, type the path to the image that you want to swap in, or click the Browse button and navigate to the file in your default images folder. Check the option for preloading images to apply the Preload Images behavior automatically.

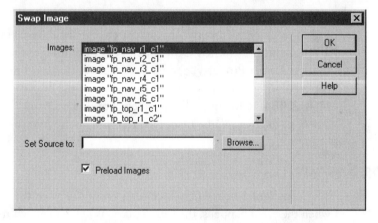

Use Swap Image and Swap Image Restore to create *disjointed rollovers,* or rollovers in which the trigger image causes a different image on the page to change sources. In a typical rollover, the trigger image replaces itself. To set up a disjointed rollover, simply choose an image other than the trigger in the Images area of the Swap Image dialog box. Whatever image you choose is the one that changes when the behavior launches.

To convert an existing rollover to a disjointed rollover, select the rollover image and double-click the Swap Image behavior in the Behaviors panel. Then, in the Images area of the Swap Image dialog box, choose a new image for the behavior to change.

Changing the Image Source

Another way to change the source of an image is to use the Change Property behavior. For this particular application, the Change Property behavior works in Netscape Navigator 3.0 and higher or Internet Explorer 4.0 and higher.

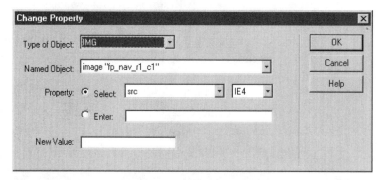

In the Change Property dialog box, choose IMG from the Type Of Object list. Then, from the Named Object list, select the image whose source you want to change. Under Property, choose the Select option, and then choose src from the corresponding drop-down list. Make sure that the next drop-down list shows NS3, NS4, or IE4. Remember that this behavior doesn't work in Internet Explorer 3.0. Then, in the New Value field, type the path to the new image source.

Playing Sounds

The Play Sound behavior associates a sound file with the trigger element so that when the event happens, the sound plays. When you attach the Play Sound behavior, the Play Sound dialog box appears (see see the next illustration). Type the path to the sound file in the Play Sound field or click the Browse button and navigate to the sound file on your site. If you haven't already embedded the sound file—that is, if you haven't added a plug-in element for the sound with the Plug-in button under the Media tab of the Insert panel—Dreamweaver automatically creates the correct embed tag, saving you the trouble.

on the job

Keep in mind that browsers vary widely in their degree of support of sound files. Don't convey mission-critical information by way of the Play Sound behavior, since some of your visitors might not be able to hear the sound files. For the best results, use only common sound-file types, like MID, WAV, and MP3.

Controlling Movies

The Control Shockwave Or Flash behavior gives the visitor the ability to perform basic stop and play operations on Shockwave and Flash movies in the page. You could add a Stop button to your page, for instance, that stops the playback of a particular Flash presentation. For this behavior to appear on the menu that drops down when you click the plus button on the Behaviors panel, a Shockwave or Flash movie must appear somewhere on the page.

From the Movie list of the Control Shockwave Or Flash dialog box (shown next), choose the name of the movie that you want the behavior to control. Choose an action for the behavior from the choices provided. The Play action causes the movie to start playing. The Stop action causes the movie to stop playing. The Rewind action causes the movie to back up to the first frame. The Go To Frame action positions the movie at the frame you specify.

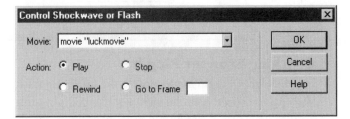

Checking for Specific Browsers and Plug-Ins

The Check Browser and Check Plugin behaviors allow your page to assess the visitor's browser and installed plug-ins, respectively. For instance, if you go against my recommendations and design a site exclusively for Internet Explorer, the Check Browser behavior can intercept users of all other browsers and direct them to a special page that explains exactly why their choice of browser isn't good enough for you. Along the same lines, if a particular page in your site requires the Flash Player plug-in and a visitor doesn't have the Flash Player, the Check Plugin behavior can direct the visitor to a different page that provides alternative content.

Checking Browsers

Use the Check Browser behavior (shown in the following illustration) to load an alternative Web page according to the visitor's browser. Type the path to the main URL in the URL field of the Check Browser dialog box or navigate to it by clicking the Browse button next to this field. Type the path or browse to the alternative URL in the Alt URL field. Then set up the conditions for loading the main URL and the alternative URL with the fields and lists at the top of the dialog box.

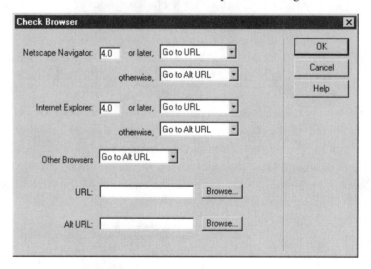

Checking Browser Plug-Ins

Use the Check Plugin behavior (see the following illustration) to load an alternative Web page according to the visitor's installed plug-ins. Select the plug-in that you want to detect from the Plugin list. If you know the exact name of the plug-in, you can choose the Enter option and type the name in the field to the right. In the If Found field, type the path to the page that should load if the behavior detects the correct plug-in, or navigate to the page by clicking the Browse button to the right of the field. Leave this field blank if you want the visitor to stay on the current page. In the Otherwise field, type the path or browse to the page that loads when the visitor doesn't have the correct plug-in installed.

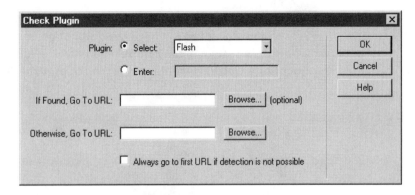

This behavior works best when the visitor uses a Netscape browser, because JavaScript doesn't detect plug-ins in Internet Explorer. If the visitor uses Internet Explorer for Windows, your page can detect the Flash Player and Shockwave Player plug-ins by way of VBScript, not JavaScript. Choosing Flash or Shockwave from the Plugin list causes Dreamweaver to add an extra JavaScript function to your page. This function has an interesting purpose: It causes your Web page to write a VBScript on the fly for Flash and Shockwave detection! That's right—your page writes its own VBScript by executing a JavaScript. Now that's sophistication.

If the visitor uses Internet Explorer for Mac, this behavior doesn't work at all— not even for Flash and Shockwave.

Changing the Status Bar

The status bar of a browser window usually contains the destination URL when the visitor hovers over a link on the page. You can find the status bar at the bottom left of Internet Explorer and Netscape windows. The Set Text Of Status Bar behavior's dialog box allows you to change the message in the status bar to any piece of text. To attach this behavior, choose Set Text | Set Text Of Status Bar from the menu that drops down when you click the plus button on the Behaviors panel. In the Message field of the dialog box, type the text that should appear in the browser's status bar.

on the
Think twice before you change the text of the browser's status bar. Many visitors rely on the status bar to check the destination of a link. Also, the status bar isn't part of IE's default configuration on some Windows XP systems, so nontechnical-oriented visitors might not realize that the status bar exists.

Calling JavaScripts

Use the Call JavaScript behavior (shown next) to execute a JavaScript function. In the JavaScript field of the Call JavaScript dialog box, type the name of the function that should execute. Make sure that your page contains either the script itself or a link element to the correct script file, or the Call JavaScript behavior will cause an error.

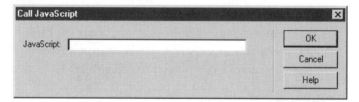

Controlling Layers

Dreamweaver provides a number of behaviors to use for controlling layers on your page, including Drag Layer, Show-Hide Layers, Set Text Of Layer, and Change Property. In addition, you can animate layers and use Timeline behaviors to control the playback of the animation.

Dragging Layers

Use the Drag Layer behavior to allow the visitor to drag a layer around the browser window. To attach this behavior, your page must already have at least one layer. You must also use the body tag of the page as the trigger, not the layer tag, so make sure that the Behaviors panel shows *<body> Actions* before you choose Drag Layer from the list of behaviors.

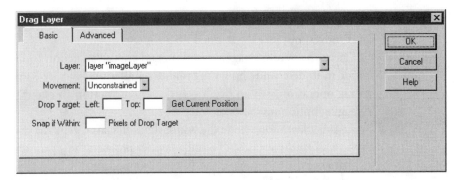

Look under the Basic tab of the Drag Layer dialog box and, from the Layer list, choose the name of the layer that you want to make draggable. From the Movement list, choose either Constrained or Unconstrained. Unconstrained movement allows the visitor to drag the layer anywhere in the browser window. Constrained movement establishes boundaries. Supply maximum values for up, down, left, and right movement in the corresponding fields, which appear when you choose Constrained from the Movement list.

You can define a *drop target* for the layer, which is a location on the page to which the visitor should drag the layer for a special result. Define the drop target in terms of its position from the top and left sides of the browser window. Type these values in the Left and Top fields of the Drop Target area. To use the layer's current position as the drop target, click the Get Current Position button. Afterward, be sure to move the layer to a different position in the document window. To cause the layer to jump to the drop target when the visitor drags the layer within a certain range, type the range, in pixels, in the Snap If Within field. This range is the *snap-to zone* of the drop target.

Look under the Advanced tab of the Drag Layer dialog box for more options. In the Drag Handle list, determine where on the layer the visitor can position the mouse pointer in order to drag. If you want the visitor to be able to drag the layer from anywhere on the layer, set this list to Entire Layer. If you want to create a specific drag zone, choose Area Within Layer, and then define the area in the L, T, W, and R fields that appear. These fields correspond to the distance from the left side of the browser window, the distance from the top of the browser window, the width of the drag region, and the height of the drag region. The visitor will be able to drag the layer only when the mouse pointer sits inside this region, but the entire layer moves, not just the defined drag zone.

Check the While Dragging option, and choose an action from the drop-down list beside it, to determine how the browser handles the layer's z-index during and after a drag operation. If you don't want a specific action to occur, leave the While Dragging option unchecked.

To call a JavaScript while the visitor drags the layer, type the name of the function in the Call JavaScript field. To call a JavaScript when the visitor drops the layer, type the name of the function in the When Dropped field. Check the Only If Snapped option if you want the function to launch only if the visitor drops the layer into the snap-to zone.

Controlling Layer Visibility

Make layers appear and disappear on the fly with the Show-Hide Layers behavior. To use this behavior, select a layer from the Named Layers area of the Show-Hide Layers dialog box. Then click the Show button to cause this layer to become visible when the behavior activates. Click the Hide button to make the layer disappear. Click the Default button to set the layer's visibility to its default state, which you defined in the Layers panel.

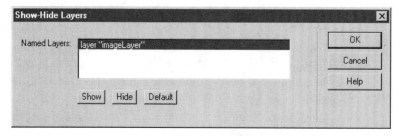

Changing Layer Content

Not only can you change the visibility of a layer on the fly, you can also change the content inside the layer. To do so, use the Set Text Of Layer behavior by selecting a trigger element, clicking the plus button at the top of the Behaviors panel, and choosing Set Text | Set Text Of Layer.

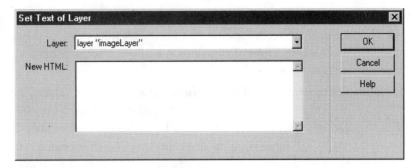

First select a layer from the Layer drop-down list on the Set Text Of Layer dialog box. Then type the new content of the layer in the New HTML field. As the name of this field suggests, you can use HTML tags, not just plain text, in the layer's content.

Changing Layer Properties

You can also change certain layer properties such as the background color and font without swapping in a whole new block of HTML. Use the Change Property behavior for this task. This behavior was discussed earlier in the chapter in the context of changing the source of an image. Here I discuss a different application of the same behavior.

In the Type Of Object list in the Change Property dialog box (shown earlier in this chapter in the section "Changing the Image Source"), select the layer tag that you used to create the layer. Click the Select option and from the Select list, choose the property that you want to change. Then type the new value of the property in the New Value field.

Since browsers vary in their support of layers, be sure that you test this behavior thoroughly before you use it on your live site.

Animating Layers

When you animate a layer, you essentially ask the computer to drag the layer from one location on the screen to another over a certain amount of time. If you put an image of a car in a layer and then animate the layer, for instance, the car appears to drive around the screen, unhindered by whatever other content appears on the page. The end result is an imperfect but nonetheless serviceable alternative to Flash and

Shockwave movies. On the plus side, your visitor doesn't need a media plug-in to view your layer animation. On the minus side, you face the typical incompatibility problems that even the most recent browsers seem to have with rendering layers.

Using the Timelines Panel The first step to creating an animated layer is to open the Timelines panel (see the following illustration) by choosing Window | Others | Timelines. Then select a layer, and choose Modify | Timeline | Add Object To Timeline; or drag the layer into the Timelines panel. Dreamweaver creates a timeline object for the layer and assigns it 15 *frames* by default. Note that a frame in this context is *not* the same thing as the strategy for creating page layout. Rather, a frame in the Timeline panel represents a unit of time in the animation, similar to a frame in a movie.

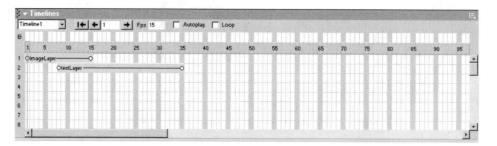

Fifteen frames works out to a one-second animation, since the animation plays back at 15 frames per second. To change the number of frames per second, type a new value into the Fps field on the Timelines panel. If you want the animation to play automatically when the page loads, check the Autoplay option. Leave this option unchecked if you want to launch the animation with a behavior. If you want the animation to repeat indefinitely once it starts playing, check the Loop option.

The white circles in the starting and ending frames are the *keyframes* of the timeline object. Keyframes represent the position of the layer at the start and end of a particular motion. To create an animation, all you have to do is put the layer in its start position for the first keyframe and in its ending position for the last keyframe. Dreamweaver automatically fills in the positions for the intermediate frames—this process is called *tweening*.

To move the layer from the top-left corner of the browser window to the bottom-right corner, for instance, you would position the layer in the top left of the document window for the first keyframe and the bottom right of the document window for the last keyframe. Dreamweaver tweens the intermediate steps, creating a smooth, straight motion path from one position to the next.

Here's how to do it.

1. In the Timelines panel, select the first keyframe for the layer by clicking the first white circle in the timeline object and drag the layer to its starting position in the document window.

2. Select the last keyframe for the layer by clicking the last white circle in the timeline object and drag the layer to its ending position.

3. Drag the salmon-colored playback head back and forth and test the motion of the layer.

4. To edit the starting or ending position of the layer, select the corresponding keyframe and then drag the layer elsewhere on the screen.

To change the position of a keyframe in the Timelines panel, simply click the keyframe, hold down the mouse button and drag. By doing this, you can change the way the animation plays back.

To increase the duration of the animation, increase the distance between the starting and ending keyframes. To shorten the duration, decrease the distance between the keyframes.

To change position of the timeline object in the Timelines panel while preserving the distance between the starting and ending keyframes, select the object by clicking in the blue area between the keyframes, hold down the mouse button, and drag.

To add a frame to the timeline object, thereby pushing the ending keyframe one position to the right, select the object in the Timelines panel and choose Modify | Timeline | Add Frame, or right-click the object and choose Add Frame from the context menu. Dreamweaver adds the frame at the position of the playback head.

To remove a frame from the timeline object, thereby bringing the ending keyframe one position to the left, select the object in the Timelines panel and choose Modify | Timeline | Remove Frame, or right-click the object and choose Remove Frame from the context menu. Dreamweaver removes the frame at the position of the playback head.

To change the source of the timeline object without resetting the keyframes, select the object in the Timelines panel and choose Modify | Timeline | Change Object, or right-click the object and choose Change Object from the context menu.

The Change Object dialog box appears. Set the Object To Animate field to the layer that you want to animate and click OK.

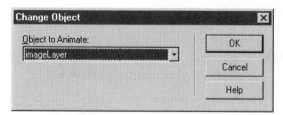

Remove the timeline object from the Timelines panel entirely by selecting the object and choosing Modify | Timeline | Remove Object or by right-clicking the object and choosing Remove Object from the context menu.

Editing the Motion Path   You can edit the path that the layer takes during its journey by adding keyframes to its object in the Timelines panel. Here's how to add a keyframe:

1. Select the object in the Timelines panel by clicking anywhere in the blue region between the existing keyframes.

2. Position the salmon-colored playback head at the point at which you want to add the new keyframe.

3. Choose Modify | Timeline | Add Keyframe, press F6, or right-click the object and choose Add Keyframe from the context menu. Dreamweaver adds a new white circle to the layer's object.

4. Select this keyframe and move the layer to a different position on the screen. The motion path bends accordingly.

To remove a keyframe from the timeline object, select the keyframe, and choose Modify | Timeline | Remove Keyframe or right-click on the object and choose Remove Keyframe from the context menu. You can remove only middle keyframes from the timeline object. You can't remove the starting or ending keyframes.

Recording a Motion Path   You can create a motion path for the layer by dragging the layer across the document window exactly as you want the layer to move, recording the motion path as you go.

1. Select the layer, drag it to its starting position in the document window, and position the salmon-colored playback head on the Timelines panel in the frame in which you want to start the animation.

2. Choose Modify | Timeline | Record Path Of Layer or right-click inside the Timelines panel at the position of the playback head and choose Record Path Of Layer from the context menu.

3. Go back to the document window and drag the layer exactly the way you want it to move. A motion path appears behind the layer as you drag. Don't release the mouse button until you're finished creating the entire path.

4. When you release the mouse button, Dreamweaver automatically adds a new object for the layer to the Timelines panel along with the necessary keyframes to reproduce the layer's motion path.

Working with Multiple Objects   You can add as many layers to the Timelines panel as you like. Each layer receives its own object and keyframes, allowing you to animate multiple layers simultaneously. By putting the timeline objects in different rows on the Timelines panel, you can synchronize the motions of the various layers, so that Layer 2 begins moving at Frame 20, for instance, when Layer 1 reaches the middle of the screen.

If you don't want more than one layer moving at the same time, keep all the objects in the same row on the Timelines panel.

Working with Multiple Timelines   A timeline represents a single set of motions for a single set of objects. You can add as many timelines to your page as you want. By creating multiple timelines, you can cause a set of layers to move one way when the visitor clicks one button and another way when the visitor clicks another button, for instance.

To add a new timeline to your page, choose Modify | Timeline | Add Timeline, or right-click anywhere inside the Timelines panel and choose Add Timeline from the context menu. The new timeline appears in the drop-down list at the upper-left corner of the Timelines panel. Add objects to this timeline as you did for the previous one. You can go back to the first timeline by choosing that timeline from the drop-down list.

Dreamweaver names timelines sequentially by default: Timeline 1, Timeline 2, Timeline 3, and so on. To change the name of a timeline to something more descriptive, select the timeline from the drop-down list at the top-left of the Timelines panel and choose Modify | Timeline | Rename Timeline or right-click anywhere in the Timelines panel and choose Rename Timeline from the context menu.

To remove a timeline from your page, select the timeline from the drop-down list, and choose Modify | Timeline | Remove Timeline or right-click anywhere in the Timelines panel and choose Remove Timeline from the context menu.

The first timeline (Timeline 1 by default) controls the frame rate, Autoplay, and Loop settings for all the timelines on the page. You can't adjust these values in any other timelines. (See the next Scenario and Solution sidebar to help you figure out when to use multiple timelines.)

Controlling Playback   If you don't select the Autoplay feature on the Timelines panel, you can use timeline behaviors to play back the animation. Attaching the Play Timeline behavior to a button, for instance, causes the animation to start when the visitor clicks the button.

Three timeline behaviors are available: Go To Timeline Frame, Play Timeline, and Stop Timeline. With the Go To Timeline Frame behavior, the browser jumps to a particular frame in the timeline. In the Go To Timeline Frame dialog box, choose the timeline that you want to control. Type the frame to which to jump in the Frame field, and set the number of times to loop the animation in the Loop field.

SCENARIO & SOLUTION

When do you need to add multiple timelines to your page?	When you want to create different animations that play at different times or under different conditions
When can you get away with a single timeline?	When you want to animate multiple layers at the same time

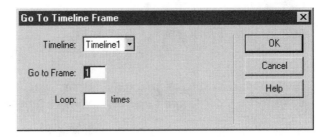

With the Play Timeline behavior, the browser plays a timeline of your choice from start to finish, looping according to the option that you set on the Timelines panel.

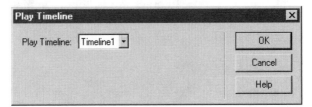

With the Stop Timeline behavior, the browser stops the playback of a single timeline or all the timelines on the page. Choose your poison from the Stop Timelines list on this behavior's dialog box.

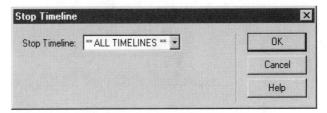

Using a Timeline Frame as the Trigger   The frame of a timeline can serve as the trigger for another behavior. If you attach a behavior to Frame 15 of a timeline, for instance, the behavior launches as soon as the browser plays Frame 15 of that timeline.

To attach a behavior to a frame in a timeline, choose the timeline from the drop-down list at the top left of the Timelines panel. Then click a frame in the row marked *B*—for *behavior*. Go to the Behaviors panel, click the plus button, and choose the behavior that you want to launch. After you fill in the appropriate dialog box information, Dreamweaver marks this frame in the Timelines panel so that you remember which one has the behavior.

To remove a behavior from the Timelines panel, click the frame with the behavior in the row marked *B*. Then choose Modify | Timeline | Remove Behavior, or right-click the object and choose Remove Behavior from the context menu.

exam ***Remember that the row marked B on the Timelines panel is for frame***
ⓦatch ***behaviors only. You can't add keyframes or timeline objects to this row.***

You may note that the Modify | Timeline menu and the right-click-activated context menu have Add Behavior commands. These commands do nothing more than show a pop-up message that states, "To add a behavior to the timeline, select a behavior from the '+' menu." In other words, these commands do absolutely nothing other than jog your memory about the correct procedure to follow.

Changing Frame Content

Just as you can change the content of a layer on the fly if your site uses layers, you can change the content of a frame on the fly if your site uses frames. (*Frames* in this context is the familiar definition: the strategy for page layout that divides the browser window into separate rectangular areas.) Use the Set Text Of Frame behavior, which you can find in the Set Text submenu of the list that drops down when you click the plus button on the Behaviors panel.

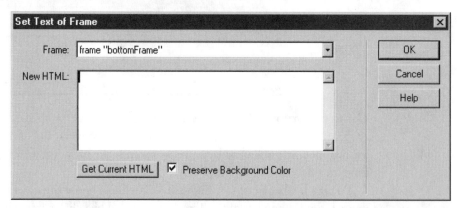

Choose a frame from the Frame list on the Set Text Of Frame dialog box. Then type the new content for the frame into the New Content field. As with the Set Text Of Layer behavior, this new content can include HTML tags. Retrieve the existing HTML content of the selected frame by clicking the Get Current HTML button. To preserve the background color of the existing frame, check the Preserve Background Color option.

exam
ⓦatch *Remember that the Set Text Of Layer and Set Text Of Frames behaviors allow new HTML content, while the Set Text Of Text Field and Set Text Of Status Bar behaviors allow plain text only.*

Controlling Forms

Dreamweaver offers three behaviors for controlling forms and form elements: Validate Form, Set Text Of Text Field, and Change Property.

Validating Form Input

By attaching the Validate Form behavior (see the following illustration) to the Submit button of a form on your page, you create a JavaScript function to screen the data that the visitor is trying to submit. If this data doesn't appear to be correct, such as when the visitor types the word *hello* instead of a credit card number or when the visitor forgets to fill in a required field, the Validate Form behavior stops the submission procedure and asks the visitor to check the information in the form. The behavior doesn't submit the form to the server until all the fields pass their validation tests.

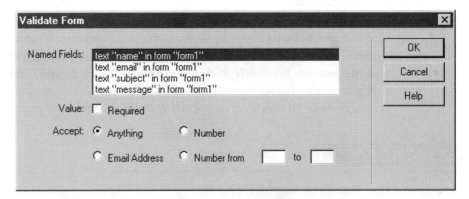

By attaching the Validate Form behavior to individual text fields and specifying the onBlur event, validation for that field happens as soon as the visitor moves on to the next field in the form. If the field fails its validation test, your page alerts the visitor immediately. However, unless you also attach a Validate Form behavior to the Submit button, the visitor can submit the form without changing the bad field.

on the
ⓙob *It can be annoying to the visitor if the form tries to validate itself before the visitor clicks the Submit button, especially if many fields need to be filled out.*

After you select this behavior from the Behaviors panel, the Validate Form dialog box appears. In the Named Fields area, choose the field that you want to validate. If this field is required, check the Required option. Then, in the Accept area, choose from four options: Anything, Number, Email Address, or Number From. The Anything option allows the visitor to type anything in the field. As long as the field isn't blank, it passes the validation test. The Number option requires that the visitor type a numeral into the field. The Email Address option requires that an at sign (@) be located somewhere in the field. The Number From option accepts all numbers that fall between a minimum value and a maximum value. Type these values in the fields next to this option.

If you're attaching the behavior to the Submit button, continue selecting fields from the Named Field area and defining their validation tests. When you finish, click OK. If you're attaching the behavior to an individual text field, you don't need to choose any other fields to validate. Click OK to close the Validate Form dialog box.

After you apply this behavior, double-check that Dreamweaver has assigned the correct event. If you attached the behavior to a Submit button, the correct event is onClick. If you attached the behavior to an individual text field, the correct event is onBlur.

on the
Öob

When the Validate Form behavior detects an erroneous submission, it causes the browser to display a pop-up message with the details of the error. This error message is generic and somewhat technical, as you'll see in Exercise 8-2. If you know JavaScript, you can modify the MM_validateForm *function in the source code to display a customized, more user-friendly error message.*

EXERCISE 8-2

Extending the Validate Form Behavior

In this exercise, you expand the scope of the Validate Form behavior that you added in Exercise 8-1.

1. Launch Dreamweaver, open the Site panel, and set the site to Mad Science LLC.

2. Open the folder *contact* and double-click the file *index.htm.* The Contact Us page opens in a document window.

3. Open the Behaviors panel. You can find this panel in the Design panel group or choose Window | Behaviors.

4. Select the Send E-mail button in the document window. The Behaviors panel shows the Validate Form behavior that you added in Exercise 8-1. Double-click this behavior to open the Validate Form dialog box.

5. In the Named Fields area, click the *text "Email"* item. Make this field required by checking the Required option. Under Accept, check the Email Address option. This causes the page to look specifically for an e-mail address in the field when the visitor clicks the Submit button.

6. Go back to the Named Fields area, and click the *text "phoneno"* item. Make this field required, but don't create an addition validation test. Dreamweaver's Validate Form behavior doesn't offer a suitable test. If you choose the Number option under Accept, this field would accept only number values, not parentheses, slashes, or hyphens, which people often use to format phone numbers.

7. Click the *text "message"* item. Make this field required. Your Validate Form dialog box should look like this:

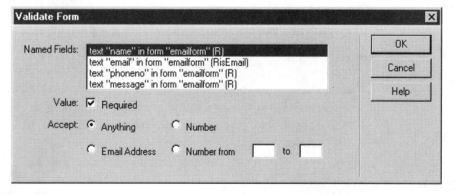

8. Press F12 to test the page in a browser. Enter bad information in the fields, and watch your page catch the errors. Then try to beat the validation. See if you can trick the Email field into accepting a value that isn't an e-mail address. Here's a hint: The behavior looks mainly for an at-sign (@), not necessarily what comes before or after it.

9. Close the browser window.

10. Choose File | Save. Good work!

Changing Text Field Content

The Set Text Of Text Field behavior changes the content of a single-line text field or text area. To apply this behavior, choose a text field or text area as the target, click the plus button on the Behaviors panel, and choose Set Text | Set Text Of Text Field.

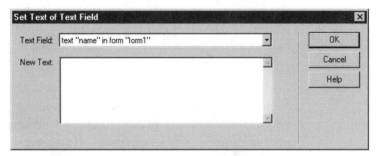

From the Text Field list of the Set Text Of Text Field dialog box, choose the text field whose content you want to change. Then type the new content in the New Text field. This content should be text only, not HTML.

Changing Properties of Forms and Form Objects

The Change Property behavior that relates to image sources and layers also works with forms and form objects. Using this behavior, you can change certain properties of form tags, checkboxes, radio buttons, single-line text fields, text areas, password fields, and select objects (lists and menus). By attaching this behavior to a scripting button, for instance, you could allow the visitor to check several checkboxes with a single click.

In the Type Of Object list on the Change Property dialog box, choose the type of object whose property you want to change. Then select the specific object to change from the Named Objects list. Choose the property to change from the Select list and type the new value of this property in the New Value field. If you like, continue selecting objects and properties from the lists and supplying new values. You don't have to stop at one. When you finish, click OK.

The results of this behavior on forms and form objects are very reliable across browsers. When you use Change Property on image sources and layers, the results aren't nearly as reliable.

Now that you've explored two different behaviors for changing form objects, see the following Scenario and Solution sidebar a quick reference to help you sort them out.

SCENARIO & SOLUTION

When should you use the Set Text Of Text Field behavior?	When you want to change the value of a single-line text field or text area
When should you use the Change Property behavior?	When you want to change the properties, including the values, of single-line text fields, text areas, password fields, checkboxes, radio buttons, lists, and menus

Creating Pop-Up Menus

The Show PopUp Menu behavior (Figure 8-4) brings up a menu of links when the visitor interacts with the trigger element. If you apply this behavior to a graphical button in your main navigation, for instance, you can produce a list of links to the subpages in that particular navigational category when the visitor hovers over the button image. For best results, use a hyperlink or an image as the trigger of this behavior.

The Show Pop-Up Menu dialog box has four tabs: Contents, Appearance, Advanced, and Position. Start with the Contents tab. Type the text of the link in Text field. Type the path to the destination page in the Link field or click the folder icon and browse to the desired Web page. If you want to target the link, choose a value from the Target list.

Click the plus button to add a new item to the pop-up menu. Use the Outdent Item and Indent Item buttons to the right of the plus and minus buttons to set up a visual hierarchy of menu items. To change the position of an item in the menu, select it and click the up-arrow and down-arrow buttons. To edit a menu item, select it and change the values in the Text, Link, and Target fields. To remove an item from the menu, select it and click the minus button.

Under the Appearance tab, choose a vertical or horizontal pop-up menu from the list at the top of the dialog box. Set the properties of the font and choose colors for the up-states and over-states of the menu items. Keep your eye on the preview window as you design the pop-up menu.

Under the Advanced tab, set the width, height, padding, and spacing for the cells in the menu, as well as the properties of the pop-up menu's border. You can also specify the amount of delay in milliseconds. The delay determines how long the

FIGURE 8-4

Use the Show
Pop-Up Menu
behavior to call
up a menu of
links when the
visitor interacts
with the trigger
element.

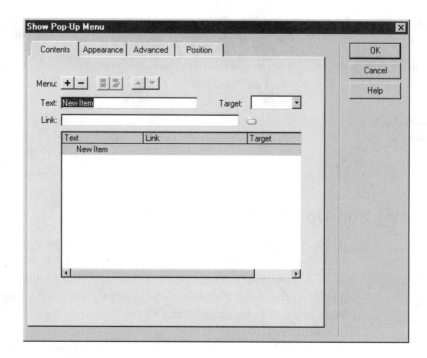

browser waits before displaying the pop-up menu. Typing 1000 in this field causes
a 1-second delay, since 1000 milliseconds equals 1 second. Having a delay is usually
a good idea, since the pop-up menu may partially conceal another clickable element
on the page. You want to give the visitor the opportunity to click the element before
the menu comes up.

Under the Position tab, choose where the pop-up menu should appear in relation
to the trigger element. Then fine tune the position by typing values into the X and Y
fields. To close the menu automatically after the visitor mouses away, check the Hide
Menu option.

Click OK to create the pop-up menu. By default, Dreamweaver assigns the
onMouseOver event to this behavior. You can change this event on onClick
or a handful of others in version 4.0 browsers and up.

If you checked the Hide Menu option, Dreamweaver automatically added the Hide
Pop-Up Menu behavior to your page. If you didn't check this option, you can still
apply the Hide Pop-Up Menu behavior manually by choosing it from the list that
drops-down when you click the plus button on the Behaviors panel.

CERTIFICATION SUMMARY

In this chapter, you learned about Dreamweaver behaviors. Behaviors are client-side JavaScript functions that perform various useful tricks and tasks. A behavior has three components: the *trigger*, or the element on the page that launches the behavior; the *event*, or the thing that happens to the trigger to launch the behavior; and the *action*, or the function that the behavior performs. While behaviors can shift some of the processing burden to the visitor's browser, the visitor can disable your behaviors by turning off JavaScript. For this reason, I urged you to add noscript content to your page if you decide to use behaviors.

You learned that the trigger helps to determine what kinds of behaviors you can attach. Not all triggers support the same behaviors. You also learned that the visitor's browser determines which events can launch the behaviors. Early versions of popular browsers offer relatively few events, while more recent versions offer scores of them. However, to keep your site cross-browser-compatible, restrict yourself to events commonly supported in version 4.0 browsers.

I explained that you can't attach certain events to certain triggers. However, Dreamweaver can nest the trigger element between opening and closing anchor tags, thereby giving you a wider selection of events. When an event appears in parentheses on the Behaviors panel, you know that Dreamweaver has to nest the trigger between anchor tags and attach the behavior to the anchor, not the trigger itself.

You then explored the various behaviors that Dreamweaver offers. You saw that behaviors can perform marvelous feats, everything from opening pop-up messages and pop-up windows to managing images, checking browsers and plug-ins, validating forms, adding HTML content on the fly, and animating layers. In spite of this functional arsenal, I explained why it's usually better to develop your own client-side functions in a professional setting.

TWO-MINUTE DRILL

Working with Triggers, Events, and Actions

❑ A trigger is the element on the page that launches the behavior.

❑ An event is the thing that happens to the trigger to launch the behavior.

❑ An action is the function that the behavior performs.

❑ Not all triggers support the same behaviors.

❑ Older browsers generally support few events.

❑ In general, Dreamweaver behaviors aren't useful in version 3.0 browsers.

❑ If a trigger has multiple behaviors with the same event, the order in which the behaviors appear in the Behaviors panel is the order in which the behaviors execute.

❑ Be sure to include noscript content if you add behaviors to your site, since your visitors can deactivate all the functions by turning off JavaScript in their browser preferences.

Exploring Behaviors

❑ For pop-up windows and messages, create text-only messages in system dialog boxes with the Popup Message behavior or open new browser windows containing Web-page content with the Open Browser Window behavior.

❑ The Check Plugin behavior doesn't always work on Microsoft Internet Explorer.

❑ Set Text Of Frame and Set Text Of Layer allow you to specify new HTML content on the fly, while Set Text Of Text Field and Set Text Of Status Bar allow plain text only.

❑ When you attach the Validate Form behavior to a Submit button, the form doesn't send its data to the server until all the fields pass their validation tests.

❑ Use the Change Property behavior to change the properties of forms and form objects reliably.

❑ Use layer behaviors to control the visibility, mobility, and properties of layers on your page and to animate layers using the Timelines panel and timeline behaviors.

❑ The frame of an animation can serve as the trigger of another behavior.

SELF TEST

The following questions will help you measure your understanding of the material presented in this chapter. Read all the choices carefully because there might be more than one correct answer. Choose all correct answers for each question.

Working with Triggers, Events, and Actions

1. You want to launch a behavior when the visitor moves the mouse pointer away from the trigger element after hovering over it. What's the correct event?

   A. `onMouseOver`

   B. `onMouseAway`

   C. `onMouseOff`

   D. `onMouseOut`

2. What is a behavior's action?

   A. The function that the behavior performs

   B. The element on the page that launches the behavior

   C. The interaction that causes the behavior to launch

3. You attach two behaviors to a button: Go To URL and Call JavaScript. You test the page in a live browser window. The URL loads fine when you click the button, but the JavaScript doesn't seem to work. What's going on here?

   A. You can't attach two behaviors to the same trigger.

   B. The Go To URL behavior doesn't allow any other behaviors on the same trigger.

   C. The Call JavaScript behavior doesn't allow any other behaviors on the same trigger.

   D. When you select the button in the document window, the Go To URL behavior is at the top of the Behaviors panel.

4. Which of the following statements about trigger elements are true?

   A. You can attach any behavior to any trigger.

   B. The type of trigger you select determines the kinds of behaviors you can attach.

   C. You can choose timeline frames as triggers.

   D. You can choose the body tag of the page as the trigger.

   E. Each trigger must call a different behavior.

5. When an event in the Behaviors panel appears inside parentheses, what does it indicate?

    A. The event isn't supported on older browsers.

    B. Dreamweaver will add a pair of anchor tags to your page and attach the behavior to the anchor.

    C. The selected trigger element will receive the behavior.

    D. The event may backfire and crash the behavior.

6. How do you set up Dreamweaver to show events for Netscape 6.0 only?

    A. Double-click a behavior in the Behaviors panel.

    B. Double-click a behavior in the Behaviors panel and choose Edit | Preferences.

    C. Select a behavior in the Behaviors panel and choose Edit | Preferences.

    D. Select a behavior in the Behaviors panel, click the button to the right of the event, and choose Show Events For | Netscape 6.0.

7. What's the main difference between `href="#"` and `href="javascript:;"` as null links? Choose the best answer.

    A. The null link `href="#"` causes the browser to jump to the top of the page.

    B. The null link `href="javascript:;"` is the only one that works in behaviors.

    C. The null link `href="#"` is the only one that works in behaviors.

    D. The null link `href="javascript:;"` causes a JavaScript function to execute.

8. Which of the following are commonly supported events for version 4.0 browsers?

    A. `onClick`

    B. `onMouseOver`

    C. `onFocus`

    D. `onAfterPrint`

    E. `onBlur`

9. What are the disadvantages to targeting events to version 3.0 browsers?

    A. These events don't work in later versions of the same browsers.

    B. You don't get many events.

    C. Behaviors don't work reliably in version 3.0 of Internet Explorer anyway.

    D. After you attach a behavior with one of these events, you can't change the event, even after you target a different browser.

10. Why might you want to add behaviors to your Web site?

    A. You want to reduce the amount of server-side scripting.

    B. You want to enhance the interactivity of your page.

    C. You want to connect with a database.

    D. You want reliable, cross-browser–compatible JavaScripts.

Exploring Behaviors

11. Which of the following behaviors can you use specifically to create rollover effects for images?

    A. Change Property

    B. Swap Image

    C. Show Pop-Up Menu

    D. Preload Images

12. Which of the following behaviors allow you to swap in new HTML content?

    A. Set Text Of Frame

    B. Set Text Of Status Bar

    C. Set Text Of Text Field

    D. Set Text Of Layer

13. What's the difference between attaching the Validate Form behavior to a text field and attaching the Validate Form behavior to a Submit button?

    A. When you attach this behavior to a Submit button, the behavior launches while the visitor fills out the form.

    B. When you attach this behavior to a text field, the behavior prevents erroneous input from reaching the server.

    C. When you attach this behavior to a Submit button, you can validate only a single field.

    D. When you attach this behavior to a text field, the behavior launches while the visitor fills out the form.

14. Why doesn't the Check Plugin behavior work in Internet Explorer?

    A. IE doesn't support VBScript.

    B. IE doesn't allow you to check plug-ins using JavaScript.

    C. IE doesn't support plug-ins.

    D. The Check Browser behavior automatically checks installed plug-ins in IE.

15. Which of the following behaviors can you use to change form objects?

    A. Change Property

    B. Show Pop-Up Menu

    C. Set Text Of Text Field

    D. Set Text Of Textarea

16. What's a keyframe?

    A. The target frame in a frameset

    B. An object in the Timelines panel representing an animated frame on the page

    C. A frame in the Timelines panel representing the starting point or ending point of an animated layer

    D. A frame in the B row of the Timelines panel

17. How can you change the motion path of an animated layer without deleting the motion path and starting again?

    A. Choose Modify | Timeline | Change Object.

    B. Choose Modify | Timeline | Add Keyframe.

    C. Choose Modify | Timeline | Remove Keyframe.

    D. Choose Modify | Timeline | Add Object.

    E. Choose Modify | Timeline | Remove Object.

18. Why might you want to use the Check Browser behavior?

    A. Your visitors will always have multiple browsers installed on their systems.

    B. Some features on your site might not work on older browsers.

    C. You want to determine whether the browser has the Flash Player plug-in.

19. What happens to the behaviors on your page if a visitor turns off JavaScript in the browser preferences?

    A. Nothing happens to your behaviors.

    B. Your page writes VBScripts on the fly to compensate.

    C. Your page automatically produces a warning message.

    D. Your behaviors cease to function altogether.

20. What's a pop-up menu?

    A. A message that appears in a system dialog box

    B. A list of links

    C. A bare-bones browser window

    D. A set of graphical buttons for navigation

LAB QUESTION

Your Web site's response time is slower than you'd like. Visitors are complaining that it takes forever to place an order, which isn't good, since you bill your site as "The Fastest Way on Earth to Buy Computer Software." You're beginning to suspect that the pages request too much information from the server, and it occurs to you that you might be able to use Dreamweaver behaviors to shift some of the processing to the client side.

Your site includes Web apps and CGI scripts for the following tasks: (1) Checking the available stock for a particular item; (2) Checking the fields of the order form for valid input; (3) Allowing the visitor to track an order; (4) Opening menus of additional links when the visitor hovers over a graphical button in the nav bar; (5) Preselecting certain items in the menus, radio buttons, and checkboxes of the order form as the *Softwaire Du Jour*; (6) Checking that the visitor has the Flash Player plug-in; (7) Loading a pop-up coupon when the visitor hits the home page; and (8) Customizing the content on the page to reflect the visitor's buying preferences.

Which of these functions could you conceivably implement with behaviors instead, and which behaviors would you use? Make a list, and check it twice. Then check your list against mine in the Lab Answer section.

SELF TEST ANSWERS

Working with Triggers, Events, and Actions

1. ☑ **D.** The `onMouseOut` event launches the behavior when the visitor moves the mouse pointer away from the trigger element after first hovering over it.

☒ **A** is incorrect because the `onMouseOver` event launches the behavior when the visitor hovers over the trigger element with the mouse pointer. **B** and **C** are incorrect because these aren't events.

2. ☑ **A.** The action is the function that the behavior performs.

☒ **B** is incorrect because this choice describes the trigger of the behavior. **C** is incorrect because this choice describes the event of the behavior. **D** is incorrect because only choice **A** is the correct answer.

3. ☑ **D.** The top behavior in the Behaviors panel launches first. If this behavior transfers control to a new Web page, as it does with the Go To URL behavior, the pending behaviors on the old page don't execute. To solve this problem, simply change the order of the behaviors in the Behaviors panel. Launch the Call JavaScript behavior first.

☒ **A, B,** and **C** are incorrect because these aren't true statements. All three of them are false.

4. ☑ **B, C,** and **D.** The type of trigger that you select determines the kinds of behaviors that you can attach, you can attach behaviors to frames in the Timelines panel, and you can attach behaviors to the body tag of the page.

☒ **A** is incorrect because different triggers allow different behaviors. **E** is incorrect because different triggers can call the same behavior. If not, you couldn't have more than one rollover button in your nav bar.

5. ☑ **B.** When the event in the Behaviors panel appears inside parentheses, Dreamweaver must add a pair of anchor tags to your page and attach the behavior to the anchor.

☒ **A, C,** and **D** are incorrect because the parentheses indicate choice **B**.

6. ☑ **D.** Select a behavior in the Behaviors panel, click the button to the right of the event, and choose Show Behaviors For | Netscape 6.0.

☒ **A** is incorrect because double-clicking the behavior causes the behavior's dialog box to appear. **B** and **C** are incorrect because nothing in the Preferences dialog box allows you to target events for specific browsers.

7. ☑   **A.** The null link `href="#"` causes the browser to jump to the top of the page.
    ☒   **B** is incorrect because previous versions of Dreamweaver used the null link `href="#"` with behaviors, so `href="javascript:;"` isn't the only one that works. **C** is incorrect because Dreamweaver MX uses the null link `href="javascript:;"` with behaviors, so `href="#"` isn't the only one that works. **D** is incorrect because the null link `href="javascript:;"` doesn't supply the name of a function to execute.

8. ☑   **A, B, C,** and **E.** These events work well in version 4.0 browsers.
    ☒   **D** is incorrect because the `onAfterPrint` event works only in later versions of Internet Explorer.

9. ☑   **B** and **C.** You don't get many events, and Dreamweaver behaviors don't work reliably in Internet Explorer 3.0 anyway.
    ☒   **A** is incorrect because events that work in 3.0 browsers work exactly the same in later browsers. **D** is incorrect because you can always change the event after you change the target browser.

10. ☑   **A, B,** and **D.** All three of these choices are good reasons for adding behaviors to your Web site.
    ☒   **C** is incorrect because you can't use client-side behaviors to connect with a server-side component like a database.

Exploring Behaviors

11. ☑   **A** and **B.** Use the Swap Image and Change Property behaviors to create rollover effects for images.
    ☒   **C** is incorrect because the Show Pop-Up Menu behavior doesn't give you rollover effects for images. **D** is incorrect because while the Preload Images behavior improves the performance of rollover images, this behavior by itself doesn't create the rollover effect.

12. ☑   **A** and **D.** The Set Text Of Layer and Set Text Of Frame behaviors allow you to swap in new HTML content.
    ☒   **B** and **C** are incorrect because these behaviors allow you to swap in only plain text.

13. ☑   **D.** When you attach the Validate Form behavior to a text field, the behavior launches while the visitor fills out the form. When you attach this behavior to a Submit button, the behavior launches when the visitor clicks the button.
    ☒   **A** is incorrect because attaching the behavior to a text field causes this effect. **B** is incorrect because attaching the behavior to the Submit button causes this effect. **C** is incorrect because you can validate any number of fields when you attach this behavior to the Submit button.

14. ☑ **B.** Internet Explorer doesn't allow you to check plug-ins with JavaScript.
☒ **A, C,** and **D** are incorrect because all three of these statements are false.

15. ☑ **A** and **C.** The Change Property and Set Text Of Text Field behaviors allow you to change form objects.
☒ **B** is incorrect because the Show Pop-Up Menu behavior doesn't change form objects.
D is incorrect because there is no such behavior in Dreamweaver.

16. ☑ **C.** A keyframe is a frame in the Timelines panel representing the starting point or ending point of an animated layer.
☒ **A, B,** and **D** are incorrect because these choices don't describe a keyframe.

17. ☑ **B** and **C.** Adding or removing keyframes changes the motion path of the animated layer.
☒ **A** is incorrect because changing the object doesn't change the motion path. It changes the layer that follows the motion path. **D** is incorrect because adding a new object to the timeline doesn't change the motion path of an existing object. **E** is incorrect because removing the object deletes the motion path entirely.

18. ☑ **B.** Use the Check Browser behavior if some of the content on your site doesn't work in older browsers.
☒ **A** is incorrect because the Check Browser behavior doesn't take an inventory of all the browsers on the visitor's system. **C** is incorrect because the Check Plugin behavior determines whether the visitor's system has the Flash Player plug-in installed, not the Check Browser behavior.

19. ☑ **D.** If the visitor turns off JavaScript, your behaviors cease to function.
☒ **A** is incorrect because your behaviors stop working. **B** is incorrect because your page doesn't write VBScripts on the fly to compensate. You might be thinking of the Check Plugin behavior, where Dreamweaver adds a JavaScript function that writes VBScripts on the fly to check for Flash and Shockwave plug-ins on IE for Windows. **C** is incorrect because your page doesn't automatically produce warning messages. You should specifically create warning messages by adding noscript content to your page.

20. ☑ **B.** A pop-up menu is a list of links.
☒ **A** is incorrect because this description applies to a pop-up message. **C** is incorrect because this description applies to a new browser window with all the browser attributes turned off. **D** is incorrect because this description applies to a navigation bar.

LAB ANSWER

You can use Dreamweaver behaviors for the following tasks: checking the fields of the order form for valid input with Validate Form; opening menus of additional links when the visitor hovers over a graphical button in the nav bar with Show Pop-Up Menu; preselecting certain items in the menus, radio buttons, and checkboxes of the order form as the *Softwaire Du Jour* with Change Property; checking that the visitor has the Flash Player plug-in with Check Plugin; and loading a pop-up coupon when the visitor hits the home page with Open Browser Window.

You can't use Dreamweaver behaviors to check the available stock of an item, track an order, or customize the content to reflect a particular visitor's buying preferences.

Dreamweaver®

CERTIFIED DREAMWEAVER DEVELOPER

9

Managing Styles

N
o matter how many graphics you add to your site, you'll eventually find yourself working with text. As a conscientious Web builder, you want to give the same level of attention to the appearance and format of the text as you do the images, animations, and navigation. To this end, you'll find Dreamweaver styles extremely helpful.

A *style* in Dreamweaver is a set of attributes that defines the appearance of a particular piece of text. Defining styles saves you time and effort, and it helps you to maintain design consistency across your site. You don't have to keep applying the same appearance attributes by way of the Properties panel. Define a style, and you can achieve consistent formatting with a few clicks of the mouse button.

Two types of styles are used in Dreamweaver: HTML styles and Cascading Style Sheet (CSS) styles. This chapter shows you how to create and use both.

CERTIFICATION OBJECTIVE 9.01

Managing HTML Styles

An *HTML style* is a collection of HTML formatting tags and appearance attributes that are used for defining the look of a particular piece of text. Dreamweaver doesn't use CSS style definitions to create these styles—they're purely HTML.

This has two effects, one positive, one negative. On the plus side, HTML styles are more reliable across browsers. Different browsers are notoriously inconsistent in their support of CSS, but all browsers handle formatting tags in much the same way. On the down side, though, HTML styles don't give you nearly as many formatting options, while CSS provides a vast number of design choices with better, more precise control and unbeatable editability.

An HTML style is, in essence, Dreamweaver's shorthand for a collection of tags and attributes. When you apply an HTML style to a piece of text, Dreamweaver adds the appropriate tags and sets the appropriate attributes. You don't need HTML styles to accomplish this. You could format the text yourself using nothing more than the Insert and Properties panels and achieve the same results. HTML styles are a convenience more than anything else. They save you the hassle of adding the same tags and defining the same attributes over and over again.

Defining HTML Styles

Here's how to define an HTML style.

1. Open the Design panel group and click the HTML Styles tab. This opens the HTML Styles panel, as shown in Figure 9-1. Choosing Window | HTML Styles does the same thing.

2. To the left of the trashcan icon at the bottom of the HTML Styles panel is the new-page icon. Click this icon to open the Define HTML Style dialog box, shown in Figure 9-2. If you don't want to bother with the HTML Styles panel at all, you can access this dialog box by choosing Text | HTML Styles | New Style.

3. Type a descriptive name for the style in the Name field. Dreamweaver doesn't use this name anywhere in the source code of the page. Remember that an HTML style is just a collection of tags and attributes. Try to coordinate the style name with its function on the page instead of its appearance. For instance, *Main Headline* is probably a better name than *Green Text,* especially if more than one kind of green text appears on the page. Functional style names help others on the development team to follow your work, and these names don't require editing if the client decides that blue text for the main headline is better.

Remember that functional style names work better than purely descriptive ones.

4. Under Apply To, choose whether to create a selection style or a paragraph style. A *selection style* applies only to the currently selected text in the document window. You must highlight a string of text to apply a selection style. A *paragraph style* applies to all the text in a given paragraph—that is, all the text

between opening and closing paragraph tags, <p> and </p>. You don't have to select the text manually in the document window. Clicking anywhere inside the paragraph suffices. (See the Scenario and Solution sidebar for a quick reference to help you remember the two types of HTML styles.)

5. Under When Applying, determine how Dreamweaver should add the style to your selection. If you choose the Add To Existing Style option, Dreamweaver doesn't replace the current formatting tags when it applies the style. A piece of boldface text remains boldface, in other words, even if you don't specify boldface in the attributes of the style. Watch out, though, if you set this option for paragraph styles, because you may get unexpected or undesired results. The Clear Existing Style option behaves better in general. This option causes Dreamweaver to remove any existing formatting in the selection before applying the style.

6. Finally, select the attributes of the style. Choose a set of fonts from the Font drop-down list and choose a font size and color, just as if you were setting the appearance of the text on the Properties panel. Choose boldface or italic for the style if you want, or specify a different HTML formatting tag by clicking the Other button and choosing a value from the menu that drops down.

What is a selection style?	An HTML style that applies to a selected string of text
What is a paragraph style?	An HTML style that applies to an entire paragraph, heading, or block of preformatted text

It's worth pointing out here that the boldface and italic forms of HTML styles come by way of the bold tag, `<b>`, and the italic tag, `<i>`. You'll recall that the B and I buttons on the Properties panel use the strong tag, `<strong>`, to produce boldface and the emphasis tag, `<em>`, to produce italics. For example, if you apply boldface and italic through the HTML Styles panel, your code looks like this:

```
<p>This paragraph has a word in <b>boldface</b> and a word in <i>italic</i>.</p>
```

Applying the same styles through the Properties panel gives you this:

```
<p>This paragraph has a word in <strong>boldface</strong> and a word in
    <em>italic</em>.</p>
```

If you're creating a paragraph style, you can specify the format of the text, such as Paragraph, Heading 1, and Heading 2, as well as left, right, or center alignment. These values are precisely the same as the ones on the Properties panel. Specifying Heading 1 as the format, for instance, causes Dreamweaver to nest the paragraph between opening and closing level-one heading tags, `<h1>` and `</h1>`.

e x a m
ⓦ a t c h
You can apply paragraph styles to paragraphs, headers of all levels, and preformatted text, not just paragraphs.

Now click OK to create the style. Dreamweaver adds it to the list in the HTML Styles panel. The underlined *a* icon to the left of the style name designates a selection style, while the paragraph-character icon means a paragraph style. A small plus sign to the right of the style icon indicates that you selected the Add To Existing option instead of Clear Existing Style from the HTML Styles dialog box.

You can use your HTML styles with every Web page in your current site. Dreamweaver stores the style definitions in an XML file in your local root folder.

If you switch sites, the HTML Styles dialog box reconfigures itself to the HTML styles (if any) in that particular site. This XML file is created for Dreamweaver's purposes only. You don't have to upload this file with your site to the remote server.

Applying HTML Styles

To apply a selection style, select a string of text in the document window, go to the HTML Styles panel, and click the name of the style that you want to apply. To apply a paragraph style, click anywhere inside the paragraph and click the name of the style.

At the bottom left of the HTML Styles panel is a checkbox next to an Apply button. This checkbox is checked by default, meaning that Dreamweaver automatically applies the style whenever you click a style name in the panel. If you would rather apply the style manually, uncheck this box. Then, to apply a style, select a style name from the panel and click the Apply button.

Another way to apply an HTML style is to select a string of text or a paragraph and choose the appropriate style name from Text | HTML Styles.

Removing Formatting Tags

You can also use the HTML Styles panel to remove existing formatting tags from a selected string of text or a paragraph, even if you didn't use HTML styles to format the text in the first place. To remove the formatting from a string of text, select the text in the document window. Then, in the HTML Styles panel, click Clear Selection Style, which is the first option in the list. If you unchecked the checkbox next to the Apply button, click the Apply button. Otherwise, Dreamweaver automatically removes all the formatting tags from the selection, reducing the text to its default appearance. This operation does nothing to the formatting tags outside the selection. Therefore, if all the text in a given paragraph is font size 5 and you clear the formatting from just three words inside the paragraph, the rest of the paragraph remains font size 5.

To remove the formatting from a paragraph, click anywhere inside the paragraph and choose Clear Paragraph Style from the HTML Styles panel. Click the Apply button as needed. Unlike clearing the style from a selected string of text, clearing the style from a paragraph removes all its formatting tags.

Choosing Text | HTML Styles | Clear Selection Style or Text | HTML Styles | Clear Paragraph Style performs the same task.

EXERCISE 9-1

Creating an HTML Style for Mad Science LLC

In this exercise, you use Dreamweaver to create an HTML style.

1. Launch Dreamweaver, open the Site panel, and select the Mad Science LLC site.
2. Double-click the *index.htm* file of the home page. The home page loads in a new document window.
3. Go to the Design panel group and click the tab for the HTML Styles panel.
4. Click the New Style button at the bottom of the panel, to the left of the trashcan icon. The Define HTML Style dialog box appears.
5. Type **Monster Name** in the Name field.
6. Under Apply To, choose the Paragraph option.
7. Under When Applying, choose the Clear Exiting Style option.
8. Choose the first set of fonts from the Font list.
9. Set the Size to 5.
10. Click the color square next to the Color field and choose a shade of purple. I'm going with #663399.
11. Under Style, click the B button for boldface.
12. Under Format, choose Paragraph from the list.
13. Under Alignment, click the first button on the left, the Align Left button.
14. Click OK. Dreamweaver adds the style to the HTML Styles panel.
15. To test your style, click any paragraph in the document window, go to the HTML Styles panel, and click the Monster Name style. Your document window should look something like Figure 9-3.

FIGURE 9-3

Test your new HTML style by applying it temporarily to some text on the home page.

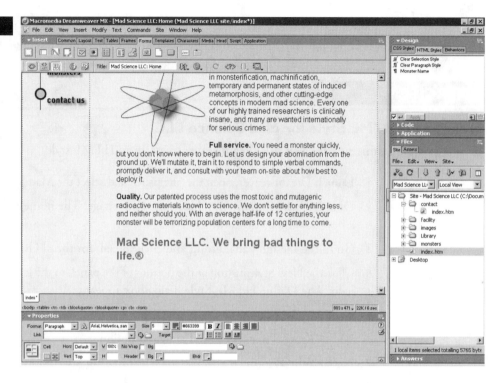

16. Choose Edit | Undo to remove the style for now. You'll use it later.

17. Choose File | Save. Good job!

Editing HTML Styles

You can edit the definition of an HTML style at any time. To do so, uncheck the checkbox next to the Apply button and double-click the style that you want to edit. Then right-click the style name and choose Edit from context menu, or open the HTML Styles panel menu and choose Edit. (If you use the context menu, you don't have to uncheck the checkbox next to the Apply button.)

All three roads lead to the same place. The Define HTML Style dialog box reappears. Make your changes to the style definition and click OK. All future uses of this HTML style reflect the new definition. Recheck the checkbox next to the Apply button if you prefer applying HTML styles automatically.

Unfortunately, editing a style doesn't affect your existing page at all. If you change a style from boldface to italic, for instance, the text to which you applied this style remains boldface. If you want to update the text on the page, you must go through manually and reapply the edited style.

To duplicate the attributes of an existing HTML style as the basis for a new style, open the context menu or the HTML Styles panel menu and choose Duplicate. Supply a new name for the style in the Name field of the Define HTML Style dialog box, and make any necessary adjustments to the attributes.

Deleting HTML Styles

To remove a style from the HTML Styles panel, select the style and click the trashcan icon at the bottom of the panel or open the panel menu and choose Delete. You can also right-click the name of the style and choose Delete from the context menu. This way, you don't have to uncheck the checkbox next to the Apply button. Deleting an HTML style is not doable, so look (and think) before you leap.

Keep in mind that deleting an HTML style doesn't automatically remove the formatting of the text to which you applied the style, just as editing an HTML style doesn't automatically update your page.

CERTIFICATION OBJECTIVE 9.02

Managing CSS Styles

CSS styles have the same effect as HTML styles. You use CSS styles to control the formatting of particular pieces of text. Under the hood, though, in the source code of your page, CSS styles and HTML styles couldn't be more different. CSS styles use a different set of HTML tags and CSS style definitions to format the text.

e x a m
ⓦ a t c h

Take note of the format of CSS code in the examples of this chapter, and pay close attention to its differences from HTML. CSS code appears several times on the exam.

Using Cascading Style Sheets has some undisputed advantages. First, they give you a bewildering variety of formatting possibilities. Where HTML offers seven possible text sizes, CSS offers every possible text size. Where HTML gives you just a few alignment options, CSS allows you to align the text exactly where you want it on the screen. You can even use CSS to redefine the way HTML tags work! In addition, CSS styles make editing the format of your text incredibly easy. Recall that when you edited an HTML style, the appearance of the existing text on your page didn't change. Not so with CSS styles. When you make a change to the style, you automatically update every instance of that style on your page or across your entire site, depending on how you set up the CSS.

Unfortunately, as you know, browsers still haven't gotten their act together with regard to CSS. Different browsers can interpret the same style sheet in annoyingly different ways. This is especially true for some of the more advanced formatting possibilities that CSS offers. CSS styles aren't readily backward compatible, either. Test your CSS-style–enhanced page in version 4 browsers, and you often find even greater inconsistencies in presentation.

When you work with CSS styles, it's important to watch out for two common problems. The first is setting up conflicting style definitions. This can happen whenever two or more style sheets control the appearance of the same piece of text, in which case the browser tries to apply all the attributes of all the styles. You run into problems sometimes when one style definition contradicts another—like if one style sheet gives the text color as green and another style sheet gives the text color of orange, or if one style sheet specifies boldface and another style sheet specifies normal text weight. In general, the style that comes closest to the text in the source of the page is the one that prevails when style sheets conflict, but you may experience unexpected results.

The second common problem is mixing HTML formatting tags and CSS styles. HTML styles automatically override CSS. If you apply an HTML text size to a CSS-controlled paragraph, for instance, the HTML text size determines the size of the text, not the CSS. Therefore, for best results with CSS styles, clear all the HTML formatting tags from a paragraph or selection before you apply the style.

o n t h e
ⓙ o b

Most professional sites use at least some CSS.

In spite of the drawbacks, don't dismiss CSS styles out of hand. I encourage you to experiment with them. Begin to incorporate them into your projects. Once you start working with Cascading Style Sheets, I think you'll find their potential too great to ignore.

Defining CSS Styles

Open the CSS Styles panel (Figure 9-4) in the Design panel group to define a CSS style. Click the New CSS Style button at the bottom of the panel, or choose Text | CSS Styles | New CSS Style. (The New CSS Style button is the second button from the left.) This opens the New CSS Style dialog box, shown in the following illustration. From this dialog box, you can choose to create a class, redefine an HTML tag, or use a CSS selector.

A *class* is a CSS style that doesn't apply to any HTML tag in particular. That is, you can use this kind of style with any textual element—a paragraph, a heading, or what have you. These styles are the most versatile. When in doubt, create a class.

By redefining an HTML tag, you create a style that works only with a particular tag, such as `<p>` or `<h1>`. The text in your document needs to appear between opening

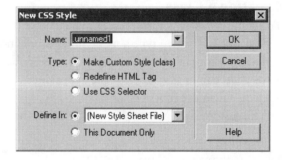

FIGURE 9-4

Use the CSS Styles panel to create and manage CSS styles.

and closing tags of this type for the style to take effect. You can use this kind of style to change all the instances of that tag in your page or on your site, or you can change some instances but leave others alone.

A *selector* is the beginning part of the CSS style definition in the source code of the page. It determines the element to which the style applies. All CSS styles have selectors. The name of a class is a CSS selector, as is the name of the HTML tag that you want to redefine, so the Use CSS Selector option on the dialog box is somewhat misleading. Choose this option when you want to create a style that applies to a certain series of HTML tags, defines link attributes, or controls all tags with a particular `id` attribute.

Be sure you know the differences between CSS styles and how best to use each type.

Creating a Class

To create a class, select the Make Custom Style (Class) option from the New CSS Style dialog box. Then type a name for the style in the Name field, preceded by a period. As with HTML styles, names that describe the function of the style work better than names that describe the appearance, since the appearance is more likely to change than the function.

The custom style *.navtext* looks like this in the code:

```
.navtext {
   background-color: #FF0000;
}
```

The name *.navtext* is the selector for this particular style definition. The curly braces ({ and }) contain the appearance attribute of this style, which sets the background color of the navigation text to red. Notice that a colon (:) follows the attribute name and that a semicolon (;) appears at the end of the value. Contrast this with HTML attribute/value pairs, which use equal signs and quotes instead (bgcolor="#FF0000").

Redefining an HTML Tag

To redefine an HTML tag, select the Redefine HTML Tag option from the New CSS Style dialog box. The Name field becomes a Tag field. Choose the HTML tag to which you want to apply the style from this field's drop-down list.

If you want your custom definition to apply to all instances of this tag, make sure that only the name of the tag appears in the Tag field. If you want your definition to apply only to particular instances of this tag, click to the right of the tag name in the Tag field, type a period, and then add a descriptive class name. For instance, you might create the style *p.copyright* for the copyright message at the bottom of your page. By adding a class name to the tag, you prevent all the paragraphs on the page from acquiring the same formatting as the copyright message.

This HTML-tag style definition applies to all level-one heading tags. It makes the color of the text green:

```
h1 {
    color: #00FF00;
}
```

By contrast, this style definition applies only to level-one heading tags that belong to a class called `special`:

```
h1.special {
    color: #00FF00;
}
```

To apply this style to a heading on your page, you must set the `<h1>` tag's `class` attribute like this:

```
<h1 class="special">This is a green headline</h1>
```

The *h1.special* style doesn't affect the text in the following example at all because the `class` attribute appears in a paragraph tag, not a level-one heading tag:

```
<p class="special">This paragraph is the default color because the special
    class only applies to h1 tags.</p>
```

Using a CSS Selector

I mentioned before that class names and HTML tags are CSS selectors in their own right. These aren't the only kinds of selectors, though. To create styles for other selectors, choose the Use CSS Selector option from the New CSS Style dialog box. The Name field becomes a Selector field.

If you want to create a style that applies to a particular series of tags, type the HTML tags without angle brackets into the Selector field. Separate each tag with a space, like this: p strong. Such a style applies whenever the browser encounters a strong tag, <strong>, inside a paragraph tag, <p>. The style does nothing to strong tags that you haven't nested inside paragraph tags, nor does it affect the appearance of a paragraph that doesn't also contain a strong tag.

In this example, the combination of paragraph and strong tags makes the boldface text appear in red:

```
p strong {
    color: #FF0000;
}
```

If you want to define a link attribute, choose a preset selector from the drop-down list. The *a:link* selector defines the appearance of unvisited links. Similarly, *a:visited* and *a:active* determine the appearance of visited and active links, respectively. Use the *a:hover* selector to define a hover state for text hyperlinks. The hover state appears when the visitor moves the mouse pointer over the link. Netscape Navigator 4 is notorious for not supporting the hover state, although Netscape 6 fully supports it.

This example sets up a hover state that turns off the underline of the link:

```
a:hover {
    text-decoration: none;
}
```

As with redefined HTML tags, you can specify that link states apply only to links of a particular class. To do so, click to the left of the colon character in the Selector field, type a period, and then type the class name. The CSS selector looks like this in the code:

```
a.effect:hover {
    text-decoration: none;
}
```

Now, only link elements that belong to the effect class have the hover:

```
<p><a href="http://www.taotezing.com" class="effect">This link</a> has a
    hover effect, while <a href="http://www.taotezing.com">this link</a>
    does not.</p>
```

If you want to create a style that applies to any tag with a specific id attribute, type a hash mark (#) followed by the name of the id attribute in the Selector field. To apply this style, you must define the id attribute of the HTML tag that controls the text. For instance, you might create the selector #content to apply to the running text on the page, whether that text appears in paragraphs, lists, or cells of layout tables. The CSS selector looks like this:

```
#content {
    font-size: 12pt;
}
```

Applying this style to a paragraph is simply a matter of selecting the appropriate paragraph tag in the Tag Inspector and typing **content** (without the hash mark) as the id attribute, so that your paragraph tag looks like this:

```
<p id="content">This paragraph uses the #content selector. It has
    12-point type.</p>
```

Apply the same style to a table cell like this:

```
<td id="content">This table cell uses the #content selector. It has
    12-point type.</td>
```

Now that you've examined the different types of CSS styles, see the next Scenario and Solution sidebar for a quick reference to help you remember which is which.

Creating the Declaration

If the selector of a CSS style is the element to which the style applies, the *declaration* of the style is the set of attribute/value pairs that appears between the curly braces of

SCENARIO & SOLUTION

When should you create a class style?	When you want a versatile style that doesn't restrict itself to a single tag or set of tags
When should you redefine an HTML tag?	When you want every occurrence of the tag to look the same way
When should you choose the Use CSS Selector option?	When you want to create a style for a specific combination of tags, when you want to create a style for link colors and effects, or when you want to create a custom selector that requires the id attribute in its corresponding HTML tag

the style definition. To create the declaration from the New CSS Style dialog, first choose where to define the style, either in the current page or in a separate CSS file. I'll talk more about this option in the "Using External CSS Files" section of this chapter. If you're testing out the software while you're reading, choose the This Document Only option for now. Doing so embeds the style definition into the source code of the page.

Click OK in the New CSS Style dialog box, and the CSS Style Definition dialog box appears. Choose from among the categories on the left side of the dialog box, and fill in the fields and options that appear on the right. You can define as many or as few options as your style requires. When you finish, click OK.

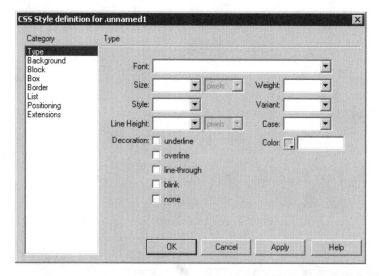

When you embed the style sheet in the source code of the page, all the style definitions appear in the head section between style tags, `<style>` and `</style>`, like this:

```
<head>
<title>My Page</title>
<style type="text/css">
<!--
    #content {
        font-size: 12pt;
        color: #CCFFFF;
        font-weight: bold;
    }
```

```
   1.special {
      color: #00FF00;
   }
-->
</style>
</head>
```

Notice that each attribute/value pair sits on its own line in the declaration and that comment tags nest the entire chunk. These comment tags prevent non–CSS-enabled browsers from displaying the CSS code as literal text in the browser window.

Occasionally, depending on how you add styles to the page, Dreamweaver puts each definition between its own set of style tags, like this:

```
<head>
<title>My Page</title>
<style type="text/css">
<!--
   #content {
      font-size: 12pt;
       color: #CCFFFF;
      font-weight: bold;
   }
</style>
<style>
   h1.special {
      color: #00FF00;
   }
-->
</style>
</head>
```

This doesn't affect the way the page works, although it's not the best coding practice.

Remember that browsers give inconsistent and unreliable support for CSS, so don't get too carried away with elaborate style definitions, and always test your work in several browsers before you upload it to the Web.

Applying CSS Styles

The CSS Styles panel has two views: Apply Styles and Edit Styles. To apply a CSS style to text on your page, switch to the Apply Styles view.

Under Apply Styles, you'll find all the class names for your styles in the panel. Redefined HTML tags and custom CSS selectors don't appear in this list.

To apply a class style, select the element to which you want to apply the style, and go to the Tag Selector at the bottom of the document window to choose specifically which HTML tag should receive the `class` attribute. For instance, if you click a link in the document window but want to apply the class style to the paragraph in which the link appears, click the paragraph tag, `<p>`, in the Tag Selector bar.

After you choose the correct tag, go to the CSS Styles panel and click the name of the class style that you want to apply, or choose the name of the style from Text | CSS Styles. Dreamweaver adds the appropriate `class` attribute to the selected tag.

FROM THE CLASSROOM

Form Letters

Once Web builders start creating forms, it doesn't take long for them to want to change the appearance of those ugly form objects. Unfortunately, HTML doesn't provide a way for this to happen. Fortunately, CSS does. Here's a quick list of methods you can use to spruce up text fields, password fields, lists, menus, and buttons:

- By attaching a style with the attribute `background-color`, you can supply a background color value for the form object (`background-color: #CCCCFF;`).

- By attaching a style with the attribute `color`, you can change the color of the text inside the object (`color: #003366;`).

- By attaching a style with the attribute `font-face`, you can change the font of the text inside the object (`font-face: Arial;`).

- By attaching a style with the attribute `font-weight`, you can change the font inside the object to boldface (`font-weight: bold;`).

- By attaching a style with the attribute `font-style`, you can change the font inside the object to italic (`font-style: italic;`).

- By attaching a style with the attribute `font-size`, you can change the size of the text inside the object (`font-size: 12px;`).

Bear in mind, of course, that these styles might not work on all browsers, so make sure that your forms look respectable, even without your CSS flourishes.

If you don't want to apply the class to a particular tag, you can select a string of text in the document window instead. When you do this, Dreamweaver inserts a special span tag, <span>, into the code and adds the class attribute to this tag:

```
<p>This paragraph highlights <span class="highlight">three words only</span>
   with a CSS style.</p>
```

To apply a redefined-tag style, you don't have to do anything. If you set up the style to affect all tags of that kind, every time you insert this tag the style automatically applies. If you specified a particular class for a redefined tag, proceed as if you're applying a class style.

Likewise, do nothing special to apply styles for multi-tag selectors. All occurrences of that particular combination of tags automatically receive the style you defined. The same holds true for link definitions, unless you specifically supplied a class name, in which case you follow the method for class styles above. To apply an id attribute style, you must add the id attribute to the appropriate element's HTML tag and set the value of this attribute to the name of the selector.

EXERCISE 9-2

Creating a CSS Style for Mad Science LLC

In this exercise, you use Dreamweaver to create a CSS style.

1. Launch Dreamweaver, open the Site panel, and select the Mad Science LLC site.

2. Double-click the *index.htm* file of the home page. The home page loads in a new document window.

3. Go to the Design panel group and click the tab for the CSS Styles panel.

4. Click the New CSS Style button at the bottom of the panel. This button is the second one from the left. The New CSS Style dialog box appears.

5. Type **.monsterbox** in the Name field.

6. Under Type, choose the Make Custom Style (Class) option.

7. Under Define In, select the first option and choose New Style Sheet File from the list.

8. Click OK. The Save Style Sheet File As dialog box appears. Navigate to the top of your local root folder so that you see the folders for *contact, monsters,* and *facility* in the window. Type **styles.css** in the File Name field and click Save. The CSS Style Definitions dialog box appears.

9. Click the Background category on the left of the dialog box. Click the color square next to the Background Color field and choose a shade of lime green. (I chose #66FF00.)

10. Click the Box category. Choose the Auto options from the Width and Height lists. Check the Same For All checkbox under Padding, choose Value from the list, and type **10**. Set the units to Pixels.

11. Click the Border category. Check all three Same For All checkboxes at the top of the dialog box. Then choose Solid from the list under Style. Choose Thick from the list under Width. Click the color square under Color and choose a dark shade of blue. (I picked #003366.)

12. Click OK to create the style. Dreamweaver adds the style to the CSS Styles panel.

13. To test your style, click any paragraph in the document window, go to the CSS Styles panel and click the *.monsterbox* style. Dreamweaver places the paragraph inside a bright green box with a thick blue border. Nice! Your document window should now look something like Figure 9-5.

14. Click Clear CSS Style in the CSS Styles panel to remove this style for now.

15. Choose File | Save. You did it!

Modifying CSS Styles

Switch to the CSS Style panel's Edit Styles view to modify CSS style definitions. When you switch to this view, all your style definitions appear—not just the classes. Double-click the name of a style to recall the CSS Style Definition dialog box for that particular style, or right-click the name of the style and choose Edit from the context menu. Make as many or as few changes as you like and click OK. As promised, every piece of text that uses this style automatically changes in the document window.

FIGURE 9-5

Try out your new CSS style on some text from the home page.

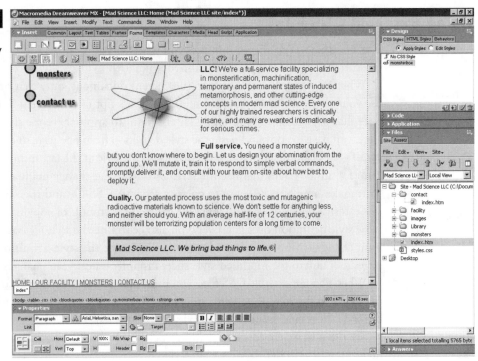

Removing CSS Styles

To clear the effects of a class style on a particular piece of text, select the text in the document window. Then, for best results, go to the Tag Selector at the bottom of the document window and select the tag to which you applied the style. In the CSS Styles panel, switch to Apply Styles view and click the No CSS Style option at the top of the styles list. Dreamweaver removes the `class` attribute of the appropriate tag or deletes the corresponding span tags from the code.

Removing `id` attribute styles is not quite as fast but just as straightforward. Manually remove the `id` attribute from the appropriate tag.

To remove a redefined-tag style that doesn't have a class, modify the style's definition by double-clicking its name in Edit Styles view.

To delete a CSS style entirely, switch to Edit Styles view, select the style to delete, and click the trashcan icon at the bottom of the CSS Styles panel. You can also right-click the name of the style and choose Delete from the context menu. Deleting the style automatically removes this style from all elements on the page.

Using External CSS Files

The New CSS Style dialog box asks you whether you want to add the style sheet to the current page or a separate document.

When you add the CSS style to the current document, only that document can use your style definitions, just like adding a JavaScript to the current document allows only that page to run the function. If you want to apply the same style to a different page, you have to copy and paste the style definition from one page to the other. Worse yet, if your client decides to change the look of a style at the last minute, you have to hunt for all the pages that use the style and make the change manually.

It makes much more sense to create a separate CSS file and then link each page to this external file. Not only do you save yourself the trouble of copying and pasting the same style definition over and over, you also centralize the style so that when eleventh-hour changes come up, all you have to do is change the style definition once. All the pages that link to the modified style sheet instantly reflect your changes.

When you use external CSS files, you must upload the CSS file with the rest of your site assets to the remote server. Otherwise, the visitor's browser won't be able to find the style sheet, and none of your style definitions will work.

See the next Scenario and Solution sidebar for a quick reference to help you determine how to define your CSS styles.

Creating External CSS Files

To create an external CSS file and link it automatically to the current page, choose the New Style Sheet File option under Define In on the New CSS Style dialog box. When you click OK, the Save Style Sheet File As dialog box appears. Navigate to a convenient location in your local root folder, supply a name for the file in the File Name field, and click Save. Then build the declaration from the CSS Style Definition dialog box.

SCENARIO & SOLUTION

When should you embed the style definitions in the current page?	When you want to create a quick style that you don't plan on using anywhere else
When should you create the style definitions in a separate CSS file?	When you plan on using the same styles elsewhere on your site

Dreamweaver adds a link tag, `<link>`, to the head section of the page, like this:

```
<head>
<title>My Page</title>
<link href="../css/mystyles.css" rel="stylesheet" type="text/css">
</head>
```

The `href` attribute provides the path to the external CSS file. The `rel` attribute explains that the relation of the linked file to the page is that of a style sheet, and the `type` attribute declares the type of style sheet.

Cascading Style Sheets aren't the only kind of style sheet in use today. JavaScript style sheets are also popular.

Attaching and Importing Existing CSS Files

If you already have an existing CSS file that you want to link to the current page, or if you want to import the style definitions from an external CSS file, click the first icon on the left at the bottom of the CSS Styles panel. This is the Attach Style Sheet button, and clicking it opens the Link External Style Sheet dialog box (shown here).

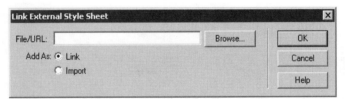

At the bottom of the dialog box, choose whether Dreamweaver should link to the file or import the style definitions. Then click the Browse button, navigate to the CSS file, and click OK.

If you chose to link to the file, Dreamweaver adds a link tag to the head section of the page, as before. If you chose to import the file, Dreamweaver adds a peculiar bit of code to the style definition:

```
<style type="text/css">
<!--
    @import url("../css/mystyles.css");
-->
</style>
```

The `@import` command works much like a link tag. Netscape browsers don't support `@import`, so use link tags instead for better cross-browser compatibility.

Remember that `@import` ***doesn't work in Netscape browsers.***

Editing External CSS Files

To edit an external CSS file in Dreamweaver, choose Test | CSS Styles | Edit Style Sheet. The Edit Style Sheet dialog box appears, as shown in the following illustration. Choose the name of the style sheet that you want to edit. Then click Duplicate to create a new copy of the selected style sheet, click Remove to detach the selected style sheet, or click Edit to edit the style definitions in the selected style sheet. If you click Edit, a new dialog box appears with the CSS styles of the selected style sheet, along with commands for duplicating, removing, and editing the style definitions.

Exporting an Embedded Style Sheet

To export the current embedded style sheet as an external CSS file, choose File | Export | CSS Styles or open the CSS Styles panel menu and choose Export Style Sheet. Type a name for the CSS file in the File Name field of the Export Styles As CSS dialog box, and navigate to a convenient location in your local root folder. Click Save to create the file.

Using Design Time Style Sheets

Design Time style sheets are external CSS files that you can attach to Dreamweaver's Design view. These style sheets don't affect the code or appearance of your page in a live browser window. Instead, Design Time style sheets allow you test different CSS files in Dreamweaver before attaching them to your page.

Design Time style sheets apply to your page in Dreamweaver only.

To add or remove Design Time style sheets, first make sure that you save the current document. Then choose Text | CSS Styles | Design Time Style Sheets, or right-click in the CSS Styles panel and choose Design Time Style Sheets from the context menu. The Design Time Style Sheets dialog box appears.

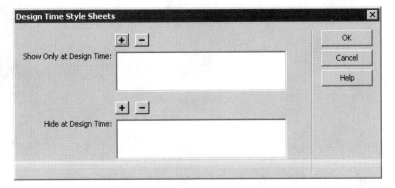

Click the plus button above the Show Only At Design Time area and browse to the location of a CSS file that you want to try out. This style sheet appears in the large field at the top of the dialog box. To remove a style sheet from this field, highlight the name of the file, and click the minus button.

You can also hide the effects of style sheets while you design your page. To do so, click the plus button above the Hide At Design Time area and browse to the location of the CSS file that you want to hide. None of this file's style definitions appear in Design view, nor do they show up in the Apply Styles view of the CSS Styles panel.

If you switch the panel to Edit Styles view, you can review the styles that Dreamweaver is currently showing or hiding.

Remember that Design Time style sheets are for preview purposes only. They affect the appearance of your page in Dreamweaver's document window, but they don't do anything to your page as it appears in a browser. If you want to add the styles from a Design Time style sheet to your page, you must attach or import the style sheet as described earlier in the chapter.

Converting CSS Styles to HTML Styles

In the interest of cross-browser compatibility, you can create a version of your page that works in older browsers and non–CSS-enabled browsers by converting CSS styles to HTML styles.

To do this, choose File | Convert | 3.0 Browser Compatible. This opens the Convert To 3.0 Browser Compatible dialog box (see the next illustration). Select either the CSS Styles To HTML Markup option or the Both option, depending on whether layers appear on your page. Then click OK. The 3.0-compatible page opens in a new document window. Dreamweaver converts your page fairly accurately, although not perfectly, since CSS offers many more design choices than HTML tags and attributes can render.

Working with CSS in the Properties Panel

By default, the font controls on the Properties panel apply HTML tags to the source code of your page. Choosing a value from the Size list, for instance, adds the `size` attribute to the font tag that controls the text.

If you want to use the Properties panel to apply CSS styles instead, click the A icon on the Properties panel. The icon changes into Dreamweaver's CSS symbol, and the font list becomes a CSS-style list, from which you can apply CSS styles to selected elements, define new CSS styles, edit existing CSS styles, or attach external Cascading Style Sheets. When you switch to CSS, you lose the ability to change the color and alignment of the selection from the Properties panel (shown in the following illustration), since the CSS style that you choose controls these design elements. However, you can still apply boldface and italic HTML tags to CSS-controlled text.

Click the CSS icon on the Properties panel to switch back to HTML-based styles.

CERTIFICATION SUMMARY

In this chapter, you learned the difference between HTML styles and CSS styles.

Dreamweaver creates HTML styles with HTML tags and attributes. HTML styles are more cross-browser compatible than CSS styles, but they don't offer as many formatting options. Moreover, when you edit HTML styles, the existing text in your document window remains exactly the same. Only new text created after you edit the styles is affected.

CSS styles come from Cascading Style Sheet style definitions, which aren't HTML at all. These styles appear in the head section of a page between style tags, `<style>` and `</style>`, or in the form of a link to an external CSS file. CSS styles aren't as compatible across browsers as HTML styles, but they offer many additional formatting options, including the ability to redefine HTML tags. When you edit a CSS style, the existing text in your document window automatically changes to reflect the new style definition.

If the editability of CSS intrigues you but you find the lack of consistent browser support annoying, you can convert your CSS-enhanced pages into HTML styles by invoking File | Convert | 3.0 Browser Compatible.

TWO-MINUTE DRILL

Managing HTML Styles

- ❑ HTML styles are styles created by HTML tags and attributes.
- ❑ Use the HTML Styles panel to manage and create HTML styles.
- ❑ HTML styles are more cross-browser compatible than CSS styles but offer fewer design choices.
- ❑ Selection styles are styles that you can apply to selected strings of text.
- ❑ Paragraph styles are styles that you can apply to an entire paragraph.
- ❑ When you delete or modify existing HTML styles, the text in the document window doesn't change.
- ❑ You can use your HTML styles on any page of your current site.

Managing CSS Styles

- ❑ CSS styles are created with Cascading Style Sheet style definitions.
- ❑ The selector of a CSS style is the element to which the style applies, while the declaration of the style is the set of attribute/value pairs that defines the appearance of the style.
- ❑ CSS attribute/value pairs don't look like HTML attribute/value pairs.
- ❑ Dreamweaver allows you to define three kinds of CSS styles: classes, redefined HTML tags, and miscellaneous CSS selectors.
- ❑ A class style requires the `class` attribute in the corresponding HTML tag, while some kinds of CSS selector styles require the `id` attribute.
- ❑ You can add class names to redefined-tag styles to prevent the styles from applying to every instance of the HTML tag in your page.
- ❑ Attaching a style sheet as a separate CSS file, rather than embedding the style definitions in the source code of the page, allows you to use the same style definitions for any number of pages.
- ❑ When you edit or delete a CSS style in Dreamweaver, the text in the document window automatically changes.

SELF TEST

The following questions will help you measure your understanding of the material presented in this chapter. Read all the choices carefully because there might be more than one correct answer. Choose all correct answers for each question.

Managing HTML Styles

1. Which of the following is an advantage to using HTML styles?
   A. HTML styles give you more than seven text sizes.
   B. HTML styles offer more formatting choices than CSS styles.
   C. HTML styles update automatically when you edit them.
   D. HTML styles offer better cross-browser compatibility.

2. Which of the following HTML tags create boldface text in most browsers?
   A. `<em>`
   B. `<strong>`
   C. `<b>`
   D. `<weight>`

3. You want to apply a paragraph style to a paragraph on your page. What do you do? Choose the best answer.
   A. Click anywhere inside the paragraph, go to the HTML Styles panel, and click the name of the style that you want to apply.
   B. Select all the text of the paragraph, go to the HTML Styles panel, and click the name of the style that you want to apply.
   C. Click the name of the style that you want to apply, go to the document window, and click anywhere inside the paragraph.
   D. Click the name of the style that you want to apply, go to the document window, and select all the text of the paragraph.

4. What is a selection style?
   A. A style that applies to the visitor's selections
   B. A style that applies to a string of text

    C. A style that applies to a paragraph of text

    D. An HTML style selector

5. On the HTML Styles panel, how can you tell whether an HTML style adds its attributes to the current attributes of the selected text?

    A. A plus sign appears to the right of the name of the style.

    B. A plus sign appears to the right of the style's icon.

    C. A red exclamation point appears to the right of the name of the style.

    D. A red exclamation point appears to the right of the style's icon.

6. When you delete an HTML style, what happens to the text in the document window that you had formatted with this style?

    A. Nothing.

    B. Dreamweaver deletes the text.

    C. Dreamweaver returns the text to its default appearance.

    D. None of the above.

7. How does Dreamweaver keep track of your HTML styles?

    A. It doesn't.

    B. It stores the styles in a separate CSS file in your local root folder.

    C. It stores the styles in a separate DW file in your local root folder.

    D. It stores the styles in a separate XML file in your local root folder.

8. You created an HTML style called *caption* for the picture captions on your page. What is the correct HTML markup for a paragraph tag that uses the *caption* style?

    A. `<p>`

    B. `<p class="caption">`

    C. `<p id="caption">`

    D. `<p.caption>`

    E. `<#caption>`

9. What kinds of formatting can you achieve with HTML styles?

    A. Boldface

    B. Headline level

C. Text color

D. Alignment

E. Link color and hover effects

10. You just created an HTML style for a page in your site. To which page or pages can you apply the style?

A. Any Dreamweaver document

B. Any Dreamweaver document in any site

C. Any Dreamweaver document in the current site

D. Only the current Dreamweaver document

Managing CSS Styles

11. What or who is the selector in a CSS style definition? Choose the best answer.

A. The person, usually a Web site visitor, who makes a style selection

B. The element to which the CSS style applies

C. The designer of the style sheet

D. An external style sheet

12. You created an external CSS file to control the appearance of text on your site. You uploaded your site, and now you're visiting it on the Web with Microsoft Internet Explorer 6. The style sheet worked perfectly offline. Now you see nothing but plain, unformatted HTML text. What is the likely problem?

A. You used CSS style definitions that IE 6 doesn't support.

B. You attached your style sheet to the pages of your site with the `@import` method instead of the `link` method.

C. You forgot to upload the CSS file.

13. You want to redefine an HTML tag using CSS, but you want the style to affect only certain instances of the HTML tag. What should you do?

A. Add a class name to the tag in the Tag field of the New CSS Styles dialog box.

B. Add an `id` attribute to the appropriate tags.

C. Forget about redefining HTML tags. You need to create a class style from the New CSS Styles dialog box.

D. Choose Text | CSS Styles | Redefine HTML Tag.

14. You want to maximize the cross-browser compatibility of your site. Which of the following statements best describes your policy toward styles?

    A. You will use CSS styles only.

    B. You will use HTML styles only.

    C. You will use HTML styles for all but the hover effects on the page.

15. What does a non–CSS-enabled browser do when it encounters Dreamweaver's CSS code?

    A. It ignores the code.

    B. It displays the code as text in the browser window.

    C. It may cause unexpected browser crashes.

    D. It converts the CSS styles to HTML styles.

16. Which of the following are valid CSS selectors?

    A. `#special`

    B. `b`

    C. `td p`

    D. `a:hover.special`

    E. `.special`

    F. `special`

17. Which of the following are valid CSS declarations?

    A. `font-size: 10pt;`

    B. `font-size="10pt"`

    C. `color="#FFFF00"`

    D. `color: #FFFF00;`

    E. `bgcolor: #FFFFFF;`

    F. `bgcolor="#FFFFFF"`

18. What is the command for converting CSS styles to HTML styles in Dreamweaver?

    A. File | Convert | 2.0 Browser Compatible

    B. File | Convert | 3.0 Browser Compatible

    C. File | Convert | 4.0 Browser Compatible

    D. File | Convert | CSS To HTML

19. When you attach an external CSS file to a page in your site, what tag does Dreamweaver use to achieve this? Choose the best answer.

    A. `<head>`

    B. `<style>`

    C. `<script>`

    D. `<link>`

20. How is a Design Time style sheet different from an attached CSS file?

    A. The Design Time style sheet affects only the design of the page, while the CSS file affects the design and the attributes.

    B. The Design Time style sheet works only in a live browser window, while the CSS file works in Dreamweaver and the browser window.

    C. The Design Time style sheet works only in Dreamweaver, while the CSS file works in Dreamweaver and the browser window.

    D. You can hide Design Time style sheets, but you can't hide CSS files.

    E. You can hide CSS files, but you can't hide Design Time style sheets.

LAB QUESTION

Sports coaches often advise their players to be the ball, whatever that means. In this lab question, I'm going to ask you to be the browser. Knowing what you know about CSS styles, look over the following style sheet and HTML snippet. Write down on a piece of paper what the text will look like in a browser. Check your answer against the real deal in the Lab Answer section.

Here is the style sheet:

```
.styleA {
   text-decoration: line-through;
}
p.styleB {
   text-decoration: underline;
   font-size: large;
}
#styleC {
   font-style: italic;
}
```

Here's the HTML snippet:

```
<h1 class="styleB">The ABCs</h1>
<p class="styleA">A B C D E F G</p>
<p class="styleB">H I <span class="styleC">J</span> K
    <span id="styleC">L M N</span> O P</p>
<p id="styleC">Q R S <span class="styleB">T U V</span></p>
<p class="styleB">W X <span class="styleA">Y</span> Z</p>
```

SELF TEST ANSWERS

Managing HTML Styles

1. ☑ **D.** HTML styles offer better cross-browser compatibility.

☒ **A, B,** and **C** are all advantages, but they're advantages to using CSS styles, not HTML styles.

2. ☑ **B and C.** The tags `<strong>` and `<b>` create boldface.

☒ **A** is incorrect because the emphasis tag, `<em>`, creates italic text. **D** is incorrect because there is no `<weight>` tag in HTML.

3. ☑ **A.** Click anywhere inside the paragraph, go to the HTML Styles panel, and click the name of the style that you want to apply.

☒ **B** is incorrect because this is the procedure you'd follow to apply a selection style to the paragraph. **C** and **D** are incorrect because neither choice applies a style. You must select the text first and then click the name of the style.

4. ☑ **B.** A selection style is a style that applies to a string of text.

☒ **A** is incorrect because there is no selection style for this effect. **C** is incorrect because this choice describes a paragraph style. **D** is incorrect because there is no such thing as an HTML style selector. You could be thinking of a CSS style selector, which is the element to which you attach the style.

5. ☑ **B.** A plus sign appears to the right of the style's icon in the HTML Styles panel to signify that the style adds its attributes to those of the selected text.

☒ **A** is incorrect because the plus sign appears to the right of the style's icon, not its name. **C** and **D** are incorrect because there is no red exclamation point in the HTML Styles panel.

6. ☑ **A.** Not a blessed thing happens to the text in your document window if you delete an HTML style.

☒ **B** is incorrect because Dreamweaver doesn't delete your text. **C** is incorrect because Dreamweaver doesn't restore the text to its default appearance. You might be thinking of the Clear Selection Style or Clear Paragraph Style choices on the HTML Styles panel. **D** is incorrect because choice **A** is the correct answer.

7. ☑ **D.** Dreamweaver stores your HTML styles in a separate XML file in your local root folder. You don't have to upload this file to your remote site.

☒ **A, B,** and **C** are incorrect because Dreamweaver stores your HTML styles in a separate XML file in your local root folder.

8. ☑ **A.** The correct HTML markup is simply `<p>`. HTML styles are regular HTML tags with regular HTML attributes.

 ☒ **B** is incorrect because this markup indicates a CSS class style called *caption*. **C** is incorrect because this markup indicates a custom CSS selector style called *#caption*. **D** and **E** are incorrect because neither of these are proper HTML tags.

9. ☑ **A, B, C,** and **D.** You can achieve boldface, headline level, text color, and alignment with HTML styles, among many other formatting choices.

 ☒ **E** is incorrect because you need CSS to create styles for link colors and hover effects.

10. ☑ **C.** You can apply your HTML style to any document in the current site.

 ☒ **A, B,** and **D** are incorrect because you can apply your HTML style to any document in the current site.

Managing CSS Styles

11. ☑ **B.** The selector is the element to which a CSS style applies.

 ☒ **A, C,** and **D** are incorrect because, in terms of a CSS style definition, the selector is the element to which the CSS style applies.

12. ☑ **C.** You probably just forgot to upload the CSS file to the remote server. It happens to the best of us.

 ☒ **A** is incorrect because if the style definitions were the problem, your pages would look unformatted offline, as well as online. **B** is incorrect because the `@import` method doesn't work on Netscape, and you would have noticed before you uploaded your site to the remote server.

13. ☑ **A.** Add a class name to the tag in the New CSS Style dialog box.

 ☒ **B** is incorrect because this procedure applies to custom CSS selector styles, not redefined-tag styles. **C** is incorrect because you can add a class name to a redefined HTML tag. **D** is incorrect because there is no such command in Dreamweaver.

14. ☑ **B.** To maximize the cross-browser compatibility of your site, you will use only HTML styles.

 ☒ **A** is incorrect because CSS is less cross-browser compatible than HTML. **C** is incorrect because Netscape browsers as recent as Netscape 4 don't support hover effects.

15. ☑ **A.** Non-CSS-enabled browsers ignore Dreamweaver's CSS code because Dreamweaver nests it between comment tags.

 ☒ **B** would be correct only if Dreamweaver didn't nest the code between comment tags. **C** is incorrect because it's highly unlikely that ignored code will cause a crash. **D** is incorrect because, while Dreamweaver can convert CSS styles to HTML styles, a browser cannot.

16. ☑ **A, B, C,** and **E.** All four of these choices are valid CSS selectors.
    ☒ **D** is incorrect because the class name goes after the a selector, not after the `hover` part. **F** is incorrect because this selector doesn't have a hash sign (#) or period in front of it.

17. ☑ **A** and **D.** These declarations are properly formatted.
    ☒ **B, C,** and **F** are incorrect because these choices appear in something like HTML-style attribute/value pairs. CSS attribute/value pairs look like choices **A** and **D. E** is incorrect because `background-color` is the correct attribute in CSS, not HTML's `bgcolor`.

18. ☑ **B.** The correct command is File | Convert | 3.0 Browser Compatible.
    ☒ **A, C,** and **D** are incorrect because these commands don't exist in Dreamweaver.

19. ☑ **D.** Dreamweaver uses the link tag, `<link>`, to attach a separate CSS file to a page.
    ☒ **A** is incorrect because, while Dreamweaver nests the link tag in the head section, the head tag by itself doesn't link to the external file. **B** is incorrect because the style tag is for embedded CSS style definitions and the `@import` method. **C** is incorrect because script tags are for attaching client-side scripts, not style sheets.

20. ☑ **C** and **D.** Design Time style sheets appear only in Dreamweaver's document window, and you can hide them.
    ☒ **A, B,** and **E** are incorrect because none of these choices are true statements. Choice **A** also contains empty jargon. Watch out for that!

LAB ANSWER

Here's the text from a live browser window:

<h2 style="text-align:center">The ABCs</h2>

A̶B̶C̶D̶E̶F̶G̶

<u>H I J K L M N O P</u>

Q R S T U V

<u>W X ¥ Z</u>

Notice that the headline doesn't have an underline. Why not? Because `p.styleB` applies only to paragraph tags, not headline tags. Therefore, the formatting of the headline in the browser window has nothing to do with the `class` attribute and everything to do with the standard appearance of level-one headlines in HTML. The *J* doesn't appear in italic like the *L, M,* and *N* because `#styleC` is a custom CSS selector, for which you need the `id` attribute, not the `class` attribute. The *T, U,* and *V* don't appear large and underlined because, once again, `p.styleB` applies only to paragraph tags, not span tags.

Dreamweaver®

CERTIFIED DREAMWEAVER DEVELOPER

10

Speeding Up Production

Few professions move as fast as Web building. It seems like there's always an impossible deadline rapidly approaching. The client wants more, more, more, now, now, now. The 30-hour workday is the rule. Slouches don't last long in this business, nor do people with outside interests, hobbies, friends, family, or lives of their own.

If you've come this far already, you're not afraid of hard work. Now let Dreamweaver ease the burden a little. Employing the features and techniques that are described in this chapter can help you to produce more sooner, which may mean the difference between a working weekend and being first in line at the next *Lord of the Rings*.

CERTIFICATION OBJECTIVE 10.01

Managing Content

Maintaining the content on your site can be a chore. Macromedia realizes this, and as a result, Dreamweaver helps you reduce the inherent tediousness of common management action items like searching dozens of files for a particular string of text, finding typos, and organizing assets. You can even record and create your own Dreamweaver commands. How's that for convenience?

Finding and Replacing Text

To search for text or a particular piece of source code on your page, use the Find And Replace dialog box. This dialog box opens when you choose Edit | Find And Replace.

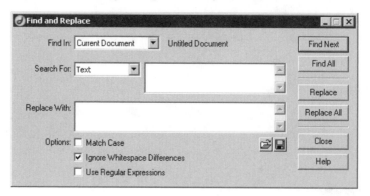

In the Find In list at the top of the dialog box, specify where you want Dreamweaver to search. You can target the search to the current document, the entire current local site, or selected files in the current local site. If you want to choose certain files, open the Site panel, hold down CTRL (Windows) or COMMAND (Mac) and click each file in which you want to search.

In the Search For list, specify what type of text you want to find from among four options: Text, Text (Advanced), Source Code, and Specific Tag. Type the target string in the field to the right of the Search For list and type the replacement string in the Replace With field. Press SHIFT-ENTER or SHIFT-RETURN to insert a carriage return in these fields, if necessary.

Check the Match Case option at the bottom of the dialog box if you want Dreamweaver to skip potential matches that don't use the same capitalization style as the search string. Check the Ignore Whitespace Differences option if you want Dreamweaver to overlook carriage returns and instances of multiple spaces. This option is especially helpful when you search the source code. However, if you entered carriage returns in the Search For or Replace With field, be sure to uncheck the Ignore Whitespace Differences option, or Dreamweaver will ignore the whitespace that you added to the search or replace strings!

Click Find Next to find the next occurrence of the target string or click Find All to find every occurrence, one at a time. Click Replace Next to replace the next occurrence of the target string with the replacement string or click Replace All to replace every occurrence in one fell swoop.

Searching for Text   In the Search For list, the Text option, which is the default, ignores all source code and concentrates solely on the text of the page. Selecting this option and searching for the word *able*, for example, returns a match in this line of code:

```
<p>We are ready, willing, and able.</p>
```

However, Dreamweaver returns no match from this line of code because the occurrence of the search string appears inside the table HTML tag:

```
<table width="100%">
```

Choosing the Text (Advanced) option allows you to target your search even more precisely. When you choose this option, Dreamweaver adds fields and controls to the Find And Replace dialog box.

From the list to the right of the plus and minus buttons, choose where to look for the search string: Inside Tag or Not Inside Tag. When you select Inside Tag from this list, you restrict the search to text that falls inside a particular tag that you indicate in the second field to the right of the plus and minus buttons. For example, searching for the word *able* inside paragraph tags `<p>` finds a match here:

```
<p>We are ready, willing, and able.</p>
```

The same condition doesn't find a match here, however, because the target text isn't inside a paragraph tag:

```
<td>We are ready, willing, and able.</td>
```

If you choose Not Inside Tag as the condition, Dreamweaver ignores matches inside the tag that you choose from the second drop-down list.

Click the plus button to add another condition to the search. Another set of drop-down menus appears on the dialog box. Select the condition from the first new drop-down list, and choose values for the condition from the remaining lists. For instance, to search for the word *able* in paragraph tags containing the `align` attribute set to the value `left`, you'd set the first new drop-down list to With Attribute, the second list to Align, the third list to the equal sign, and the fourth list to Left.

Continue adding conditions by clicking the plus button. To remove a condition, select it and click the minus button.

Searching for Source Code Choose the Source Code option in the Search For list to look for the search string in the source code of the page. This option looks for the search string everywhere in the source, including the text, but it returns text matches only when the search string appears exactly as you type it in the Search For field. For instance, if you search for the string *table width* in the source, Dreamweaver finds a match here:

```
<table width="100%">
```

Dreamweaver also finds a match here, because *table width* appears literally in the text:

```
<p>Ever since the refugees arrived, my dinner table width is not sufficient.</p>
```

However, Dreamweaver doesn't find a match here, because a closing anchor tag separates the words *table* and *width:*

```
<p>Ever since the refugees arrived, my <a href="table.htm">dinner table</a>
   width is not sufficient.</p>
```

If you search the text instead of the source code, Dreamweaver ignores the closing anchor tag and returns a match.

Choosing Specific Tag from the Search For list replaces the text fields in the dialog box with drop-down lists, as shown in the following illustration. From the drop-down list to the right of the Search For list, select the tag that you want to find. Set conditions for the search by choosing values from the set of drop-down lists directly below the Search For list. Click the plus button to add another condition and click the minus button to remove a condition.

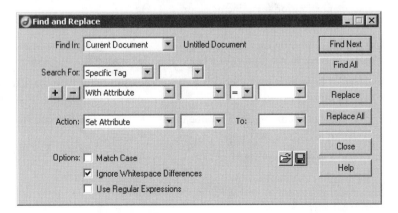

Under Action, determine what Dreamweaver will do when it finds a match. You can replace the tag and its contents, replace the contents of the tag only, remove the tag and its contents, strip the tag but leave the contents, change the tag to some other tag, set attributes of the tag, remove attributes of the tag, or add code either before or after the opening or closing tag.

Using Regular Expressions

A *regular expression* is a special code that represents a particular character or range of characters in a search string. For instance, the regular expression \t indicates the tab character, and \w indicates any alphanumeric character.

To include regular expressions in your search string, check the Use Regular Expressions option at the bottom of the Find And Replace dialog box. The quick reference in the following Scenario and Solution shows regular expressions for common searches. A complete list of regular expressions appears in Dreamweaver's online help.

exam

👁atch

Familiarize yourself with common regular expressions like the ones described in the quick reference.

SCENARIO & SOLUTION	
What is the regular expression for the tab character?	\t
What is the regular expression for a line break or carriage return?	\p
What is the regular expression for a specific character that appears at the beginning of a line?	^, as in ^a for the a character when it appears at the beginning of a line (Anything for a sale)
What is the regular expression for a specific character that appears at the end of a line?	$, as in $s for the s character when it appears at the end of a line (Where are my lawyers)
What is the regular expression to search for one item or another?	l, as in yes|no (She said yes for once; The deal is a no-go.)
What is the regular expression to search for any digit character?	\d
What is the regular expression to search for any alphanumeric character?	\w

Saving Queries

The following icons are useful in saving queries.

■ To save a set of *queries,* or search conditions, as a file on your computer, click the Find And Replace dialog box's Save Query button.

■ Click the Load Query button to retrieve a previously saved set of queries.

Saving queries for a rainy day means that you don't have to reenter a particularly complex or frequently used set of conditions the next time you need it.

Checking Spelling

Dreamweaver comes with an integrated spelling dictionary. Choose Text | Check Spelling to run the contents of the current document window through the spell checker. If Dreamweaver finds a word that it doesn't recognize, the Check Spelling dialog box appears.

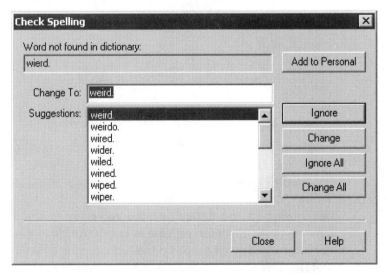

Choose from Dreamweaver's spelling suggestions on the left side of the dialog box. Then click the Change button to change this particular occurrence of the misspelled word or click Change All to change all occurrences. Click Ignore to skip over this occurrence or click Ignore All to skip over all occurrences of this word.

If the highlighted word is correct, you may add it to your personal dictionary by clicking the Add To Personal button.

Always check spelling. People who know how to spell are especially indignant toward those who don't, and a simple typo in a prominent place can cost you business. Would you rather buy from "The Smart Source for Software" or "Aplications Warehouse?"

Using the History Panel

The History panel records almost every action that you perform on a Dreamweaver document. You can use this panel to replay an action or a series of actions elsewhere on your page. Open the History panel by choosing Window | Others | History.

To play back a series of steps, choose a new insertion point on your page or select an element. Hold down CTRL (Windows) or COMMAND (Macintosh) and click the steps of the History panel that you want to replay. Then click the Replay button.

Depending on the actions or the selection in the document window, Dreamweaver might not be able to apply the History steps. The History panel doesn't record mouse movements or dragging procedures, so if your steps involve selecting different areas of the page or moving elements around, you might not get the results you want.

Undoing Multiple Actions at Once   Roll back your page to an earlier state by dragging the slider on the left of the History panel to the point at which you want to resume editing. Then simply execute a new command from that point.

Copying and Pasting Steps   You can transfer History steps from one document window to another. To do so, select the desired steps in the first document window, click the Copy button (shown here) at the bottom of the History panel, switch to the new document window, and choose Edit | Paste.

Dreamweaver attempts to paste the steps exactly as you executed them in the first document window. Again, depending on the steps, you may not get the exact results you want.

Recording Commands

Using Dreamweaver's Record feature, you can save a series of actions and replay them later. Choose Commands | Start Recording to begin recording your actions. Dreamweaver doesn't allow you to record mouse movements or dragging procedures, but you can record anything else, such as inserting a particular image or a piece of code.

When you finish, choose Commands | Stop Recording. Play back your recorded actions by choosing Commands | Play Recorded Command.

Dreamweaver remembers your recorded steps until you record over them or close the software.

Creating New Commands

You can save a series of steps in the History panel as a permanent Dreamweaver command. To do so, select the steps that you want to save and click the Save button at the bottom of the History panel.

The Save As Command dialog box appears. Type the name of the command in the Command Name field to indicate how the command will appear in the Commands menu. Then click OK.

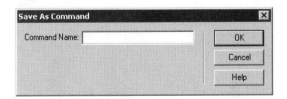

To execute your command, select its entry in the Commands menu.

To edit the name of your command or remove the command from the menu, choose Commands | Edit Command List. This opens the Edit Command List dialog box, shown next. Select a command from the list and type a new name to rename it or click the Delete button to remove it.

Using Code Snippets

Dreamweaver's Snippets panel, shown next, organizes a number of ready-made blocks of source code. You can insert these code snippets at will, edit their content, or create new snippets of your own. Look under the Code panel group for the Snippets tab or choose Window | Snippets.

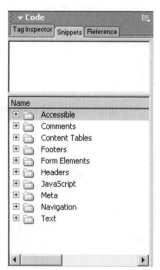

To insert a snippet, navigate the categories in the Snippets panel's main window until you find the snippet that you want. Then drag the snippet into the document window or select the snippet, choose an insertion point in the document window, and click the Insert button.

Snippets are prepackaged content. As with any content of this type, if you use it on a professional project, be sure to modify it to suit your specific needs.

Feel free to modify the appearance of the code afterward. Your changes don't affect the stored snippet. If you want to edit the stored version, select a snippet in the Snippets panel and click the Edit Snippet button.

The Snippet dialog box appears, as in Figure 10-1. Make your changes and click OK. If you inserted a previous version of this snippet, the code on your page doesn't update, so delete the old block of code and reinsert the edited version if necessary.

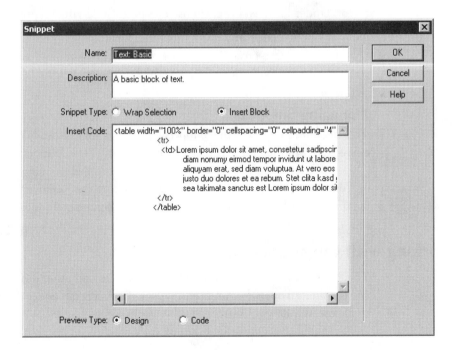

FIGURE 10-1

Use the Snippet dialog box to edit a snippet.

Creating Snippets

To create a new snippet, click the New Snippet button (shown here) which you can find at the bottom of the Snippets panel. This opens the Snippet dialog box. Type a name for the snippet in the Name field and type in a short blurb in the Description field.

Choosing Wrap Selection in the Snippet Type area allows you to break the snippet into two chunks, Before and After. When you apply your snippet to a selection on your page, the Before chunk appears to the left of the selection, and the After chunk appears to the right.

1. Type the chunk of Before code in the Insert Before field in the Snippet dialog box and type the chunk of After code in the Insert After field.

2. Choosing Insert Block in the Snippet Type area inserts the snippet as a continuous block of code. Add the code to the Insert Code field.

3. Under Preview Type, choose Design to see a visual representation of your code in the Snippets panel or choose Code to see the source.

4. Click OK to create the snippet. Dreamweaver adds your snippet to the currently open folder in the Snippets panel.

Managing Snippets

To reorganize snippets in the Snippets panel, drag them from folder to folder. Create a new folder in the Snippets panel by clicking the New Snippet Folder button.

You may delete the selected snippet by clicking the Remove button. You can find the same commands in the Snippet panel's menu.

Working with the Assets Panel

The Assets panel keeps track of external asset files and other design elements in the current site. To open the Assets panel, click the Assets tab under the Files panel group or choose Window | Assets.

The icons along the left of the Assets panel control the category of element that appears in the main list area. To switch categories, simply click a new icon. From top to bottom, the categories are Images, Colors, URLs, Flash movies, Shockwave movies, Movie files (other than Flash or Shockwave), Scripts, Templates, and the Library. I'll talk more about the Library in the next section, "Using the Library." In the meantime, see the Scenario and Solutions sidebar for a quick reference for what the Assets panel organizes.

SCENARIO & SOLUTION

What appears in the Images category?	GIF, JPEG, and PNG images
What appears in the Colors category?	Text colors, link colors, and background colors
What appears in the URLs category?	External links
What appears in the Flash category?	SWF files
What appears in the Shockwave category?	DCR files
What appears in the Movies category?	MPEG and QuickTime movies
What appears in the Scripts category?	External JavaScript and VBScript files
What appears in the Templates category?	All the template files for the site
What appears in the Library category?	All the Library items for the site

The Assets panel is a great help for at least three reasons. First, it organizes the elements of your site in a convenient place. You don't have to scour the folders in the Site panel for a particular movie, image, or script file. Second, it can help you to improve the visual consistency of your site. If you check the Colors category of the Assets panel from time to time, for instance, you can make sure that you haven't called for two similar but different shades of red. Third, the Assets panel isn't just a convenient list. You can drag an element from the Assets panel into the document window, or you can select the item and click the Insert or Apply button at the bottom of the panel. Similarly, you can edit an asset by double-clicking it or selecting it and clicking the Edit button, which is the button with the paper-and-pencil icon.

If you change the location of an asset file, or if you remove a particular asset from your site, you may need to refresh the Asset panel. To do so, click the Refresh button at the bottom of the panel.

Add a frequently used asset to your list of favorites by selecting an asset clicking the Add To Favorites button.

Review your list of favorite assets by selecting Favorites at the top of the Assets panel and choosing a category from the icons on the left. You can change the name of a favorite asset in this view by clicking the name. To remove an asset from your favorites, select the asset and click the Remove From Favorites button.

Switch back to Site view by clicking the Site option at the top of the Assets panel.

Using the Library

Dreamweaver's Library allows you to collect and store any content that appears in the body section of a page, including snippets of code, tables, layers, and pieces of text. (You can't store content that appears in the head section of a page.) The Library works in such a way that if you edit a Library item, Dreamweaver can automatically update all the references to that item throughout your site.

For example, assume that you create a Library item for the following piece of code, the tag line of your client:

```
<h1>We Want Your Business</h1>
```

You find out later that the client wanted a level-two headline instead of a level-one, but not before you added *references,* or instances of this Library item, to several hundred pages of your site. (Just humor me.) To correct this problem quickly and painlessly, simply edit the Library item to the following:

```
<h2>We Want Your Business</h2>
```

Macromedia is less than consistent in its use of the terms Library items *and* Library references. *More often than not,* Library item *can mean either.*

Everywhere Dreamweaver finds a reference to this Library item, it substitutes the edited version. If this isn't convenience, I don't know what is.

 Adding Items to the Library To create a Library item, first open the Assets panel and click the Library Category button, which is the bottom icon along the left side of the panel. Then select a portion of the page in Design view or a section of code in Code view and click the New Library Item button at the bottom of the Assets panel.

You can also drag the selection into the Assets panel, but only from Design view, not from Code view; or you can choose Modify | Library | Add Object To Library.

Dreamweaver creates a new Library item from the selection. Type a name for this item in the Assets panel and press ENTER or RETURN. Now, whenever you want to use this item on your page, create a Library reference by dragging the item from the Library onto your page or by selecting the Library item and clicking the Insert button at the bottom of the Assets panel.

Library references appear highlighted in document window, both in Design view and in Code view. This highlighting doesn't affect the page as it appears in a live browser window.

Dreamweaver stores Library items in a special *Library* folder in your site's local root folder, and each Library reference appears in the source code of your page between comment tags:

```
<!-- #BeginLibraryItem "/Library/robot.lbi" -->
   <img src="images/robot.jpg" width="100" height="100"
   alt="A picture of a robot"><!-- #EndLibraryItem -->
```

As you can see, the first comment tag contains a link to the reference's source in the *Library* folder. This link doesn't affect a live browser in any way. The browser ignores the link completely, since it appears in a comment tag. However, Dreamweaver uses the link to keep your Library references up to date. Removing the comment prevents Dreamweaver from recognizing a Library reference as such. Consequently, Dreamweaver skips over this reference when you update the content of a Library item.

When you upload your site to the production server, you don't have to send the *Library* folder, since Dreamweaver copies the Library item's source code to your page every time you add a Library reference.

Editing Items and Updating References   To edit a Library item, select the item in the Assets panel and click the pencil-and-paper icon at the bottom of the panel. Dreamweaver loads the Library item as a document window. Make your changes and choose File | Save. The Update Library Items dialog box appears (as shown in the following illustration), asking if you want to update your site's Library references at this time. Click Update for yes or Don't Update for no. If you decide to update, Dreamweaver shows an Update Pages dialog box with statistics about what it changed and where. Close this dialog box to return to Dreamweaver. Then feel free to close the Library item's document window or leave it open for additional changes.

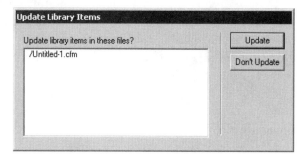

You can update Library references at any time by selecting Modify | Library | Update Current Page or Modify | Library | Update Pages. The Update Current Page command updates references on the current document window only, while the Update Pages command updates references on all pages in your site by way of the Update Pages dialog box.

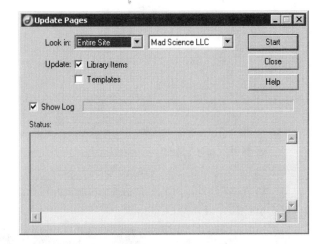

Detaching Library References   To detach a Library reference from its item, thereby preventing Dreamweaver from updating the reference if you edit its item, select the reference and click the Detach From Original button on the Properties panel.

Detaching a Library reference does nothing more than remove the comment tags around the reference in the source code. You can manually detach a Library reference by deleting the comment tags yourself in Code view.

Removing and Re-Creating Library Items   To remove an item from the Library, select the item and click the trashcan icon at the bottom of the Assets panel. This procedure doesn't remove any references to this item on your site, nor does it remove the comment tags around the references.

You can recreate a deleted Library item by selecting one of its old references in the document window and clicking the Re-create button in the Properties panel.

EXERCISE 10-1

Creating a Library Item

In this exercise, you create a Library item from an asset on the Mad Science LLC home page.

1. Launch Dreamweaver, open the Site panel and select the Mad Science LLC site.

2. Double-click the *index.htm* file of the home page. The home page loads in a new document window.

3. Go to the Files panel group and click the Assets tab to open the Assets panel.

4. Click the Library icon.

5. Select the atom image in the document window.

6. Back in the Assets panel, click the New Library Item button. Dreamweaver adds the atom image to the Library

7. Type a name for the Library item, such as **atom**, and press ENTER or RETURN. You now have a Library item. The following illustration shows a Library item like the one you created.

8. Choose File | Save. Mission accomplished! Well done.

CERTIFICATION OBJECTIVE 10.02

Working with Templates

As you remember, a Dreamweaver *template* is a page with predefined content. I've been hinting at templates for ten chapters now, implying that they can make your life easier, and it's about time I delivered on that promise.

When you create a template, you create, in essence, a Library item for an entire page layout. The template contains the overall structure of the page, along with its essential design elements, such as the nav bar, header, and footer. The template doesn't contain the guts of the page or the elements that change from page to page on your site. When you use your template to create a new page, Dreamweaver automatically adds the layout and the common design elements to the document window. You don't have to re-create the layout table or insert the nav bar. All you have to do is add the guts. Better still, if you edit the template, Dreamweaver updates all the pages in your site that refer to the template, just like when you edit a Library item in the Assets panel.

These features can save you considerable time. Not only that, but they virtually guarantee a consistent overall look and feel. You can't get more consistent than the exact same code for the exact same layout from page to page to page.

Creating a Dreamweaver Template

You can create a Dreamweaver template in one of several ways. You can select File | New from the main menu and choose the Templates Page category from the New Document dialog box, which creates a blank template file to which you add content and various template regions.

exam
ⓦatch

If you're familiar with templates in Dreamweaver 4, be sure that you pay close attention to this section, because Dreamweaver MX expands template features significantly.

Another way, which is probably the most common, is to start with an existing Web page on your site and save the page as a template for use with future pages. To do so, open the page and choose File | Save As Template, or click the Make Template button on the Insert panel under the Templates tab.

FROM THE CLASSROOM

A Time for Templates

There is a time for every purpose under heaven, according to folk singers, and that goes doubly for templates. Templates can speed up production enormously. You should definitely take advantage of them. But when is the best time?

If you're closely following this book, you may have the impression that templates should come in toward the end of production, since I waited until Chapter 10 to talk about them. In fact, templates belong at the beginning of production, as soon as the designer delivers final page models of the layout.

When you build templates from these page models instead of regular Web pages, you set up the conditions for rapid production. Create the templates and save them in the *Templates* folder as the first development task and then use the templates to create the actual pages of the site. Sure, this takes a bit of extra development time up front, but you more than make up for this time soon after. When you build a page from a template, the common features of the page are already in place because this is the content that the template supplies. You don't have to worry about reconstructing a complex table or system of layers. You don't have to reset the links in the navigation bar. You can concentrate solely on the guts of the page.

Here's another good reason to create the templates first. I have never known a client not to change direction in the middle of a project. The change is never small and is often drastic. When change comes, and it will—at least once—you can make one set of modifications to the template, and all the referring pages change accordingly. (If only you could attach a template to your client.)

What if you didn't use Dreamweaver to build your site in the first place? The same basic guideline holds true. After importing the site into Dreamweaver, your first task should be to create a set of templates from existing pages, and then you should apply your templates to the remaining pages according to their design. The sooner you switch to a template-based workflow, the sooner you can reap the rewards.

The Save As Template dialog box appears, as shown next. Supply a name for the template file in the Save As field and click the Save button.

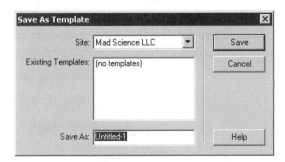

 You can also go to the Assets panel, click the Templates icon along the side of the panel, and click the New Template button at the bottom of the panel.

author's
note

Opening a new template file or converting an existing page to a template is not the same as creating a new page based on a template. To create a new page based on a template, you must first have the template file, which is what you're building now.

Adding Editable Regions

An *editable region* is an area of the template that you can change from page to page. The layout and common design elements should not appear in an editable region; the table cell or layer that holds the guts of the page should.

To create an editable region:

1. Clear out any existing content in this area.

 2. Place the cursor inside this region and choose Insert | Template Objects | Editable Region or right-click and choose Templates | New Editable Region. (If you add an editable region to a page that isn't currently a template, Dreamweaver informs you that it's going to convert the page into a template first. Click OK to continue.) You can also click the Editable Region button under the Templates tab of the Insert panel.

3. The New Editable Region dialog box appears, as shown next. Type a descriptive name for the editable region in the Name field or accept Dreamweaver's generic default name. Every editable region in the template must have a unique name, so make sure that you don't repeat the same name on the same page. You can change the name of the editable region later by selecting the region in the document window and typing a new name in the Properties panel.

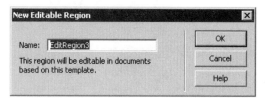

4. Click OK to close the dialog box.

Much like with Library references, Dreamweaver refers to the editable region in the source code with comment tags, like this:

```
<!-- InstanceBeginEditable name="EditRegion1" -->
   EditRegion1<!-- InstanceEndEditable -->
```

A browser ignores these comment tags, but to Dreamweaver they're vital! Don't strip out the comments, or your template won't work properly.

Making Certain Attributes Editable   You can make specific attributes editable in otherwise fixed HTML tags.

1. Select the tag whose attributes you want to make editable and choose Modify | Templates | Make Attribute Editable. The Editable Tag Attributes dialog box appears, as shown next.

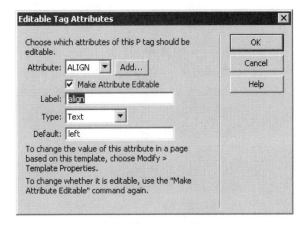

2. The Attribute list on this dialog box contains all the current attributes of the selected tag. To make an attribute editable instead of fixed, select the attribute from this list. Then check the Make Attribute Editable checkbox.

3. Type a name for the editable attribute in the Label field.

4. From the Type list, set the type of value that the attribute requires.

5. Finally, in the Default field, type the default value for the attribute. Since this attribute is editable, you'll be able to change the default value in pages based on this template.

Dreamweaver represents an editable attribute in the source code like this:

```
<p align="@@(align)@@">This paragraph has an editable alignment attribute.</p>
```

The name of the editable region appears in parentheses between a pair of double at signs (@@). Again, this is Dreamweaver-only nomenclature.

Adding Optional Regions

An *optional region* may or may not appear on a page that refers to the template. When you use a template with an optional region as the basis for a new page, you can turn on or off the optional region. Turning off the optional region makes it invisible. Turning on the optional region makes it visible.

To add an optional region to your template:

1. Select the content that you want to make optional.

2. Choose Insert | Template Objects | Optional Region, right-click and choose Templates | New Optional Region from a context menu, or click the Optional Region button under the Templates tab of the Insert panel:

3. The New Optional Region dialog box appears, as shown in the following illustration. Supply the name of the region in the Name field, and check the Show By Default option if you want the optional region to be visible when you create a page based on the template. Unchecking this option causes the optional region to be invisible when you create a page based on the template.

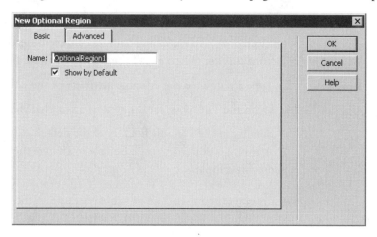

An optional region's comment tag looks like this:

```
<!-- TemplateBeginIf cond="OptionalRegion1" --><p>This is an
optional paragraph.</p><!-- TemplateEndIf -->
```

Adding Editable Optional Regions   *Editable optional regions* are editable regions on a template that may or may not appear on pages that refer to this template. As with optional regions, when you create a page based on the template, you can choose to turn on or off the editable optional regions.

To add an editable optional region:

1. Clear out the existing content in the area.

2. Choose Insert | Template Objects | Editable Optional Region or click the Editable Optional Region button (shown here) located under the Templates

tab of the Insert panel. (There is no New Editable Optional Region item in the context menu.)

3. The New Optional Region dialog box appears as before. Make your choices and click OK.

When you add an optional editable region, Dreamweaver nests an editable region comment within an optional region comment, like this:

```
<!-- TemplateBeginIf cond="OptionalRegion1" -->
    <!-- TemplateBeginEditable name="EditRegion1" -->
    <!-- TemplateEndEditable --><!-- TemplateEndIf -->
```

Adding Repeating Regions

A *repeating region* is a template area that duplicates its content a variable number of times. When you create a page based on a template with repeating regions, you can determine the number of times the repeated region duplicates itself.

To add a repeating region, select the content that you want to repeat. (If you want to repeat an editable region, select the editable region.) Then choose Insert | Template Objects | Repeating Region, right-click and choose Templates | New Repeating Region from the context menu, or click the Repeating Region button under the Templates tab of the Insert panel.

This opens the New Repeating Region dialog box, as shown next. Type the name of the repeating region in the Name field and click OK.

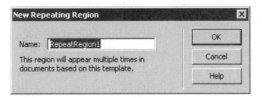

Here is the comment tag for a repeating region:

```
<!-- TemplateBeginRepeat name="RepeatRegion1" -->
    <p>I repeat myself under pressure.</p><!-- TemplateEndRepeat -->
```

Adding Repeating Tables   A *repeating table* is a table with a variable number of rows. You can specify a different number of rows in this table on every page that refers to the template.

Add a repeating table by choosing Insert | Template Objects | Repeating Table or by clicking the Repeating Table button under the Templates tab of the Insert panel, shown here. As with optional editable regions, repeating tables don't appear on the context menu.

In the Insert Repeating Table dialog box, shown in the following illustration, type the properties of the table in the Rows, Columns, Cell Padding, Cell Spacing, Width, and Border fields, as if you were filling out the Insert Table dialog box. Then determine the number of repeating rows. Type the number of the first repeating row in the Starting Row field and type the number of the last repeating row in the Ending Row field.

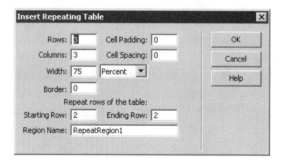

For instance, if you want a repeating table with a fixed top row, a fixed bottom row, but a variable number of middle rows, create a repeating table with three rows. Type 2 in the Starting Row field and type 2 in the Ending Row field, since you want only the middle row to repeat.

The repeated rows are editable in pages that refer to the template. Type a name for the editable region in the Region Name field and click OK. Dreamweaver creates the repeating table. Don't forget to fill in the content of the noneditable rows now, since you won't be able to do this on pages that refer to the template.

exam
ⓦatch

Remember that optional regions and repeating regions aren't editable by themselves, but repeating tables and optional editable regions are editable, since these elements contain editable regions.

Dreamweaver's code for the repeating portion of a repeating table amounts to table-row and table-data tags, with editable-region comments in each table cell. The whole construction appears between repeating-region comments, like this:

```
<!-- TemplateBeginRepeat name="RepeatRegion1" -->
  <tr>
    <td><!-- TemplateBeginEditable name="EditRegion1" -->
         <!-- TemplateEndEditable --></td>
    <td><!-- TemplateBeginEditable name="EditRegion2" -->
         <!-- TemplateEndEditable --></td>
    <td><!-- TemplateBeginEditable name="EditRegion3" -->
         <!-- TemplateEndEditable --></td>
  </tr><!-- TemplateEndRepeat -->
```

See the following Scenario and Solutions sidebar for a quick reference to help you remember which template regions are which.

Saving the Template

After you set up the various regions and build the fixed content into the template, choose File | Save. Dreamweaver prompts you for a file name and saves the template to a special folder called *Templates* in your local root folder.

As with the Library folder, you don't need to upload this folder to the production server.

SCENARIO & SOLUTION

What is an editable region?	A region that you can edit on a template-based page
What is an editable attribute?	An attribute in an otherwise fixed HTML tag whose value you can edit on a template-based page
What is an optional region?	A noneditable region that you can make visible or invisible on a template-based page
What is an optional editable region?	An editable region that you can make visible or invisible on a template-based page
What is a repeating region?	A noneditable region that you can repeat any number of times on a template-based page
What is a repeating table?	A fixed table with at least one repeating row of editable cells

Modifying a Template

To edit the content of a template file, choose File | Open from Dreamweaver's main menu, navigate to the Templates folder in your local root folder, and choose the template that you want to open. You can also look in the Assets panel and click the Templates icon. Then select the template that you want to edit and click the Edit button or double-click the name of the template.

You can modify everything in the template file, not just the editable regions. Change the fixed content as you require. Delete template regions by selecting them and pressing the DELETE key or choosing Edit | Clear.

Choose File | Save to save your changes. The Update Template Files dialog box appears, prompting you to update the files that refer to the template you just changed (see the following illustration). Click Update to update the pages or click Don't Update to leave the pages as they are. To update the pages afterward, choose Modify | Templates | Update Current Page, which updates the current document window only, or choose Modify | Templates | Update Pages, which opens the Update Pages dialog box.

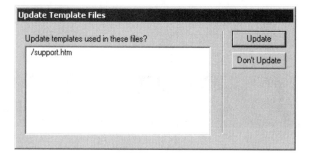

EXERCISE 10-2

Creating a Template

In this exercise, you create a template for the Mad Science LLC site.

1. Launch Dreamweaver, open the Site panel, and select the Mad Science LLC site.

2. Double-click the *index.htm* file in the *contact* folder. The Contact Us page loads in a new document window.

3. In the Title field at the top of the screen, type **Mad Science LLC Template**.

4. Choose File | Save As Template. The Save As Template dialog box appears. Supply the file name **main** and click Save. You're now editing the template file.

5. Clear out the headline and the form on the right side of the page so that the content area is empty.

6. Choose an insertion point in the empty content area and set the Format list in the Properties panel to Heading 1.

7. Look under the Templates tab of the Insert panel and click the Editable Region button.

8. The New Editable Region dialog box appears. Type **headline** in the Region Name field and click OK.

9. The flashing cursor should appear to the right of editable region.

10. Set the Format list on the Properties panel to None. The flashing cursor jumps to the right of the headline region. Add a new editable region called *content,* which appears below the headline region in its proper place on the page.

11. Check your screen against that shown in Figure 10-2.

12. Choose File | Save again to save your template, complete with the editable regions. Dreamweaver informs you that one of the editable regions is inside a block tag. This is the headline region. Click OK to close the dialog box and close the template's document window.

13. Now choose File | New. In the New Document dialog box, click the Templates tab and select the template that you just saved. Click the Create button to open a new page based on the template.

14. The document window opens with the template's content intact. Change the title of this page to **Mad Science LLC: Our Facility**.

15. You can't edit this content. However, you can add new content to the editable regions. Click inside the headline region and delete the current placeholder text. Choose the first set of fonts from the Font list on the Properties panel and type **Our Facility**.

FIGURE 10-2 The screen you have created should look something like this one.

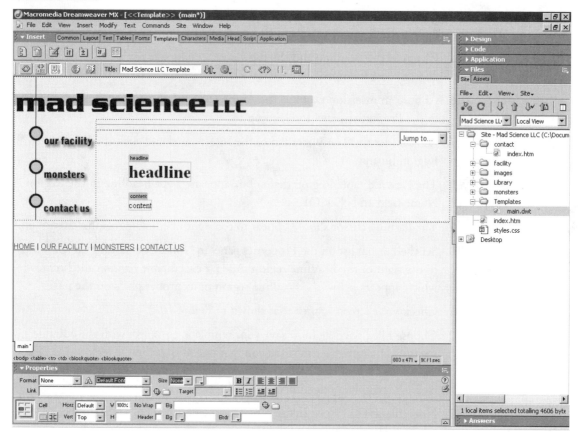

16. Click inside the content region and delete the current text. Choose the first set of fonts from the Font list again, set the Format list to Paragraph, and type **Content about facility goes here**. Your screen should look like the one shown in Figure 10-3.

17. Choose File | Save As and save this template-based page as *index.htm* in the *facility* folder, replacing the temporary *index.htm* file that currently resides there. Excellent work!

FIGURE 10-3   Here is the finished template.

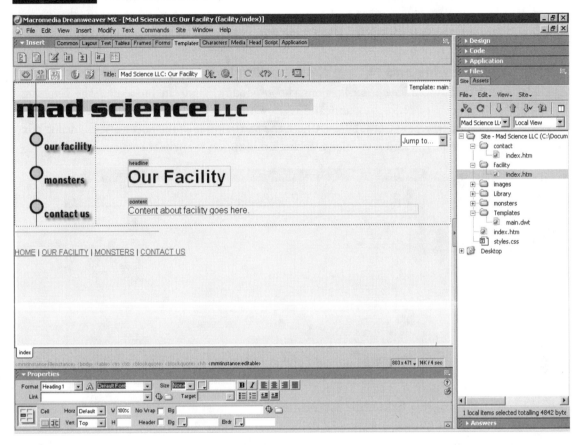

Creating Pages Based on Templates

After you create a template file and save it in the Templates folder, you can use it as the basis for a new page.

One way to do this is to choose File | New. Then click the Templates tab in the New Document dialog box, choose a site from the pane on the left, choose a template in that site from the next pane over, and click Create. Another way to do this is to open the Assets panel, click the Templates icon, select a template file, right-click it, and choose New From Template from the context menu.

When the document window loads, Dreamweaver adds all the content from the template file. You can add content only to the specific editable regions that you defined in the template. Everything else is fixed and locked.

Showing and Hiding Optional Regions

To show or hide optional regions, choose Modify | Template Properties. The Template Properties dialog box appears, as shown in the following illustration. Select an optional region from the list. Check the Show option at the bottom of the dialog box to make the region visible or uncheck this option to make the region invisible.

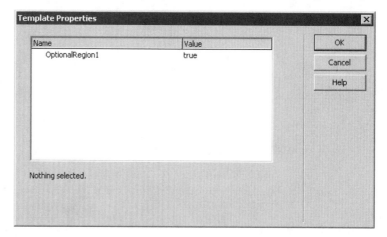

Changing Editable Attributes

Use the Template Properties dialog box to change the attributes of fixed tags with editable attributes. Select an editable attribute from the list and then fill in the desired value in the fields that appear at the bottom of the dialog box.

Managing Repeating Regions

In the document window, repeating regions and repeating tables appear with four small buttons, as shown in the next illustration. Click the plus button to duplicate the content of the repeating region or table.

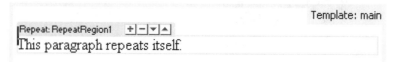

If the repeating region contains an editable region, you can click the minus button to eliminate the currently selected editable region, and you can click the up- and down-arrow buttons to change the editable region's position relative to the other repetitions. These buttons don't work on repeating regions with uneditable content.

As an alternative to the buttons, you can choose from a variety of commands under Modify | Templates | Repeating Entries in the main menu. The same commands appear under Templates in the context menu.

Creating a Nested Template

A *nested template* is a template that sits inside a page that refers to another template, the *base template*. Nested templates give you, essentially, multiple versions of the same template file. When you create a new page from a nested template, you can modify the editable regions of the nested template, as well as those that the base template supplies. However, pages that you create directly from the base template don't have the extra editable regions that the nested template supplies.

 To create a nested template, open a page that refers to the base template, and choose File | Save As Template or click the Make Nested Template button under the Templates tab of the Insert panel.

The Save As Template dialog box appears. Supply a file name for the nested template in the Save As field and click the Save button. Then add new regions to the nested template. Notice that you can add new regions in the nested template only to the existing editable regions of the base template, and you can't change the content that comes from the base template. If you want to modify the structure of the base template, you must open this file separately.

Choose File | Save to save your changes to the nested template.

Applying a Template to an Existing Page

To apply a template to an existing page on your site, open the page in Dreamweaver. Then in the Assets panel, click the Templates button, choose the template that you want to apply, and click the Apply button at the bottom of the panel. You can also choose Modify | Templates | Apply Template To Page.

Unless you're attaching the template to a completely blank page, the Inconsistent Region Names dialog box appears, as shown in the following illustration. This dialog box is Dreamweaver's not-so-polite way of asking you what you want to do with the existing content on the page. Select each item in this dialog box in turn and choose a value from the Move Content To New Region list. When Dreamweaver applies the template to the page, it moves the page's existing content to the area in the template that you specify from this list. If you choose Nowhere, Dreamweaver deletes the current content. For the transfer to proceed, none of the items in this dialog box can have a <Not Resolved> value. Click Cancel to close the dialog box without applying the template.

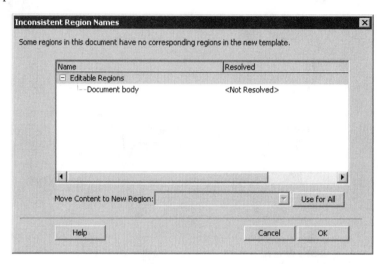

Detaching a Template from a Page

To detach a template from a page, choose Modify | Templates | Detach From Template. The page loses all its template comment tags but retains the content that it received from the template. When you edit the template file, though, this page no longer receives updates.

Exporting Your Site Without Template Markup

If you want to create a version of your site that doesn't have Dreamweaver's telltale template comments in the pages, choose Modify | Template | Export Without Markup. The Export Site Without Template Markup dialog box appears:

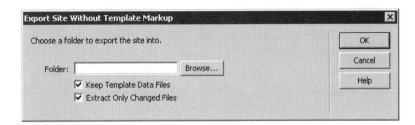

In the Folder field, specify the folder to which you want to export the site. This folder cannot reside in the local root folder of your site. Add a check the Keep Template Data Files option to preserve your template data in XML format. Add a check to the Extract Only Changed Files option to export only the files that you updated since the last time you invoked this command. If your site is large and you export comment-free documents regularly, this option is faster.

Click OK to export the site files.

on the
Job

Deliver your finished site to the client without Dreamweaver's template markup, but keep a copy of the site with this markup for your archives. This way, when you need to make changes, you can leverage the time-saving power of templates.

Leaving the template markup in the pages doesn't affect the browser at all. Web browsers ignore all comments, including the ones that Dreamweaver requires for features like templates and Library references. Because of this, the markup is dead weight on your page outside of Dreamweaver. Your page will load slightly faster without the template markup. Don't expect a massive increase in performance, though. Stripping out the template markup saves only a few kilobytes at most.

Exporting and Importing XML Data

Dreamweaver can export template data in XML format for use in external applications such as database programs. Dreamweaver can also import an external XML file into a page that refers to a template, thereby populating the template's editable regions with content, as long as you format the XML correctly.

exam
Watch

The exam may ask you about using template-based pages with XML, so study this section carefully.

Choose File | Export | Template Data As XML, and the Export Template Data As XML dialog box appears, as shown in the following illustration. Under Notation, select the Use Standard Dreamweaver XML Tags option if the template contains editable attributes, optional regions, or repeating regions. Select the Use Editable Region Names As XML Tags option if your template contains only editable regions. Click OK, and Dreamweaver prompts you for a file name. Supply one and click Save.

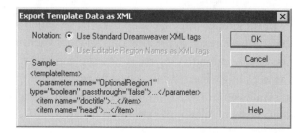

Choose File | Import | XML Into Template to populate a template-based page with the contents of an XML file. Note that for this procedure to work properly, you need to structure the XML exactly the way Dreamweaver wants it. The best way to get this structure is to export XML data from an existing template page first and then view the XML file in Dreamweaver's code view. Parrot this structure in your own XML files, and you're good to go.

CERTIFICATION SUMMARY

In this chapter, you learned various commands and features for saving you time and speeding up production.

For managing the text content on your site, you can find and replace strings of text or source-code components such as tags and attributes, and Dreamweaver's built-in dictionary keeps your spelling on track. The Snippets panel gives you dozens of pieces of prewritten code, which you can organize or augment as your needs require.

Use the History panel to repeat or undo sequences of actions and save permanent commands. You can also record and play back temporary commands with Dreamweaver's Record feature.

The Assets panel neatly organizes several categories of external files, productivity aids, and design elements. You can add frequently used assets to Favorites view, and you can drag assets from the panel onto your page. The Library category of this panel is especially helpful. You can store any kind of body-section code in the Library and recycle it by creating Library references on your page. When you update a Library item, you can automatically update every reference to that item, which makes maintaining your site not only simple but also almost enjoyable.

For true management power, look no further than Dreamweaver templates. Templates are pages with predefined content. When you use templates to control the design and layout of your site's pages, you practically guarantee a consistent look and feel.

A template file contains regions of fixed content that you can't update on the pages that refer to the template. A template also has variable areas such as editable regions, optional regions, and repeating regions, which you can modify on template-based pages. Further, by importing properly structured XML data into a template-based page, you can populate the template's editable regions with content.

TWO-MINUTE DRILL

Managing Content

❑ Use the Find And Replace dialog box to search text, source code, and tags.

❑ Regular expressions help you to search for specific characters or patterns.

❑ The History panel allows you to repeat or undo a sequence of actions.

❑ Record one set of actions at a time with Dreamweaver's Record feature, or create permanent commands by clicking the Save button on the History panel.

❑ Use the Snippets panel to add blocks of prewritten source code to your page.

❑ Use the Assets panel to keep track of site assets, templates, Library items, and color choices.

❑ When you update a Library item, you can automatically update all the references to that item in your site.

Working with Templates

❑ A template is a Dreamweaver page with predetermined content.

❑ Add editable regions, editable attributes, optional regions, optional editable regions, repeating regions, and repeating tables to your template page.

❑ When you create a page from a template file, add new content to the editable regions of the page, turn on and off optional regions, and determine how many times to present repeating regions.

❑ Create a nested template when you want to make an alternative version of an existing template file.

❑ Dreamweaver indicates most template-based content and Library references with comment tags in the source code.

❑ Choose Modify | Templates | Export Without Markup to create a version of your site without Dreamweaver's template markup.

❑ You can export template data as an XML file for use in external applications.

❑ You can import properly formatted XML data into a page based on a template to populate the template regions with content.

SELF TEST

The following questions will help you measure your understanding of the material presented in this chapter. Read all the choices carefully because there might be more than one correct answer. Choose all correct answers for each question.

Managing Content

1. How many commands can you store at a time with Dreamweaver's Record feature?

   A. One

   B. Ten

   C. Thirty-two

   D. An unlimited number

2. Which of the following can update automatically on your page when you edit the original?

   A. Code snippets

   B. Library references

   C. Regular expressions

   D. Template-based content

3. Which of the following categories appear on the Assets panel?

   A. Images

   B. Colors

   C. Library items

   D. Scripts

   E. Snippets

4. Which of the following actions don't appear on the History panel?

   A. Selecting a table cell

   B. Dragging to highlight a string of text

   C. Inserting an image

   D. Typing your name

5. You want to create a new code snippet that adds paragraph tags to unformatted text when you select the unformatted text in the document window. What is the best procedure?

   A. Create a block snippet and type <p></p> in the Insert Code field of the Snippet dialog box.

   B. Create a block snippet and type the opening paragraph tag in the Before field and the closing paragraph tag in the After field of the Snippet dialog box.

   C. Create a wrapping snippet and type <p></p> in the Insert Code field of the Snippet dialog box.

   D. Create a wrapping snippet and type the opening paragraph tag in the Before field and the closing paragraph tag in the After field of the Snippet dialog box.

6. In which panel do you view Library items?

   A. The Library panel

   B. The Assets panel

   C. The Snippets panel

   D. The Templates panel

7. How does Dreamweaver keep track of Library references in the source code?

   A. It uses comment tags.

   B. It uses Cascading Style Sheets.

   C. It uses XML.

   D. It uses JavaScript.

8. Should you upload the Library folder to the production server? Why or why not?

   A. Yes. Otherwise, the links in the source code won't work.

   B. Yes. The browser won't know where to look for the Library items.

   C. No. The browser looks in the default folder for Library items automatically.

   D. No. The code for the Library items appears in the source of the page.

9. You want to find a particular tag somewhere on your site. How can you target your search?

   A. Search the source code.

   B. Search for a specific tag.

   C. Search for text.

   D. Use advanced search criteria for text.

10. You want to replace every occurrence of the tab character in the source code of the page with a series of three spaces. After enabling regular expressions, what should you type in the Search For field of the Find And Replace dialog box?

    A. ^t

    B. ^tab

    C. \t

    D. \tab

    E. <t>

    F. <tab>

Working with Templates

11. Which of the following template regions are editable by default on a page that refers to the template?

    A. Editable region

    B. Optional region

    C. Optional editable region

    D. Repeating region

    E. Repeating table

12. What happens when you import properly formatted XML data into a page that refers to a template?

    A. The template changes.

    B. You populate the template fields with content.

    C. You create an XML file containing the existing template.

    D. You create an XML file containing the current page's template-based content.

13. You want to turn off an optional region on the current page. What command do you use?

    A. Modify | Template Regions

    B. Modify | Templates | Optional Regions

    C. Modify | Optional Regions

    D. Modify | Template Properties

14. When might you want to create a nested template? Choose the best answer.

    A. When you want to embed template content in the source code of the page

    B. When you want to create an alternative version of an existing template

    C. When you want to add a template to a nested table or layer

    D. When you want to update every page that refers to the template

15. How many times does a repeating region appear by default?

    A. One

    B. Three

    C. Five

    D. Seven

16. Why would you want to export a version of your site without Dreamweaver's template markup?

    A. Template markup can confuse older browsers.

    B. Template markup reveals that you used Dreamweaver to create the site.

    C. Template markup adds a small amount of extra download time to the page.

    D. Template markup appears in the browser window as unsightly boxes and editable regions.

17. You create an editable `width` attribute called `imgWidth` in a fixed image tag on your template. How does this attribute appear in the source of the template page?

    A. `<img src="monster.jpg" height="50" width=v@imgWidth@v alt="A picture of a monster">`

    B. `<img src="monster.jpg" height="50" width="@@(imgWidth)@@ " alt="A picture of a monster">`

    C. `<img src="monster.jpg" height="50" width="@(imgWidth)@ " alt="A picture of a monster">`

    D. `<img src="monster.jpg"height="50" width="@@imgWidth@@" alt="A picture of a monster">`

18. On a nested template, where can you add new template regions?

    A. Anywhere

    B. In any existing template region

    C. In any existing editable region

D. In any existing optional region

E. In any existing repeating region

19. What is the purpose of the Inconsistent Region Names dialog box? Choose the best answer.

A. To change the names of regions in the current template file

B. To alert you to the fact that a particular page cannot refer to a template

C. To allow you to determine where in the template to place the existing content of the page

D. To inform you that Dreamweaver is about to wipe out the existing content of the page

20. What button do you click under the Templates tab of the Insert panel to insert an optional region?

A. The button that looks like this:

B. The button that looks like this:

C. The button that looks like this:

D. The button that looks like this:

LAB QUESTION

It's the night before the big launch, and you're working late, as usual. You're running your site through the paces one more time between bites of pizza and gulps of your favorite caffeine-enhanced carbonated beverage. All the links check out. There are no broken images. The movie on the front page plays perfectly.

You're almost ready to call it quits when you glance at the Colors category of the Assets panel and find that you used three different but similar shades of red in your site: #FF0000, #CC0000, and #CC3366. You look closely at a few pages in your browser window, and, yes, now that you know what to look for, you find that you can see a difference. You think about leaving it, but you're too conscientious a Web builder—you want to give the client's visitors the best possible user experience, and that means coordinating the colors. A quick glance at the style guide for the site shows that all reds should be #CC0000.

There's only one problem. The sheer number of pages on the site makes ferreting out the color references a headache waiting to happen. You haven't slept for two days. You need to make the change, but you need to make it fast.

Your sleep-deprived fingers are still nimble enough to choose Edit | Find And Replace by instinct. Now, how can you change all the occurrences of #FF0000 and #CC3366 to #CC0000 in a single step? On a piece of paper, draw a sketch of the Find And Replace dialog box with the correct fields filled in, and check your answer against mine in the Lab Answer section.

SELF TEST ANSWERS

Managing Content

1. ☑ **A.** You can store only one command at a time with Dreamweaver's Record feature. Use the Save button on the History panel to store multiple commands.
   ☒ **B, C,** and **D** are incorrect because you can store only one command at a time with Dreamweaver's Record feature.

2. ☑ **B** and **D.** Library references and template-based content can update automatically when you edit library items and template pages, respectively.
   ☒ **A** is incorrect because code snippets on your page don't update when you edit the original snippets. **C** is incorrect because regular expressions are search codes. You can't insert them on your page, so this question doesn't apply.

3. ☑ **A, B, C,** and **D.** All of these appear on the Assets panel as icons along the left side.
   ☒ **E** is incorrect because snippets appear in their own panel, not the Assets panel.

4. ☑ **A** and **B.** Mouse movements and selection procedures don't appear in the History panel.
   ☒ **C** and **D** are incorrect because these choices don't involve moving the mouse or creating a selection. Therefore, they appear in the History panel.

5. ☑ **D.** Create a wrapping snippet and type the opening paragraph tag in the Before field and the closing paragraph tag in the After field.
   ☒ **A** and **B** are incorrect because block snippets insert a solid block of code. They don't allow you to wrap the snippet around a selection. Further, choice **B** is doubly incorrect because you don't get Before and After fields when you create a block snippet. **C** is incorrect because you don't get an Insert Code field when you create a wrapping snippet.

6. ☑ **B.** View Library items in the Assets panel.
   ☒ **A** is incorrect because there is no Library panel. **C** is incorrect because the Snippets panel shows code snippets, not Library items. **D** is incorrect because there is no Templates panel. View templates in the Assets panel, as well as Library items.

7. ☑ **A.** Dreamweaver uses comment tags to keep track of Library references in the source code of your page.
   ☒ **B, C,** and **D** are incorrect because Dreamweaver uses comment tags, which a Web browser ignores.

8. ☑ **D.** You don't have to upload the Library folder, since because Library items appear in the source code of the page.

   ☒ **A** and **B** are incorrect, and they say essentially the same thing. The Web browser doesn't follow the links in the source code—these links are for Dreamweaver only. You can confuse Dreamweaver by modifying the links, but you can't confuse a browser this way. **C** is incorrect because there is no default Library folder that the browser knows to use.

9. ☑ **A** and **B.** You can search the source code or search for a particular tag.

   ☒ **C** and **D** are incorrect because searching the text, even with advanced criteria, automatically rules out HTML tags.

10. ☑ **C.** Type the regular expression \t.

    ☒ **A** and **B** are incorrect because this regular expression doesn't search for tabs but looks instead at the beginning of a line. **D** is incorrect because the appropriate regular expression in Dreamweaver for the tab character is \t. **E** and **F** are incorrect because this character isn't a symbol for any regular expression in Dreamweaver.

Working with Templates

11. ☑ **A, C,** and **E.** By default, editable regions, optional editable regions, and repeating tables are editable on a page that refers to a template with these regions.

    ☒ **B** and **D** are incorrect because optional regions and repeating regions aren't editable unless you nest an editable region inside.

12. ☑ **B.** You populate the template regions with content.

    ☒ **A** is incorrect because importing XML data doesn't change the template itself. **C** and **D** are incorrect because importing an XML file doesn't trigger the creation of a new XML file. However, choice **D** happens when you export an XML file.

13. ☑ **D.** Choose Modify | Template Properties.

    ☒ **A, B,** and **C** are incorrect because these commands don't exist in Dreamweaver.

14. ☑ **B.** Create a nested template when you want to create an alternative version of an existing template.

    ☒ **A** is incorrect because Dreamweaver automatically embeds template content in the source of the page. **C** is incorrect because you don't add templates to objects on a page. Templates themselves are pages, or at least page models. **D** is incorrect, because when you edit a template file, you have the option of updating the pages that refer to the template. You don't need to create a nested template to do this.

15. ☑ **A.** A repeating region appears once by default. You can increase the number of repetitions by clicking the plus button here to the repeating region in the document window.
☒ **B, C,** and **D** are incorrect because a repeating region appears once by default.

16. ☑ **B** and **C.** Template markup is a telltale sign that you used Dreamweaver to build the site, and it adds a small amount of download time to the page.
☒ **A** and **D** are incorrect because template markup doesn't affect the browser one way or the other. Web browsers ignore all comments, including Dreamweaver's template markup.

17. ☑ **B.** The correct markup is `@@(imgWidth)@@`.
☒ **A, C,** and **D** are incorrect because these choices don't have the correct formatting.

18. ☑ **C.** Add new template regions in any existing editable region on a nested template.
☒ **A, B, D,** and **E** are incorrect because you can add new template regions only to existing editable regions. Dreamweaver locks the remainder of the nested template, since another template controls this content.

19. ☑ **C.** The Inconsistent Region Names dialog box allows you to determine where in the template to place the existing content of the page.
☒ **A** is incorrect because you can't rename the region names in the template from this dialog box. **B** and **D** are incorrect because you can attach a template to the page after you determine what to do with the existing content.

20. ☑ **A.** That's the Optional Region button.
☒ **B** is incorrect because that's the Repeating Table button. **C** is incorrect because that's the Repeating Region button. **D** is incorrect because that's the Editable Region button.

LAB ANSWER

To perform this feat in a single bound, Superman style, use a regular expression. Choose Edit | Find And Replace, set the Find In list to Entire Current Local Site, check the Use Regular Expressions option, set the Search For list to Source Code, and type the following the in Search For field:
#FF0000|#CC3366

Type the following in the Replace With field: **#CC0000**

Click the Replace All button. Dreamweaver searches for all occurrences of *#FF0000* or *#CC3366* in the source code and replaces them with *#CC0000*. Problem solved. Now get some sleep!

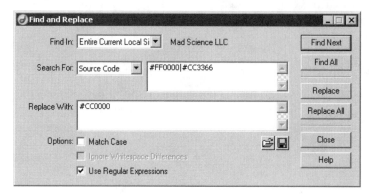

11

Building Web Applications

Adding Server-Side Functionality

So far, you've added content and built Web pages with great skill, but your pages and content have been static, according to Dreamweaver's strict understanding of the term. Even when you enhanced your pages with JavaScript behaviors, you still wound up with stasis, technically speaking. It's time now to make the leap from static pages to dynamic pages by way of Web applications.

With Web applications, or Web apps, you shift some of your site's processing chores from the client side to the server side. In so doing, you transcend many of the limitations of client-side-only scripting. Your Web apps work across browsers and platforms. You don't have to worry about your visitors turning off JavaScript, either, because Web apps execute on the server, not the browser.

The main drawback, at least from the visitor's perspective, is that server-side applications tend to reduce the performance of your site. For this reason, you should only add Web apps when you can't achieve the same functionality using client-side methods or when the client-side solution would be too difficult to manage.

This chapter walks you through Dreamweaver's application-building features and procedures.

Preparing Your Site for Web Apps

The first step to building Web applications is to install a Web server or HTTP server on your personal computer or development environment. A *Web server* is this sense isn't a piece of hardware like a production server or staging server. Instead, it's software that serves Web pages. That is, when you test your site offline using a Web server, your browser receives the pages as if they were actually on the Web.

The Windows NT Server, Windows 2000, and Windows XP Professional operating systems have a built-in Web server called IIS, for Internet Information Server. If this Web server isn't already installed on your system, you can easily add it by modifying your Windows components in the Control Panel. Windows 98 and Windows NT workstations use Personal Web Server (PWS), which you can also install from the Control Panel. If you don't want to use IIS or PWS, or if your operating system doesn't support either, you can acquire a Web server from other vendors, including Netscape and Apache.

You also need an *application server,* which is software that works with your Web server to present dynamic pages. When you create a Web application, you add special markup to the source code of your page. Browsers don't understand this markup, because it's not for the browser to interpret. The application server catches the page before it goes to the browser, processing the special markup and generating a regular HTML page from the results. Then the app server passes this HTML page to the browser, and the browser renders the page for the visitor to see.

Choose an application server that supports the brand of server-side scripting that you plan to use. Dreamweaver support five common server languages: ColdFusion, ASP.NET, ASP, JSP (JavaServer Page), and PHP. Some application servers function as their own Web servers, which means that you don't need to install IIS, PWS, or a comparable product. Macromedia ColdFusion MX is an example of this kind of app server. Speaking of ColdFusion, Dreamweaver MX for Windows ships with a developer's version of ColdFusion MX, so Windows users who need an app server in a pinch can install this one.

on the job *It should come as no surprise to anyone that Macromedia's own ColdFusion MX works extremely well with Dreamweaver MX. ColdFusion developers enjoy perhaps the most robust set of Dreamweaver features when it comes to application building.*

Whichever application server you choose needs to run on the production server. Otherwise, there's nothing to catch the pages before they go to the visitor's browser, and your Web apps don't work as a result. The application server also needs to run on your development environment, which is either your personal machine or a dedicated development server. You can't test your Web apps if the application server isn't running. You need the application server to catch the pages before they go to the browser, even if it's your own browser.

Moving the Local Root Folder

The local root folder for your site needs to sit inside the folder of your Web server, usually in a subfolder called *wwwroot, htdocs,* or something to that effect. Check with your server's documentation for more details. If you created your local root folder in another location, you should make a copy of the local root folder and paste it inside the *wwwroot* or *htdocs* folder. You should also rename this copy of the local root folder to something without spaces or to nonalphanumeric characters, as if it were a folder on an actual production server. For instance, you might change the name of the local root folder *Mad Science LLC site* to *madscience.*

After you paste a copy of the local root folder in the *wwwroot* or *htdocs* folder, redefine your site so that Dreamweaver knows where to find the new local root folder. Do this in the Site Definition dialog box.

Go to the Site panel's menu and choose Site | Edit Sites. Select a site from the list in the Edit Sites dialog box and click Edit. The Site Definition dialog box appears. Look under the Advanced tab and select the Local Info category. Click the folder icon to the right of the Local Root Folder field and navigate to the copy of the local root folder inside *wwwroot* or *htdocs.* Double-click this folder to open it and click the Select button. Then reset the default images folder by clicking the folder icon to the right of the Default Images Folder field, navigating to the *img* or *images* folder inside the new local root folder.

Configuring Your Site for Application Testing

Under the Advanced tab of the Site Definition dialog box, click the Testing Server category, as shown in Figure 11-1. The testing server is your development environment—the machine that runs your Web server and application server.

Choose your app-server language from the Server Model list. If you choose ColdFusion, the This Site Contains list activates. Dreamweaver asks if your site contains Dreamweaver MX pages only, Dreamweaver UltraDev 4 pages only, or both. Be sure to choose the most accurate option from this list, because Dreamweaver MX won't recognize UltraDev's ColdFusion markup otherwise. If you're building your Web app from scratch, select Dreamweaver MX Pages Only from this list. If you want to upgrade existing UltraDev pages to Dreamweaver MX's improved ColdFusion markup, choose Both Versions.

From the Access list, determine how you connect to your testing server. If you have to dial up to get in, choose FTP from the list, and fill in your user name, password, and host information. Normally, though, you don't have to dial up if the testing server is your personal machine or a development server on your local network. Select Local/ Network in this case, and make sure that the Testing Server Folder field contains the correct path to your local root folder.

In the URL Prefix field, type the address that you use to access the home page of your site during testing. When you run a Web server on your personal system, you can specify a *localhost* address such as *http://localhost* or a *localhost* address plus the port number, such as *http://localhost:8500.* Don't forget to append the name of the folder that contains the home page, as in *http://localhost/madscience* or *http://localhost:8500/ madscience.*

A quick way to make sure that you configured everything correctly is to copy the address from the URL Prefix field and paste it into the Address field of a live browser

FIGURE 11-1

Use the Site
Definition dialog
box to define (or
redefine) your
site for dynamic
content.

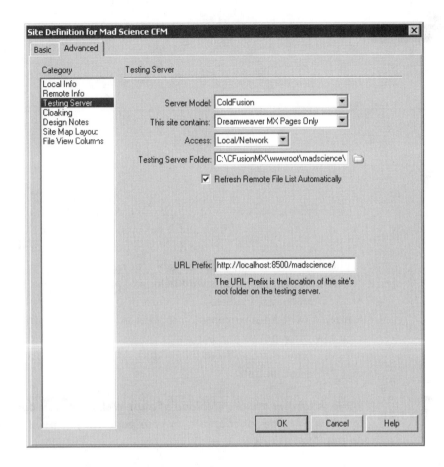

window. If your home page loads, you know that your testing server is running and
that it can see your site.

Click OK in the Site Definition dialog box to make your changes and click Done
in the Edit Sites dialog box. Feel free to delete the old version of your local root folder.

Connecting to a Database

One of the most common strategies to building Web apps is to draw from a database
application like Microsoft Access or MySQL. The database contains tables of
information like that shown in Table 11-1. When you connect your Web apps to a
database, your apps can pull any value or collection of values from the database table
or update the content of the database on the fly. To use databases on your site, you
must install a database application and create the database tables.

TABLE 11-1	Sample Database Table

A database table consists of columns and rows. The columns, also called *fields,* provide the categories of the table. The rows, or *records,* are the individual entries in the database table. You can use databases for a variety of purposes. One common application is creating a database table for registered users of your site. This table contains user name and password fields and perhaps also fields for access privileges or site preferences. Each row or record in the table corresponds to a particular registered user. Another common application is storing product information, where each row corresponds to a particular product. You can build a search function to retrieve a set of matches from the product database according to a keyword or phrase that the visitor submits.

exam
ⓦatch

While databases are the lifeblood of most Web apps, you don't need a database to add server-side functionality to your page. All you need is a Web server and an application server.

The Databases panel in the Application panel group lists the databases and tables to which your site can refer. The method for adding, editing, and removing database connections depends on the type of server language that you use. For a ColdFusion site, you go by way of the ColdFusion Administrator panel, which appears in a browser window when you click the Modify Data Sources button on the Databases panel.

For other server languages, to add a database connection, click the plus button on the Databases panel and from the menu that drops down, choose the type of connection that you want to make. If you're not sure what to choose, consult Dreamweaver's online help. A dialog box for your connection type appears, as shown next. Fill out the dialog box and click the Test button to test the database connection. If you don't get an error message, you're good to go. Click OK, and Dreamweaver adds the database to the Databases panel.

To edit a database connection in a non-ColdFusion site, select the connection in the Database panel, and right-click (Windows) or CONTROL-click (Mac) to open a context menu. Choose Edit Connection.

To delete a database connection in a non-ColdFusion site, select the connection in the Database panel and click the minus button.

Opening a Dynamic Page

A *dynamic page* contains server-specific markup for your application server. As I explained earlier, a browser can't interpret this markup. The browser needs the application server to intervene and translate the markup into pure HTML. The extension of the dynamic page is what signals the application server that the page contains markup for processing. If your application server is ColdFusion MX, for instance, the server catches all pages with the *.cfm* extension, while PHP catches pages with the *.php* extension.

Under no circumstances does the browser have anything to do with processing the server-side code. Remember that the browser handles client-side code like HTML, CSS, and JavaScript.

To create a new dynamic page, choose File | New from Dreamweaver's main menu. Select the Dynamic Page category from the New Document dialog box and choose the type of page from the pane on the right side of the dialog box. The type of page that you create should match the server language that you're using. Click the Create button or double-click the page type, and a new document window opens.

Depending on the type of dynamic page that you open, new tabs on the Insert panel appear. For instance, a ColdFusion page gives you CFML Basic, CFML Flow, and CFML Advanced tabs, while a PHP page gives you a PHP tab, (see the following two illustrations). Under these tabs are buttons for inserting server-specific elements for your Web application.

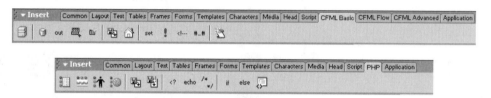

Another way to create a new dynamic page is to choose File | New File from the Site panel's menu. Dreamweaver creates a new dynamic file of the default type for your site. If ColdFusion MX is your application server, Dreamweaver creates a *.cfm* file. If PHP is your application server, Dreamweaver creates a *.php* file, and so on. Give this file a name and then double-click it to open its document window.

Converting a Static Page into a Dynamic Page

You can convert any static HTML page on your site into a dynamic page by opening the page's document window in Dreamweaver. Then expand the Application panel group and click any of the tabs in this group. A numbered list appears in the panel.

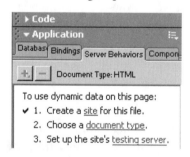

You should see a check mark next to the first step, Create A Site For This File. Click the link in the second step, Choose A Document Type, and the Choose

Document Type dialog box opens (shown next). Choose the correct server-language type from the drop-down list in this dialog box and click OK. If other pages in your site link to this page, Dreamweaver asks if you want to update the links—click Update for yes or Don't Update for no. Then choose File | Save from the main menu, and Dreamweaver adds a new file to your site with the appropriate server-language extension. You may delete the static HTML version of your page.

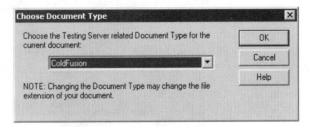

Logging In to ColdFusion RDS

If you're building a ColdFusion site, you need to log in to ColdFusion Remote Development Services (RDS) before you can add ColdFusion markup to your page. To log in, select any tab in the Application panel group and look for the numbered list of steps. Click the RDS Login link to open the Login To ColdFusion Remote Development Services (RDS) dialog box, shown next. Type your password in the Password field and click OK. Typically, you need to do this only once per site. Dreamweaver remembers your password.

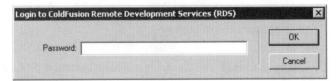

Building Dynamic Content

Dynamic content is content that the application server adds to the page as it processes the server-side markup. This dynamic content can be practically anything: the visitor's name for a personalized welcome on the front page; a product image and text description that corresponds to the visitor's selection from a menu; or specific formatting for an HTML tag, such as red boldface text on a form label to mark that the visitor didn't supply the correct information.

Defining the Source of Dynamic Content

To add dynamic content to a page, you must first set up a dynamic content source, or the container from which your site draws the dynamic content. This source can be a database, but you can define other sources as well. The Bindings panel (in the following illustration) under the Application panel group lists the dynamic content sources for the current page.

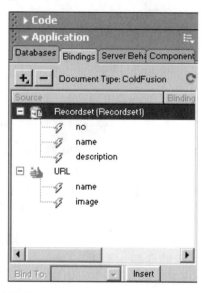

Remember that if you don't define a dynamic content source, you can't display that content on your page.

Using a Database as a Dynamic Content Source   To draw dynamic content from a database, you must add a recordset to the page on which you want to display the dynamic content. A *recordset* is a temporary container for the data of a database. Your Web app sends a *query*, or a request to the database, for a specific set of records. The database returns the desired information to the recordset for the Web app to process or display on the page.

Create a recordset by clicking the plus button on the Bindings panel and choosing Recordset (Query) from the menu that drops down. You can also click the Recordset button under the Application tab of the Insert panel.

This opens the Recordset dialog box, shown in Figure 11-2. Provide a unique name for the recordset in the Name field or use Dreamweaver's default name. From the Data

FIGURE 11-2

Use the
Recordset dialog
box to define a
recordset for the
results of a simple
database query.

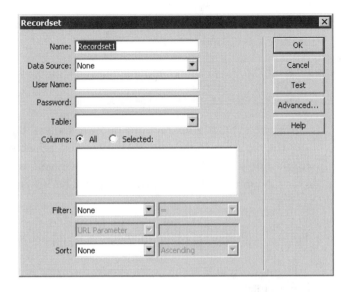

Source list, choose the database from which you want to draw the dynamic content.
Enter your user name and password for the application server in the appropriate fields
if your system administrator requires it; otherwise, you can leave these fields blank.
From the Table list, choose the database table that you want to look up. If you want
to include the values of only specific columns in the recordset, choose the Selected
option and then hold down CTRL (Windows) or COMMAND (Mac) and select the
desired table columns.

Use a filter to narrow the focus of your database query. Choose a column name from
the first Filter list and then set a conditional expression like equals or greater than
from the second list. From the third list, choose the type of value that you want to
compare, and type the value in the text field to the right. For instance, to retrieve only
the data for the record whose *product_name* value is *deluxe computer,* ignoring the rest
of the data in the database, set the first drop-down list to *product_name,* the second
to the equal sign, and the third to Entered Value. Type **deluxe computer** in the text
field, but if you want to retrieve the data whose *product_name* value matches that of
a URL parameter called *sentName,* set the third drop-down list to URL Parameter,
and type **sentName** in the text field. (For more information on URL parameters,
see "Using a URL Variable as a Dynamic Content Source" later in the chapter.)

The filter takes the form of a SQL query. SQL (read *sequel*), Structured Query
Language, is a language used for interacting with the data in a database. Assuming that

the name of the database in the above example is *my_products,* the SQL command for the filter looks like this:

```
SELECT *
FROM my_products
WHERE product_name = 'deluxe computer'
```

The line SELECT * instructs the query to look at the entire table. If you want to limit the recordset to the value in the *product_price* column, for instance, thereby returning only the price of the deluxe computer, you would choose the Selected option under Columns and click the price column. The SQL query changes as follows:

```
SELECT product_price
FROM my_products
WHERE product_name = 'deluxe computer'
```

To sort the results of the query, choose the name of a column from the Sort list and choose a method of sorting from the list to the right. This feature is handy if you want the values of a dynamic list or menu to appear in alphabetical order.

Sorting also appears in the SQL command:

```
SELECT product_price
FROM my_products
ORDER BY product_price ASC
```

The ASC keyword in the ORDER BY line indicates ascending order. This sorts the product prices from lowest to highest. If you want descending order instead, the keyword is DESC:

```
SELECT product_price
FROM my_products
ORDER BY product_price DESC
```

Now your visitors see the most expensive items first.

Remember that Dreamweaver sends queries to the database with SQL commands.

Clicking the Test button in the Recordset dialog box sends your query to the database and returns the recordset to the Test SQL Statement dialog box (Figure 11-3). If you're happy with the results, close the Test SQL Statement dialog box and click OK in the Recordset dialog box. Dreamweaver adds the recordset to the Bindings panel. You may now add the values of the recordset to your page.

FIGURE 11-3

See the results
of your query
in the Test SQL
Statement dialog
box.

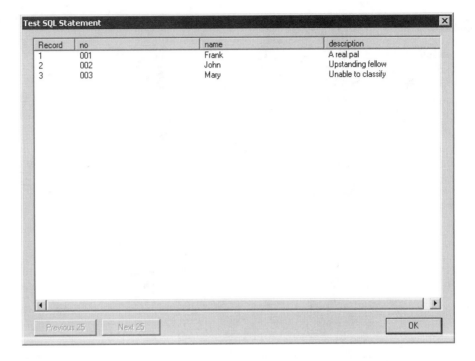

If you know SQL and want to built an advanced query, such as one that tests several conditions simultaneously, click the Advanced button in the Recordset dialog box. The dialog box changes, as shown in Figure 11-4. Use the controls at the bottom of the dialog box to assemble the statement piece by piece, or write the statement manually in the SQL field. Click the Simple button to switch the Recordset dialog box back to its original configuration.

I should point out here that in ASP.NET sites, a recordset goes by the name of *DataSet*. The Recordset dialog box becomes the DataSet dialog box, and so on. See the next Scenario and Solution sidebar for a quick reference to help you with the terminology.

SCENARIO & SOLUTION

What is a recordset?	A collection of records from a database table (ColdFusion, ASP, JSP, and PHP)
What is a DataSet?	A collection of records from a database table (ASP.NET)

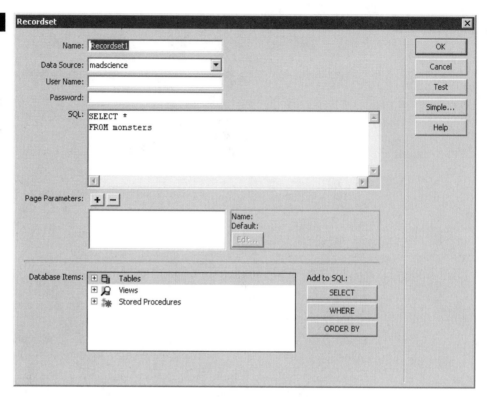

FIGURE 11-4

When you click the Advanced button on the Recordset dialog box, the dialog expands to allow you to enter or build your own SQL query.

Using a Form Variable as a Dynamic Content Source   A *form variable* is a container for a value in a posted form submission. When the visitor submits the form, the Web app on the receiving page extracts the desired value from the submission message and stores that value in the form variable.

Remember that two methods are used for submitting form data: the get method and the post method. Define form variables for post method forms only. get method forms require URL variables instead.

Defining form variables involves two steps. First, set up your post method form to submit the posted data to the page with the Web application. Select the form in the document window and set the Action field on the Properties panel to the path of the page that contains the Web app. Make sure that the Method list on the Properties panel says *post*.

Second, on the page that receives the form submission, create a new data binding. Click the plus button on the Bindings panel and choose Form Variable from the menu for ColdFusion or PHP sites, Request Variable | Request.FORM for ASP or ASP.NET sites, or Request Variable for JSP sites. This calls the corresponding dialog box, shown next. Type the name of the form variable in the Name field and click OK. The variable name should match the name of the field of the form. For instance, if you want to retrieve the value of the *creditcardNo* field, set the name of the form variable to *creditcardNo*. The form variable appears in the Bindings panel.

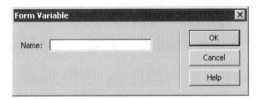

Using a URL Variable as a Dynamic Content Source
A *URL variable* is a container for a value that the Web app receives from a *query string*, which a series of *name=value* pairs called *parameters* separated by ampersand characters (&). When your visitor submits a get method form, the browser sends a query string with the form's results to the receiving page. You can also append a query string to the href attribute of a link so that when the visitor clicks the link, the destination page receives the parameters.

To configure a form to send a query string, select the form in the document window and open the Properties panel. In the Action field, type the path to the page with the Web app. This is the page that receives the form submission. Be sure to choose get from the Method list.

To attach a query string to a link, select the link and find the Link field on the Properties panel. Type the path to the page containing the Web app that receives the query string. Then type a question mark (?). The query string begins. Type the name of the parameter, an equal sign (=), and the value of the parameter. To send another parameter, type an ampersand and the next name/value pair. Dreamweaver appends the href attribute of the anchor tag in the source code accordingly:

```
<a href="receivingPage.cfm?product_name=animation%20workstation&
product_price=8995&product_color=cherry%20red">
```

Notice that Dreamweaver converts spaces and other nonalphanumeric characters into numeric codes that begin with percentage signs. The code for a space is %20.

You can also add URL parameters by way of Dreamweaver's Parameters dialog box (shown in the following illustration). The Parameters dialog box allows you to append a query string to a link without fussing over the correct format. Click the folder icon to the right of the Link field, and the Select File dialog box appears. Navigate to the destination page of the link and select this page. Then click the Parameters button to open the Parameters dialog box. Under the Name column, type the name of the parameter. Under the Value column, type the value. You can set either one to draw from a dynamic content source by clicking the lightning-bolt icon that appears when you type in the column. To add a new parameter, click the plus button. To remove a selected parameter, click the minus button. Use the arrow buttons to move a selected parameter up or down in the list. When you finish, click OK. Dreamweaver adds a set of correctly formatted parameters to the URL field.

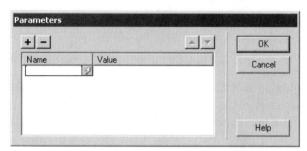

To store the URL parameters on the receiving page, click the plus button on the Bindings panel and choose URL Variable from the menu for ColdFusion and PHP sites. Choose Request Variable | Request.QueryString for ASP.NET and ASP sites or choose Request Variable for JSP sites. The corresponding dialog box appears, as shown next. Type the name of the URL variable in the Name field. This name should match the name of the parameter in the query string. If you sent a parameter called *product_price,* for example, make the name of the URL variable *product_price,* too. Click OK to add the URL variable to the Bindings panel. If you want to store all the URL parameters, you should create a separate URL variable for each.

exam
ⓦatch

Be sure that you know the difference between form variables and URL variables.

See the next Scenario and Solution sidebar for a quick reference to help you remember the difference between form variables and URL variables.

SCENARIO & SOLUTION

What is a form variable?	A variable that contains a value from a `post` method form submission
What is a URL variable?	A variable that contains a value from a `get` method form submission or a parameter value from a link's query string

Using a Session Variable as a Dynamic Content Source   A *session variable* is a visitor-specific value that the application server remembers for the duration of the visitor's session on your site. That is, the value of the session variable follows the visitor from page to page. Once you set a session variable, any subsequent page in your site can retrieve its value. The application server deletes server variables when they're no longer needed, typically after a long period of inactivity. You can also design your Web app to terminate session variables on command, similar to a Log Out button. As a security measure, your application server may require that you enable session variables or session management explicitly, so check with the documentation before defining a session variable.

One common application of session variables is storing a visitor's preferences. If on the home page of your site you ask your visitor to pick a text color, for instance, you can store this preference in a session variable and use it to determine the color of the text on every page that follows. One disadvantage to session variables is that they use cookies. If your visitor has cookies turned off, your session variables won't work.

After you enable session management, you can create a session variable in Code view by adding the proper server-side markup. In ColdFusion, you type something like this:

```
<cfset session.color_preference = "black">
```

Dreamweaver's preferred PHP equivalent is this:

```
<?php $HTTP_SESSION_VARS['color_preference'] = "black"; ?>
```

If you want the session variable to receive a value from a `post` method form submission, type the following in ColdFusion:

```
<cfset session.color_preference = form.color_pref_field>
```

In PHP, type this:

```
<?php $HTTP_SESSION_VARS['color_preference'] =
$HTTP_POST_VARS['color_pref_field']; ?>
```

If you want the session variable to receive a query-string value from a link or a `get` method form submission, type the following in ColdFusion:

```
<cfset session.color_preference = url.colorpref>
```

In PHP, type this:

```
<?php $HTTP_SESSION_VARS['color_preference'] = $HTTP_GET_VARS['colorpref']; ?>
```

As you can see, the syntax for declaring session variables varies significantly among server languages. Check your documentation for the proper markup.

Once you declare a session variable in the source code, create a new data binding. Click the plus button on the Bindings panel and choose Session Variable from the menu. The Session Variable dialog box appears, as shown in the following illustration. In the Name field, type the name of the session variable that you just declared in Code view and click OK. Dreamweaver adds the session variable to the Bindings panel.

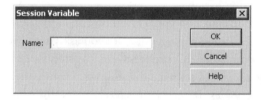

Using Other Variables as Dynamic Content Sources   Depending on your app server, you can create and use other kinds of variables as dynamic content sources, including application variables, server variables, and cookie variables.

Application variables remain in memory for the duration of the application. The application lasts until the server shuts down. Unlike with session variables, where different visitors can have different values, the value of an application variable is the same for all visitors. Declare application variables in the source code of the page with the proper markup for your server language. Then choose the Application Variable item from the Binding panel's menu. ColdFusion, ASP.NET, and ASP sites can use these variables.

Server variables remain in memory until the server shuts down, like application variables, only any Web app on the server can reference these variables. Declare server variables in the source code and choose Server Variable from the Binding panel's menu for ColdFusion and PHP sites. Choose Request Variables | Request.ServerVariable for ASP.NET and ASP sites. JSP sites can't use server variables.

Cookie variables retrieve values from cookie files. To create a data binding for this kind of variable, choose Cookie Variable from the Binding panel's menu for ColdFusion and PHP sites. Choose Request.Cookie for ASP.NET and ASP sites. You can't set cookie variables in JSP sites.

Using a JavaBean as a Dynamic Content Source   JSP sites can use JavaBeans and JavaBean collections as sources of dynamic content. *JavaBeans* are reusable software components, similar to Microsoft ActiveX controls, only they're platform-neutral. To create a data binding for a JavaBean, choose JavaBean from the Binding panel's menu. To create a data binding for a JavaBean collection, choose JavaBean Collection.

Adding Dynamic Content to a Page

After you set up a dynamic content source, you can pull from it with a few simple clicks. Dreamweaver adds the necessary *server behaviors* to the source code of your page. Much like Dreamweaver's JavaScript behaviors are prewritten client-side functions, server behaviors are prewritten server-side functions. Keep track of the server behaviors on your page with the Server Behaviors panel under the Application panel group (shown in the following illustration). This panel opens when you choose Window | Server Behaviors. To edit a server behavior, double-click its name in the Server Behaviors panel. To remove a server behavior, select it and click the minus button.

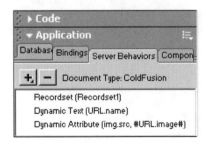

Adding Dynamic Text   To insert text from a dynamic content source, choose an insertion point on your page and then click the Dynamic Text button on the Insert panel under the Application tab.

You can also click the plus button on the Server Behaviors panel and choose Dynamic Text from the menu that slides out or go to Dreamweaver's main menu and choose Insert | Application Objects | Dynamic Text.

In the Dynamic Text dialog box that appears (Figure 11-5), select the dynamic content source from the Field list. You can also choose a preset format for the text by choosing a value from the Format list. The Code field displays the server markup that Dreamweaver will add to your page. You can tweak this code manually if you want. Click OK to insert the text. Dreamweaver makes a placeholder for the dynamic text in the document window, as Figure 11-6 shows. To see the content of the dynamic text, switch to Live Data view or preview your page in a browser window.

Another way to insert dynamic text is to drag a dynamic content source from the Bindings panel directly into the document window.

Retrieving Paths from a Data Source   Dynamic text is textual content, obviously. Then again, so is HTML. If a dynamic content source contains not plain text but the path to an image file, Flash movie, or some other asset, you can create some extremely useful effects. For instance, an image on your page can change depending on the visitor's preferences or the current stock levels in your client's warehouse.

FIGURE 11-5

Use the Dynamic Text dialog box to insert dynamic text on your page.

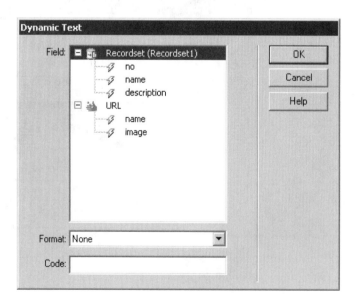

FIGURE 11-6

By default,
Dreamweaver
shows
placeholders
for dynamic text
in the document
window.

***When a dynamic content source contains a path to an image or some other
asset, root-relative paths are helpful. A root-relative path expresses the location
of the asset in terms of the site's top-level directory, as in*** `<img src="/images/
atom.jpg">` ***instead of*** `<img src="../images/atom.jpg">`, ***which is a
document-relative path, or*** `<img src="http://www.madsciencellc.com/
images/atom.jpg">`, ***which is an absolute path.***

To use the value of a dynamic content source as the `src` attribute of an image tag,
insert an image as you normally would, either by clicking the Image button on the
Insert panel under the Common tab or by choosing Insert | Image. Then, in the
Select Image Source dialog box, set the Select File Name From option to Data Sources
instead of File System. The Select Image Source dialog box changes, as Figure 11-7
shows. Select the dynamic content source that contains the path to the image and
click OK.

Dreamweaver adds a Dynamic Attribute behavior to the Server Behaviors panel
and inserts a placeholder graphic on your page. To see the image from the dynamic
content source, switch to Live Data view or preview the page in a live browser.

The server-side markup looks something like this in ColdFusion:

```
<img src="<cfoutput>#Recordset1.path_to_image#</cfoutput>" width="100" height="150">
```

FIGURE 11-7

To choose a path
to an image from
a dynamic
content source,
the Select Image
Source dialog box
changes.

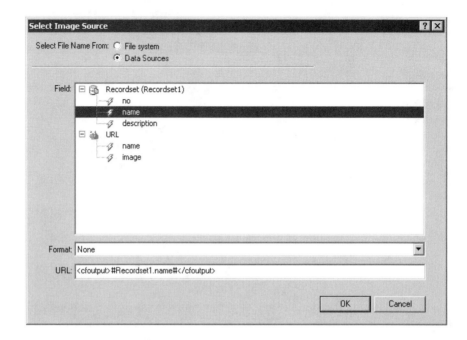

If you really want to get fancy, you can pull the `alt` text for the image from a data source, too. Drag the dynamic content source that contains the `alt` text into Code view and put the block of code inside the `alt` attribute, like this:

```
<img src="<cfoutput>#Recordset1.path_to_image#</cfoutput>" width="100"
height="150" alt="<cfoutput>#Recordset1.alt_text#</cfoutput>">
```

You can specify dynamic-attribute paths for rollover images, navigation bars, background images, Flash movies, Shockwave movies, applets, plug-ins, and hyperlinks by following the same procedure used for images.

Creating a Dynamic Table   A *dynamic table* displays the contents of a recordset in tabular form. A recordset, remember, is the result of a query to a database table, so think of a dynamic table as a visual representation of a database table.

To insert a dynamic table, first create a recordset for the information from the database table that you want to display. If you want to display the entire database table, choose the All option under Columns on the Recordset dialog box and don't specify a filter. If you want to display a portion of the database table, choose the Selected option under Columns and choose the target columns, or create a filter to display only those results that meet specific criteria.

Then click the Dynamic Table button on the Insert panel under the Application tab. You can also choose Insert | Application Objects | Dynamic Table. This opens the Dynamic Table dialog box, shown in the following illustration. Choose the recordset to display from the Recordset list. Under Show, if you want to present all the matching records at once, choose the All Records option. Otherwise, choose the other option and enter the number of records to display at a time in the appropriate field. Specify the border, cell padding, and cell spacing for the table in the fields for these and click OK. Dreamweaver inserts an HTML table with placeholders for the dynamic content. Each column in the recordset generates a Dynamic Text server behavior. The repeating row of the table is a Repeat Region server behavior.

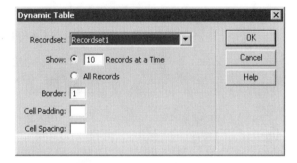

You can modify the appearance of the dynamic table to suit your needs, or you can build a dynamic table from scratch. Simply insert the recordset columns in a table of your own configuration. Then select the row or rows that contain the recordset placeholders, and click the Repeated Region button on the Insert panel under the Application tab.

You can also click the plus button on the Server Behaviors panel and choose Repeat Region from the menu that drops down or choose Insert | Application Objects | Repeated Region. The Repeat Region dialog box appears, as shown next. Choose the recordset from the Recordset list and determine how many records you want to display at a time. Click OK to create the repeated region.

If you chose to display a certain number of records at a time, you should add a recordset navigation bar to the page to allow the visitor to view the rest of the results.

A recordset navigation bar consists of text or graphical links for First, Previous, Next, and Last. To insert a recordset navigation bar, look under the Application tab under the Insert panel and click the Recordset Navigation Bar button.

You can also choose Insert | Application Objects | Recordset Navigation Bar from the main menu. This command opens the Recordset Navigation Bar dialog box, shown in the following illustration. From the Recordset list, choose the recordset that you display in the dynamic table. Under Display Using, determine whether you want text or graphical links. If you choose the Images option, Dreamweaver inserts its own generic image files and saves these files in the same directory as the current page. Using the Site panel, you should move these images to the default images folder.

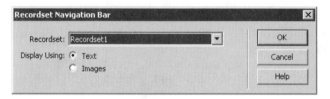

Click OK to create the navigation bar. Dreamweaver adds the Move To First Page, Move To Previous Page, Move To Next Page, and Move To Last Page server behaviors to control the `href` attribute of the links. Dreamweaver also adds a pair of Show If Not First Page and Show If Not Last Page server behaviors. The two Show If Not First Page behaviors suppress the First and Previous links when the visitor views the first set of records. Similarly, the two Show If Not Last Page behaviors suppress the Next and Last links when the visitor views the last set of records.

You can build a customized recordset navigation bar by applying the various Move To and Show If behaviors to elements in your design. Click the plus button on the Server Behaviors panel and look under the Recordset Paging submenu for the Move To behaviors, or look under the Show Region submenu for the Show If behaviors. Notice that two additional Show If behaviors appear in the Show Region submenu: Show If Recordset Is Empty, which allows you to display the selected content when the recordset is empty; and Show If Recordset Is Not Empty, which displays the selected content when the recordset isn't empty.

To improve the usability of your recordset navigation bar, add a recordset counter to your page, which displays a message such as "Records 11–20 of 37." Look under the Application tab of the Insert panel and click the Recordset Navigation Status button.

You can also choose Insert | Application Objects | Recordset Navigation Status. The Recordset Navigation Status dialog box appears, as shown next. Choose the recordset of your dynamic table from the Recordset list and click OK.

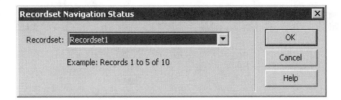

Dreamweaver adds the Display Starting Record Number, Display Ending Record Number, and Display Total Records server behaviors. You can modify the layout of the recordset counter however you like. It's also a good idea to select the entire counter and add a Show If Recordset Is Not Empty server behavior to suppress the message when the database query returns no results.

To build a customized recordset counter, insert the Display Record Count server behaviors manually by clicking the plus button on the Server Behaviors panel and choosing from the items in the Display Record Count submenu.

Inserting Dynamic Form Elements   The initial values or checked states of text fields, checkboxes, radio groups, lists, and menus can come from a dynamic content source, just like the `src` attribute of an image tag.

A *dynamic text field* is a text field whose initial value comes from a dynamic content source. The dynamic text field can be a single-line text field, a text area, a password field, or a hidden field. To change a text field into a dynamic text field, select the object in the document window. Then, on the Properties panel, click the lightning-bolt icon to the right of the Initial Value field to open the Dynamic Data dialog box (Figure 11-8). Choose the dynamic content source from the Field area and choose a formatting option if you prefer. Click OK to set the dynamic initial value.

You can also go to the Server Behaviors panel, click the plus button, and choose Dynamic Form Elements | Dynamic Text Field from the menu. The Dynamic Text Field dialog box appears, as shown next. From the Text Field list, choose the text field that you want to make dynamic and click the lightning-bolt icon to open the Dynamic Data dialog box.

FIGURE 11-8

Use the Dynamic
Data dialog box
to use a dynamic
content source
for the initial
value of a text
field.

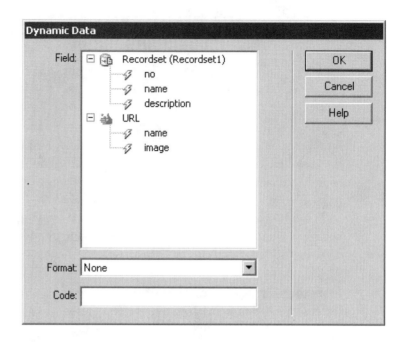

A *dynamic checkbox* is a checkbox that the Web app automatically checks under certain conditions. To change a checkbox into a dynamic checkbox, select a checkbox on your page, go to the Properties panel and click the Dynamic button. You can also click the plus button on the Server Behaviors panel and choose Dynamic Form Elements | Dynamic CheckBox.

Either method calls up the Dynamic CheckBox dialog box (shown next). Choose a checkbox from the CheckBox list and click the lightning-bolt icon next to the Check If field. Select a data source from the Dynamic Data dialog box. Then, in the Equal To field of the Dynamic CheckBox dialog box, type the target value. If the value of the dynamic content source matches this value, the Web app checks the checkbox automatically.

A *dynamic radio group* contains a radio button that the Web app automatically checks under certain conditions. To change a radio group into a dynamic radio group, select any radio button in the group. Either click the Dynamic button on the Properties panel, or click the plus button on the Server Behaviors panel and choose Dynamic Form Elements | Dynamic Radio Group.

The Dynamic Radio Group dialog box appears, as shown in the following illustration. Select the radio group from the Radio Group list and click the lightning-bolt icon to the right of the Select Value Equal To field. The Dynamic Data dialog box appears. Choose a dynamic content source from this dialog box and click OK. Then click OK in the Dynamic Radio Group dialog box.

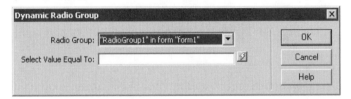

When you test the page, whichever radio button's checked value matches the value of the dynamic content source is the radio button that the Web app checks. For instance, if a radio group has three radio buttons, whose checked values are *isLarge*, *isMedium*, and *isSmall*, connecting to a dynamic content source containing the value *isMedium* causes the Web app to check the second radio button in the group.

A *dynamic list* or *dynamic menu* is a list or menu containing dynamically generated choices. To convert a list or menu into a dynamic list or menu, select the object in the document window and click the Dynamic button on the Properties panel. You can also go to the Server Behaviors panel, click the plus button, and choose Dynamic Form Elements | Dynamic List/Menu. This command calls up the Dynamic List/ Menu dialog box, shown in Figure 11-9.

Choose a list or menu from the Menu field. Set or modify the static items of this object in the Static Options area. Then, in the Options From Recordset list, choose a recordset containing the dynamic options for the object. Choose the values of the dynamic options from the Value list and choose the labels of the dynamic options from the Name list. In the Select Value Equal To field, you can determine which list or menu item the browser initially selects. Type a value in this field, and the browser selects the item with the corresponding value. For example, if you want the browser to select the item with the value *default*, type **default** in this field. To use a value from

FIGURE 11-9

Add dynamically generated choices to a list or menu with the Dynamic List/Menu dialog box.

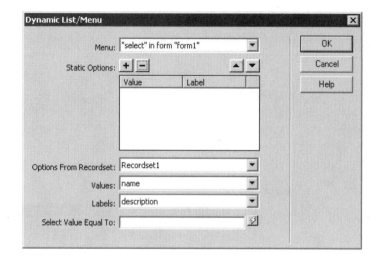

a dynamic content source, click the lightning-bolt icon to the right of the field and choose a dynamic content source from the Dynamic Data dialog box. Doing so allows you to preselect a list or menu item based on the submission of a form or a session variable, for instance.

See the next Scenario and Solution sidebar for a quick reference to help you remember how to preselect dynamic form elements.

SCENARIO & SOLUTION

How do you preselect a dynamic checkbox?	Make the value of the Equal To field in the Dynamic CheckBox dialog box the same as the value from the dynamic content source.
How do you preselect a radio button in a dynamic radio group?	Make the checked value of the radio button the same as the value from the dynamic content source.
How do you preselect an item in a dynamic list or menu?	Make the value of the Select Value Equal To field in the Dynamic List/Menu dialog box the same as the value of the item that you want to select. If the value comes from a dynamic content source, make sure that this value matches the value of the item that you want to select.

EXERCISE 11-1

Building a Web App

In this exercise, you create short Web application to add functionality to the Monsters page of Mad Science LLC site.

1. Before you begin this exercise, install a Web server and application server on your local system.

2. Pop the CD-ROM that comes with this book into your computer. Navigate to the Examples/Ch11 folder on the CD-ROM and copy the following graphics files: *gertrude.gif, molly.gif,* and *jerome.gif.* Paste these files inside the default *images* folder for Mad Science LLC.

3. Now copy the local root folder of the Mad Science LLC site and paste it in the *wwwroot* or *htdocs* folder of your Web server. Check with your server's documentation if you don't see a folder like this.

4. Change the name of the new folder to *madscience.*

5. Launch Dreamweaver, open the Site panel, and select the Mad Science LLC site.

6. Choose Site | Edit Sites from the Site panel's menu. Choose the Mad Science LLC site from the Edit Sites dialog box and click Edit. The Site Definition dialog box opens.

7. Click the Advanced tab and choose the Local Info category.

8. Click the folder icon to the right of the Local Root Folder field and navigate to the new copy of the local root folder that you created in step 3. Open this folder to select it and click Select.

9. Click the folder icon to the right of the Default Images Folder field and navigate to the *images* folder inside the new local root folder. Open this folder to select it and click Select.

10. Now choose the Testing Server category from the Site Definition dialog box.

11. From the Server Model dialog box, choose the server language that you're using.

12. From the Access list, choose Local/Network.

13. Click the folder icon to the right of the Testing Server Folder field and navigate to the local root folder of your site. Open this folder to select it and click Select.

14. In the URL Prefix field, append the folder name */madscience* to the end of the *http://localhost* address, like this: *http://localhost/madscience*. If your localhost address has a port number, retain this information in the appended address, as in *http://localhost:8500/madscience*.

15. Copy the value in the URL Prefix field. Open a browser window and paste this value into the Address field. If your Mad Science home page loads, you have the right URL prefix. If the home page doesn't load: (1) Make sure your application server and Web server are running. (2) Make sure that you spelled the URL prefix correctly. (3) Make sure that you have the right port number in the address, if required. (4) Make sure that you pasted the local root folder into the correct folder of your Web server.

16. All good? Close the browser window and return to Dreamweaver. Click OK in the Site Definition dialog box and click Done in the Edit Sites dialog box.

17. Go back to the Site panel and click the *monsters* folder. Choose File | New File from the Site panel's menu. Dreamweaver creates a new file with the extension of your server language. Rename this file to *details* plus the correct extension, as in *details.cfm*.

18. Choose File | New from Dreamweaver's main menu. Click the Templates tab on the New Document dialog box. Select the template *main* for the Mad Science LLC site and click Create. Dreamweaver opens a new document window based on this template.

19. Change the title of this page to **Mad Science LLC: Monsters.**

20. Clear out the content in the editable region for the headline. Then choose the first set of fonts from the Font list on the Properties panel and type **Monsters** in the editable region.

21. Clear out the content in the second editable region. Choose the first set of fonts from the Font list, set the Format list to Paragraph, and type **Three of our most popular configurations are Gertrude, Molly, and Jerome.**

22. Highlight the name *Gertrude* and click the folder icon to the right of the Link field on the Properties panel. The Select File dialog box opens. Select the *details* file. Then click the Parameters button. The Parameters dialog box opens.

23. Type **name** in the Name column. Press TAB twice and type **Gertrude** in the Value column.

24. Click the plus button. Type **image** in the Name column. Press TAB twice and type **/images/gertrude.gif** in the Value column. Click OK in the Parameters dialog box.

25. Click OK in the Select File dialog box. Dreamweaver adds the link plus your parameters to the Link field of the Properties panel.

26. Highlight the name *Molly* and click the folder icon to the right of the Link field. Choose the details page again and set the parameter *name* as **Molly** and *image* as **/images/molly.gif.**

27. Highlight the name *Jerome* and click the folder icon to the right of the Link field. Choose the details page and set the parameter *name* as **Jerome** and *image* as **/images/jerome.gif.**

28. Choose File | Save from the main menu to save the Monsters page.

29. Now comes the details page. Double-click this page in the Site panel. The page opens in a new document window. Type Mad Science LLC: Monster Details in the Title field.

30. Expand the Design panel group and open the CSS Styles panel.

31. Click the Attach Style Sheet button at the bottom of the panel. The Link External Style Sheet dialog box appears. Click the Browse button and navigate to the *styles.css* file. Select it and click OK. Then click the OK button on the Link External Style Sheet dialog box. Dreamweaver adds the style *monsterbox* to the CSS Styles panel.

32. Select the Apply Styles option at the top of the panel and click the monsterbox style. Dreamweaver creates a box in the document window.

33. Now expand the Application panel group and open the Data Bindings panel. Click the plus button on this panel and choose URL Variable from the menu. The URL Variable dialog box appears.

34. Type **name** in the Name field. This value corresponds to the *name* parameters you created on the Monsters page. Click OK to create the data binding.

35. Drag the URL variable name into the box in the document window. Dreamweaver inserts a placeholder for the variable. Select this placeholder.

36. Go back to the Design panel group and switch to the HTML Styles panel. Click the Monster Name style. Dreamweaver applies this style to the placeholder.

37. Press ENTER or RETURN. Dreamweaver adds a new paragraph to the page. Switch back to the CSS Styles panel and click No CSS Style.

38. In the Bindings panel, click the plus button again and choose URL Variable. This time, specify the name *image* and click OK.

39. Look under the Common tab of the Insert panel and click the Image button. The Select Image Source dialog box appears. Set the option for Data Sources at the top of the dialog box. Choose the *image* URL variable and click OK. Dreamweaver may warn you that the image doesn't exist in the current local root folder. Click No in the dialog box if this happens.

40. Dreamweaver adds an icon for a dynamic image in the document window. Select this icon, go to the Properties panel, and set the W field to **200** and the H field to **250**. Type **A picture of a monster** in the Alt field and click the Align Center button.

41. Press the down-arrow key and press ENTER or RETURN. Under the Common tab of the Insert panel, click the Horizontal Rule button. With the horizontal rule selected, go to the Properties panel and set the width to 33%. Set the height to 1. Choose Left from the Align list and uncheck the option for shading.

42. Press the down-arrow key to move the cursor to the right of the horizontal rule. Press ENTER or RETURN.

43. Set the Font list on the Properties panel to the first set of fonts and set the Size list to −1. Type **BACK.**

44. Highlight the word *BACK*. In the Link field of the Properties panel, type **index.htm**. This gives you a link back to the Monsters page.

45. That's your details page. It should look like the page shown in Figure 11-10.

46. Choose File | Save from Dreamweaver's main menu to save the details page.

47. Now for the moment of truth. Close the document window for the details page. You should still have the Monsters page in Dreamweaver. If not, open it.

48. Press F12. Click a link, and the link sends a query string to the details page. The details page captures the URL parameters, puts them in URL variables, and uses their values to generate the names and images of the monsters.

49. Close the browser window. Very well done!

FIGURE 11-10 Your details page should look like this.

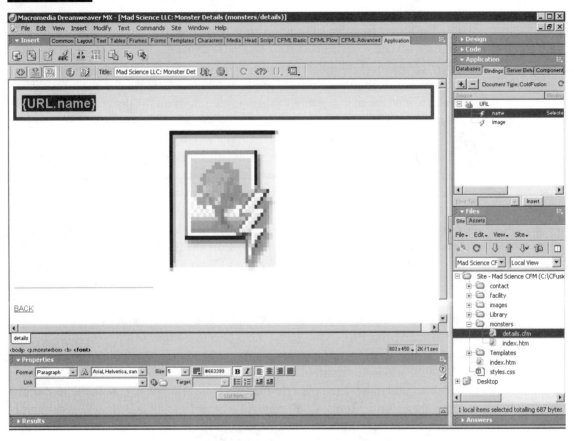

Using Live Objects

Dreamweaver comes with a few *live objects,* or ready-made Web apps, that you can add to your site by clicking a button and filling out a dialog box. These Web apps consist of a combination of server behaviors and dynamic pages. You could build the same Web apps by hand, adding the necessary server behaviors one by one to the dynamic pages, but having Dreamweaver insert them all at once automatically is a great timesaver.

Building Master/Detail Page Sets

The Master/Detail Page Set live object requires two pages: a master page and a detail page. The master page displays a recordset in a dynamic table and includes a recordset navigation bar and recordset counter. Links in the dynamic table lead to the detail page, which displays more information about the record you clicked. One common use of this strategy is to present a list of products on the master page. The visitor clicks a product and sees an image and complete description on the detail page.

You can add the Master/Detail Page Set live object to ColdFusion, ASP, and JSP sites. Dreamweaver doesn't support it in ASP.NET or PHP sites.

To add this live object, first create and design a master page and a detail page. Insert the static content and save these pages to your site. Then, in the master page's document window, create a recordset for the information that you want to display. This recordset should contain master-page data, as well as detail-page data—you can configure which information appears on which page later. Finally, click the Master Detail Page Set button in the Insert panel under the Application tab.

You can also choose Insert | Application Objects | Master Detail Page Set from the main menu.

In the Master Detail Page Set dialog box (Figure 11-11), choose the recordset from the Recordset list. Determine which recordset columns should appear on the master page in the Master Page Fields area: Click the plus button to add a column, click the minus button to remove a selected column, and use the arrow buttons to change the order of the selected column. In the Link To Detail From list, choose the record that acts as the link to the detail page. In the Pass Unique Key list, choose the record to send as the identifier to the detail page. This record should contain a unique value, like a product code, ISBN number, or SKU. If the record is nonnumeric, uncheck the Numeric option to the right of this field.

Set up the number of records to display at a time in the Show area. If you choose All, Dreamweaver doesn't add the recordset navigation bar or recordset counter to your master page.

Click the Browse button to the right of the Detail Page Name field and navigate to the detail page that you created. Finally, determine which recordset columns appear on the detail page under Detail Page Fields and click OK. Dreamweaver adds server behaviors to the master and detail pages. You may modify the layout and appearance of the master and detail pages to suit the look and feel of your site.

Modifying Database Records

Dreamweaver's Record Insertion Form and Record Update Form live objects allow your visitors to add and update rows in a database table. By way of a Record Insertion

FIGURE 11-11

Use the Master Detail Page Set dialog box to add the Master/Detail Page Set live object to your site.

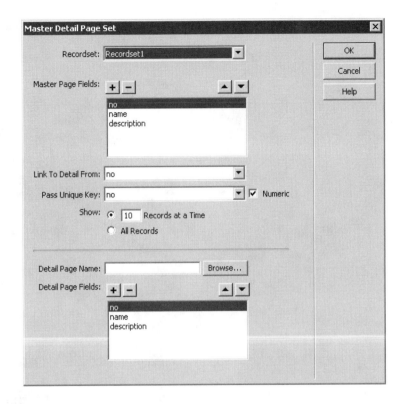

Form, a visitor can register with your site by adding his or her user name, password, and preferences to your site's user database. By way of a Record Update Form, the visitor can modify his or her record in the database. Don't add Record Insertion Forms and Record Update Forms to the same page, or your site won't function properly.

Inserting Records   To add the Record Insertion Form live object, you need two pages: the start page, or the page that contains the form, and the destination page, or the page that loads after the visitor submits the form. Open and create pages for both. Then, on the start page, go to the Insert panel, look under the Application tab, and click the Record Insertion Form button.

You can also choose Insert | Application Objects | Record Insertion Form.

In the Data Source list on the Record Insertion Form dialog box (Figure 11-12), choose the database to which you want to add a record and pick the database table from the Table list. Supply your app server's user name and password, if required, in the appropriate fields.

FIGURE 11-12

Create a form for inserting new records into a database with the Record Insertion Form dialog box.

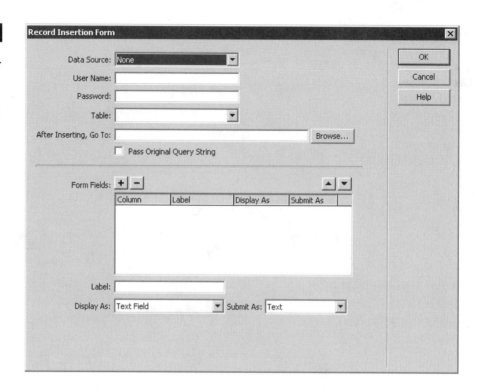

Click the Browse button to the right of the After Inserting, Go To field and navigate to the destination page that you created. Then, in the Form Fields section of the dialog box, choose which fields to display and the order in which to display them. If you don't want to display a particular field, select it and click the minus button. This prevents the visitor from adding information to that particular column of the database table.

Change the label of the selected form field in the Label field. In the Display As list, change the type of form object that accepts the visitor's input. In the Submit As list, determine how you want to submit the information of the selected field. Make the selected field dynamic by clicking the lightning-bolt icon.

Click OK to insert the form. Dreamweaver adds an HTML form with a Submit button to the start page, along with the Insert Record server behavior.

If this form is a registration form for your Web site, you'll probably want to check that the visitor's user name is unique. You can achieve this by adding the Check New Username server behavior to your page. To apply this server behavior, click the plus button on the Server Behaviors panel and choose User Authentication | Check New Username. The Check New Username dialog box appears (shown next). From the

Username Field list, choose the field of the Record Insertion Form that contains the visitor's user name. Then click the Browse button to the right of the If Already Exists, Go To field and choose a page to load when someone else has already taken the user name in question. Click OK to add this server behavior to your page.

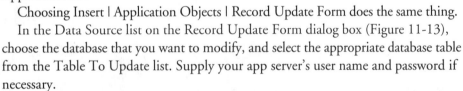

Updating Records   You need two pages to insert the Record Update Form live object: a start page and a destination page, just as with the Record Insertion Form app. In addition, the start page should contain a filtered recordset containing only the row of the database table that you want the visitor to modify. Create these pages and then, on the start page, click the Record Update Form button on the Insert panel under the Application tab.

Choosing Insert | Application Objects | Record Update Form does the same thing.

In the Data Source list on the Record Update Form dialog box (Figure 11-13), choose the database that you want to modify, and select the appropriate database table from the Table To Update list. Supply your app server's user name and password if necessary.

From the Select Record From list, choose the recordset that you inserted for this app. Choose the column that contains the unique identifier for this record from the Unique Key Column list, and check the Numeric option if this identifier is a number. The visitor won't be able to update this value in the database.

Click the Browse button to the right of the After Updating, Go To field, and navigate to the destination page. Then fill out the Form Fields area. The controls here work exactly the same as those on the Record Insertion Form dialog box. When you finish, click OK to create the form. Dreamweaver adds an HTML form plus the Update Record server behavior to your page.

on the **Job**

If you're delivering a database-enabled site to a client who has little technical expertise, it's always a nice touch to include special administrator-only pages that allow the client to add and modify database records from a browser window. This saves the client from having to learn to use the database software. You can easily create maintenance pages like these with the Record Insertion Form and Record Update Form live objects.

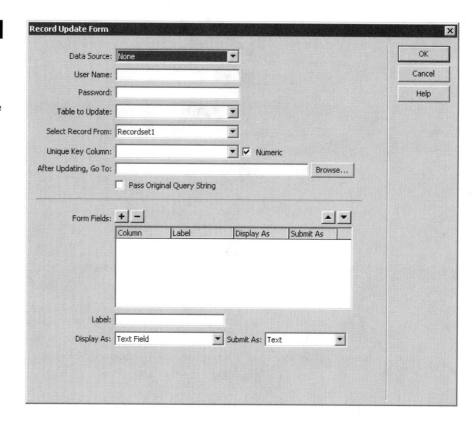

FIGURE 11-13

The Record Update Form dialog box gives you a ready-made Web app for updating the content of a database record.

Using Server Behaviors to Authenticate Users

Dreamweaver provides server behaviors for restricting visitor access to certain areas of your site and creating login and logout procedures. These behaviors work in ColdFusion, ASP, and JSP sites but not in ASP.NET or PHP sites.

Logging Visitors In and Out

If your site has a user database, you can add login and logout functionality with the Log In User and Log Out User server behaviors.

To insert the Log In User behavior, first create a login page with a form that contains fields for user name and password, plus a Submit button. Then go to the Server Behaviors panel, click the plus button, and choose User Authentication | Log In User. The Log In User dialog box appears, as shown in Figure 11-14.

Choose the login form from the Get Input From Form list. Then specify the fields that contain the user name and password from the Username Field and Password Field lists. Choose the user database from the Validate Using Data Source list and select

Use the Log In User dialog box to attach a login procedure to a form on your page.

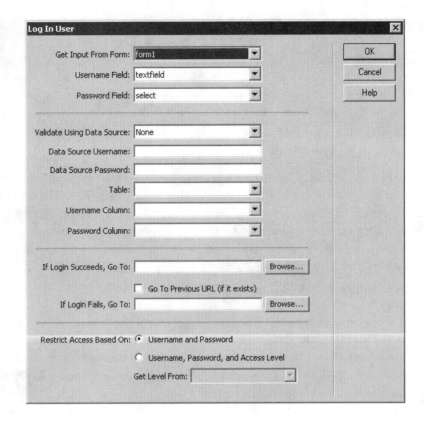

the appropriate database table from the Table list. Then choose the column of the table that contains user names and the column that contains passwords from the Username Column and Password Column lists. Don't forget to supply your app server's user name and password in the Data Source Username and Data Source Password fields, if required.

Click the Browse button next to the If Login Succeeds, Go To field and choose the appropriate page. If you want to send the visitor back to the page that called the login page, check the Go To Previous URL (If It Exists) option. Choose a page to load if login fails by clicking the second Browse button.

Under Restrict Access Based On, determine the conditions for successful login. If user name and password are sufficient, select the Username And Password option. If you want to require a specific access level in addition to user name and password, select the second option, and choose the table column that contains the visitor's access level from the Get Level From list. See the next section for more information about access levels.

FROM THE CLASSROOM

Search functions are standard fare on the Web. The visitor expects them. You can add a simple search feature to display matching results from a database with a few quick steps.

Building a Search Function

Search functions usually consist of two pages: the search page, which contains the search form, and the results page, which displays the results. Design both pages in Dreamweaver. Add a form to the search page with a text field and a Submit button. Give the text field a name and make a note of it—you'll use this name on the results page. Set the method of the form to get or post. get is more common for search functions, but post is more secure.

Interestingly enough, the results page is the page that actually performs the search. The first step is to add a recordset to the results page. In the Recordset dialog box, select the database and database table that you want to search. If you want to display all the columns of the database table in your results list, choose the All option under Columns. If you want to display only particular columns, choose the Selected option and choose the desired columns from the list.

The recordset filter is the workhorse. The filter decides which records in the database are matches. From the first drop-down list under

Filter, choose the column that you want to test for matches. From the second drop-down list, choose Contains. This expression allows the visitor to type in partial search strings like *te*, returning results for *teeth, coyote, miter,* and so on.

From the third drop-down list, select URL Parameter if you used a get method form or Form Parameter if you used a post method form. Finally, in the text box to the right, type the name of the text field from the search page. The filter now uses the visitor's search string to scour the database table. Click OK to create the recordset.

Now simply add a dynamic table to the results page to display the contents of the recordset. For a touch of class, create a new URL variable or form variable, depending on the type of form you built on the search page. Set the value of this variable to the name of the text field, just like you did in the recordset. Drag the variable from the Bindings panel into the document window, and add a message like "Your search for the keyword *x* returned the following results."

You can apply the Log Out User behavior to a link or a page. If you apply this behavior to a link, clicking the link logs out the visitor. If you apply this behavior to a page, the Web app logs out the visitor automatically when the page loads.

Go to the Server Behaviors panel, click the plus button, and choose User Authentication | Log Out User. The Log Out User dialog box appears, as shown next. Under Log Out When, choose to insert a new Log Out link or to trigger logout automatically when the page loads. Then click the Browse button next to the When Done, Go To field and choose the appropriate page. Click OK to apply the behavior.

Restricting Access to a Page   The Restrict Access To Page server behavior forces visitors to log in before they can access the page. To apply this behavior, click the plus button on the Server Behaviors panel and choose User Authentication | Restrict Access To Page. The Restrict Access To Page dialog box appears.

Under Restrict Based On, determine the criteria for prohibiting the visitor from accessing the page. If you want the visitor to log in first, choose the Username And Password option. If you want to check the visitor's access level as well, choose the second option. Then choose the required access level from the Select Level(s) window, holding down CTRL (Windows) or COMMAND (Mac) to choose more than one.

To add or remove access levels, click the Define button. This opens the Define Access Levels dialog box, shown in the following illustration. In the Name field, type the name of the access level. This name should match the value that you store for visitor access levels or privileges in the user database. To add a new access level, click the plus button.

Change the order of a selected access level by clicking the arrow buttons and remove a selected access level by clicking the minus button. Click OK to return to the Restrict Access To Page dialog box.

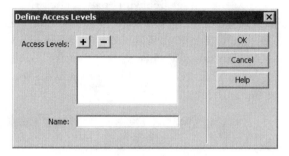

Click the Browse button to the right of the If Access Denied, Go To field and choose the appropriate page. Typically, you should choose the login page if all you need from the visitor is a user name and password. If you require a higher access level than the visitor owns, you can link to the home page of the site or an Access Denied page. Click OK to apply the behavior.

Don't restrict access to your login page! That defeats the purpose of a login page.

Using ColdFusion Server Debug

As a final insult to non-ColdFusion developers, Dreamweaver's extremely convenient Server Debug feature allows you to test your entire ColdFusion site inside Dreamweaver. That's right—you can test rollovers, fill out forms, click hyperlinks, execute Web apps, and do everything I swore you couldn't do in Dreamweaver, right inside the document window.

This feature works only on ColdFusion sites developed in Dreamweaver MX for Windows. Sorry, Mac users. Sorry, PHP developers. Sorry, ASP.NET developers and the rest. I'm sure this is just an unfortunate oversight, even though certain parties may have a vested interest in getting you to develop for ColdFusion Server.

To enter Server Debug mode, look to the left of the Live Data View button for the Server Debug button.

Click this button, and your document window behaves like a browser instance of Internet Explorer. You see all the live data, and all the functionality on your page works exactly as it would in IE. If ColdFusion runs into any problems in the server-side code, the Server Debug panel appears in the Results panel group with information about the error.

Click the Server Debug button again to resume editing in Dreamweaver.

CERTIFICATION SUMMARY

In this chapter, you learned how to add server-side functionality to your pages to create a dynamic site.

You need at least a Web server and an application server to build server-side apps or an application server that also functions as a Web server, such as ColdFusion MX. You also need a database like Microsoft Access or MySQL if you want to use recordsets from the database as sources of dynamic content.

Use the Bindings panel in the Application panel group to add dynamic content sources like form variables, URL variables, and session variables. Use form variables to retrieve values from a `post` method form submission and use URL variables to retrieve values from a `get` method form submission or parameter values from a link's query string. Use session variables to set information that pertains to a particular visitor during a particular session on your site. You can draw from all these sources to create dynamic text, dynamic `src` or `href` attributes, and dynamic form elements.

To use a database with your site, create a connection to the database from the Databases panel. Then, from the Bindings panel, add a recordset. A recordset contains the results of a query to a database table. You can filter the records so that the recordset shows only the records that you want. Display the recordset in a dynamic table and add a recordset navigation bar and a recordset counter to improve usability.

Dreamweaver's live objects give you ready-made Web apps for creating master/detail page sets, inserting new records in a database, or updating existing records in a database. Dreamweaver also provides server behaviors to authenticate your visitors. You can register new users with the Record Insertion Form live object and the Check New Username server behavior. You can log in registered visitors with the Log In User behavior, and you can log them out with the Log Out User behavior. Restrict a visitor's access to certain pages of your site with the Restrict Access To Page behavior.

TWO-MINUTE DRILL

Adding Server-Side Functionality

❑ Web applications are functions that execute on the server, not the browser.

❑ You need a Web server and an application server to build and test Web apps.

❑ If you want your site to connect to a database, you must install database software like Microsoft Access or MySQL.

❑ Configure your dynamic site's connections in the Testing Server category of the Site Definition dialog box.

❑ Dynamic content is content that the application server adds to your page before sending the page to the browser.

❑ Create a recordset, or a collection of records from a database table, by establishing a database connection, adding a Recordset (Query) data binding, and writing a query to the database in the Recordset dialog box.

❑ Create a URL-variable binding to receive values from query strings sent by links and get method form submissions.

❑ Create a form-variable binding to receive values from post method form submissions.

❑ Use session variables to store information about a particular visitor during the visitor's session on your site.

❑ Add dynamic text to your page to display the value of a dynamic content source.

❑ If a dynamic content source provides the correct path to an asset file like a graphic, you can add dynamic src attributes to your page.

❑ Use dynamic tables to display the records of a recordset and add recordset navigation bars and recordset counters to improve the usability of your app.

❑ Dynamic form elements have dynamically determined initial values, checked states, or selections.

❑ Use the Record Insertion Form live object to create a form to add new records to a database and use the Record Update Form live object to update existing records.

❑ Apply User Authentication server behaviors to create login and logout procedures and restrict user access to certain pages in ColdFusion, ASP, and JSP sites.

SELF TEST

The following questions will help you measure your understanding of the material presented in this chapter. Read all the choices carefully because there might be more than one correct answer. Choose all correct answers for each question.

Adding Server-Side Functionality

1. What is a form variable? Choose the best answer.

   A. A variable that retrieves a particular value from a `post` method form submission

   B. A variable that retrieves a particular value from a `get` method form submission

   C. A variable that contains the action of a form

   D. A variable that contains the method of a form

2. You want to display multiple records from a recordset on your page. Which of the following should you insert? Choose the best answer.

   A. Dynamic radio button

   B. Dynamic `src` attribute

   C. Dynamic table

   D. Recordset counter

3. When does it make sense to declare a session variable?

   A. When you want to assign different values to different visitors

   B. When you want to assign the same value to all visitors

   C. When you want to query a database

   D. When you want to turn off session management

4. Which of the following must you install before you can develop and test a dynamic site?

   A. A Web server

   B. An application server

   C. A database

   D. A JavaScript-enabled browser

5. You want to query a particular database, but the database doesn't appear in the Recordset dialog box's drop-down list. What's the likely cause of this problem?

   A. You forgot to create a recordset.

   B. You forgot to connect to the database.

   C. You can create only one recordset per page.

   D. You forgot to shut down the current database.

6. Which of the following can send a value to a URL variable?

   A. A recordset

   B. A `get` method form submission

   C. A `post` method form submission

   D. A link

7. You want your Web app to check a dynamic checkbox on your form when the dynamic content source returns the value *yes*. What should you do?

   A. Change the name of checkbox to *yes*.

   B. Change the checked value of the checkbox to *yes*.

   C. Type **yes** in the Equal To field on the Dynamic CheckBox dialog box.

8. Now you want your Web app to select a particular radio button in a dynamic radio group when the dynamic content source returns the value *isLarge*. What should you do?

   A. Change the name of the radio button to *isLarge*.

   B. Change the checked value of the radio button to *isLarge*.

   C. Neither **A** nor **B**.

9. What's the correct format for a query string appended to a link's `href` attribute when the destination page is *index.htm* and the parameters to pass are `name` and `iq`?

   A. `index.htm:name=George+iq=75`

   B. `index.htm?name=George+iq=75`

   C. `index.htm+name=George+iq=75`

   D. `index.htm&name=George&iq=75`

   E. `index.htm?name=George&iq=75`

10. How can you use a database to add dynamic images to a Dreamweaver page?

   A. Attach image files to a column of the database table.

   B. Embed image files in a column of the database table.

   C. Supply paths to image files in a column of the database table.

   D. Type image names into a column of the database table.

11. Which of the following pages should never receive the Restrict Access To Page server behavior?

   A. The home page

   B. The login page

   C. The administrator page

   D. The members-only home page

12. Which of the following is a typical application of Dreamweaver's Record Insertion Form live object?

   A. Registering new visitors

   B. Recording the movements of a visitor throughout your site

   C. Allowing registered visitors to change their passwords

   D. Deleting an unused database table

13. What is a recordset? Choose the best answer

   A. A collection of all the records in a single column of a database table

   B. A collection of all the records in a database table

   C. A collection of database records returned by a query

   D. A single row of a database table

14. How does your Web app request information from a database?

   A. It sends DHTML.

   B. It sends a recordset.

   C. It sends an HTTP request.

   D. It sends a SQL command.

15. How do you display a value from a query string?

    A. Create a data binding for a URL variable in the Bindings panel and insert it as dynamic text.

    B. Open a database connection, create a recordset, and insert it as dynamic text.

    C. Create a data binding for a form variable in the Bindings panel and insert it as dynamic text.

    D. Add the Display Query String server behavior to the page.

16. Which of the following can be dynamic content sources?

    A. A URL variable

    B. A form variable

    C. An application server

    D. A Web server

    E. A JavaBean

    F. A session variable

    G. A recordset

17. How do you represent a space character in a query string?

    A. `%20`

    B. `#20`

    C. `!20`

    D. `?20`

18. Which of the following components processes server-side markup?

    A. The Web browser

    B. The Web server

    C. The application server

    D. The visitor's operating system

19. Under which file extension should you save a dynamic page?

    A. *.htm*

    B. *.css*

    C. *.js*

    D. None of the above

20. How can you preview the dynamic content on your page?

    A. Switch to Design view.

    B. Switch to Live Data view.

    C. Press F12.

    D. Press CTRL-F12 (Windows) or COMMAND-F12 (Mac).

    E. Switch to Database view.

LAB QUESTION

You're designing an application for your site that allows the visitor to search a product database. The database has five columns: *product_sku, product_name, product_image, product_description,* and *product_price.*

Here's how your application works: The visitor types a search string in a text field and submits it by the get method. You want the application to search the product names in the database against the search string and display the names and prices of the matching records.

You design a search page, which contains a form called *searchForm,* a text field called *searchString,* and a Submit button called *submitSearch.* You set the form's submission method to get.

Now you design the results page. You want to use a dynamic table to display the results, but first you need a recordset, so you click the Recordset button and get down to business. What columns should you include in the recordset, and what are the parameters of the filter? Jot down your answers on a piece of paper and check your results against mine.

SELF TEST ANSWERS

Adding Server-Side Functionality

1. ☑ **A.** A form variable retrieves a value from a post method form submission.
   ☒ **B** is incorrect because a URL variable retrieves a value from a get method form submission. **C** and **D** are incorrect because, while form variables could conceivably contain this information, so could any other variable type. Choice **A** is the best answer.

2. ☑ **C.** Insert a dynamic table to display multiple records from a recordset.
   ☒ **A** and **B** are incorrect because these objects don't allow you to display multiple records from a recordset. **D** is incorrect because a recordset counter displays the total number of records in a recordset, not the records themselves.

3. ☑ **A.** Declare a session variable when you want to assign different values to different visitors.
   ☒ **B** is incorrect because it describes an application variable, not a session variable. **C** is incorrect because a recordset contains the results of a database query, not a session variable. **D** is incorrect because setting a session variable doesn't turn off session management. In fact, without session management, session variables don't work.

4. ☑ **A** and **B.** You need a Web server and an application server to develop dynamic sites.
   ☒ **C** is incorrect because a database isn't necessary, although it's often an integral part of a dynamic site. **D** is incorrect because you don't need JavaScript to develop dynamic sites. Server-side code executes on the server, not in the browser.

5. ☑ **B.** You forgot to connect to the database. Go to the Databases panel and do the deed.
   ☒ **A** is incorrect because when you query a database, you create a recordset. **C** is incorrect because you can have as many recordsets on your page as you like. **D** is incorrect because you can connect to as many databases as you like.

6. ☑ **B** and **D.** URL variables can retrieve data from get method form submissions and links with query strings.
   ☒ **A** is incorrect because a recordset contains database records. It doesn't send data to URL variables. **C** is incorrect because form variables retrieve data from post method form submissions.

7. ☑ **C.** Type **yes** in the Equal To field.
   ☒ **A** and **B** are incorrect because the name and value of the checkbox don't have to match the value that the dynamic content source provides.

8. ☑ **B.** Set the radio button's checked value to *isLarge.*
   ☒ **A** and **C** are incorrect because the checked value of the radio button, not the name, has to match the value that the dynamic content source provides.

9. ☑ **E.** Add a question mark after the destination page and separate parameters with ampersands.
   ☒ **A, B, C** and **D** are incorrect because these aren't in the correct format.

10. ☑ **C.** Supply paths to image files in a column of the database table.
    ☒ **A, B,** and **D** are incorrect because Dreamweaver wants the column of the database table to contain paths to image files, not digitized images or image names.

11. ☑ **B.** Never restrict access to the login page. The purpose of a login page is to grant visitors access to restricted pages.
    ☒ **A, C,** and **D** are incorrect because, under certain conditions, you might want to restrict access to these pages.

12. ☑ **A.** Use the Record Insertion Form live object to register new visitors to your site. This app creates a new row in the user database table.
    ☒ **B** is incorrect because the Record Insertion Form app is for adding new records to a database table, not tracking site movements. **C** is incorrect because you'd use the Record Update Form Web app for this task. **D** is incorrect because the Record Insertion Form app doesn't remove unused database tables.

13. ☑ **C.** A recordset is a collection of database records returned by a query.
    ☒ **A, B,** and **D** are correct only in certain instances, while choice **C** is always correct.

14. ☑ **D.** Your Web app sends a SQL command to request information from a database.
    ☒ **A** is incorrect because DHTML is a client-side markup language. It doesn't interface with databases. **B** is incorrect because a recordset is what receives the results of the query from the database. **C** is incorrect because an HTTP request is what a browser sends to a Web server to request a Web page.

15. ☑ **A.** Create a URL variable data binding on your page and display the URL variable as dynamic text.
    ☒ **B** is incorrect because the recordset contains database records, not query strings. **C** is incorrect because form variables receive `post` method form submissions, not query strings. **D** is incorrect because there is no such server behavior.

16. ☑ **A, B, E, F,** and **G.** All of these are potential sources of dynamic content.
    ☒ **C** and **D** are incorrect because application servers and Web servers don't store dynamic

content. The application server adds the dynamic content to the page, and the Web server presents the page to the browser.

17. ☑ **A.** Represent a space character in a query string with %20.
☒ **B, C,** and **D** are incorrect because the proper code is %20.

18. ☑ **C.** The application server processes server-side markup.
☒ **A** is incorrect because the Web browser interprets HTML, not server-side markup. **B** is incorrect because the Web server sends pages to the browser. **D** is incorrect because the visitor's operating system doesn't process server-side markup.

19. ☑ **D.** The file extension depends on the server language that you use. A ColdFusion page gets the *.cfm* extension, while a PHP page gets the *.php* extension, and so on.
☒ **A, B,** and **C** are incorrect because these file extensions are for static pages only.

20. ☑ **B, C,** and **D.** Preview dynamic content in your document window by switching to Live Data view, pressing F12 to launch your default preview browser or pressing CTRL-F12 or COMMAND-F12 to launch your secondary preview browser.
☒ **A** is incorrect because Design view shows placeholders, not actual dynamic content. **E** is incorrect because there is no such thing as Database view in Dreamweaver.

LAB ANSWER

Here's what you know:

- You want to display two of the five columns: *product_name* and *product_price*.
- You want to search the *product_name* column against the visitor's input.
- You created a text field called *searchString* to solicit the visitor's input, which the form submits as a URL parameter, thanks to the get method.

This means that you want to limit the recordset to the *product_name* and *product_price* columns. The rest of the data in the database is extraneous as far as this Web app is concerned. Therefore, in the Recordset dialog box under Contains, you'd click the Selected option and choose *product_name* and *product_price*.

In addition, you want the filter to extract only those records whose *product_name* column contains the visitor's input from the *searchString* field. To specify this, in the Recordset dialog box under Filter, you'd choose *product_name* from the first drop-down list, Contains from the second, and URL Parameter from the third. In the text field to the right, you'd type **searchString**.

CERTIFIED DREAMWEAVER DEVELOPER

Part III

Solution Testing, Deployment, and Maintenance

12

Testing and Troubleshooting

A s you build your site, it's often helpful to perform some diagnostic checks on the source code, just to make sure everything's running smoothly. If at no other time, then certainly before the big launch, reserve some time in your schedule for analyzing and fine-tuning the code.

While nothing replaces good old-fashioned elbow grease when it comes to testing and troubleshooting, Dreamweaver provides a number of features that can help you save time or point you in the right direction. This chapter discusses these features and their benefits to you and your clients.

CERTIFICATION OBJECTIVE 12.01

Checking and Fixing Your Site

This certification objective lumps together a number of different procedures under the general heading of checking and fixing your site. You can launch many of these procedures from the Results panel group, while you have to look elsewhere to launch the others. Dreamweaver MX does much to consolidate the various checks and reports, but you shouldn't rely on the Results panels in the same way you rely on the tabs of the Insert panel. Often, the Results panels don't provide the precise reporting or checking procedures that you need, especially during crunch time, for some reason.

The next Scenario and Solution sidebar quick reference gives you a breakdown of when to use the Results panels according to the topics of discussion in this objective.

Checking the Design for Different Screen Sizes

You can set Dreamweaver's document window to display at common width and height ratios. This allows you to check your design against different screen sizes.

First make sure that the document window isn't maximized. Then click the size list at the bottom of the document window and choose a new configuration from the menu that appears, as shown in Figure 12-1.

You can add or remove window sizes by choosing Edit | Preferences and clicking the Status Bar category.

SCENARIO & SOLUTION

When do you use the Results panels?	For validation checks, compatibility checks, link checks, changing individual links, accessibility checks, and custom reports
When don't you use the Results panels?	For changing links sitewide, formatting the code, cleaning up the code, debugging JavaScript, changing the default connection time, or checking the design for different screen sizes

Checking Download Time for Different Connections

The download-time indicator at the bottom right of the document window tells you approximately how long the current page takes to download over the default connection type, which is 28.8 Kbps (kilobits per second). If you want to change the default

FIGURE 12-1

Change the size of the document window to match common screens.

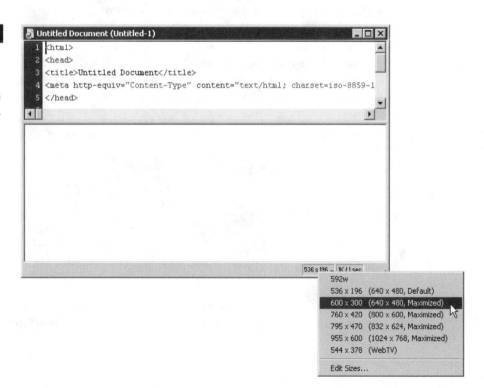

connection type, choose Edit | Preferences, click the Status Bar category, and choose a new value from the Connection Speed list.

It's better to underestimate your target audience's typical connection than to overestimate it, so don't go beyond 56 Kbps, which is the fastest dial-up connection speed. Choose the highest value only if you're designing an intranet site and users all have a T1 connection.

exam
ⓦatch
Unlike the screen size, you can't change the default connection type from the document window.

Checking Markup for Browser Compatibility

Dreamweaver allows you to check the markup of your site for compatibility with various browsers. To do so, open the Target Browser Check panel (Figure 12-2) in the Results panel group by choosing Window | Results | Target Browser Check.

Click the green arrow button at the top left of the Target Browser Check panel, and select an option from the menu that slides down. If you want to check the current page only, choose Check Target Browsers. If you want to check the current site, choose Check Target Browsers For Entire Site. If you want to check only certain files or folders in your site, first highlight these in the Site panel, and then click the green arrow button in the Target Browser Check panel and choose Check Target Browser For Selected Files/Folders In Site.

The Check Target Browser dialog box appears, as shown next. Choose a browser from the list and click Check. The results appear in the Target Browser Check panel.

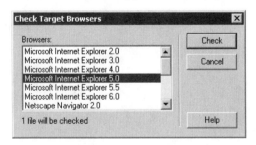

 Double-click a result in the list to open the corresponding page in Dreamweaver. To see more information about a result, select it and click the More Info button.

To view the entire report in more detail, click the Browse Report button.

To save a copy of the report, click the Save Report button.

To check the current page against a target browser without opening the Check Target Browsers panel first, choose File | Check Page | Check Target Browsers.

Validating Markup

Use Dreamweaver's Validation panel (Figure 12-3) in the Results panel group to check the tags in your site for syntax errors and standards compliance. Choose Window | Validation to open the Validation panel.

Click the green arrow button at the top of the Validation panel and select an option from the menu that slides out. Choose Validate Current Document to check the current page or choose Validate As XML to check the current page against XML standards instead of HTML. Choose Validate Entire Site to check all the pages in the current site. Choose Validate Selected Files In Site to check the selected files in the Site panel.

Dreamweaver runs the report and displays the results in the Validation panel. Double-click a result in the list to open the corresponding page. Click the More Info button to see more information about the selected result or click the Browser Report button to see a detailed report. To save the report, click the Save Report button.

You can adjust the settings of the validation check to fine-tune the results for your particular needs. Click the green arrow button on the Validation panel and choose Settings from the menu. The Preferences dialog box appears with the Validator category preselected, as shown in Figure 12-4. You can validate your site against various versions of HTML and XML with and without proprietary extensions, as well as ColdFusion

FIGURE 12-2

The Target Browser Check panel lets you verify your site's markup for compatibility with a variety of browsers.

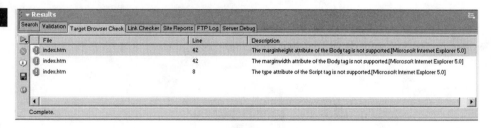

FIGURE 12-3

Use the
Validation panel
to check the tags
in your site for
syntax and
standards
compliance.

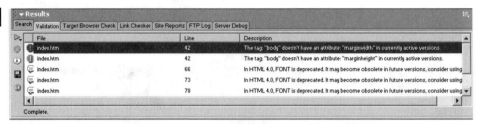

and JSP server-side markup. Click the Options button to change the level of scrutiny
of the validation or to suppress certain kinds of errors.

Comparing Validation with Browser Compatibility

Although validation and browser compatibility would seem to have much in common,
the truth of the matter is that they hardly ever do. A page that fails a validation check
miserably can work perfectly well in a variety of browsers.

FIGURE 12-4

Change the
settings of
the validation
check in the
Preferences
dialog box.

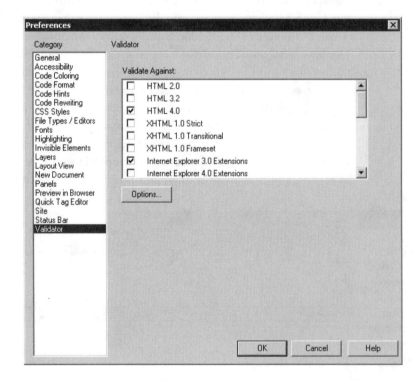

The Validation panel displays problems with the structure of the code according to official standards, but standards committees aren't in the business of producing browser software. Internet Explorer in particular is notorious for letting sloppy HTML code slide, while Netscape has the bad habit of ignoring little-used tags such as `<legend>` and `<label>`. Some tags, such as `<optgroup>`, have yet to receive support from any of the major browsers.

In theory, the best cross-browser, cross-platform, cross-device-compatible code should always comply with markup standards, but in practice you can get away with much. The cross-browser-compatible code that Dreamweaver produces routinely fails validation checks! If you have to choose between validation and compatibility, go with compatibility.

See the next Scenario and Solution sidebar for a quick reference to sum up the differences between compatibility reports and validation reports.

EXERCISE 12-1

Comparing Validation and Compatibility Reports

The time has come to run some diagnostics on the Mad Science LLC site. You didn't do any hand coding for this project, so it should be interesting to see how well Dreamweaver fared.

1. Launch Dreamweaver, open the Site panel, and select the Mad Science LLC site. Double-click the *index.htm* file of the home page. It opens in a new document window.

2. Now open the Validation panel group by choosing Window | Results | Validation.

3. Click the green arrow button on the Validation panel and choose Validate Current Document.

   Dreamweaver validates away, and in a moment, your results appear in the Validation panel. Don't be alarmed if you see many warnings or alerts. One of them says something to the effect that the body tag shouldn't have a `marginwidth` attribute, yet Netscape uses the `marginwidth` attribute in the body tag. Blame Netscape on that one, not you or Dreamweaver. Another one says that HTML 4.0 deprecates the use of the font tag, which is true enough, although Dreamweaver uses the font tag in HTML styles, and all the major browsers still support the font tag. The moral of the story is this: Validation is not the same thing as compatibility.

4. Speaking of compatibility, click the Target Browser Check tab and click the green arrow button. Choose Check Target Browsers from the menu and choose Microsoft Internet Explorer 4.0 from the Check Target Browsers dialog box that appears. Click OK to run the compatibility check.

   More false positives here. One warning says that Internet Explorer 4.0 doesn't like the `marginheight` and `marginwidth` attributes, which is absolutely correct. You added those attributes to satisfy Netscape users.

5. Another warning states that the target browser doesn't support the `type` attribute of the script tag. Double-click the result for this, and the corresponding page opens in a new document window. Remove the highlighted type attribute from the script tag. Choose File | Save and then choose File | Check Page | Validate Markup. The Validation panel reappears.

6. Wouldn't you know it? The very `type` attribute you just removed causes a validation error! Since Internet Explorer 4.0 simply ignores attributes that it doesn't understand, there's no harm leaving the `type` attribute in the style tag. Choose Edit | Undo to replace the deleted attribute and choose File | Save again. Some days you just can't win.

Checking and Changing Links

Use the Link Checker panel in the Results panel group (Figure 12-5) to scour your site for broken links, external links, and orphaned files. A *broken link* is a link for which there is no corresponding page in your site. In other words, a link to the page

SCENARIO & SOLUTION

What is a compatibility report?	An assessment of how well your page works in a live browser of a particular type, even if the code strays from official standards
What is a validation report?	An assessment of how well the markup of your page adheres to official standards of syntax and usage, even if the code isn't compatible in any browsers

FIGURE 12-5

Use the Link
Checker panel to
find broken links,
external links,
and orphaned
files in your site.

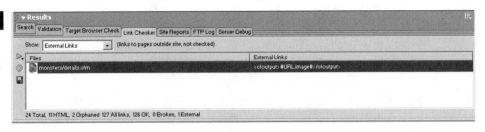

store.htm is broken if you don't have a *store.htm* page in your site or if you don't specify the correct path to this page. An *external link*, as you know, is a link whose destination is outside the root folder of the current site, while an *orphaned file* is a file in your site to which no link points. For example, the file *bunny.jpg* in your local root folder is orphaned if none of the image tags in your site declare this image as the source.

Click the green arrow button at the top left of the Link Checker panel and choose an option from the menu that appears. You can check the links in the current document, the entire site, or the currently selected files in the Site panel. If you want to check specifically for orphaned files, make sure that you choose the Check Links For Entire Site option.

After you make your selection, Dreamweaver runs the link report. Pull Broken Links, External Links, or Orphaned Files from the Show list at the top of the Link Checker panel to see the results for a particular category. Notice that Dreamweaver counts JavaScript and dynamic links as external when they might not actually be external at all. Dreamweaver also doesn't correctly assess server-side code, so that a great many orphaned files may show up in a dynamic site that aren't actually orphaned files. Go over the results carefully to weed out inaccuracies.

To fix a broken link, select its entry in the results list. A folder icon appears to the right of the link in the Broken Links column. Click the folder and browse to the correct destination or simply type the correct path in the Broken Links column.

exam
Watch

If you want to change all occurrences of a link, choose the Change Links Sitewide command.

Double-click an entry in the results list to open the corresponding page in Dreamweaver. To save a copy of the report, click the Save Report button.

To run a link report on all the files in your site without opening the Link Checker panel first, choose Site | Check Links Sitewide from the Site panel's menu. To run a link report on the current page without opening the Link Checker panel first, choose File | Check Page | Check Links from the main menu.

Changing Links Sitewide

Dreamweaver allows you to find and replace all occurrences of a particular link in your site. Use this feature to batch-process inaccurate links or update a number of incorrect paths automatically.

Close any currently open document windows and choose Site | Change Links Sitewide from the Site panel's menu. The Change Links Sitewide dialog box appears, as shown here:

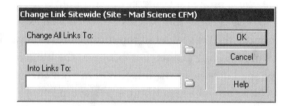

Type a root-relative path in the Change All Links To field or click the folder icon to the right of this field and browse to the appropriate page. If you're changing an incorrect link, you won't be able to browse for the file, so type the root-relative path that would exist if the link were correct. For example, assume that you want to change links to the nonexistent file *contact/contact.htm* into links to the correct file, *contact/ index.htm,* which resides in the *contact* folder. The correct root-relative path is */contact/ contact.htm,* even though this file doesn't exist.

exam

Ⓦatch

Make sure that you supply root-relative paths for all internal links in the fields of the Change Links Sitewide dialog box. Document-relative paths don't work.

If you're changing an e-mail, JavaScript, FTP, or null link, don't bother typing a root-relative path or browsing for a file. Simply type the full text of the path, such as *mailto:marc@taotezing* or *javascript:myFunction( ).*

Then, in the Into Links To field, click the folder icon and browse to the desired file, or type the full text of the replacement path, using root-relative format for URL links. Click OK to proceed.

If Dreamweaver finds at least one match, the Update Files dialog box appears, as shown next. Choose the files to update and click Update to make the change. Click Don't Update to leave the files as they are.

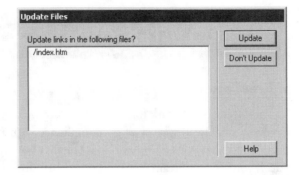

Checking Accessibility

To check the current page for accessibility problems, choose File | Check Page | Check Accessibility. Dreamweaver returns the results to the Site Reports panel (Figure 12-6) in the Results panel group.

Double-click a result to go to the corresponding line in the page's source code. For more information on a particular result, click the More Info button on the Results panel. The Reference panel in the Code panel group opens, displaying the relevant entry in the UsableNet Accessibility Reference online book. To save a copy of the report, click the Save Report button in the Site Reports panel.

You can modify the accessibility report to show only particular results by way of the Reports dialog box. See "Running Custom Reports," in the next section, for more information.

Running Custom Reports

Dreamweaver allows you to build a custom report by choosing options from the Reports dialog box (Figure 12-7). This dialog box opens when you select Site |

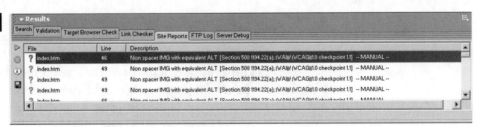

FIGURE 12-6

The Site Reports panel shows results for accessibility tests and customized reports.

FROM THE CLASSROOM

An Ounce of Prevention

Accessibility is an important benchmark for your site. At the same time, Dreamweaver's coding conventions aren't always accessibility-friendly by default. If you rely on Dreamweaver to provide the bulk of your HTML markup, there's a good chance that an accessibility check on your site will cough up all sorts of little problems.

If your contract hinges on you delivering an accessible site, you would be wise to enable Dreamweaver MX's accessibility dialog boxes. These dialog boxes appear when you insert problematic elements such as tables and images, providing additional fields and options. By filling out these dialog boxes completely, you improve the accessibility of your site.

The advantage to using Dreamweaver's accessibility dialog boxes during the design and development phase is that they help you to avoid a lengthy list of warnings when you run an accessibility check during the troubleshooting phase. What's more, these dialog boxes show

you exactly what you need to supply for strict compliance with accessibility standards.

The disadvantage to using these dialog boxes is that they slow down production. Every time you insert an image, no matter how insignificant, the Image Tag Accessibility Options dialog box appears. After you insert a table, the Accessibility Options For Tables dialog box appears. You get twice the amount of paperwork, so to speak. Of course, if you need to deliver an accessible site, this is a small price to pay, at least until you have a better idea about exactly which attributes require values to make your code accessible.

To turn on Dreamweaver's accessibility dialog boxes, choose Edit | Preferences, and select the Accessibility category. Under Show Attributes When Inserting, check the dialog boxes that you want to use. There are five: Form Objects, Frames, Media, Images, and Tables.

Reports from either the main menu or the Site panel's menu or when you click the green arrow button on the Site Reports panel.

From the Report On list at the top of the dialog box, select the page or pages that you want to include in the report. You can choose the current document, the entire local site, the currently selected pages in the Site panel, or all the pages in a particular folder. When you select the Folder option, a new field appears in the Reports dialog box.

FIGURE 12-7

Choose options
from the Reports
dialog box to run
a custom report.

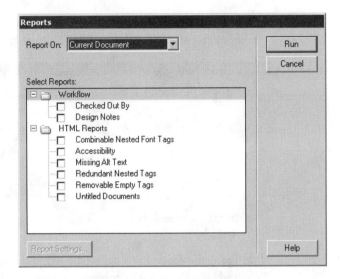

1. Click the folder icon to the right of this field and browse to the desired folder.

2. Then, under Select Reports, choose the report components that you want to include in your test. There are eight options: Checked Out By, Design Notes, Combinable Nested Font Tags, Accessibility, Missing Alt Text, Redundant Nested Tags, Removable Empty Tags, and Untitled Documents. The first two options, Checked Out By and Design Notes, apply specifically to workflow in a collaborative environment.

   ■ The **Checked Out By dialog box** shows all the documents that a team member has currently signed out. Select this option and click the Report Settings button to enter the user name of the team member.

   ■ The **Design Notes report** returns all the design notes associated with the file or files in the Report On list. Select this option and click the Report Settings button to filter the results. The Design Notes dialog box appears, as shown next. As you can see, this is not the same Design Notes dialog box that opens when you choose File | Design Notes from the main menu.

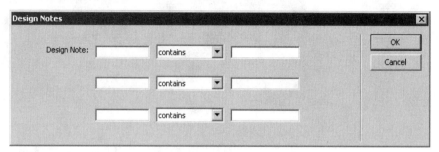

   a. In the first field, type the category name of a design note, such as *status* or *notes*.

   b. From the drop-down list to the right, choose a comparison statement and type the value to compare in the third field.

   c. Repeat this process for the next two rows in the dialog box if you want to filter the results further.

- The Combinable Nested Font Tags report finds font tags that Dreamweaver can combine to streamline your code.

- The Accessibility report looks for problems with the accessibility, just like the File | Check Page | Check Accessibility command.

   a. Select this option, click the Report Settings button to open the Accessibility dialog box (Figure 12-8), and choose the parameters of the report.

   b. Select a category or subcategory in the dialog box and click the Disable button to turn off that particular test. Likewise, click the Enable button to turn on that test.

   c. If you want to display the accessibility tests that your site passes, not just the ones that it fails, click the Show "PASSED" Tests option.

   d. Save these settings for future use by clicking the Save button. If you don't click Save, Dreamweaver reverts to the default settings the next time you launch the software.

- The **Missing Alt Text report** looks for image tags that don't have `alt` attributes.

on the
Job

Remember that supplying `alt` ***text for images is one of the best ways to improve accessibility on your site.***

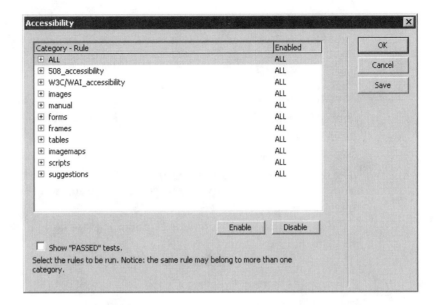

FIGURE 12-8

The Accessibility dialog box allows you to choose and save the parameters of your accessibility report.

■ The **Redundant Nested Tags report** looks for duplicate sets of tags that have no bearing on the presentation of your page, such as this:

```
<p><strong>This text isn't getting any <strong>stronger</strong>
   by piling on tags.</strong></p>
```

■ The **Removable Empty Tags report** looks for tags with no function, like this:

```
<p>There is nothing here <em> </em> to emphasize.</p>
```

■ Finally, **the Untitled Documents report** returns all the pages that don't have titles.

After you choose the reports that you want, click the Run button. Dreamweaver returns the results to the Site Reports panel.

Polishing the Code

Dreamweaver provides features for formatting and cleaning up the source code of the current page. The Apply Source Formatting command makes it easier for humans to follow the logic of the code, and the Clean Up HTML command helps you to streamline the code, fixing the problems that the Combinable Nested Font Tags, Redundant Nested Tags, and Removable Empty Tags reports identify, among other things.

Formatting the Source Code

Choose Command | Apply Source Formatting to format the code of the current document, or select a block of code and choose Commands | Apply Source Formatting To Selection. In practical terms, formatted code doesn't perform any better than unformatted code. The browser looks for HTML syntax, not formatting. Just the same, format your code regularly as a courtesy to your team members. Nobody likes trying to figure out messy code.

To modify the default formatting options, choose Edit | Preferences and select the Code Format category.

Cleaning Up the Source Code

Choose Commands | Clean Up HTML to streamline the source code of the current document. The Clean Up HTML/XHTML dialog box appears:

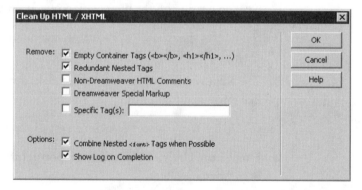

Under Remove, choose the coding problems that you want the procedure to fix:

- The **Empty Container Tags option** removes tags that have no function on the page.

- The **Redundant Nested Tags option** combines extraneous duplicate tags.

- The **Non-Dreamweaver HTML Comments option** removes comment tags that Dreamweaver doesn't use for features such as templates and Library items.

- The **Dreamweaver Special Markup option** removes Dreamweaver's comment tags. Cleaning up these tags removes the functionality of features such as templates and Library items, so think twice before you choose this option.

- The **Specific Tags option** removes a tag or series of tags. Type the tags in the field to the right of this option, separating them with commas, like this: **b, i, font**.

Under Options, check Combine Nested <font> Tags When Possible to streamline the use of font tags in your code. Check Show Log On Completion if you want Dreamweaver to tell you exactly what it changed.

Click OK to clean up the code. If you checked Show Log On Completion, Dreamweaver shows a summary of the procedure in a pop-up window.

on the
Job

If you rely on Dreamweaver to supply most or all of your source code, you should clean the code often. Dreamweaver isn't as skilled a programmer as you might think.

To help you remember the reasons for formatting and cleaning the code, I provide the next Scenario and Solution sidebar for a quick reference.

Cleaning Up Word HTML   Dreamweaver's Clean Up Word HTML feature takes the highly problematic HTML that Microsoft Word generates and converts it into something more suited to the Web.

To use this feature:

1. Open an HTML page that came from Word and choose Commands | Clean Up Word HTML. The Clean Up Word HTML dialog box appears, as shown in Figure 12-9.

2. Under the Basic tab, choose the version of Microsoft Word that created the HTML and choose cleaning options.

3. Look under the Detailed tab for more specific criteria with regard to fixing Word's markup and Cascading Style Sheet (CSS) conventions.

4. Click OK to clean the code.

exam
Watch

The Clean Up Word HTML command works specifically with HTML that comes from Microsoft Word. It doesn't work with HTML from other applications.

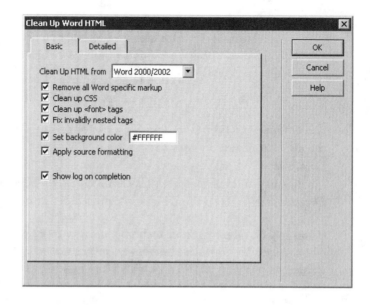

FIGURE 12-9

Use the Clean Up Word HTML dialog box to convert Microsoft Word HTML into something more suited to the Web.

Using the JavaScript Debugger

If you write your own JavaScript functions, use Dreamweaver's JavaScript Debugger feature to find and fix errors in the source code. The JavaScript Debugger looks for two kinds of errors: syntax errors and logical errors. Syntax errors are the easier of the two to identify because they always cause the script to crash. The following function contains a syntax error in the second line:

```
function showAlert() {
    alert"This is poor syntax. The alert statement requires
parentheses.";
}
```

SCENARIO & SOLUTION

Why should you format the code?	To make the logic of the code easier to follow. Formatting the code doesn't affect the performance of the page in a browser.
Why should you clean up the code?	To remove or repair unnecessary markup. Cleaning up the code doesn't necessarily improve the presentation of the code's logic, but it often makes the code more readable.

When you preview a page with syntax errors in the JavaScript, a warning icon appears in the status bar of your browser, along with a message like "Error on page." The browser continues to work, although without the benefit of your script. To fix a syntax error, all you have to do is locate the bad line of code and supply the correct syntax, like this:

```
alert("This is correct syntax. The alert statement now has parentheses.");
```

exam
ⓦatch

Crashed scripts don't cause the browser to crash, although the crashed script doesn't function on the page.

Logical errors are more insidious, because they don't always cause the script to crash. To fix these problems, you must often go through the script line by line and determine where the logic has gone wrong. Here is an example of a script with a logical error:

```
function showAlert() {
    var x = 1;
    var y = 2;
    alert("The value of x = " + y);
}
```

If you run this script in a browser, the script doesn't crash. There's nothing wrong with the syntax. The problem comes in the logic of the fourth line, when the script announces that the value of the variable *x* is the variable *y*. To get this script to function correctly, you must change the fourth line to read:

```
alert("The value of x = " + x);
```

To use the JavaScript Debugger, open a page containing JavaScript and choose File | Debug In Browser. Then choose a preview browser from the menu that slides out. You may choose any version of Internet Explorer or Netscape Navigator version 4, but not Netscape version 6.

The JavaScript Debugger first checks for syntax errors in the code. If it finds any, a document window opens, listing the type of error and the line in which it appears, as shown in Figure 12-10. Select an entry in the list to see a detailed description of the error. To jump to a faulty line in the source code, select an entry in the list, and click the Go To Line button. Dreamweaver's Code view opens, and Dreamweaver automatically highlights the line in question.

Next, the JavaScript Debugger looks for logical errors your scripts. Your preview browser launches, and a security warning dialog box may appear. If this happens, click

The JavaScript
Debugger checks
for syntax errors
in your code first.
If it finds any, the
errors appear in
this dialog box.

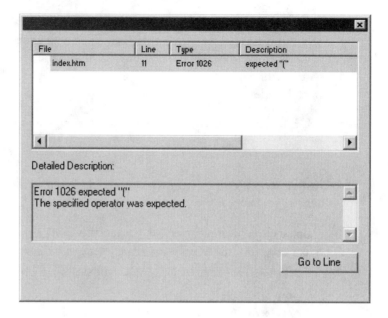

Yes or OK to give the JavaScript Debugger permission to execute and then click OK
to start debugging.

The JavaScript Debugger dialog box opens, as shown in Figure 12-11, containing
the source code of the page. The first step is to set breakpoints. A *breakpoint* is a line
at which the script pauses temporarily, allowing you to assess the values of different
variables before continuing. You may add a breakpoint to any line with JavaScript
code, including JavaScript event handlers in the HTML.

- **To set a breakpoint,** highlight a line of code by clicking the line number along
the left side of the dialog box and click the Set/Remove Breakpoint button.

- **To remove a breakpoint,** highlight the line with the breakpoint and click the
Set/Remove Breakpoint button again. To remove all the breakpoints at once,
click the Remove All Breakpoints button.

The next step is to include the variables that you want to monitor. When the
Debugger reaches a breakpoint, it displays the current value of the variable. To add
a variable to the monitor list, click the plus button and enter the variable's name.
Remove a variable by highlighting it in the list and clicking the minus button.

When you're ready to debug, click the Run button, shown here. This causes Control
to revert to the browser window, which loads the HTML of the page and executes

The JavaScript Debugger dialog box lets you set breakpoints in the code and assess the values of variables.

```
15  function MM_swapImgRestore() { //v3.0
16    var i,x,a=document.MM_sr; for(i=0;a&&i<a.length&&(x=a[
17  }
18
19  function MM_preloadImages() { //v3.0
20    var d=document; if(d.images){ if(!d.MM_p) d.MM_p=new A
21      var i,j=d.MM_p.length,a=MM_preloadImages.arguments;
22      if (a[i].indexOf("#")!=0){ d.MM_p[j]=new Image; d.MM
23  }
24
25  function MM_findObj(n, d) { //v4.01
26    var p,i,x; if(!d) d=document; if((p=n.indexOf("?"))>0
27      d=parent.frames[n.substring(p+1)].document; n=n.subs
```

Variable Name	Value

the automatic scripts. If your script waits for an event like onClick or onMouseOver before executing, perform this action in the browser window.

As soon as the script reaches a breakpoint, the JavaScript Debugger dialog box regains focus. Check the current values of the variables in the list at the bottom of the dialog box, or add and modify breakpoints as needed. Change the value of any variable in the list by clicking the Value column of the variable's entry and typing in the new value.

 To continue running your script, click one of the code-stepping buttons. Click the Step Over button to execute the current line and pause again at the next line.

When you click the Step Over button at a line that calls a new function, the new function executes from start to finish, and the Debugger pauses the code at the next line in the main function. If you want to enter the new function and pause at its first line instead, click the Step Into button.

 Use the Step Over button to continue line by line through the new function. To return to the main function at any time, executing the rest of the current function, click the Step Out button.

 If you don't want to step line-by-line through the functions, clicking the Run button again causes the script to execute until the next breakpoint.

 To close the JavaScript Debugger dialog box, click the Stop Debugging button (shown here) and then close the preview browser.

CERTIFICATION SUMMARY

In this chapter, you learned how to check your site for various conditions and fix problem areas. The panels in the Results panel group provide many of the commands that you need. Use the Validation panel to check the structure of your code against official standards. Use the Target Browser Check panel to check for compatibility with various browsers and use the Link Checker panel to find broken links, external links, and orphaned files in your site.

However, it's often the case that you need to look outside the Results panel group for the appropriate commands. If you want to change all the occurrences of a link, you should use the Change Links Sitewide command, which appears under the Site panel's Site menu. If you want to set up a custom report, open the Reports dialog box by choosing Site | Reports. If you want to run an accessibility report on the current page, choose File | Check Page | Check Accessibility from the main menu.

For formatting and cleaning up the code, use the Apply Source Code and Clean Up HTML commands, respectively. Formatting makes the logic of your code easier to follow, while cleaning up the code streamlines it and improves its readability.

Finally, use the JavaScript Debugger, accessed by choosing File | Debug In Browser, to identify and troubleshoot syntax errors and logical errors in your scripts. The JavaScript Debugger allows you to set breakpoints and track the values of variables to pinpoint mistakes.

TWO-MINUTE DRILL

Checking and Fixing Your Site

- ❑ Check your site for different screen settings by changing the screen size list at the bottom of the document window.

- ❑ Change the default connection speed for your site by choosing Edit | Preferences and selecting the Status Bar category.

- ❑ Use the Target Browser Check panel to check the compatibility of your HTML markup with a variety of browsers.

- ❑ Use the Validation panel to check the structure of your markup against official standards of syntax and usage.

- ❑ Validation and browser compatibility are two different tests: Validation assesses the formal structure of your site, while compatibility assesses your site's performance in practical terms.

- ❑ Use the Link Checker panel to find broken links, external links, and orphaned files.

- ❑ A broken link is a link without a recognizable destination; an orphaned file is a page without an incoming link.

- ❑ To change a particular instance of a link, type the new path into the corresponding result in the Link Checker panel.

- ❑ To change all instances of a link throughout your site, use the Change Links Sitewide command.

- ❑ Check the accessibility of the current document by choosing File | Check Page | Check Accessibility from the main menu.

- ❑ Use Dreamweaver's Accessibility dialog boxes to help make your site more accessible as you build it.

- ❑ To build a customized report, including expanded accessibility options, choose Site | Reports.

- ❑ Formatting the code of a page doesn't improve performance in a browser, but it makes the code easier to read by humans.

- ❑ Clean up redundant nested tags, combinable font tags, empty container tags, and comments with the Clean Up HTML command.

- ❑ Use the JavaScript Debugger to identify and fix errors in your client-side scripts.

SELF TEST

The following questions will help you measure your understanding of the material presented in this chapter. Read all the choices carefully because there might be more than one correct answer. Choose all correct answers for each question.

Checking and Fixing Your Site

1. Which of the following is the correct formatting for a path in the Change Links Sitewide dialog box if you want to change an internal URL link?

   A. *contact/contact.htm*

   B. *http://www.madsciencellc.com/contact/contact.htm*

   C. */contact/contact.htm*

   D. *contact.htm*

2. How to you check the accessibility of all the pages in your site with a single command?

   A. Choose File | Check Page | Check Accessibility.

   B. Open the Site Reports panel and click the green arrow button.

   C. Open the Accessibility panel and click the green arrow button.

   D. Choose File | Check Page | Check Accessibility In Entire Local Site.

3. Which of the following reports can you generate from the Reports dialog box?

   A. Dreamweaver-specific markup

   B. Redundant nested tags

   C. Combinable font tags

   D. Empty container tags

   E. Broken links

4. Which of the following items can you remove or fix with the Clean Up HTML command?

   A. Dreamweaver-specific markup

   B. Redundant nested tags

   C. Combinable font tags

   D. Empty container tags

   E. Broken links

5. What does the command File | Debug In Browser allow you to troubleshoot?

    A. HTML markup compatibility

    B. HTML syntax

    C. Server-side code

    D. JavaScript

6. Why should you format the source code of a page? Choose the best answer.

    A. To improve the performance of your page in multiple browsers

    B. To improve the performance of your page in the target browser

    C. To prepare the page for a battery of reports

    D. To make your code easier to follow

7. What is a breakpoint in the JavaScript Debugger? Choose the best answer.

    A. A line of code that causes the script to crash

    B. A line of code at which the script pauses

    C. The set of variables that you assess

    D. A line of code that the JavaScript Debugger ignores

8. When would you want to clean up Word HTML? Choose the best answer.

    A. When you want to include an HTML file from Microsoft Word on your site

    B. When your page contains many words

    C. When your page contains few words

    D. When you want to format a page for use in Microsoft Word

9. In practical terms, which is the more important virtue for most sites and why?

    A. Validation because even slightly invalid code crashes the browser

    B. Validation because the W3C will fine you for noncompliance

    C. Compatibility because compatible code is always on spec

    D. Compatibility because browsers themselves often vary from official compliance standards

10. How do you change the default connection speed for your site?

   A. Click the current connection speed at the bottom of the document window.

   B. Double-click the current connection speed at the bottom of the document window.

   C. Choose Edit | Preferences and look under the Connection Speed category.

   D. Choose Edit | Preferences and look under the Status Bar category.

   E. None of the above.

11. What kind of error in client-side scripting always causes the script to crash? Choose the best answer.

   A. Syntax errors

   B. Logical errors

   C. JavaScript errors

   D. Scripting errors

12. What happens when a JavaScript crashes?

   A. The visitor's browser crashes.

   B. The visitor's computer crashes.

   C. The Web server crashes.

   D. The Internet crashes.

   E. None of the above.

13. What tag-based languages can Dreamweaver validate?

   A. HTML

   B. XML

   C. CFML

   D. CSS

   E. JSP

14. You run a report from the Target Browser Check panel, and you discover an incompatible tag on one of the pages of your site. Which of the following methods automatically removes the tag?

   A. Double-click the result in the Target Browser Check panel.

   B. Click the result in the Target Browser Check panel and click the green arrow button.

C. Open the page, choose Commands | Clean Up HTML, and set up the procedure to remove this specific tag.

D. Choose Edit | Find And Replace, set up the procedure to find the specific tag, and strip it out.

15. Which of the following panels appear in the Results panel group by default?

A. Accessibility

B. Link Checker

C. Target Browser Check

D. Validate

E. Site Reports

F. Invalid Nested Tags

G. JavaScript Debugger

H. Reference

16. When you check links on the current page, which of the following doesn't appear in the results?

A. Broken links

B. External links

C. Orphaned files

D. None of the above

17. Which statement best describes Dreamweaver's reporting capabilities?

A. The results are always 100 percent accurate.

B. You must periodically run reports on your site for Dreamweaver to work correctly.

C. You should examine the results carefully for possible false positives.

D. Yet another useless feature.

18. Which of the following reports helps you to improve the accessibility of your site?

A. Broken Links

B. Missing Alt Text

C. Design Notes

D. Target Browser Check

19. Which of the following reports apply specifically to working in a collaborative environment?

   A. Design Notes

   B. Untitled Documents

   C. Checked Out By

   D. Combinable Nested Font Tags

20. How do you fix an individual occurrence of a broken link?

   A. Click the Broken Links column of the Link Checker panel and browse to the new link.

   B. Click the Broken Links column of the Link Checker panel and type the new link.

   C. Choose Site | Change Links Sitewide from the Site panel's menu.

   D. Choose Site | Change Link from the Site panel's menu.

LAB QUESTION

You're having one of those days. You just ran a validation check on your site, and you received 142 identical results. They all say this: "In HTML 4.0, FONT is deprecated. It may become obsolete in future versions. Consider using style sheets instead."

At least you know how many paragraphs you have on your site: 142—one for every result in the Validation panel. You took great pains to nest a pair of font tags between every pair of paragraph tags on your site, like this:

```
<p><font face="Arial, Helvetica, sans-serif">This is a sample
    paragraph.</font></p>
```

Without sinking into self-pity, you open your site's external CSS style and add a style called pg to replace the obsolete font tag:

```
.pg {
    font-family: Arial, Helvetica, sans-serif;
}
```

Believe it or not, that was the hard part. Jot down a procedure for fixing your entire site by applying the Find And Replace command twice.

SELF TEST ANSWERS

Checking and Fixing Your Site

1. ☑   C. Use the root-relative path.
   ☒   A is incorrect because it gives a document-relative path. B is incorrect because it gives an absolute path. Use absolute paths for external links, not internal ones. D is incorrect because it doesn't supply a path at all.

2. ☑   B. Open the Site Reports panel and click the green arrow button. Then, in the Reports dialog box, choose the accessibility report and set the report to check the entire site.
   ☒   A is incorrect because this command checks only the accessibility of the current document. C is incorrect because there is no Accessibility panel in Dreamweaver. D is incorrect because there is no such command in Dreamweaver.

3. ☑   B, C, and D. You can run reports on redundant nested tags, combinable font tags, and empty container tags from the Reports dialog box
   ☒   A is incorrect because you can't run a report on Dreamweaver-specific markup. However, you can remove Dreamweaver-specific markup with the Clean Up HTML command. E is incorrect because you can't run a report on broken links from the Reports dialog box. Use the Link Checker panel instead or choose Site | Check Links Sitewide from the Site panel's menu.

4. ☑   A, B, C, and D. You can clean up Dreamweaver-specific markup, redundant nested tags, combinable font tags, and empty container tags with the Clean Up HTML command.
   ☒   E is incorrect because you can't fix broken links with the Clean Up HTML command. Use the Link Checker panel or choose Site | Change Links Sitewide from the Site panel's menu.

5. ☑   D. The File | Debug In Browser command launches the JavaScript Debugger.
   ☒   A is incorrect because the Target Browser Check panel alerts you to markup incompatibilities. B is incorrect because the Validation panel alerts you to potential syntax errors in the markup. C is incorrect because JavaScript is a client-side scripting language, not a server-side scripting language.

6. ☑   D. Formatting your code makes the code easier to follow.
   ☒   A and B are incorrect because code formatting doesn't affect the performance of your page in any browser. C is incorrect because you don't need to format the code to run reports on the page.

7. ☑ **B.** A breakpoint is a line of code at which the script pauses.

   ☒ **A** is incorrect because a breakpoint isn't necessarily located on the same line of a script that causes a crash. **C** is incorrect because the list of variables that you assess doesn't control the pausing of the script. **D** is incorrect because the JavaScript Debugger doesn't allow you to ignore a line of code in the script.

8. ☑ **A.** Clean up Word HTML when you want to include a page of Word-generated HTML on your site.

   ☒ **B** and **C** are incorrect because the number of words on the page doesn't necessarily determine when to clean up Word HTML. **D** is incorrect because the Clean Up Word HTML command moves the HTML away from Word's preferred style, not closer toward it.

9. ☑ **D.** Compatibility is more important than validation for most sites, because browsers themselves don't always follow official guidelines.

   ☒ **A** is incorrect because invalid code often works perfectly well in many browsers. **B** is incorrect because the W3C doesn't fine anybody for anything. **C** is incorrect because compatible code isn't necessarily valid in the sense of adhering strictly to standards.

10. ☑ **D.** Choose the Status Bar category in the Preferences dialog box.

    ☒ **A** and **B** are incorrect because clicking the current connection speed on the document window doesn't have any effect. **C** is incorrect because there is no Connection Speed category in the Preferences dialog box. **E** is incorrect because **D** is the correct answer.

11. ☑ **A.** Syntax errors always cause the script to crash.

    ☒ **B** is incorrect because logical errors don't necessarily cause a crash. **C** and **D** are incorrect because they are too vague. Choice **A** is the best answer.

12. ☑ **E.** None of the above. The browser continues to work, although the script does not.

    ☒ **A, B, C,** and **D** are incorrect because the only thing that crashes when the script crashes is the script. If the Internet crashed every time I crashed a JavaScript, Microsoft would have probably sued me by now.

13. ☑ **A, B, C,** and **E.** Dreamweaver can validate HTML, XML, CFML, and JSP.

    ☒ **D** is incorrect because CSS isn't a tag-based language, and Dreamweaver doesn't validate it.

14. ☑ **C** and **D.** Use either Clean Up HTML or Find And Replace.

    ☒ **A** is incorrect because double-clicking a result in the Target Browser Check panel opens the page in Dreamweaver and highlights the offending line. You must remove the tag manually. **B** is incorrect because clicking the green arrow button simply allows you to perform another check.

15. ☑ B, C, D, and E. These panels all appear in the Results panel group by default.

☒ A, F, and G are incorrect because these aren't panels in Dreamweaver. H is incorrect because the Reference panel appears in the Code panel group by default.

16. ☑ C. Orphaned files don't appear in the results when you check links on the current page.

☒ A and B are incorrect because broken links and external links appear in the results. D is incorrect because orphaned files don't appear in the results.

17. ☑ C. Examine the results closely for false positives.

☒ A is incorrect because Dreamweaver doesn't always give 100 percent accurate results. B is incorrect because you don't need to run reports at all for Dreamweaver to function properly. D is incorrect because, while not perfect, Dreamweaver's report capabilities can yield valuable feedback on your site.

18. ☑ B. The Missing Alt Text report can help you to improve the accessibility of your site, since screen readers and other user agents look for `alt` text to describe images.

☒ A, C, and D are incorrect because these reports don't necessarily help you to improve the accessibility of your site.

19. ☑ A and C. Design Notes and Checked Out By apply specifically to working in a collaborative environment.

☒ B and D are incorrect because these reports don't have anything to do with working in a collaborative environment.

20. ☑ A and B. Either browse for the desired page or type the path to the desired page in the Broken Links column of the Link Checker panel.

☒ C is incorrect because this command changes all occurrences of the broken link, not just an individual occurrence. D is incorrect because there is no such command in Dreamweaver.

LAB ANSWER

The first Find And Replace should strip out all the font tags in your site, so set up the Find And Replace dialog box like this:

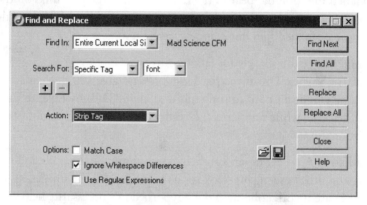

Click Replace All to strip out the font tags. Then add the class attribute to all the existing paragraph tags in your site. Set up the Find And Replace dialog box like this:

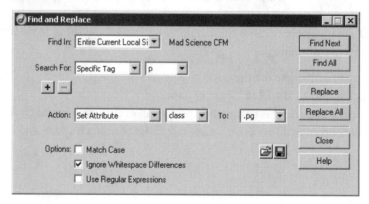

Click Replace All, and your site is fixed. Run that validation check again for a victory lap.

Dreamweaver®

CERTIFIED DREAMWEAVER DEVELOPER

13

Managing
Your Web Site

CERTIFICATION OBJECTIVES

D reamweaver's usefulness doesn't stop after you've built your last page and added the last bit of content to your site. This software is also a site-management tool, as you'll recall from the early chapters in this book. I mentioned many of Dreamweaver's management tools in passing earlier in the book, but the time has come to take a closer look. This chapter demonstrates how Dreamweaver can help you to juggle the various versions of your site during and after the launch.

CERTIFICATION OBJECTIVE 13.01

Managing Your Web Site

Site management comes in three phases. The first phase is the initial building of the structure of your site and the shuffling around and shifting that follows. The second phase is the launch, when you publish your site to the Web for the first time. The third phase is the maintenance of your site, when you tweak its structure and send regular content updates. While the first two phases have definite beginnings and endings, the third phase begins immediately after the launch and continues for the life of your site.

This exam objective looks mainly at site-management phases two and three. It covers everything from configuring your connection to the production server to keeping your live site up to date and running smoothly.

Setting Up a Remote Site

As you know, a *remote site* is the live version of your site that resides on the production server. This is the version that loads when visitors browse to your URL. After you've built, tested, and debugged your site locally, you must upload the files and folders to the production server to publish them to the Web.

Dreamweaver helps you to accomplish this, naturally, but first you need to tell Dreamweaver where to find the production server, or the *remote server,* as Dreamweaver calls it. The Site Definition dialog box is the place to start. Choose Site | Edit Sites from either the Site panel's menu or Dreamweaver's main menu or choose Edit Sites from the list of sites in the Site panel to open the Edit Sites dialog box. Select the site whose definition you want to edit and click the Edit button to open the Site Definition dialog box.

On the Advanced tab of the Site Definition dialog box, choose the Remote Info category. At first, you see a single Access drop-down list. From this list, select the way that you connect to the remote server. The two most common methods are FTP (for File Transfer Protocol) and Local/Network. FTP is typically the way you connect when the remote server belongs to an ISP (Internet service provider), and you rent the Web space for your site. With a Local/Network connection, the remote server is part of the network to which your personal computer belongs. If you or your employer owns your site's production server, this could be the method that you use to connect. When in doubt, check with your system administrator—you know, the only person on staff who puts in more hours than you, and the one who's always scowling.

Depending on your choice, Dreamweaver provides additional fields for you to fill out, as Figure 13-1 shows. The Remote Info category is much like the Testing Server category in this regard. Your ISP or network administrator can help you configure

FIGURE 13-1

After you choose a method of access from the Remote Info category of the Site Definition dialog box, Dreamweaver gives you additional fields to fill out.

this connection properly, since what you need to type here depends on the setup of the remote server.

If you choose FTP as the connection method, the Host Directory field should contain the path to your Web site's *remote root folder,* which is the folder that contains all the folders and files for the site on the remote server. For instance, if your ISP stores your Web site in a folder called *html,* you'd type **/html/** in the Host Directory field. If your site resides in a subfolder of the host directory, append the name of the subfolder, as in /html/madscience/. If you don't type the first forward slash, Dreamweaver adds it for you.

If you choose Local/Network as the connection method, type the path to the remote root folder in the Remote Folder field or click the folder icon to the right of the field, and browse to the remote root folder (see Figure 13-2).

FIGURE 13-2

If you choose Local/Network as the connection method, type the path to the remote root folder in the Remote Folder field.

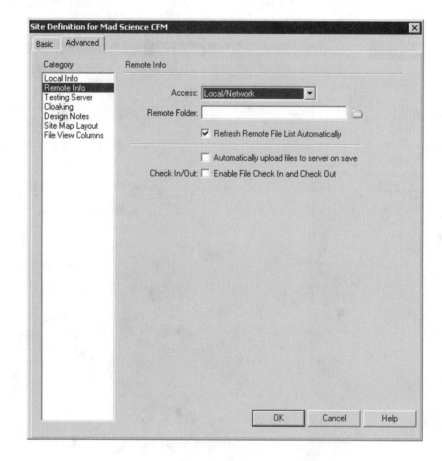

Check the Automatically Upload Files To Server On Save option if you want Dreamweaver to send fresh copies of your files to the remote server after you save changes to the local versions. This feature can save you a few extra steps, but I don't recommend that you choose it. You should save regularly when you edit a file in Dreamweaver, especially if you need to make a number of changes, and you don't want to send the world your works in progress. It's much better to wait until your file is ready for public consumption before you deploy it to the remote server.

Connecting to the Remote Site

If the remote server is on your local network, you're ready to upload files, since you're already connected to the server. If you use FTP, though, you need to establish a connection manually before you can start uploading files. Clicking the Connect button on the Site panel does the trick.

You can also choose Site | Connect from the Site panel's menu. If your computer's Internet connection isn't currently activated, Dreamweaver may give you an error message. Simply turn on your Internet connection and click the Connect button again.

Dreamweaver connects to the remote server and shows the structure of the remote site in the Site panel, shown in the following illustration.

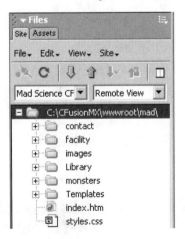

If you want to see the remote site and the local site side by side, expand the Site panel by clicking the Expand/Collapse button.

The remote site appears on the left of the expanded Site panel, and the local site appears on the right, as you can see in Figure 13-3. Dreamweaver displays remote folders in yellow and local folders in green.

FIGURE 13-3   In the expanded Site panel, the remote site appears on the left, and the local site appears on the right.

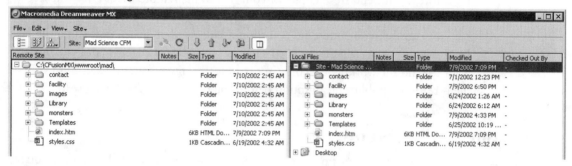

To disconnect from the remote server, click the Connect button again or choose Site | Disconnect from the Site panel's menu.

As mentioned, if the remote server is on your local network, you don't need to click the Connect button. To call up the structure of the remote site from the collapsed Site panel, choose Remote View from the drop-down menu to the right of the list of sites. When you expand the Site panel, the remote site should appear on the left automatically. If it doesn't, click the Site Files button.

Synchronizing Your Site

The fastest way to update your site is to use Dreamweaver's Synchronize command. When you synchronize your site, Dreamweaver examines the files on the remote site and uploads the corresponding files from the local site with more recent last-modified dates. The theory here is that a modified local file contains changes that you want to publish to the Web.

To synchronize your site, choose Site | Synchronize from the Site panel's menu. The Synchronize Files dialog box appears, as shown here:

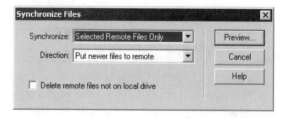

From the Synchronize list, choose the Entire Site option to synchronize all the files in the remote site or choose the Selected Remote Files Only option to synchronize the currently selected files in the remote site. Selecting files from the remote site is just like selecting them from the local site.

In the left side of the expanded Site panel (or choose Remote View in the collapsed Site panel), hold down CTRL (Windows) or COMMAND (Mac) and click the names of the remote files in the Site panel. A convenient way to select all the newer versions of the remote files is to choose Edit | Select Newer Remote from the Site panel's menu. Likewise, choose Edit | Select Newer Local from the Site panel's menu to select all the newer versions of local files.

From the Direction list, choose the Put Newer Files To Remote option to upload newer versions of local files to the remote site. Check the Delete Remote Files Not On Local Drive option to remove all remote files that don't have a local counterpart.

The Get Newer Files From Remote option in the Direction list replaces your local files with newer versions from the remote site, if any newer versions exist. Use this option if you're working with a team of developers and you need to refresh your local version of the site with the most recent updates that your colleagues published to the Web. If you want Dreamweaver to remove all local files that don't have a remote counterpart, check the Delete Local Files Not On Remote Server option.

Choose the Get And Put Newer Files option from the Direction list if you want Dreamweaver to refresh both the local and remote sites with the newest files from both. If one file is newer on the local site, Dreamweaver puts it on the remote site. If another file is newer on the remote site, Dreamweaver gets it for your local site.

exam
Watch

Remember that you can synchronize the local version of your site to the remote version, as well as the remote version to the local version.

Click the Preview button to proceed. After Dreamweaver determines which files to get and put, another dialog box appears, as shown in Figure 13-4. This dialog box shows a list of the files that Dreamweaver plans to synchronize. Examine this list *very* carefully! Now is not the time to be taking shortcuts, especially when you're deleting files. If you would rather not include a file in the synchronization, uncheck its entry in the list, and Dreamweaver adds the note *Skip* to the Status column. Click OK to synchronize the site.

FIGURE 13-4

Preview the files that Dreamweaver plans to synchronize and make changes as necessary.

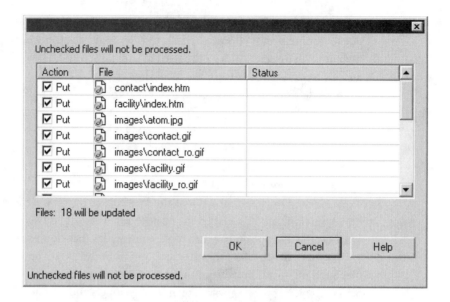

Dreamweaver synchronizes the files and adds the note *Updated* to the Status column for each file. Click the Save Log button to save a copy of the synchronization report or click Close to close the dialog box (see Figure 13-5).

FIGURE 13-5

After you synchronize the files of your site, you can save a copy of the synchronization report by clicking the Save Log button.

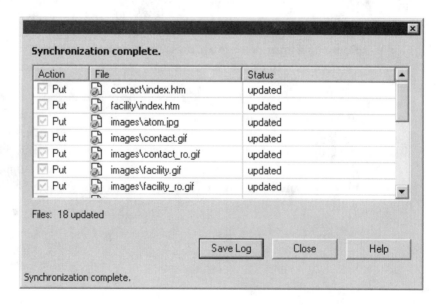

FROM THE CLASSROOM

FROM THE CLASSROOM

Cutting the Dead Weight

A newly launched site is a beautiful thing. Its folders are clean. Every file has a purpose. The structure is agile and lean.

Inevitably, after a few update cycles, a site begins to take on weight. Unused graphics files clutter up the default images folder. Orphaned Web pages start appearing when you run site reports. Folders with half-forgotten purposes show up in the file list.

Growth is good. It's the sign of a healthy site. But clutter is bad. It hogs up valuable server space, and it creates confusion, not only for you but also for your colleagues. There's nothing worse than trying to figure out somebody's personal filing system, except when you have to do it by 3 P.M. or else.

Getting rid of the clutter is a three-step process in Dreamweaver. Start with the local site. Use the Results panels to track down broken links and orphaned files. Separate the test versions or prototypes of new pages from the final versions. Archive if you wish, but delete everything in the local root folder that you no longer need, or at least move the clutter to a cloaked folder.

After you tidy up the local root folder, use the Synchronize command to send your changes to the remote server, and check the Delete Remote Files Not On Local Drive option to kill the orphaned files and temporary pages that you pruned from the local site.

Finally, just like you schedule regular content updates, schedule regular site tune-ups. Reevaluate the contents of your local root folder often. Remember that trim sites are easier to manage than bloated ones.

See the next Scenario and Solution sidebar for a quick reference to help you remember the functions of the Synchronize command.

SCENARIO & SOLUTION

What does the Put Newer Files To Remote option do?	It looks for more recent versions of files on the local site and updates the remote site accordingly.
What does the Get Newer Files From Remote option do?	It looks for more recent versions of files on the remote site and updates the local site accordingly.
What does the Get And Put Newer Files option do?	It updates the local and remote sites with the most recent versions from both.

Getting and Putting Files

If batch operations make you nervous, you can use the Site panel to transfer files manually between the local and remote sites.

Select the folders and files that you want to transfer. To select multiple items, hold down CTRL (Windows) or COMMAND (Mac) as you click. Then, to download the selected folders and files to the local site, choose Site | Get from the Site panel's menu, or click the Get button.

To upload the selected folders and files to the remote site, choose Site | Put from the Site panel's menu or click the Put button.

Normally, when you want to get files and folders from the remote site, you select from the remote view, and when you want to put files and folders on the remote site, you select from the local view. However, you can select a remote file and click the Put button to replace the remote file with the current local version, or you can select a local file and click the Get button to replace the local file with the current remote version. Just remember that the Get button always downloads files from the remote server, and the Put button always uploads files to the remote server. See the next Scenario and Solution sidebar for a quick reference to help you.

The Get button always downloads files from the remote server, and the Put button always uploads files to the remote server, no matter which view of the Site panel you used to select the files.

When you initiate a file transfer, Dreamweaver asks whether you want to include dependent files, as shown in the next illustration. *Dependent files* are files that the

SCENARIO & SOLUTION	
What happens when you select a local file and click the Put button?	You upload the file to the remote site.
What happens when you select a local file and click the Get button?	You replace the file with its counterpart on the remote site.
What happens when you select a remote file and click the Get button?	You download the file to the local site.
What happens when you select a remote file and click the Put button?	You replace the file with its counterpart on the local site.

selected items need for proper display or operation, such as images, media files, or external Cascading Style Sheets. Including dependent files causes Dreamweaver to transfer these files along with whatever folders or files you selected. Be careful! If the dependent files that Dreamweaver transfers are out of date, you can wind up with an inaccurate site and lost data. If you don't include dependent files, Dreamweaver transfers only the selected folders and files.

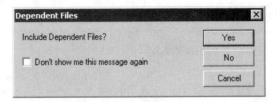

 Linked pages are not dependent files. Dependent files are images, media assets, and Cascading Style Sheets.

You can also drag files and folders from one side of the expanded Site panel to another. Dragging from local to remote puts files, and dragging from remote to local gets files.

Managing Remote Files and Folders

You can delete, rename, and move folders and files on the remote site just as you would on the local site. Just switch to the Site panel's remote view or expand the Site panel and work on the left side. Open the Site panel's File menu to access Rename and Delete commands and drag files and folders to new locations in the remove site to move them.

 Remember that deleting a folder simultaneously deletes all its contents.

To find the local version of a selected remote folder or file, choose Edit | Locate In Local Site. Likewise, to find the remote version of a selected local folder or file, choose Edit | Locate In Remote Site.

To open the local version of a remote file in Dreamweaver, double-click the remote file in the Site panel. Keep in mind that any changes you make to this document affect only the local version of the file. You must synchronize your site or put the edited file on the remote server manually to publish your changes to the Web, or you must check the Automatically Upload Files To Server On Save option from the Site Definition dialog box.

Unfortunately, you can't check and change links or run reports on your remote site. You can perform these functions only on the local version of your site. Similarly, if you move or rename something on the remote site, Dreamweaver doesn't ask if you want to update the files that refer to the item that you edited. It's better to make these kinds of changes locally and then put the edited site structure on the remote server.

EXERCISE 13-1

Launching the Mad Science LLC Site

In this exercise, you configure a bogus remote connection for the Mad Science LLC site and transfer the local files for the big rollout.

1. Launch Dreamweaver, open the Site panel and select the Mad Science LLC site.

2. Choose Site | Edit Sites from the Site panel's menu. The Edit Sites dialog box appears.

3. Select the Mad Science LLC site and click Edit. The Site Definition dialog box appears.

4. Click the Advanced tab and select the Remote Info category.

5. From the Access list, choose Local/Network.

6. Click the folder icon to the right of the Remote Folder field. In the dialog box that appears, navigate to a convenient spot on your hard drive and click the Create New Folder button. Provide a name for the new folder such as **mad** and then double-click this folder to open it. Click the Select button, and the dialog box closes.

7. Click OK in the Site Definition dialog box.

8. Click Done in the Edit Sites dialog box.

9. Now, go to the Site panel and click the Expand/Collapse button to expand the panel.

10. You should see the folder you just created on the left side of the panel. If you don't, click the Site Files button at the top of the panel.

11. Choose Site | Synchronize from the Site panel's menu. The Synchronize Files dialog box appears.

12. From the Synchronize list, select the Entire Site option.

13. From the Direction list, select Put Newer Files On Remote.

14. Click Preview. Normally, I'd advise you to look closely at the list of scheduled operations in the dialog box, but since there aren't any remote files to delete, you have nothing to fear. Click OK with confidence.

15. Click Close after Dreamweaver synchronizes the site. The remote view of the Site panel fills with the folders and files from the local view (see Figure 13-6). If your remote folder were on a production server, your site would be live as of right now. Congratulations!

FIGURE 13-6 Your Site panel should look like this after you synchronize the remote version of Mad Science LLC with the local version.

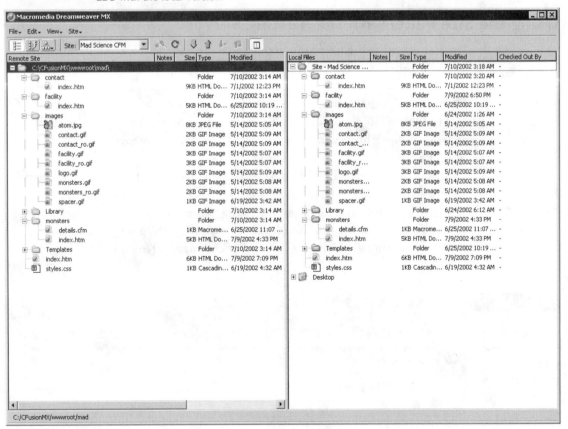

Viewing the FTP Log

If you connect to the remote server by FTP, Dreamweaver keeps a running log of all the connections and file transfers. Reviewing this log can help you figure out when or if you made a scheduled content update or what happened to a particular remote file.

To open the FTP log, click the View Site FTP Log button on the expanded Site panel.

You can also choose View | Site FTP Log from the Site panel's menu or choose Window | Results | FTP Log from Dreamweaver's main menu.

The FTP Log panel opens, as shown in Figure 13-7. Browse the log by dragging the scrollbar on the right of the panel. The most recent entries appear at the bottom of the list. If you're currently connected, you can send FTP commands directly to the server by typing them in the FTP Command field and pressing ENTER or RETURN.

Using the Site Panel with the Testing Server

If you're managing a dynamic site, you can view the files and folders on the development server, or *testing server,* by choosing Testing Server from the drop-down list to the right of the list of sites in the collapsed Site panel, as shown in Figure 13-8. On the expanded Site panel, click the Testing Server button.

The files and folders on the testing server appear on the left, and the local site appears on the right, as you can see in Figure 13-9. Dreamweaver displays testing-server folders in red and local folders in green.

See the next Scenario and Solution sidebar for a quick reference to help you interpret the Site panel's color coding.

Manage the files and folders of the testing server as you would on the remote server. You can synchronize your local site with the testing server, and you can transfer files manually with the Get and Put commands. Keep in mind that if the

---

FIGURE 13-7

Use the FTP Log panel to review your FTP sign-ins and file transfers.

```
Results
Search | Validation | Target Browser Check | Link Checker | Site Reports | FTP Log | Server Debug
FTP Command:
NOOP
200 NOOP command successful.
QUIT
221 Goodbye.
```

FIGURE 13-8

Choose Testing
Server from the
drop-down list
on the right of
the collapsed Site
panel to view the
files and folders
on your testing
server.

testing server is your personal computer, remote-server view and local view probably
show the exact same files.

Using the Site Map

Dreamweaver's site map shows you which pages link to which other pages in your
local site, but it's more than just a helpful diagram. You can use the site map to modify
your site's navigation.

exam
ⓦatch   ***The site map works only with local sites.***

FIGURE 13-9   Expand the Site panel and click the Testing Server button to view the structures of the testing
server and the local server side by side.

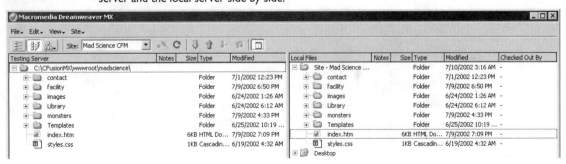

SCENARIO & SOLUTION

Which view of the Site panel shows green folders?	Local view
Which view of the Site panel shows red folders?	Testing-server view
Which view of the Site panel shows yellow folders?	Remote view

To open the site map in the collapsed Site panel, choose Map View from the drop-down menu to the right of the list of sites, as in Figure 13-10, or choose View | Site Map from the Site panel's menu. In the expanded Site panel, choose View | Site Map, or click the Site Map button.

The site map appears on the left side of the expanded Site panel, as Figure 13-11 shows. The right side of the panel shows the standard file list as reference. To hide this list, hold down the mouse button on the Site Map button and choose Map Only from its menu. Bring back the file list by choosing the Map And Files command from the same menu.

on the job

Use the site map to help you troubleshoot problems with your site's navigation. One quick check is to make sure that the home page appears among the links of every other page in the site map.

Configure the appearance of the site map with commands in the Site panel's View menu. Choose View | Show Page Titles to list the pages by title, not by file name. This feature is handy if a number of your pages share the same file name, such as *index.htm.* Choose View | Show Dependent Files to include dependent files such as images and Flash movies in the site map. Otherwise, Dreamweaver displays Web-page documents only.

To change the layout of the site map, choose View | Layout, and the Site Definition dialog box appears. Select the Site Map Layout category and change the maximum number of columns and the width of each column in the appropriate fields (see Figure 13-12). You can also change the *home page,* or the default page from which Dreamweaver builds the site map, by clicking the folder icon next to the Home Page field and selecting a different page in your site.

Another way to change the home page of your site is to select a page in the file list and choose Site | Set As Home Page or right-click the page and choose Set As Home Page from the context menu.

FIGURE 13-10

Choose Map
View from the
drop-down list
on the right in
the collapsed Site
panel to view
the site map.

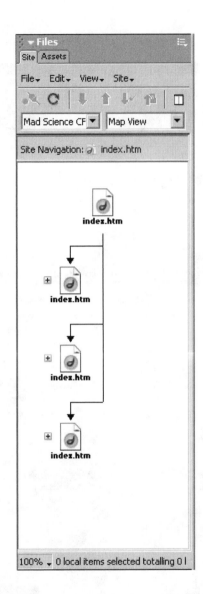

To create a new file as the home page, deselect everything in the file list and
choose Site | New Home Page. The New Home Page dialog box appears, as shown
next. Supply a file name in the File Name field and give the page an HTML title in

FIGURE 13-11   View a larger site map in the expanded Site panel.

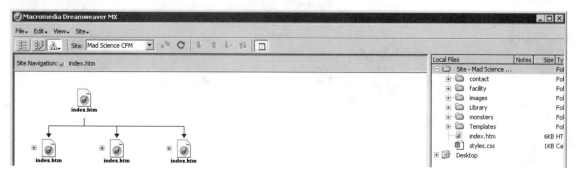

FIGURE 13-12

Display the Site Map Layout category of the Site Definition dialog box to change the layout of the site map.

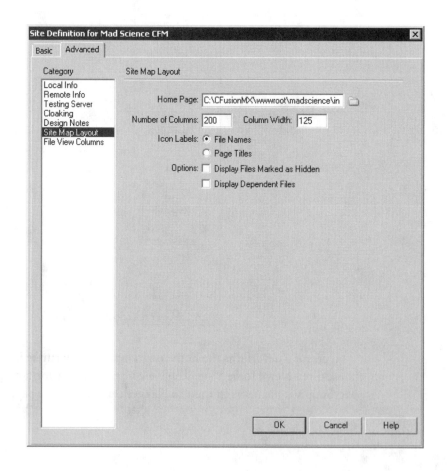

the Title field. Click OK to add the new file to the file list and designate it as the home page. The site map changes accordingly.

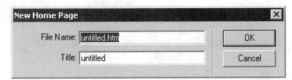

If you want to adjust the configuration of the site map without redefining the home page of your site, select the page in the site map that you want to use as the *root,* or the basis of the map, and choose View | View As Root. You can also right-click the page and choose View As Root from the context menu. Dreamweaver redraws the site map according to the new root file but leaves your current home-page definition intact. Dreamweaver also adds the name of the root page to the Site Navigation bar above the site map, as shown in Figure 13-13. Click the name of a page in this bar to change the site map's root.

Editing Navigation from the Site Map

The page at the top of the site map is the map's root, which is, by default, the home page of your site. The solid arrows represent existing links from the root page to other pages in your site. These are the *branches* of the site map. Pages with red labels indicate broken links—either the link to this page gives the incorrect path, or this page doesn't exist.

View the links of a secondary page in the map by clicking the plus button to the left of the page's icon. The links appear in list form, and the plus button becomes

FIGURE 13-13

When you change the root of the site map without changing the home page, Dreamweaver adds the name of the new root page to the Site

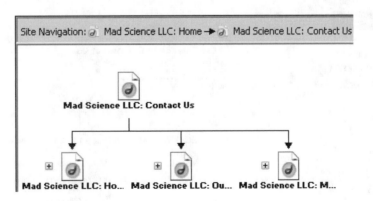

a minus button, as shown in Figure 13-14. Collapse the list of links by clicking the minus button.

To link to an existing page in your site from any page in the site map, select the page's icon in the site map and choose Site | Link To Existing File. You can also right-click the page's icon and choose Link To Existing File from the context menu. The Select HTML file dialog box appears, as shown in Figure 13-15. Navigate to the page to which you want to link and click OK. Dreamweaver adds a text hyperlink to the bottom of the page that you selected in the site map and includes the newly linked page in the site map's layout. If you want to change the format, content, or appearance of the text hyperlink that Dreamweaver added, double-click the page to open it in a document window and look for the link at the bottom of the page.

Here's another way to link to existing pages. Select a page in the site map and notice that a round target icon appears beside the page, as shown in Figure 13-16. Drag this target to any page in the site map or file list and release the mouse button to create the link.

To create a new page and add a link to it, select a page in the site map and choose Site | Link To New File or right-click the page and choose Link To New File from the context menu. The Link To New File dialog box opens, as shown here:

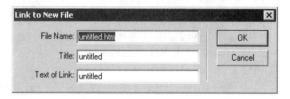

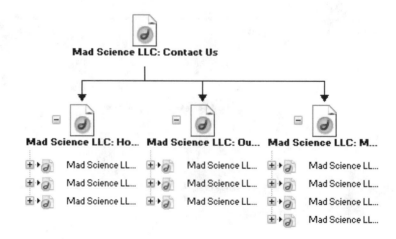

FIGURE 13-14

The site map can display the links of secondary pages.

FIGURE 13-15

Choose an
existing file
to link to the
currently selected
page in the site
map with the
Select HTML File
dialog box.

Supply a file name for the new page in the File Name field and type an HTML title for the page in the Title field. In the Text Of Link field, type the text that you want to add to the bottom of the page that you selected. Click OK to create the new page. Dreamweaver places the new page in the same folder as the page that you selected and updates the site map to show the new link. Keep in mind that the new page has no content, so open it in Dreamweaver and add some. You should also open the page to which you added the link and format the link's appearance.

To replace a linked page in the site map, select the page and choose Site | Change Link, or right-click the page and choose Change Link from the context menu. The Select HTML File dialog box opens. Navigate to the replacement page and click OK. The new page takes the place of the old one in the site map, and Dreamweaver updates the appropriate links in the HTML.

FIGURE 13-16

Drag a selected
page's target icon
to any other page
in the site map or
file list to create a
link to that page.

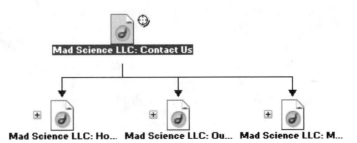

To remove a linked page from the site map, select the page and choose Site | Remove Link or right-click the page and choose Remove Link from the context menu. Dreamweaver eliminates links to this page in the HTML, and the page disappears from the site map.

on the **Job**

Be careful about replacing and removing linked pages in the site map because you can't undo these operations.

To hide a page in the site map, select the page and choose View | Show/Hide Link or right-click the page and choose Show/Hide Link from the context menu. The page disappears, along with its branch of the site map, but Dreamweaver doesn't rewrite any of the links in the HTML code. To show the hidden pages of the site map, choose View | Show Files Marked As Hidden—hidden pages appear in the site map with italicized labels. To switch the status of a page from hidden to unhidden, select the page and invoke the Show/Hide Link command again.

exam **Watch**

Always select the linked page when you want to change or remove links in the site map. Don't select the page that contains the link.

While you can hide any page in the site map, you can only remove or replace linked pages or pages in the branches of the site map. You can't remove or replace the root page.

CERTIFICATION SUMMARY

In this chapter, you learned how to coordinate the local and remote versions of your site. First, you need to configure a connection to the remote server in Dreamweaver. Depending on the type of connection, you may also need to click the Connect button on the Site panel before you start uploading files.

To publish your site to the Web, you can either synchronize the remote site to the local site, or you can manually select files and folders and click the Put button on the Site panel. To download files from the remote site to the local site, use a different kind of synchronization or click the Site panel's Get button.

You saw that the remote and testing server views of the Site panel work much like the local view, in that you can delete, rename, and move files with ease. However, I recommended that you perform these operations on the local version of your site, since Dreamweaver can automatically update the relevant links.

You also worked with the site map. Dreamweaver's site map shows you which pages link to which other pages in the local site. The site map's root is, by default, the home page of your site. You can change the root by changing the home page, or you can temporarily define another page in the site map as the root without changing the home page. By way of the site map, you can modify the navigation of your site. Dreamweaver gives you commands for adding linked pages, removing linked pages, and changing or replacing linked pages.

TWO-MINUTE DRILL

Managing Your Web Site

❑ Configure your connection to the remote server under the Remote Info category of the Site Definition dialog box.

❑ If you connect to your remote server by FTP, you must click the Connect button on the Site panel before you can transfer files and folders.

❑ If the remote server is part of your local network, you don't have to click the Connect button.

❑ Use Dreamweaver's Synchronize command to update files with their most recent versions.

❑ Use the Get and Put buttons in the Site panel to transfer files and folders manually.

❑ Dependent files are files like images, media assets, and Cascading Style Sheets that a Web page requires for proper display or operation.

❑ You can choose to include dependent files in file-transfer operations.

❑ You can delete, rename, and move files in the Site panel's remote and testing-server views, just like you can in local view.

❑ If you connect to the remote server by FTP, use the FTP Log panel to review your file transfers.

❑ In the Site panel, folders are green in local view, red in testing-server view, and yellow in remote view.

❑ Dreamweaver's site map shows you which pages link to which other pages in your local site.

❑ Dreamweaver draws the site map in reference to the site's home page by default, although you can change the root of the map without changing the home page by selecting a page and choosing View | View As Root.

❑ Broken links appear in the site map as pages with red labels.

❑ When you drag a page's target icon from the site map to any other page in the site map or file list, Dreamweaver adds a link to that page.

❑ Use commands in the Site panel's menu to remove, replace, or hide linked pages in the site map.

SELF TEST

The following questions will help you measure your understanding of the material presented in this chapter. Read all the choices carefully because there might be more than one correct answer. Choose all correct answers for each question.

Managing Your Web Site

1. You glance at the Site panel and see red folders. What view of your site are you seeing?

   A. Local view

   B. Testing-server view

   C. Remote view

   D. Map view

2. What is the home page in the site map? Choose the best answer.

   A. The *index.htm* file in the top-level directory

   B. The page with the title *Home*

   C. The page from which Dreamweaver builds the site map by default

   D. All of the above

3. Which of the following could be dependent files of a page in your site?

   A. Images

   B. Cascading Style Sheets

   C. Pages to which the page links

   D. Flash movies

4. How do you open the FTP log in Dreamweaver?

   A. Click the View Site FTP Log button in the collapsed Site panel.

   B. Click the View Site FTP Log button in the expanded Site panel.

   C. Choose View | Site FTP Log from Dreamweaver's main menu.

   D. Choose View | Site FTP Log from the Site panel's menu.

   E. Choose Window | Results | FTP Log.

5. What does FTP stand for?

   A. Fast Transaction Process

   B. File Transfer Protocol

   C. Folder Transmission Procedure

   D. First Testing Platform

6. You want to rename a file on your site. Should you rename the local or remote version of the file, and why?

   A. Rename the local version, because you can't rename the remote version.

   B. Rename the remote version, because, if you don't, you won't be able to synchronize your site.

   C. Rename the local version, because this way Dreamweaver can automatically update the affected links in local site.

   D. Rename the remote version, because this way Dreamweaver automatically updates the file name of the local version.

7. When you want to change a link in the site map, which page should you select?

   A. The page that contains the link

   B. The linked page

   C. Either the page that contains the link or the linked page

   D. Neither the page that contains the link nor the linked page

8. When you remove a link from the site map, what happens to the linked page?

   A. Dreamweaver deletes the linked page from your site.

   B. Dreamweaver moves the linked page to a different location in your site.

   C. Nothing happens to the linked page.

9. In what ways can you synchronize your site in Dreamweaver?

   A. You can update the remote site with the most recent versions of local files.

   B. You can update the local site with the most recent versions of testing-server files.

   C. You can update the local and remote sites with the most recent files from both.

   D. You can update the testing-server site with the most recent versions of remote files, as long as the testing-server site isn't the same as the local site.

10. You select a file on the remote site. You want to send this file to the local site. Which button do you click on the Site panel?

    A. Get

    B. Put

    C. Check In

    D. Check Out

11. You select a file on the local site. You want to replace this file with the version on the remote site. Which button do you click on the Site panel?

    A. Get

    B. Put

    C. Check In

    D. Check Out

12. If your local site isn't the same as your testing-server site, where do you probably store your testing-server site?

    A. On your personal computer

    B. On a development server

    C. In your local root folder

    D. None of the above

13. What color are folders in the Site panel's remote view?

    A. Red

    B. Green

    C. Yellow

    D. Blue

14. The root page of your site map is currently unhidden. You select the root page and choose View | Show/Hide Link. What happens?

    A. You hide the root page in the site map.

    B. You hide the root page in the file list.

    C. You hide the entire site map.

15. You're building a static site. Which of the following views on the Site panel can you use?

    A. Local view

    B. Remote view

    C. Testing-server view

    D. Map view

16. When you add a link from the site map, where does Dreamweaver place the link?

    A. At the bottom of the page.

    B. At the top of the page.

    C. At the location you specify.

    D. It depends on the design of the page.

17. When is the root of the site map not the same as the home page of the site?

    A. When you select a page in the file list and choose Site | Set As Home Page

    B. When you choose Site | New Home Page

    C. When you change the home page in the Site Definition dialog box

    D. When you select a page in the site map and choose View | View As Root

18. What happens when you click the name of a page in the Site Navigation bar above the site map?

    A. You remove that page from the site map.

    B. You open that page in a new document window.

    C. You set that page as the root of the site map.

    D. You set that page as the home page of your site.

19. Which of the following commands can you use on the root page of the site map?

    A. Site | Change Link

    B. Site | Remove Link

    C. Site | Link To New File

    D. View | Show/Hide Link

20. Which version of your site does the site map show?

    A. Local

    B. Testing

    C. Remote

LAB QUESTION

You're tooling around a site that your predecessor designed, developed, and launched a few months ago, and you notice some problems with the navigation. The site doesn't flow the way it should. It's your job to update and streamline the site, and you reason that a quick look at the site map might help you pinpoint the source of the navigational rough spots.

That's when you realize that your predecessor deleted everything in the local root folder! Who knows where that chowder head archived the data, if he even bothered to archive it at all.

You don't have time for a fiasco. Your new employer wants results, results, results. You can connect to the remote site from Dreamweaver just fine, but you can't run a site map, because Dreamweaver builds the site map from local files. How should you proceed? Jot down a plan of action, and compare your solution with mine in the Lab Answer section.

SELF TEST ANSWERS

Managing Your Web Site

1. ☑ **B.** You're looking at testing-server view, because folders in this view are red.
   ☒ **A** is incorrect because folders in local view are green. **C** is incorrect because folders in remote view are yellow. **D** is incorrect because the site map doesn't show folders.

2. ☑ **C.** The home page is the page from which Dreamweaver draws the site map.
   ☒ **A** is incorrect because the home page isn't necessarily the top-level *index.htm* file. **B** is incorrect because the home page isn't necessarily the one with the title *Home*. **D** is incorrect because choice **C** is the best answer.

3. ☑ **A, B, and D.** Images, Cascading Style Sheets, and Flash movies are all possible dependent files of a page in your site.
   ☒ **C** is incorrect because the pages to which your page links aren't dependent files of your page.

4. ☑ **B, D, and E.** These three methods open the FTP Log panel.
   ☒ **A** is incorrect because there isn't a View Site FTP Log button on the collapsed Site panel. This button appears on the expanded Site panel. **C** is incorrect because there isn't a Site FTP Log command in Dreamweaver's main View menu. This command appears in the Site panel's View menu.

5. ☑ **B.** FTP stands for File Transfer Protocol.
   ☒ **A, C, and D** are incorrect because FTP stands for File Transfer Protocol.

6. ☑ **C.** Rename the local version because this way Dreamweaver can update the affected links on the local site. Then synchronize your remote site with the local site to transfer the changes.
   ☒ **A** is incorrect because you can easily rename files on the remote site. **B** is incorrect because renaming files doesn't affect your ability to synchronize your site. **D** is incorrect because Dreamweaver doesn't automatically rename the local version of a file if you rename its remote counterpart.

7. ☑ **B.** Select the linked page to change (or remove) a link in the site map.
   ☒ **A, C, and D** are incorrect because you should select the linked page, nothing more, nothing less.

8. ☑ **C.** Nothing happens to the linked page, other than it disappears from the site map.
   ☒ **A** is incorrect because Dreamweaver doesn't delete the page from your site. **B** is incorrect because making changes to the site map doesn't affect the location of pages in your site.

9. ☑ A, B, and C. You can synchronize your site in all three of these ways.
   ☒ D is incorrect because you can't update the testing-server site with the most recent versions of remote files. However, if the testing-server site and the local site are one and the same, you can update the local site and therefore also the testing-server site with the most recent versions of remote files.

10. ☑ A. Click the Get button. To move a file from the remote site to the local site, always click the Get button.
    ☒ B is incorrect because the Put button uploads local files to the remote server. C and D are incorrect because Check In and Check Out don't apply to transferring files between the local and remote sites.

11. ☑ A. Click the Get button. Remember, the Get button always transfers files from the remote site to the local site.
    ☒ B is incorrect because clicking the Put button would upload the local file to the remote site. C and D are incorrect once again because Check In and Check Out still don't apply to transferring files between local and remote sites.

12. ☑ B. In this case, you probably store your testing-server site on a development server.
    ☒ A is incorrect because, if you stored your testing-server site on your personal computer, the local site and the testing-server site would probably be the same. C is incorrect because if your testing-server site is in your local root folder, your testing-server site is the same as your local site. D is incorrect because choice B is the best answer.

13. ☑ C. Folders are yellow in the Site panel's remote view.
    ☒ A is incorrect because folders are red in testing-server view. B is incorrect because folders are green in local view. D is incorrect because folders aren't blue in any view of the Site panel.

14. ☑ C. You hide the entire site map, since the Show/Hide Link command hides the selected page and all its branches, and the root page is the reference point for the whole enchilada.
    ☒ A is incorrect because the Show/Hide Link command hides the entire site map when you use it on the root page. B and D are incorrect because the Show/Hide Link command doesn't affect the file list at all.

15. ☑ A, B, and D. For a static site, use the local, remote, and map views.
    ☒ C is incorrect because you use testing-server view only with dynamic sites.

16. ☑ C. Dreamweaver places the link at the bottom of the page.
    ☒ A, B, and D are incorrect because Dreamweaver always places the link at the bottom of the page.

17. ☑ **D.** The root of the site map isn't the home page of the site when you select a page in the site map and choose View | View As Root.

☒ **A, B,** and **C** are incorrect, because while these procedures create a new home page for the site map, the root of the site map is still the home page.

18. ☑ **C.** Clicking the name of a page in the Site Navigation bar sets that page as the root of the site map.

☒ **A, B,** and **D** are incorrect because clicking the name of a page in the Site Navigation bar sets that page as the root of the site map.

19. ☑ **C** and **D.** You can link to a new file from the root page, and you can show or hide the page and its branches.

☒ **A** and **B** are incorrect because you can change or remove only linked pages, not the root page of the site map.

20. ☑ **A.** The site map shows the local version of the site.

☒ **B** and **C** are incorrect because the site map always shows the local version of the site.

LAB ANSWER

You need a local site to run a site map, but you can connect to the remote site, so your problem is as good as solved. All you have to do is copy the remote site to the empty local root folder, either by synchronizing the local site to the remote site or by getting the folders and files from the remote server manually. Transfer the files, and you rebuild the local site. Run that site map.

Part IV

Appendixes

A

Coding Reference

Being a well-rounded Web builder means knowing enough about the source code to understand what's going on when you look under the hood, so to speak. You don't necessarily have to write code off the top of your head, but being able to read it is important. Not surprisingly, a good portion of the certification exam asks code-related questions.

Source Codes

In examples throughout this book, I showed you the source code in action. Here, I collect the elements of the code for your convenience in three tables.

Table A-1 contains common HTML tags.

Table A-2 contains common cross-browser-compatible CSS declarations.

Table A-3 contains common cross-browser-compatible JavaScript event handlers.

TABLE A-1	Tag	Description
Common HTML Tags	`<a></a>`	Anchor
	`<abbr></abbr>`	Abbreviation
	`<acronym></acronym>`	Acronym (IE only)
	`<address></address>`	Address formatting
	`<applet></applet>`	Applet
	`<area></area>`	Client-side image map area or hotspot
	`<b></b>`	Boldface (not recommended)
	`<base>`	Base element
	`<basefont>`	Default font face
	`<bgsound>`	Background sound (IE only)
	`<big></big>`	Bigger text
	`<blockquote></blockquote>`	Indented text
	`<body></body>`	Body of page
	` `	Line break
	`<button>`	Button element (IE only)
	`<caption></caption>`	Table caption
	`<cite></cite>`	Citation-style text

TABLE A-1	Tag	Description
Common HTML Tags *(continued)*	`<code></code>`	Code-style text
	`<col>`	Table column (IE only)
	`<colgroup></colgroup>`	Table-column group (IE only)
	`<dd></dd>`	Definition-list definition
	`<del></del>`	Deleted text (IE only)
	`<dfn></dfn>`	Defining instance of a term (IE only)
	`<div></div>`	Layer division
	`<dl></dl>`	Definition list
	`<dt></dt>`	Definition-list term
	`<em></em>`	Emphasized text (recommended for italics)
	`<embed></embed>`	Embedded asset file (not recommended)
	`<fieldset></fieldset>`	Logical grouping of form fields (IE only)
	`<font></font>`	Font
	`<form></form>`	Form
	`<frame></frame>`	Frame definition
	`<frameset></frameset>`	Frameset definition
	`<h1></h1>`	Headline level 1 (not recommended)
	`<h2></h2>`	Headline level 2 (not recommended)
	`<h3></h3>`	Headline level 3
	`<h4></h4>`	Headline level 4
	`<h5></h5>`	Headline level 5
	`<h6></h6>`	Headline level 6
	`<head></head>`	Head section
	`<hr>`	Horizontal rule
	`<html></html>`	HTML document
	`<i></i>`	Italics (not recommended)
	`<iframe></iframe>`	Inline or floating frame (IE only)
	`<ilayer></ilayer>`	Inline or floating frame (NS only)

Tag	Description
`<img>`	Image
`<input>`	Form object (button, checkbox, file, hidden image, password, radio, reset, submit, text)
`<ins></ins>`	Inserted text (IE only)
`<kbd></kbd>`	Keyboard-style text
`<label></label>`	Form-element label (IE only)
`<layer></layer>`	Layer (NS only)
`<legend></legend>`	Legend of fieldset (IE only)
`<li></li>`	List item
`<link>`	Linked document
`<map></map>`	Client-side image map
`<meta>`	Meta element
`<noframes></noframes>`	Noframes content
`<noscript></noscript>`	Noscript content
`<object></object>`	Embedded asset file (recommended)
`<ol></ol>`	Ordered list
`<option></option>`	Option of list or menu
`<p></p>`	Paragraph
`<param>`	Parameter of applet or object
`<pre></pre>`	Preformatted text
`<q></q>`	Inline quote (IE only)
`<samp></samp>`	Sample-output text
`<script></script>`	Client-side script
`<select></select>`	List or menu
`<small></small>`	Small text
`<span></span>`	Section of text
`<strong></strong>`	Strong emphasis (recommended for boldface)
`<style></style>`	Style definition
`<sub></sub>`	Subscript

Tag	Description
`<sup></sup>`	Superscript
`<table></table>`	Table
`<tbody></tbody>`	Logical grouping of table cells (IE only)
`<td></td>`	Table data
`<textarea></textarea>`	Multiline text field
`<title></title>`	Title of page
`<tfoot></tfoot>`	Table cells at bottom of table (IE only)
`<th></th>`	Table header
`<thead></thead>`	Table cells at top of table (IE only)
`<tr></tr>`	Table row
`<tt></tt>`	Teletype-style text
`<ul></ul>`	Unordered list
`<var></var>`	Variable

Declaration	Description
`background-color`	Background color of element
`background-image`	Background image of element
`border-color`	Color of element's border
`border-style`	Style of element's border
`border-width`	Width of element's border
`clear`	Position element on a different line than a nearby floating element
`clip`	Clipped region of element
`color`	Foreground color of element
`display`	Display property of element
`float`	Float property of element
`font-family`	Typeface of element

TABLE A-2

Common
Cross-Browser-
Compatible CSS
Declarations
(*continued*)

Declaration	Description
font-size	Font size of element
font-style	Font style of element (usually italic)
font-weight	Font weight of element (usually bold)
height	Height of element
left	Left position of element
line-height	Height of inline box
margin	Margin widths of element
margin-bottom	Width of element's bottom margin
margin-left	Width of element's left margin
margin-right	Width of element's right margin
margin-top	Width of element's top margin
padding	Padding width of element
padding-bottom	Width of element's bottom padding
padding-left	Width of element's left padding
padding-right	Width of element's right padding
padding-top	Width of element's top padding
position	Positioning of element
text-align	Alignment value of element
text-decoration	Decoration style of element (usually underline)
text-indent	Amount of element's indent
text-transform	Casing of element (usually uppercase, lowercase, or capitalized)
top	Position of element's top edge
visibility	Visibility value of element
width	Width of element
z-index	Stacking order of element

	Event Handler	**Occurs**
TABLE A-3	onAbort	The user aborts the image or Web page download.
	onBlur	Focus moves away from the element.
Common Cross-Browser-Compatible JavaScript Event Handlers	onChange	The user changes the contents of a list, menu, text field, or text area.
	onClick	The user clicks the element.
	onDblClick	The user double-clicks the element.
	onDragDrop	The user drags something onto the element.
	onError	The image or Web page fails to load.
	onFocus	The element receives focus.
	onKeyDown	The user presses a key.
	onKeyPress	The user presses and holds down a key.
	onKeyUp	The user releases a key.
	onLoad	A Web page or an image loads.
	onMouseDown	The user clicks a button, document, or link object.
	onMouseMove	The user moves the mouse pointer.
	onMouseOut	The user moves the mouse pointer away from the element.
	onMouseOver	The user hovers over the element with the mouse pointer.
	onMouseUp	The user releases the mouse button on a button, document, or link object.
	onMove	The user moves the browser window or frame.
	onReset	The user clicks the Reset button.
	onResize	The user resizes the browser window or frame.
	onSelect	The user selects text in the text field or text area.
	onSubmit	The user clicks the Submit button.
	onUnload	The user exits the page.

B

About the CD-ROM

The CD-ROM included with this book comes complete with MasterExam, the electronic version of the book, and Session #1 of LearnKey's online training for Dreamweaver, Fireworks, and Flash integration. The software is easy to install on any Windows 98/NT/2000 computer and must be installed to access the MasterExam feature. You may, however, browse the electronic book directly from the CD without installation. To register for LearnKey's online training and a second bonus MasterExam, simply click the Online Training link on the main page and follow the directions to the free online registration.

System Requirements

The software requires Windows 98 or higher and Internet Explorer 5.0 or above, plus 20MB of hard disk space for full installation. The electronic book requires Adobe Acrobat Reader. To access the Online Training from LearnKey, you must have RealPlayer Basic 8 or the RealOne plug-in, which will be automatically installed when you launch the online training.

LearnKey Online Training

The LearnKey Online Training link will allow you to access online training from *www.osborne.onlineexpert.com*. The first session of this course is provided at no charge. Additional sessions for this course and other courses may be purchased directly from. *www.LearnKey.com* or by calling 800-865-0165.

The first time that you run the Online Training, you must register the online product. Follow the instructions for a first-time user. Please make sure to use a valid e-mail address.

Prior to running the Online Training, you will need to add the Real plug-in and the RealCBT plug-in to your system. This will automatically be optimized to your system when you run the training the first time.

Installing and Running MasterExam

If your computer CD-ROM drive is configured to AutoRun, the CD-ROM will automatically start up when you insert the disc. From the opening screen, you can install MasterExam by clicking the MasterExam button. This will begin the installation process and create a program group named LearnKey. To run MasterExam, choose Start | Programs | LearnKey. If the AutoRun feature did not launch your CD, browse to the CD and click the RunInstall icon.

MasterExam provides a simulation of the actual exam. The number of questions, the type of questions, and the time allowed are intended to be an accurate representation of the exam environment. You have the option of taking an open-book exam that includes hints, references, and answers; a closed-book exam; or the timed MasterExam simulation.

When you launch MasterExam, a digital clock display will appear in the upper-left corner of your screen. The clock will continue to count down to zero unless you choose to end the exam before the time expires.

Electronic Book

The entire contents of the Study Guide are provided in PDF format. A downloadable version of Adobe Acrobat Reader is included on the CD.

Help

A help file is provided through the Help button on the main page in the lower-left corner. Individual help features are also available through MasterExam and LearnKey's Online Training.

Removing Installation(s)

MasterExam is installed to your hard drive. For best results for removal of programs choose Start | Programs | LearnKey | Uninstall and click the appropriate options to remove MasterExam.

If you want to remove the Real Player, use the Add/Remove Programs Icon available from your Control Panel. You may also remove the LearnKey training program from this location.

Technical Support

For questions regarding the technical content of the electronic book or MasterExam, please visit *www.osborne.com* or e-mail *customer.service@mcgraw-hill.com.* For customers outside the 50 United States, e-mail: *international_cs@mcgraw-hill.com.*

LearnKey Technical Support

For technical problems with the software (installation, operation, or removing installations) and for questions regarding LearnKey Online Training content, please visit *www.learnkey.com* or e-mail *techsupport@learnkey.com.*

Dreamweaver®

CERTIFIED DREAMWEAVER DEVELOPER

Glossary

Absolute Path   A path containing the full URL of the destination file.

Action   The function of a behavior.

Alt Text   Alternate descriptive text for a variety of elements, particularly images.

Applet   A short application written in Java.

Application Server   A piece of software that interprets server-side markup in a dynamic Web site.

Asset   An external file such as an image or movie for use on a Web page.

Attribute   An optional value that gives a property of a tag.

Base Template   In a nested template, the template to which the main page refers.

Behavior   One of Dreamweaver's prewritten JavaScript functions. Use behaviors to achieve sophisticated interactive effects quickly.

Breadcrumb Trail   A navigational technique that shows the visitor's current location on a Web site in relation to the hierarchical structure of the site.

Breakpoint   In the JavaScript Debugger, a line at which the script temporarily pauses.

Broken Link   A link whose destination page doesn't exist in the specified location.

Cache   In Dreamweaver, a record of the files and assets in a site.

Class   A CSS style that doesn't apply to any HTML tag in particular.

Cloaking   In Dreamweaver, hiding a file, folder, or file type from site-management functions.

Content   Anything that appears in the guts of a Web page.

CSS (Cascading Style Sheet)   A document or section of a page that contains style definitions for various elements. CSS is also the name of the specific markup style for Cascading Style Sheet style definitions.

CSS Style   A style written in CSS markup.

DataSet   The name for a recordset in ASP.NET sites.

Data Table   A table that displays rows and columns of data, as opposed to a layout table.

Declaration   In CSS, the set of attribute/value pairs that defines the style.

Development Server   A piece of hardware that hosts the local version of a Web site.

Disjointed Rollover   An image that changes its source file when the visitor hovers over a different image with the mouse pointer.

Document-Relative Path   A path expressed in terms of the destination file's location in relation to the current page.

Document Window   In Dreamweaver, the window that contains the layout of a Web page, the source code of the page, or both.

Drop Target   A location on the page to which the visitor should drag a layer for a special result.

Dynamic Checkbox   A checkbox that a Web application automatically checks or unchecks.

Dynamic Content   Customized or processed content that an application server adds to a dynamic page before sending the page to a Web browser.

Dynamic List/Dynamic Menu   A list or menu with at least one dynamically generated choice.

Dynamic Page   In Dreamweaver, a page that contains server-side markup for processing by an application server. Pages with client-side functionality, such as JavaScript and CSS, may be interactive, but they aren't dynamic.

Dynamic Radio Group   A group of radio buttons from which a Web app automatically chooses.

Dynamic Site   A Web site that contains at least one and usually several dynamic pages.

Dynamic Table   A table that visually presents the results of a recordset on a dynamic Web page.

Dynamic Text Field   A text field, text area, password field, or hidden field that contains dynamically determined initial content.

Editable Region   A portion of a Dreamweaver template to which you can add new or customized content.

Event   The thing that happens to a trigger to cause a behavior to activate.

External Links   Links to files outside the current Web site.

Field   A column in a database table.

File Path   A path that begins with *file://*. Dreamweaver inserts this type of path if you create a link or add an asset to an unsaved document.

Fixed Frame   A frame with a determined width or height.

Fixed Width   A design element, particularly a table, that has a set width value.

Focus The state of an element when it receives control of the page. A text field receives focus, for instance, when the visitor clicks it and enters text.

Form Variable In a dynamic site, a container for data received from a POST-method form submission.

Frame In page layout, a region of the browser window that loads its own Web page. In layer animation, a unit of time.

Frameset An HTML document that establishes a system of frames.

Functional Requirements A document containing the necessary functionality of a Web site.

Functionality The description or capacity of what an application does.

Get To download a file from a remote server.

Get Method A method of form submission in which the browser sends a query string to the server.

GIF (Graphics Interchange Format) A common file format for Web graphics, best suited to images with large areas of flat color.

Head Content Typically invisible content that appears between the opening and closing head tags of a page.

Hotspot A clickable region on an image map.

HTML (Hypertext Markup Language) The computer language that defines the structure and content of a Web page.

HTML Style A style consisting of various HTML appearance tags and attributes.

Image Map   A graphic with multiple clickable regions.

Inline Content   Content that appears in running text or on a line of its own, not in the cell of a layout table.

Inline Frame   An independent frame that you can position anywhere in the browser window. Also called *floating frame*.

Inline Image   An image that sits inside a line of text or on a line of its own.

Internal Links   Links to Web pages inside the current site.

Invisible Tag   A tag that appears in the source code of the page but doesn't have a corresponding visual element in the page itself.

JavaBean   A reusable Java component, similar to an ActiveX control but platform-neutral.

JavaScript   A popular and well supported client-side scripting language for adding interactivity and functionality to your page.

JPEG (Joint Photography Experts Group)   A common file format for Web graphics, best suited to photographs or images with a large amount of color information.

Jump Menu   A drop-down list of navigational choices.

Keyframe   In layer animation, a frame that represents the start or end of a particular motion.

Layer   A chunk of HTML code that defines the content and position of a particular element on the page.

Layout Cell   A portion of a layout table that contains part of the content of a page.

Layout Table   An HTML table whose structure determines the design of a page.

Library Item   An asset or design element stored in the Library panel for reuse.

Live Object   One of Dreamweaver's prebuilt, ready-to-use Web applications.

Local   Pertaining to the version of the site that resides on the developer's personal computer or development server.

localhost *Address*   The HTTP address that refers to your personal computer system.

Local Root Folder   The folder on the developer's personal computer or development server that holds all the files of a particular Web site.

Low-Source Image   A temporary image that appears on your page while another, larger image downloads in the background.

Malicious User   A user who deliberately tries to crash an application.

Media   In Dreamweaver, a generic name for assets such as movies and sound clips that require special browser plug-ins.

Meta Tag   A tag that contains descriptive information about a Web page or instructions for the HTTP header of the page.

Monospace Font   A font whose characters all have the same width.

Motion Path   The path along which an animated layer moves.

Named Anchor   An invisible element that marks off a section of a page.

Navigation Bar   An element containing graphical buttons linked to the various pages of your site.

Nested Frame   A frame that appears inside an existing frame.

Nested Layer   A layer that appears inside another layer.

Nested Table   A table that appears inside the cell of another table.

Nested Template   A template that sits inside a page built from another template. Use nested templates to create different versions of the same basic template-driven page.

Noframes Content   Alternate text that appears on your page when a browser can't process frames.

Noscript Content   Alternate text that appears on your page when a browser can't or won't process a client-side script.

Null Link   A link such as `href="#"` that specifies no destination.

Optional Region   An area of a template that may or may not appear on pages built from the template.

Orphaned File   A file to which no link points.

Overflow   Content in a layer that exceeds the layer's default holding capacity.

Page Layout   The arrangement of visual elements on a Web page.

Page Model   A graphic designer's conceptual sketch of what a finished Web page will look like.

Panel   In Dreamweaver, an interface element that collects various commands and options for building a page and organizing a site. You can open and close panels as you need them.

Panel Group   A collection of related panels.

Paragraph Style   An HTML style that formats the entire paragraph or headline to which you apply the style.

Parameter   In a dynamic site, a name/value pair such as `color=green`. You must separate multiple parameters with an ampersand sign, as in `color=green&size=large`.

Parent   In regard to layers, the element that contains the layer.

Path   Instructions for a browser to find a particular file on the Web.

Peripheral Browser   A browser for which you design a passable if not optimized user experience on your site.

Plug-In   An optional piece of software that adds functionality to another piece of software.

Post Method   A method of form submission in which the browser sends a private message to the server.

Preformatted Text   A block of text that retains its whitespace.

Production Server   A piece of hardware that hosts the live version of a Web site.

Proportional-Pitch Font   A font whose characters have different widths.

Put   To upload a file to a remote server.

Query   In a dynamic site, a request to a database for specific records. The database returns the results of a query as a recordset. In Dreamweaver's Find And Replace command, a set of search conditions.

Query String   In a dynamic site, a sequence of parameters passed by URLs and GET-method forms. The query string begins with a question mark, as in `?color=green`.

Record   A row in a database table.

Recordset   A collection of records from a database table.

Reference   An instance of a Library item in a Dreamweaver document.

Regular Expression   A special code that represents a particular character or range of characters in a search string.

Remote   Pertaining to the version of the site that resides on the production server.

Repeating Region   An area of a template that duplicates its content a certain number of times on pages built from the template.

Repeating Table   In a template, a table with at least one repeating row.

Rollover Image   An image that appears to change when the visitor rolls over it with the mouse pointer.

Root-Relative Path   A path expressed in terms of the destination file's location in relation to the root folder or top-level directory of the current site.

Sans-Serif Font   A font whose characters don't have small decorations or flourishes on the extremities.

Selection Style   An HTML style that applies to the currently selected text in the document window.

Selector   The beginning part of a CSS style definition. The selector determines the element to which the style applies.

Serif Font   A font whose characters have small decorations or flourishes on the extremities.

Server Behavior   One of Dreamweaver's blocks of prewritten server-side code. Use server behaviors to build Web applications quickly.

Server-Side Include   A snippet of client-side code that the Web server inserts into a page before the browser receives the page.

Session Variable   In a dynamic site, a container for visitor-specific information. Different visitors may have different values for the same session variable.

Site Definition   In Dreamweaver, a collection of basic information about a Web site.

Site Map   A page on a Web site with links to every other page on the site, usually organized by topic.

Slicing   In Web design, the practice of dividing a larger graphic into several smaller pieces that the browser reassembles, usually in the cells of a layout table.

Snap-To Zone   The area around a drop target that automatically snatches a dragged layer and places it on the target.

Source   In a link, the clickable element.

Spacer Image   A small graphics file, usually a one-pixel-by-one-pixel GIF, that helps to reinforce the structure of a layout table.

SQL (Structured Query Language)   A computer language for interacting with data in a database.

Staging Server   A piece of hardware that approximates the typical conditions of a production server.

Strategic Goals   The reason for a Web site's existence and its plan for achieving this.

Style A set of attributes that defines the appearance of a particular piece of text.

Style Definition The CSS description of a particular set of visual formatting options.

Synchronize To update the files on one server, usually the development server, to match the most recent versions on another server, usually the development server.

Tag A component of a markup language such as HTML that identifies a particular piece of content with a particular function or appearance.

Target Browser A browser to which you optimize your site's user experience.

Template A Dreamweaver document containing predefined content and various types of editable regions.

Text Equivalence The principle of providing alternate descriptive text for purely visual elements to give visually impaired visitors a comparable user experience.

Tracing Image An image that Dreamweaver places in the background of a document window. Use tracing windows as a guide when building the layout of your page.

Trigger The element to which you attach a behavior.

Tweening In layer animation, the process by which Dreamweaver automatically calculates the position of a moving layer, given the start point and end point of the layer and the length of time between the two keyframes.

URL Variable In dynamic sites, a container for data received from a link's query string or a GET-method form submission.

User Agent A tool for accessing a Web site.

Variable Width   A design element, particularly a table, with an unspecified width. The browser determines the actual width of the element.

Version Control   The process of preventing more than one developer in a collaborative environment from working on the same file at the same time.

Web Application   A computer program that manipulates live data on a Web site.

Web Page   An individual destination in a Web site, consisting of a source-code file such as an HTML document and external assets such as images and movies.

Web Server   A piece of software that handles HTTP requests from a browser.

Web Site   A collection of related Web pages, applications, and assets.

Whitespace   Extraneous spacebars or carriage returns in a source-code listing.

INDEX

B

E

G

H

M

S

T

INTERNATIONAL CONTACT INFORMATION

AUSTRALIA
McGraw-Hill Book Company Australia Pty. Ltd.
TEL +61-2-9415-9899
FAX +61-2-9415-5687
http://www.mcgraw-hill.com.au
books-it_sydney@mcgraw-hill.com

CANADA
McGraw-Hill Ryerson Ltd.
TEL +905-430-5000
FAX +905-430-5020
http://www.mcgrawhill.ca

**GREECE, MIDDLE EAST,
NORTHERN AFRICA**
McGraw-Hill Hellas
TEL +30-1-656-0990-3-4
FAX +30-1-654-5525

MEXICO (Also serving Latin America)
McGraw-Hill Interamericana Editores S.A. de C.V.
TEL +525-117-1583
FAX +525-117-1589
http://www.mcgraw-hill.com.mx
fernando_castellanos@mcgraw-hill.com

SINGAPORE (Serving Asia)
McGraw-Hill Book Company
TEL +65-863-1580
FAX +65-862-3354
http://www.mcgraw-hill.com.sg
mghasia@mcgraw-hill.com

SOUTH AFRICA
McGraw-Hill South Africa
TEL +27-11-622-7512
FAX +27-11-622-9045
robyn_swanepoel@mcgraw-hill.com

**UNITED KINGDOM & EUROPE
(Excluding Southern Europe)**
McGraw-Hill Education Europe
TEL +44-1-628-502500
FAX +44-1-628-770224
http://www.mcgraw-hill.co.uk
computing_neurope@mcgraw-hill.com

ALL OTHER INQUIRIES Contact:
Osborne/McGraw-Hill
TEL +1-510-549-6600
FAX +1-510-883-7600
http://www.osborne.com
omg_international@mcgraw-hill.com

Well-practiced

Osborne's Certification Press line offers the only classroom-based training and self-assessment materials available for certification study. We cover a wide variety of certifications, including Microsoft, Cisco, CompTIA, Sun, Macromedia, Citrix, and more.

TEST YOURSELF

Hundreds of practice questions with in-depth answers

Accelerated review of all exam topics

Exam Watch features point out the most frequently missed questions

Test Yourself CCNA, 2nd Ed.
Syngress

Test Yourself Network+
Syngress

Test Yourself MCDBA SQL Server 2000 Administration, 2nd Ed.
Stephen Giles & Glen Martin

STUDY GUIDE

0% complete overage of all official xam objectives

ands-on exercises ith step-by-step struction modeled ter classroom labs

D featuring ertTrainer interactive torials, ExamSim sting engine, nd full e-book

ColdFusion Certified Developer Study Guide
Syngress

Linux+ Certification Study Guide
Drew Bird & Mike Harwood

MCSE Windows XP Professional Study Guide
Curt Simmons

CERT TRAINER

Interactive, instructor-led training and testing system on DVD

Hundreds of practice questions within ExamSim

E-book for corresponding Certification Press Study Guide

CCNA Cisco Certified Network Associate DVD CertTrainer
Syngress

MCSE Windows 2000 Core Four DVD CertTrainer
Syngress

A+ Certification DVD CertTrainer
Syngress